D1172004

So Many Roads

ALSO BY DAVID BROWNE

SO MANY

THE LIFE AND TIMES

of the

GRATEFUL DEAD

ROADS

David Browne

DA CAPO PRESS

A Member of the Perseus Books Group

Designed by Timm Bryson
Set in 12 point Fournier by The Perseus Books Group

Cataloging-in-Publication data for this book is available from the Library of
Congress.
978-0-306-82170-7 (hc.)
978-0-306-82171-4 (e-book)

Published by Da Capo Press
A Member of the Perseus Books Group
www.dacapopress.com

Da Capo Press books are available at special discounts for bulk purchases
in the U.S. by corporations, institutions, and other organizations. For more
information, please contact the Special Markets Department at the Perseus
Books Group, 2300 Chestnut Street, Suite 200, Philadelphia, PA 19103, or
call (800) 810-4145, ext. 5000, or e-mail special.markets@perseusbooks.
com.

10 9 8 7 6 5 4 3 2 1

FOR MY MOTHER,
RAYMONDE LELLA BROWNE

*who instilled in me a love of reading and writing
and tolerated all those years of loud records
(by the Dead and many others) in our home.*

CONTENTS

TUNING UP (OR, INTRO)

Leave it to the ever-perceptive Mountain Girl, also known as Carolyn Adams, to articulate one of the goals for this book better than I could at the time. During one of many research trips to various points on the West Coast, I visited MG at her home in Oregon. It wasn't the first time she welcomed yet another writer wishing to pick her brain about the Dead and her relationship with Jerry Garcia.

As we sat down at her dining room table, a tape of a vintage Dead concert playing in the background, I told her I was also in search of not merely the story and music of the band but a bigger picture as well— their fascinating dynamic. To clumsily show what I meant, I put my two hands together, interlocked my fingers, pulled them apart and joined them together again.

"Oh, that's the mystery!" she said, picking up on what I was trying to get at. "How those guys did what you just did with your fingers. How *did* they get together and relate to each other?" Then she partly answered her own question: "They really worked on it. They wanted it badly. They were glued to the enterprise."

The how and why of that enterprise has captivated me since I first discovered the Dead's music. Actually, I *saw* the Dead before I heard them. In the early seventies, when I was just a little kid, I came across one of those early rock history books in a local library in my New Jersey shore town. Flipping through it, I came upon a photo of the Dead circa 1969, the lineup that included both Pigpen and Tom Constanten. They looked like a welcoming bunch of hippie-cowboys, and I was as intrigued by the photo as only a kid who grew up with Old West myths and pop music could be. One of the albums in my fledgling record collection was Crosby, Stills, Nash & Young's *Déjà vu*, so I knew Garcia's name and photo from the liner notes, thanks to his guest role on "Teach Your Children." But I needed to know more about his day job.

Not long after, I received my first FM radio, and if memory serves, one of the first songs I heard on it, by way of WPLJ-FM in New York, was "Casey Jones." "Oh," I thought, *"that's* the Grateful Dead." I loved the groove and lead guitar in the song—and couldn't believe I heard the word "cocaine" in a song on the radio—and I soon bought my first Dead album, *Workingman's Dead* (home, of course, to "Casey Jones"). From that point on I kept up with the new releases, and even when I swerved into other artists and genres in the decades ahead, from indie rock to Celtic folk to electronica, I often found myself circling back to the Dead: from the time that college buddy taught me how to play the riff to "China Cat Sunflower" (so much fun that we played it over and over for maybe a half-hour) to the phone call I received in 1987 from an editor at *Rolling Stone* asking if was interested in reviewing their new album, *In the Dark*. I'll also never forget the sight of another college buddy, a guy named Phil, who wore a Dead yarmulke during the Jewish holidays—and these were in the late-seventies infancy days of rock merchandise.

Having grown up hearing singer-songwriters and folk rock, I naturally loved *Workingman's Dead*, *American Beauty*, and *Garcia*, three of my first Dead-related purchases. (I'm also one of those people who feels the Dead made many, many terrific albums, even though, as I learned, the musicians themselves generally disparaged their studio work and only thought their songs truly came to life before or after they appeared on vinyl or CD.) I thought I had the Dead figured out, but, of course, I was wrong. From hearing their albums to eventually seeing them live, starting in the eighties, I realized what a wide swath they cut in music and the culture. Their forays into country, bluegrass (Garcia with Old and in the Way), experimental music (Lesh with *Seastones*), and improvisation (good chunks of concerts and live albums) helped introduce a naïve kid like myself to those styles and approaches. From record to record, side project to side project, you never knew what you would get with these guys, and that was part of the fun (and sometimes the exasperation). At least they weren't predictable. For me the Dead also refuted the argument that England has given us the legendary rock *bands* (the Beatles, the Who, the Rolling Stones) while America has largely contributed classic *solo* performers (Chuck Berry, Buddy Holly, Dylan, Springsteen). The Dead were a great band, and very much American.

In the many, many years since my introduction to the Dead world I saw the band live and also kept up with its post-Garcia offshoots. Starting in 2008 I was fortunate enough to interview the surviving members for numerous stories for *Rolling Stone*, where I found myself on the—pardon the pun—Dead beat. Each man was never less than sharp, opinionated, and candid about the band's past and present, which, in a public-relations-manipulated world, was absolutely refreshing. They called it as they saw it, and it was easy to respect that.

In some ways those conversations were the launch point for this book, which presented me with the most daunting challenges of my career. So much has been written about the Dead: in print, online, in liner notes, you name it. The books, articles, websites, blogs, and academic papers devoted to them are mountainous. Longtime historians and journalists have written authoritative, superbly researched accounts that every Deadhead should read and study. What in the world could I, a relative outsider, bring to this story?

A different structure, for one. When I ran the idea of doing a Dead biography (pegged to their fiftieth anniversary) past my wife, Maggie, an always astute and insightful editor, she had an immediate idea:

fifty years, fifty vital days. A great if overwhelming idea, it nonetheless sparked something: What if one painted a selective portrait of the
band—its music, its members, and the times around them—by making
each chapter about one significant or representative day, using it as a
window into what was happening with the Dead during that period?
Given the colorful, multihued characters and settings that comprise
the Dead saga, I tucked the idea in the back of my brain and began my
research. In the end I went with a somewhat curtailed version of that
concept (not quite fifty, but enough). I'm sure every Deadhead or band
or family member will have their own ideas about which days should
have been selected, and I welcome feedback. But for me these were
ones that give this epic saga some shape, and these are the tales I heard
along the way.

Of course, the Dead story is not just many days but many stories.
Their narrative takes in the rise of an alternative culture; the changes in
rock 'n' roll as music and business; the role of technology, especially on
stage; the beginnings of a shared community that would lead to social
media. In the late seventies Bob Weir bristled when the TV interviewer
pegged the Dead as "a sixties band." He was right to be irked: as my
research began making clear, the Dead mirrored their times—from
the free-living sixties to the rehab-friendly eighties—more than they
probably ever intended.

As Mountain Girl also suggested, it's also a story about people: young
men from disparate musical and cultural backgrounds who joined together, helped transform the sound of popular music, grew together into
older men, and shunned responsibility yet had it thrust upon them in
any number of ways. It's about the ways in which they coped with that
success and each other as time, lifestyles, and financial weight pressed
down upon them. It's not always a serene story: as I learned over three
years and interviews with over a hundred friends, family members, musical colleagues, business executives, and employees, the Dead world

was inordinately badass, and only the heartiest survived. Their story is comedy, drama, and tragedy all in one. As Mickey Hart told me, "We all played well when we got to that group-mind place. When the music played, everything made sense. When the music stopped, things started getting weird." I hope you enjoy this particular ride.

Pigpen, manager Jon McIntire, Garcia, and Weir at the Fillmore East in New York, a few days before the start of the Workingman's Dead *sessions.*
© AMALIE R. ROTHSCHILD

SAN FRANCISCO, FEBRUARY 16, 1970

The target-practice gunfire had silenced, the women who fed and tended to them were home, and their Hells Angels buddies were swaggering around elsewhere. On this chilly, drizzly day the members of the Grateful Dead straggled in from different parts of Marin County, crossed the Golden Gate Bridge, and buzzed an intercom at a purple door on Brady Street. Tucked away in a grimy, industrial section of San Francisco, the building didn't remotely hint at rock-star glamour, and squatters had taken over a crumbling building next door. To attain the proper head-shop mood at Pacific High Recording, the bandmates lit candles and draped multicolored cloths over their amps, brightening up the burlap sacks the studio owner had hung on the walls.

Starting in 1966 outside Los Angeles and continuing in the Bay Area two years later, the West Coast had been rattled by a series of unsolved murders attributed to an anonymous slasher calling himself, with cinematic flair, the Zodiac Killer. The killings had freaked out many in the Bay Area, and Jerry Garcia, the Dead's lead guitarist and reluctant leader, was among them. During at least one drive home to his rented house in Larkspur he'd stopped at a red light, glanced over, and wondered whether the person who'd pulled up alongside him was the killer. "Please don't murder me," he thought, words that would wind up in the song they would be putting on tape that February night at Pacific High Recording. "Dire Wolf," a wintry tale of mangy animals and a card game in the woods, may have been born of fear and murder. But Garcia's folkish melody was sprightly and jaunty, as if he were daring the Zodiac maniac to come after him. Onstage at Winterland a few months before, he'd even dedicated one of its earliest performances to "the Zodiac."

The Dead weren't easily startled; after all, they'd already witnessed plenty. They'd met in and around Palo Alto over the course of the last decade and, by sheer will if not always musical aptitude, had transformed themselves from folkies, blues fanatics, and classical-music players into a rock 'n' roll band. Along the way they'd been busted and endured jail time. They'd fought with record company bosses. They'd laughed and gotten high together, but they'd also flashed moments of anger and frustration with each other. At one point a few of them had fired some of the others, although the split lasted barely a few weeks.

Little of that turmoil seemed to derail them; if anything, troubles only made them stronger. About two weeks before, the band had been in their hotel rooms in New Orleans, partying after a show, when a barrage of narcotics cops burst in, resulting in drug-charge arrests of most of the band and some of their crew. Eventually they'd dodged that bullet as well: the head of their label would spring them by contributing to the reelection fund of a local politician—hardly legal, as he would later admit with a laugh. According to drummer Mickey Hart, even the arrests worked to their advantage. "We became famous for getting busted, and every time we did, we raised our price," he says. "After we were busted we had a meeting with everyone, girls and wives, and said, 'We should double [our concert fees].' Back then just getting your name known was a big thing, and we never got *any* press." One of their most popular songs, 'Truckin'," would even emerge from the whole mess.

The musicians who began assembling at the studio on Brady Street were more complex than their public images. At twenty-six, his face encircled by a mustache, beard, and Brillo-pad-thick head of dark hair, Garcia exuded a beatific papa-bear openness, like a particularly benign guru. (The year before, *Rolling Stone*, a relatively new counterculture magazine that wedded a love of rock 'n' roll with deep journalistic reportage, had put Garcia on the cover by himself, the first major signal that the guitarist was becoming the group's public persona.) At twenty-nine, bassist Phil Lesh had an easy laugh and could flash a prankster's grin, but his shag haircut and glasses lent him the look of a hip but strict professor, and aptly so: beneath that affable exterior lay a taskmaster and perfectionist. At twenty-two, Bob Weir was the most classically handsome and gracious of the bunch—the women in the audiences couldn't get enough of his pony tail and girlish frame—but beneath his calm-river exterior was a genuine eccentric, heard in his pick-and-strum approach to rhythm guitar and his unapologetic penchant for practical jokes.

The rhythm section players were comparatively clear-cut. Setting up his collection of percussion instruments, including maracas and congas, was Hart, twenty-six, who combined the mustache and hat of a Cossack with the bucking-bronco energy of the Brooklynite he was. Bill Kreutzmann, the other drummer, was the least hippie-looking of the bunch, although his surly ranch-hand smirk made him almost as charismatic as Garcia; at twenty-three, Kreutzmann was already on his second marriage.

In terms of public image versus private life, however, none of the Dead had anything on Ron McKernan, the singer, harmonica player, and keyboard player known affectionately as Pigpen. The previous year he'd shown up for a photo shoot in a scrunched-up cowboy hat and carting along a firearm and bullets. Riding horses on one of the band's ranches, Pigpen, all of twenty-four, looked the most natural in that role—less like a musician and more like a posse member about to give chase to a bank robber—but as everyone learned, he was actually the most sensitive of the bunch. When one of the women who crashed at their home woke up in the middle of the night and saw Pigpen in her doorway, she needn't have worried; he came over and put an extra blanket on her.

The road they were traveling was still full of potholes. They were largely broke and in debt to their record company to the tune of almost $200,000. Their small but loyal road crew was stretched to the limits by slapdash planning that saw the Dead sometimes playing consecutive shows hundreds of miles apart. One of those busted with them in New Orleans was their sound engineer and former financial backer, whose future—both personally and with the Dead—was now uncertain. Some within their scene—a world that appeared loose and mellow but was, in fact, guarded and suspicious of outsiders—were growing wary of their new business manager, who happened to be related to one of the band members. Thanks to any number of in-flight pranks—like the time Weir pulled out a fake gun and "shot" Pigpen and Lesh, after which a pillow fight ensued—every airline except TWA had banned them. That fact hardly surprised one journalist, who accompanied them on a commercial flight and saw them openly sniffing cocaine off a knife being passed around their seats.

And yet for all the drama and craziness, which were as much a part of their world as quality weed, the Dead were preparing for a wilder and bigger ride as the decade began. Their newly hired road manager was promising them more work and better organized tours, and he had the experience and brazenness to make it happen. They were on the verge of moving into a new building, a shingled two-story house in San Rafael, complete with a few palm trees on the property, that would become their base of operations for over three decades.

Most importantly, their music was expanding in scope and power. Less than a week before this February recording session the band had returned to New York's Fillmore East, a former vaudeville hall that promoter Bill Graham, both the Dead's champion and sometimes adversary, had transformed into the city's leading rock 'n' roll theater, its counterculture church. In 1967 *Time* magazine had dubbed the Dead's music "acid rock," but as those seminal Fillmore shows revealed, that description was now as outmoded as their previous band name, the Warlocks. At the Fillmore they could play one of their own dirgy country ballads, "High Time," or a lanky, vampy cover of Martha and the Vandellas' "Dancing in the Street." They could strip it down, strumming an acoustic version of the Everly Brothers' "Wake Up, Little Susie" or Lightnin' Hopkins's "Katie Mae," the latter a showcase for Pigpen's country blues side. (Decades later "unplugged" segments at concerts would be de rigueur; in 1970 the changeover was almost unheard of.) They could also dive into "Dark Star," which sounded like nothing else in rock 'n' roll at that moment: its lilting, dainty melody gradually whipped itself into a group whirlwind, collapsed into itself, stripped down to bits of feedback and drums, and then began rebuilding, instrument by instrument, finally finishing one night just nineteen seconds shy of a half-hour.

During the same shows, the drummers would get ample time for tribal duets during "Alligator," and Lesh was rarely as unobtrusive as bass players were in more traditionally minded bands; from time to time his bass would pop like a gopher sticking its head up from different parts of a lawn. (It was almost as if he were taking solos while the others were still playing.) During "China Cat Sunflower" Garcia's guitar danced a sweet jig around the melody; other times, reflecting his own mood swings, his playing could be testy and terse. By the end of each night it was clear the Dead weren't just West Coast weirdoes; their repertoire made them the most eclectic, fearsome, and versatile American rock band of its time, perhaps ever.

As Fillmore East manager Kip Cohen saw for himself, the scene wasn't merely about the music; the Dead were beginning to symbolize a new lifestyle paradigm. The Dead had first played the venue in June 1968, and with each run since, they'd attracted larger, more impassioned crowds. To Cohen, many of them seemed like kids from Connecticut suburbs who'd ventured into the nasty big city to see the Dead and get wasted. When the sets ended, often in the early morning hours, the Fillmore staff found itself with "a roomful of people freaking out on acid," Cohen says, and the staff did what it could to make sure the kids wound up on the right train home or had a place in town to crash. Those fans were an early sign that the Dead were on the verge of transforming from a cult band to a larger, more national one. Indeed, in 1970 they were preparing to play the most shows—about 150—they would ever do in a year by that point. That number meant more travel, more employees, and more temptations once they were out on the road, but during that early period no one yet knew how it would all impact them.

Sam Cutler, who popped into the Pacific High sessions now and then, should have been accustomed to rock 'n' roll madness. He himself was a road-dog buccaneer; with his thin face and mustache, he looked like Captain Hook after a visit to a leather-jacket emporium. Cutler had worked for the Rolling Stones the year before, helping shepherd them around America on the band's first tour of the States in four years. Starting in January 1970, he'd begun a new job, tour manager for the Dead, a task that also involved plenty of opportunity to hang with what he first thought were a group of loosey-goosey West Coast hippies.

About two years earlier most of the Dead had fled the Haight (or "Hashbury," as the *New York Times Magazine* had dubbed their former neighborhood) for Marin County, just north of San Francisco. They relished the sprawling area's meandering, tree-shrouded streets, which looked like paths running through Muir Woods, and one by one they settled into various ramshackle houses, ranches, and quasi-communes in towns like Novato and Larkspur. In the privacy of the Marin woods they could do whatever they wanted, or at least close enough to it. Cutler witnessed that for himself during one of his early visits to Hart's Novato ranch. A television had been dragged out of the house and, with long extension cords, had been set up in a dry creek, and one hundred rounds had been loaded into various guns. With the TV on, there suddenly was Ronald Reagan, the actor turned politician who was now the governor of their state, the man who embodied everything the Dead despised about the straight world. Normally they'd shoot up concrete blocks or records, but now they took aim at Reagan's image on the small screen and let loose. Cutler estimates they fired off "about three hundred times," obliterating the set once and for all. Other times the victims were sales plaques their label, Warner Brothers, had presented to the band.

For a time Weir was living in what he would later call a "self-imposed dustbowl of a ranch" in Nicasio in western Marin County. Named Rukka Rukka, it was home as well to Weir's girlfriend, Frankie (soon to take his last name even though they weren't married), and various members of the Dead's crew, along with random wandering chickens and horses. Tales of the origins of the ranch's name were appropriately bawdy: according to one account, someone they'd known at another hangout would chase after women, squeeze their breasts, and say, "Rukka, rukka!" The Dead thought the story was hilarious, and the name stuck.

Even more than their music, Hart's ranch became a symbol of the way the Dead could build their own remote community outside the normal confines of society. Whoever had found it first—either manager Rock Scully or road manager Jonathan Riester—Hart was now the overseer of the rambling thirty-two-acre property tucked away beyond a wooden entry gate nearly hidden by trees. Dubbed Hart's Delight by some, it became the go-to place for the band, friends, roadies, and their increasingly expanding family unit to congregate, get high, and record music. With its large barn (soon filled with recording gear), horses, working water pump, and occasional displays of excitable-boy gunfire, the ranch felt like something straight out of the previous century—though with a few contemporary twists. Mike (nicknamed Josh) Belardo, an afternoon-drive DJ for KMPX in San Francisco, ventured onto the ranch one day to interview the band and had his mind blown even without hallucinogens. "Everybody's walking around stoned, and the chicks are naked," he recalls. "Topless women. Horses. It was unbelievable." Hart had a beloved Arabian white horse named Snorter, a name that took on additional meaning when Snorter would be dosed now and then—"Oh, there were many times with something or another," Hart admits. The horse didn't seem all that affected while under the influence, even dodging a herd of trampling cows once during a ride.

Unlawful activity wasn't always tolerated at Hart's Delight. They'd already been burned by the law at least once, not to mention driven out of the Haight by a tidal wave of tourism, drugs, and increasing police scrutiny. When Hart learned that certain people living on the ranch were expert pickpockets, he scolded them. "They would come home with things, wallets and stuff," he recalls, "and I'd say, 'First, if you're gonna live here, that's not the right thing to do, and second, it will bring the heat on the Dead.'" After all their busts, "under the radar" was the operative phrase.

Among those living at the ranch were Rhonda, Sherry, and Vicki Jensen, three sisters who moved onto the ranch after their previous home had burned down. The sisters cleaned, swept floors, prepared breakfast for anyone who crashed there, and fed horses: "It made the music work," says Vicki, "and that was the inspiration to do it." The only irksome part of the job involved the women the road crew would bring to the ranch. The Jensen girls had to pick out which horses the girls would ride—and, just as important, find ways to keep the women busy once the roadies left for somewhere or someone else. "They'd just sit there and think that looking pretty was enough," Vicki says with a laugh. "I used to tell them, 'You need to join in and help out here!'"

At Hart's ranch the Dead and their extended family were able to live out their fantasies as cowboys and outliers who played by their own rules without worrying about societal norms. Even the local police were skittish about stopping by. The fantasy did have its learning curve, like the day Garcia went riding on a horse whose cinch hadn't been tightened. As his girlfriend, Carolyn Adams, otherwise known as Mountain Girl, watched, Garcia fell off and broke a few ribs. "First and last time he was on a horse," she recalls. "He didn't like horses after that." Sometimes even the fantasies had limits.

"Dire Wolf," the song they were scheduled to start recording that February night at Pacific High, was symbolic in and of itself. If Hart's ranch was the Dead's almost-anything-goes headquarters, the Garcia and Mountain Girl house on Madrone Avenue in Larkspur was its creative hub. Set on a flat acre with sizable redwood trees and a creek out back, the house was far from ostentatious. Garcia had moved in first with Mountain Girl, who was now, in the parlance of the times, Garcia's "old lady." MG, as everyone called her, already had a child with writer Ken Kesey and in 1969 had given birth to Garcia's daughter, Annabelle. The two weren't technically wed, as both had been married before and hadn't yet obtained divorces, but no one seemed to mind.

One day Garcia brought up the idea of a new roommate: "I want my friend Bob Hunter to move in," he told Mountain Girl, who hadn't even met Hunter yet but knew his history with Garcia: the two men, who both could flash wide, welcoming grins, had met in the early days of the Palo Alto folk and literary scene nearly a decade before, living in adjacent cars when they were homeless, and had put their friendship through its share of inspired highs and head-butting lows. With his bookish glasses and brain-of-a-poet intensity, Hunter could be as bristly and intense as Garcia could seem affable and casual. After going their separate ways in the middle of the sixties they'd reconvened when Garcia asked Hunter to sign up as the Dead's resident lyricist.

Along with their respective girlfriends, Hunter and Garcia were now roommates in Larkspur, and one night they and Mountain Girl were watching one of the original black-and-white Sherlock Holmes movies, *The Hound of the Baskervilles*. As Hunter would later recall, they all pondered what a "ghostly hound" would look like, and the phrase "dire wolf" emerged. Just the thought of a big wolf called Dire was enough to inspire Hunter, who began writing lyrics, and in no time they had a song.

Financially, life at the house on Madrone could be a daily survival challenge. Although the Dead were technically rock stars, they didn't have the cash flow that went with that job. Their rent was an affordable several hundred dollars a month, but Garcia and Mountain Girl relied on welfare and food handouts courtesy of the WIC (Women, Infants and Children) program and often settled for meals of peanut butter, honey, and sacks of rice. Other relationships in the generally fraught Dead world were on fairly steady ground. With his second wife, Susila, Kreutzmann had just welcomed a baby boy, William Justin, who came to be known simply as Justin. (Kreutzmann already had a daughter, Stacy, from his first marriage.) Weir had settled into a relationship with Frankie, a sparkplug who'd been a dancer for the TV shows *Hullabaloo* and *Shindig!* and briefly an employee of the Beatles' Apple Records. Pigpen was into the third year of his relationship with Veronica "Vee" Barnard.

As soon as Hunter moved in during the first months of 1969 Mountain Girl saw how intense he could be: she would sometimes look outside and see Hunter using an axe handle to thwack away at a car tire dangling from an apple tree. "Bob had a pretty high need to release his physical energy," she says. "He had a lot of juice." Yet the two men complemented each other creatively and temperamentally. Garcia never relished the idea of spending hours working on lyrics; Hunter loved nothing better, even if it meant staying up all night. Mountain Girl recalls "a lot of wine and playing guitars until two in the morning." Many days, she says, Hunter would bound into the kitchen during breakfast, carrying a stack of papers: "I've got a bunch of new ones for ya!" Garcia might flash a vaguely irritated look, as if irked by his meal being interrupted, but would then start sifting through the poems: "Like this one. Like that one," he'd say. In five minutes Garcia would select up to a dozen lyrics, and soon he'd have the melodies to match.

In June 1970, a few months after the "Dire Wolf" session, Hunter beheld a particularly arresting example of the way he and Garcia collaborated. The Dead, along with Delaney and Bonnie, the Band, Janis Joplin, Ian and Sylvia, and others, embarked on a wild tour of Canada by private train. Everyone was partying and playing music even when they weren't on stage, so much so that the train had to periodically stop so more liquor could be bought. During one stop Garcia sat on the tracks, grabbed Hunter's latest lyrics—for "Ripple"—and worked out a melody. For decades to come this would remain one of Hunter's most cherished memories of a time when their creativity seemed as unstoppable as a locomotive.

◆　◆　◆

The Dead's world could be a constant lurch between light and dark, and nothing captured the latter mood better than another song that took shape during the same sessions as "Dire Wolf." If "Dire Wolf"

was a merry, if dark-humored, stroll, "New Speedway Boogie" snarled;
Garcia's guitar poked at the melody, and his voice was a little frazzled
around the edges at times. The song was testy and aptly so: it docu-
mented a moment when the darkness threatened to overshadow them.

The speedway in question was Altamont, where the Dead had been
scheduled to play in December 1969 as part of a mammoth free concert
with a formidable lineup: the Stones, Jefferson Airplane, Santana, the
Flying Burrito Brothers, and Crosby, Stills, Nash & Young. The Dead
and Stones' camps had been in discussion about doing some sort of free
show, somewhere, and the end result, after two venue cancellations, was
at Altamont. (As Scully would later write, "We actually talk[ed] the
Stones into doing a free concert in Golden Gate Park," the original site
until the city of San Francisco nixed the idea and the speedway became
the organizers' last resort.) The day-long show was ostensibly a way to
celebrate the end of the Stones' American tour, give them a filmed finale for their in-progress concert movie, *Gimme Shelter*—and help them
ward off accusations of high ticket prices by presenting one concert for
free. The Dead weren't just scheduled to perform the show but also supplied their PA system and crew, who helped set up the recording gear
and speakers. One of Hart's ranch mates was in a truck backstage rolling
hundreds of joints for Keith Richards and anyone else who wanted one.

Even when the music finally started up, the vibe felt sour. Chris Hill-
man, the former Byrds bass player then in the Flying Burrito Brothers,
walked through the crowd to the stage to play his set, stumbling over
participants who already seemed wasted. Arriving at the stage, he was
stopped by a Hells Angel, who asked who he was and almost didn't let
him up. At the airport Sue Swanson, a longtime friend and fan of the
Dead's, saw fear in the faces of other musicians who'd played and were
on their way out. "Crosby, Stills, Nash & Young were there with their
big coats on," she recalls. "The looks on everyone's faces were just very
serious. Everyone wanted the hell out of there."

The Dead had forged an alliance of sorts with the Angels several years before, during the early, untroubled days hanging with band friend Kesey in the Palo Alto hills. Some in the band weren't rattled by the sight of tattooed, hairy, and burly Angels backstage; others were less pleased, though there wasn't much they could do about it. As much as anything, that relationship between these two seemingly dissimilar camps spelled out the growing duality in the Dead's world: a seemingly sunny gentility with an undercurrent of hardened swagger that wasn't remotely for the faint of heart. A reporter covering a 1970 show noticed that Garcia's case sported a sticker that read, "Blackjack Garcia, the baddest fucking guitarist in the world." For all the field-of-flowers beauty of their music, the world of the Dead was unsentimental and demanding; to survive, one had to adapt and hold on tight.

At a Fillmore East show that January stagehand (and future movie director) Allan Arkush, an NYU student who worked part time at the theater, heard a knock on the backstage door, and he and a few other employees found themselves confronting a bunch of Hells Angels from the nearby Lower East Side chapter. The Angels name-dropped one of the Dead's road crew—Lawrence Shurtliff, otherwise known as "Ram Rod," a muscular, wiry man with old-sage eyes and strong-silent-type demeanor. But even if the Angels hadn't been on the guest list, Arkush and his fellow Fillmore employees wouldn't have dared turn them away. That night they had come bearing gifts. As Arkush watched in astonishment, the Angels began lugging nitrous oxide tanks to the dressing rooms, no easy feat given that each one probably weighed about two hundred pounds and had to be dragged up several flights of stairs. A short while later Arkush popped his head into one of the dressing rooms to alert the band that showtime had arrived. What he saw—everyone sucking on nitrous tubes—was so cartoonish it was almost funny. The band happily stumbled their way down to the stage, took their places with their instruments, and waited; Graham had arranged for Richard

Strauss's "Also Sprach Zarathustra," best known in 1970 as the theme song to the sci-fi sensation *2001: A Space Odyssey*, to blast out of the speakers before the show started. When it finished, the Dead just stood there, gazing up at a screen and giggling in a nitrous haze. To make his guitar sound like it too was laughing, Garcia began stroking the strings.

By the time the Dead were helicoptered onto the Altamont site the festivities were no longer festive. After the Airplane's Grace Slick had mentioned to Mick Jagger the role the Angels had played in security for Airplane shows, the Angels had been recruited for Altamont; whether it would be for security or to hang out in front of the stage and protect generators (as Angels had done at so many free area shows before) would be debated for years. Fights broke out early, and it became clear that some of the instigators weren't Angels but so-called "prospects," not full-on Angels. It didn't help that many in the crowd upfront were wasted. The uniformed local cops on hand were cowering at the idea of dealing with the Angels. As soon as they arrived on site the Dead were informed that an Angel had punched out Airplane singer Marty Balin. (Vicki Jensen, backstage with the crew, saw Balin come flying through the back of the stage after he'd dared to stand up to Angels beating on someone in the audience. "I'm sorry, man," one Angel was overheard saying, "but you don't say 'fuck you' to an Angel.") Walking through the dusty air and sun-scorched crowd on their way toward the stage, Lesh and Garcia saw dazed fans sprawled all over, and Lesh accidentally hit Garcia on the head with the back of his bass. It was that kind of day.

Although Woodstock had transpired a few months before, Altamont would not be the good-vibes sequel many had hoped it would be. Freaked out by a scene becoming gnarlier and more menacing by the moment, the Dead retreated to a bus behind the stage, deciding whether or not to play. At one point Dead roadie Rex Jackson, an imposing cowboy who was no pushover, was seen walking around with a black eye, which Cutler presumed was delivered by an Angel. (It's possible he received it when he intervened on Balin's behalf during the Angels skirmish, and Jackson was smart enough to know not to fight back.) Ultimately, in what even Lesh would call a mistake—and Cutler would sharply criticize as an act of "cowardice"—the Dead decided not to venture anywhere near the stage. As nighttime arrived and the Stones cranked up, the Dead returned to a helicopter and flew off while most of their crew retreated to their equipment truck and drove back to San Francisco, where the band was due to play at the Fillmore West that same night. Soon after, Meredith Hunter, a young African American, rushed the stage with a gun and was stabbed to death by an Angel. The Dead were too unnerved to even show up at the Fillmore, and Graham wound up screaming at the crew instead of the band. An after-party at the theater, which was never firmed up but was pitched to the Dead by a local promoter as "the most memorable evening in San Francisco ballroom history," never materialized. Given the Dead's role in the show, paranoia ensued. Some at Hart's ranch fled, fearing for their safety from angry Angels.

Another reminder of the dark side of the Dead could be found in an office closer to home. A year earlier, the band was fairly dazzled when Hart's father, Lenny, a former drummer and now self-ordained minister, reappeared in his son's life after leaving Hart's mother during their Brooklyn years. With his short hair and southern-car-salesman vibe, Lenny Hart didn't look much like his son or anyone on the scene. At first Mickey seemed thrilled to have his father around, at least to those who saw their interaction, and Lenny promised to help the Dead's shaky business operation. At the ranch the previous spring Lenny would spout lines like "I've seen the light!" while holding a Bible, and somehow he convinced the band and its entourage he could be their financial savior. In 1969 Garcia had spoken with *Rolling Stone* writer Michael Lydon about their business and admitted, "Mickey's father is now doing it. He's fronting our whole management thing. He's taken charge. We've given him the power to do what we want to." Garcia added, somewhat less optimistically, "Right now, things are looking good. But the whole thing about money is still something weird."

Since then the situation with Lenny had only grown stranger. "He looked like the straightest white man you ever saw," says a member of the Dead world at the time, "but he had a good goddamn rap. Some people, you can't read truth or falsity in their face." Jon McIntire, another member of the Dead organization, was suspicious of Lenny, as was Ram Rod. Garcia would tell McIntire, "I believe what people tell me." But not everyone was convinced. Mountain Girl once said to Hunter, "Why can't you just trust Lenny? We need a manager who understands business." Hunter reacted with what Mountain Girl recalls as "utter scorn at my naiveté and unwarranted confidence."

For the first time the air was filled with the promise of more income. Feeling guilty after the Altamont debacle, Garcia had asked Cutler to be the Dead's tour manager; Cutler accepted and soon realized the band needed to play more gigs than ever to shore up their finances. Throughout 1969 they would make only a few thousand dollars a show: $5,000 for two nights at the Fillmore West; $7,500 for two nights at the Pavilion in Flushing, Queens; and $1,059.50 for appearing on Hugh Hefner's TV series *Playboy After Dark*. "They knew that if they didn't start to make serious money, the Dead would cease to exist," says Cutler. "Every penny counted. We were living on $10-a-day per diems."

It would take Cutler months to get the Dead out of hock. Until then, when the musicians would ask where the money was, Lenny would tell them their "old ladies" had spent it, which wasn't the case. When some in the organization asked Lenny to show them the books, he hesitated, then eventually turned over ledgers with entries that had clearly been erased and written over. (Lesh and Mickey Hart also confronted him at a Bob's Big Boy restaurant and realized he also had two different sets of books.) When questioned, Lenny had a habit of veering into extended Bible talk, almost as a way of zoning them out. The thought of dealing forcefully with Lenny Hart didn't sit right with any of them—Garcia and Weir especially were not the most confrontational—but something had to give.

At the same time, other parts of their operation were to some degree or another in jeopardy. Owsley Stanley, their acid-king soundman and quality-control inspiration, would soon find himself behind bars after the New Orleans bust. Those close to Garcia were beginning to notice that he could unexpectedly fall into grumpy, blackened moods. When Garcia came home at night he'd frequently grumble to Mountain Girl about one thing or another having to do with the band, then ask when dinner would be ready. Although Mountain Girl didn't know it then, later she wondered whether this was the beginning of what she calls Garcia's "secret drug life." Cocaine was already on the scene; in fact, the band would give it a plug in "Casey Jones," another new song they'd record for the new album. No one considered the drug even vaguely addictive.

■   ◆   ▲

Three months after "Dire Wolf" was cut, a few Deadheads managed to slither in backstage at a show at Temple University in Philadelphia. No one knew how, but in the early days of rock 'n' roll security, crashers were always possible. One of the fans found Garcia and asked what the band was working on, and Garcia boasted about the new album they'd just finished, *Workingman's Dead*. "I like it better than any album we've done," he told them.

"That's all we do, is sit around and get smashed and listen to that album," the fan said.

Even though the album wasn't in stores yet, Garcia let that odd comment slide—he was growing accustomed to remarks like that from their budding fan base—and amiably replied, with a smile, "We get smashed and make 'em."

Sometimes they did; the nitrous tanks at Pacific High were testament to those habits. But something rare and miraculous was happening with these new songs. Everyone in the Dead had complaints about their first three studio albums: too rushed, too overproduced, way too expensive. It was impossible to satisfy them all at once. As they began filing into Pacific High, though, the mood was uncommonly optimistic. "We had pushed the envelope in experimental," Hart says. "We had to simplify. That's why that record was acoustic. There wasn't a lot of percussion. Bill and I played it very straight. Maracas, congas—light stuff." Garcia would be singing all but one of the songs, and he was eager to, in his words, "boogie" and not be bogged down in the tape-montage experimentation that ran through their last two albums.

From its inception the new album was mapped out. Bob Matthews, who had introduced Garcia and Weir before the Dead was even a glimmer in anyone's imagination, would be engineering, along with Betty Cantor. Matthews taped the band working on the songs, put the material in what he thought was a proper sequence, then gave a copy to each band member, who practiced the songs in that order. Omitted at the onset was "Mason's Children," another song about death and collapse, this one swathed in campfire harmonies and a folk-rock bounce. (Like "New Speedway Boogie," it had been written directly after Altamont.) "It was a no-brainer," says Matthews. "It didn't fit. That was by agreement."

Hunter and Garcia had crafted indelible songs before, yet something about these new ones, many written at the Larkspur house, had a special cohesiveness, a sustained vision. They were littered with images of hard-working, hard-living Americana types—the miners in "Cumberland Blues," the jack-hammering highway worker in "Easy Wind," the careening conductor in "Casey Jones"—along with a mysterious character, "Black Peter." "Dire Wolf" was set in "Fennario," an imaginary burgh overrun with the creatures. Like classic folk songs, the tunes were both down to earth and mythical. Tapping into themes of community, terror, darkness, woozy love, and trains, the songs felt more universal and timeless than anything they'd done before.

By early 1970 less electric, more organic-sounding records were in vogue, as opposed to the post–*Sgt. Pepper* approach of extravagant sonic creations. Hunter was particularly taken with the music of the Band, but according to Cutler, financial considerations also played a part in their change of direction. Having put themselves in the hole during the making of *Aoxomoxoa*, the Dead simply couldn't spend indiscriminately, at least not for a long time. "Garcia and I analyzed what they'd done in the past and why it wasn't successful and what could be done about that," says Cutler. "I kept banging on Jerry and saying, 'Do your album in one bang. Minimal recording cost. Do the two-week album. Just get in there.' And that's what they did."

As they began to record in February, the preproduction work paid off. The sessions began around the time of "Dire Wolf," paused for more touring, resumed in early March, and wrapped up around March 16. They bore down on two songs in particular. "Uncle John's Band" had started life as a long band jam on a cassette given to Hunter; he then fashioned lyrics about the band and its scene that were the most hopeful he'd written. ("Goddamn, Uncle John's mad!" went his first line, perhaps a nod to Garcia's shifting moods, but Hunter later deleted that line.) "Cumberland Blues," the mining-story song, had a chugging-locomotive rhythm propelled by Lesh's bobbing bass. "Dire Wolf" was itself ready to go. They'd been playing it live since the previous June, and Weir had even sung lead on one version. Garcia had taken up the pedal steel guitar with the Dead's country offshoot band, the

New Riders of the Purple Sage, and the instrument pranced its way through the song.

The other songs were equally filled with exquisite touches—the "oooh" harmonies in "Dire Wolf," Pigpen's warm organ in "Black Peter," the modest rave-up in "Easy Wind." But most emblematic of their heightened single-mindedness were their harmonies. The Dead were never known for them; Garcia, Lesh, and Weir each had a distinctive voice with unique creaks and crevices. But the new, folksier approach to their songs begged for vocal blends. Egged on by their friend in esoteric chords and hedonism, David Crosby (also living in a rented house in Novato, the backyard of which was seen on the cover of Crosby, Stills, Nash & Young's *Déjà vu*), the Dead began working harder than ever on their singing. "They were expected to sing all those parts, and it didn't go well," laughs Mountain Girl. "It sounded like cats howling."

In another sign of their focus, Garcia, Lesh, and Weir decided to have the last laugh and bore down on the singing. "We said, 'You're gonna have to sing this right!'" says Cantor (now Cantor-Jackson). "We worked on them until they weren't flat or sharp and were hitting the notes." The effort paid off; the mix of voices sounded natural, lending the songs a radiance and a sense of comforting teamwork. A slender brunette with a warm smile, long hair, and sharp ears that had earned her the nickname "Bettar" (as in, "She can make things sound better"), Cantor, then twenty-one, embodied another aspect of the Dead's rule-breaking approach: she was well on her way to becoming possibly the first woman recording engineer in a largely male business (and in the predominantly male Dead crew). She adored and championed the band and its music—even if she viewed the nitrous tanks in the studio with great skepticism, as she recalls with a laugh years later: "I'm sitting there going, 'I don't like this.' I'm catching the tank as it's falling over so it doesn't hit the tape machine. I'm like, 'Jesus, guys!'"

Everyone in the Dead camp had his or her spiky opinion about every aspect of their organization, but the sessions for *Workingman's Dead* marked a rare moment of genuine, yes-we-can Grateful Dead consensus: people seemed *happy* with the results. Cutler recalls they were "never more focused and on the ball" than during those sessions. "I liked it right off the bat, as soon as I heard the basics," says Bill "Kidd" Candelario, who had joined the Dead crew two years earlier. Few were more euphoric than Warner Brothers head Joe Smith. The Dead had driven Smith fairly crazy over the previous four years—from overspending to trying to dose him—but when he heard the finished record he was ecstatic. "I had been on their back," Smith says. "They saw they weren't getting any royalties. We were sticking with them, but we also said, 'Please give us something we can sell.' They wanted to prove they could do it." According to Matthews, the final bill for the album was less than $15,000. Garcia would never be happy with his singing on "High Time," thinking he hadn't nailed it. But when Smith heard the record he gave Matthews a hug and gushed about how thrilled he was to hear the vocals. The feeling behind the album was so optimistic that members of the band stopped by the offices of *Rolling Stone* to play the record for the staff. "That was a turning point," Lesh says of the making of the album. "It was kind of exciting to focus, to make such a left turn."

Outside the studio doors their world could be chaotic, disorganized, and messy. But as this music-making experience showed, they could escape it all. "Being able to do that was *extremely* positive in the midst of all this adverse stuff that was happening," Garcia would tell *Rolling Stone* editor Jann S. Wenner the following year. "It was definitely an upper . . . it was the first record that we made together as a group, all of us. Everybody contributed beautifully, and it came off really nicely."

As they worked on "Dire Wolf" and prepared for several more weeks of recording, they had the songs, the music, and the hope that they could ward off the bad mojo that threatened to engulf them. It was neither the first nor the last time the Dead would find themselves in that place. As their diffident leader knew, everything could change in the same amount of time it took to strum a chord. It had before; it could happen again.

Jerry Garcia and Robert Hunter, circa 1961.
PHOTOGRAPHER UNKNOWN; COURTESY JERRYGARCIA.COM

CHAPTER 1

MENLO PARK, CALIFORNIA, OCTOBER 27, 1962

He couldn't have picked a lovelier setting in which to die. On the West Coast the work day was drawing to a close, but Jerry Garcia's task was only beginning. With his girlfriend, Barbara Meier, he left the Chateau, the three-story home in Menlo Park where he'd been living, and walked to the adjoining Sand Hill Road. From there the two began a long, exhausting hike up a hill. With a pine ridge saluting them to the west, the warmth of the Indian summer afternoon embraced them, and as Meier would recall, the light was "infused with honey."

To anyone who passed them on the road Garcia and Meier must have seemed a study in contrasts. At twenty, Garcia sported short, thick, dark hair and a goatee that lent him "that Latin lover look, like [actor] Cesar Romero," recalls one of his later musician friends, Tom Constanten. The image wholly matched the person Garcia was at that moment: part-time music teacher, fledgling banjo picker, budding bohemian. A man of few needs, he was wearing one of the two buttoned, short-sleeve shirts that comprised the bulk of his wardrobe. In contrast, Meier, three years younger than him, was an effervescent brunette with a sun-bursting-through-the-clouds smile. Thanks to models who'd given her their cast-offs after they'd all worked together at photo shoots, Meier, who was still in high school, often dressed in what she calls "elegant baby beatnik crossed with Chanel." By contrast, Garcia was pure beatnik.

On this late afternoon neither one of them was contemplating clothes or jobs. They were leaving behind Menlo Park and its more prosperous neighboring town, Palo Alto, along with their families, friends, and favorite bookstores and hangouts. If everything happened the way the news reports said it might, none of that would exist after that night anyway.

Like everybody in the Peninsula area south of San Francisco and on the rest of the planet, Garcia and Meier had heard the alarming, apocalyptic news somewhere. Maybe on TV or the newspapers or maybe by way of local, politically conscious friends like Roy Kepler, the former War Resistors League executive director so ahead of his time that he was a conscientious objector during World War II. (Kepler ran Kepler's Books & Magazines, where all the local bohemians and intellectuals gathered to read and sip coffee; the cash register was manned by another local peace activist, Ira Sandperl.) Eleven days before, John F. Kennedy, their vibrant president, had learned of the existence of missile bases in Cuba, each installed with Soviet missiles. On October 22 Kennedy had addressed the nation about the discovery; the following day US ships headed for Cuba just as Soviet subs moved into the area as well. On October 24 Nikita Khrushchev, first secretary of the Communist Party of the Soviet Union and not a man known for subtlety, sent a letter to Kennedy that practically had bile spit on it: "You are no longer appealing to reason, but wish to intimidate us." On October 25 came a testy confrontation at the United Nations between the American representative, Adlai Stevenson, and the Soviet Union's, Valerian Zorin: "Don't wait for the translation—yes or no?" asked Stevenson, demanding to know whether the Soviets had indeed placed missiles there.

On October 26 the situation had barely improved and bordered on incendiary: additional photos taken by American U2 planes chillingly revealed construction of the sites, and Khrushchev fired off another letter to Kennedy: "What would a war give you? You are threatening us with war. But you well know that the very least which you would receive in reply would be that you would experience the same consequences as those which you sent us. . . . If indeed war should break out, then it would not be in our power to stop it, for such is the logic of war. I have participated in two wars and know that war ends when it has rolled through cities and villages, everywhere sowing death and destruction." Robert McNamara, Kennedy's secretary of defense, told his boss that American forces could carry out an air strike "in a matter of days," but Kennedy was reluctant to attack Cuba. Now, the morning of October 27, the situation had taken another turn for the ominous: the Soviets shot down a U2 plane over Cuba, and Air Force carriers were put in place in the event of war.

By ghoulish coincidence, a recently completed federal government study revealed that Palo Alto could accommodate 37,818 fallout shelters if needed. But if the world were to end, Garcia and Meier were going to be alone, together, in a radiant spot they could call their own for eternity. "If this was the end of the world, a very real probability in our teenage minds," says Meier, "we wanted to be together, awake, and face it head on." They didn't bring camping gear or food, just themselves and their fears.

The two had met the previous year in Menlo Park. Meier, then a fifteen-year-old high school student, had been invited for a hike with a friend, who first stopped by an art supply store; on the porch outside was a mysterious man in a goatee, holding a banjo. Initially he seemed reluctant to join them, but their mutual friend later told Meier that the guy, whose name was Jerry Garcia, was instantly smitten: "Oh, tell her I love her," he'd told their friend. Eventually he climbed into the backseat of the car and sang the traditional murder ballad "Silver Dagger," which Joan Baez had popularized on her first album two years before. Meier didn't know who he was, but she couldn't deny his magnetism. "Jerry was singing just to me, and it was so seductive," she says. "There was this incredible promise in his eyes of 'I know about worlds you've never dreamed of, and I'll bet you're dying to try them.'"

Although he was just another twentysomething bumming around the area and trying to figure out his next move, Garcia already exuded more than a patina of magnetism. Not long before this October night another transplant, a Seattle kid named David Nelson who was himself mastering guitar, spotted Garcia in a bookstore. Cradling a twelve-string guitar, Garcia was strumming quietly, almost to himself, but at least to Nelson he was the focus of the room. In his open-buttoned shirt, Garcia seemed "incredibly hairy," Nelson later recalled, and he struck Nelson as "kind of dark and surly," complete with a stare that zeroed in on his target. Nelson couldn't take his eyes off the guy, and Garcia also seemed preternaturally mature. "Jerry was this guy who to all of us looked like an adult, like a grownup, where we kind of looked like kids," he told writer David Hajdu. "There's this *man* here, you know. He was very advanced at the time compared to everybody else."

After being casual pals for six months, Garcia and Meier had inevitably become a couple in the fall of 1961. The relationship was merely one aspect of the new life Garcia had built for himself in the Peninsula. (He'd also followed Meier to San Francisco in the summer of 1961 when she attended art school there, then returned to the Peninsula with her.) By now Garcia had distanced himself from his family and his often painful past. When he wasn't teaching he'd be killing time at Kepler's or a nearby coffeehouse, St. Michael's Alley, or playing in an ever-evolving group of bluegrass and string bands. No longer the chubby, short-haired kid, Garcia had reinvented himself.

Nearly from the moment she found herself in the same car as Garcia, Meier had been swept up in his universe, a largely male world of folk music, poetry, coffee, cigarettes, and spontaneous car-fueled adventures. When her high school let out for the day she'd see a familiar old black heap in the parking lot; unlike the Corvettes and Lincolns owned by the wealthier students, this one had doors that were held together, in Meier's memory, by rope. Waiting for her would be Garcia and another of his new friends, Robert Hunter. (Later it would be Hunter who took each of them aside and told them their feelings were mutual.) Another friend on the scene was Alan Trist, an eighteen-year-old Brit who'd arrived in the States with his father, who was then in the midst of a fellowship at Stanford. The car was most likely Hunter's 1940 Chrysler, purchased for all of $50, and the gaggle of friends would start it up and go in search of one party or another. They were living the relatively carefree life of Kennedy-era kids who sought nothing more than to reject the draining daily jobs and lives of their parents: too young to be beatniks, too early in history to be called anything close to "hippies." As Meier says, "We got together because we didn't fit in anywhere else."

The Chateau was a world unto itself. Once the owner began renting out rooms, the house, which overlooked Los Alamos Highway, became a gathering place for seemingly every outlier in the area. "The owner liked us better than the students," says Laird Grant, a friend of Garcia's who joined him in crashing there. "We brought young girls around." All sorts of oddball characters wandered in and out, jazz often blasting from its rooms and weekly poker games on the schedule. Although the place had an illicit air, the police mostly stayed away.

Based on all the reports in and around Cuba, Garcia and Meier realized those carefree days could be numbered. From what they'd heard, that Saturday in October could be the moment tensions would either simmer down or erupt in nuclear catastrophe. For Meier the feeling was overwhelming, but Garcia had almost grown accustomed to sudden, unexpected loss. It had already haunted the first twenty years of his life, and each episode had left irrevocable scars on his body or his psyche.

■ ◆ ▲

The first tragedy was so painful he couldn't talk about it. In August 1947 Joe Garcia, the son of a Spanish immigrant and owner of a bar in downtown San Francisco, was fishing in the Trinity River in northwest California. (The first Garcias had come to America from Spain less than thirty years before Jerry's birth.) With Joe on the trip were his wife, Ruth Marie (nicknamed Bobbie, possibly to avoid confusion with her sister-in-law, Ruth), and his five-year-old son, Jerry. Whether his son was watching or not—and his older brother, Clifford, or Tiff, would long believe he wasn't—Joe slipped, fell in the water, and drowned after being trapped underwater. Tiff had been staying with grandparents in the Santa Cruz Mountains when the horrific accident happened. When Tiff saw his younger brother at the funeral, all Jerry could talk about was the fish hatchery they'd seen on the trip. "I'm thinking, 'Your dad dies and all you can remember is the fish hatchery wherever they were?'" Tiff says. "He had something good to tell me, and it was about the fish hatchery."

It may have been the only way for the youngest Garcia in the family to process the ways in which the life he'd once known was effectively over. He'd been born John Jerome Garcia on August 1, 1942—his middle name a salute to composer Jerome Kern. Born José, Jerry's father, Joe, was a musician himself, playing the clarinet and saxophone in several local bands, even once touring the country. After marrying his second wife, Ruth, he opened a bar, Joe Garcia's, in 1937. Although Joe was no longer a full-time musician (Jerry would later say Joe had been "blackballed by the [musicians] union" over an infraction), music was still in the air in other forms: one of Jerry's grandmothers would listen to Grand Ole Opry broadcasts on the radio, introducing him to country music, and both Jerry and Tiff, born in 1937, took piano lessons at home, albeit briefly. Tiff (whose nickname derived from the way his younger brother would unintentionally mangle his name) remembers Jerry as more of a voracious reader, devouring comic books twice as fast as he did.

Although it wasn't as psychically scarring as his father's death, young Jerry dealt with another loss mere months before Joe's drowning. At the family's summer home in Santa Cruz County in the spring of 1947 the two Garcia boys were tending to one of their regular chores, chopping the wood: Jerry would put the splinters down, and Tiff would hack. But one time Jerry didn't pull his finger back fast enough, and Tiff's ax bit into the middle finger of his brother's right hand. Jerry was rushed to a hospital, where part of his finger was amputated, and Tiff remembers the bandages becoming smaller and smaller until all that was left was a stub with a tiny bandage. "It was an accident," Tiff says. "I knew I'd done something wrong, but when you're kids, you just go, 'Sorry it happened.'" (Many years later, on a trip in Hawaii, a diving instructor's son would see Garcia's missing finger and ask what had happened. Garcia relayed the story of the accident simply and sweetly, as if it were a storybook tale, and the kid asked whether it would grow back. "Jerry just laughed and said, 'Nah, I don't think so,'" recalls his friend Debbie Gold, who was aboard the boat. "He wasn't the least bit self-conscious about it.")

As scarring as that incident was, it would seem trivial compared to what happened in the Trinity River. At Joe Garcia's open-casket funeral neither son could bring himself to look at their father's body; it was too painful and too disturbing. For at least a year after Joe's death Ruth would put Jerry and Tiff to bed at night and say, "God bless Daddy in heaven." The words became a standard nightly prayer and routine, along with Jerry and Tiff's regimen of hopping a streetcar, bringing flowers to the cemetery, and heading back home.

After Joe died and Ruth took over running the bar, Tiff and Jerry moved in with their maternal grandparents. (In a foreshadowing of Jerry's later, rock-star life, his grandfather, who owned a laundry, would take the boys' clothes and wash and return them to the boys.) Ruth remarried twice, and the second marriage, to Wally Matusiewicz, was especially difficult on Jerry, as Wally was a seaman who, as Dead biographer Dennis McNally wrote, "expected his stepsons to work alongside him on home projects." Already artistically inclined, Jerry had little interest in that type of labor. After Union Oil bought out Joe Garcia's, the company built a new bar for Ruth across the street, and soon the family left the city and moved to Menlo Park in the Peninsula area south of San Francisco.

From the moment Laird Grant transferred into the Menlo Oaks Middle School in the fall of 1955, the prematurely hardened kid, who'd grown up in San Francisco before his family relocated south, heard about that Garcia kid and his "stay-away reputation." Garcia was neither hood nor greaser, neither school-level criminal nor oily haired biker. In Grant's memory he was a chubby kid with hair so short it made his head seemed like it came to a point. In spite of his last name, Garcia didn't strike Grant or any of their friends as Hispanic; he didn't, for instance, speak with an accent. The rumors of Garcia as a bad boy were confirmed the day Grant walked across a field to school and was jumped by a couple of kids, including Garcia, who was a year older than Grant. As Garcia sat on Grant's chest and smeared his face with lipstick, another of the kids tried to pull Grant's pants off. "That was a big thing in those days," Grant says. "Run back to school and you'd have to show up in your tighty-whities, lipstick all over your face." It was a harmless initiation prank, and luckily Grant lived close enough to the park to be able to race back home, change, and return to school.

Later he saw Garcia again, but instead of feeling angry, he sensed a bond with the kid who'd just roughed him up. "We looked at each other and said, 'Ha, I know you!'" Grant recalls. Even at that age Garcia could get away with almost anything.

The accident that cost Jerry his finger would haunt his older brother for years after: "It's one of those things you don't ever get over," Tiff says. "It never goes away." But Tiff's little brother loved nothing better than to devise ways of having fun with his abnormality and messing with people's heads along the way—like poking his truncated digit into the ears of fellow classmates and watching their scared reaction. "He'd go up to kids and grab 'em and stick that knobby bony piece of weirdness in 'em," Grant says. "Made them freak." Garcia might also jam that finger into his nostril to make it look as if he was sticking his finger all the way up his nose. The missing finger only added to his image, especially when he would boast, wrongly, that the absent part of his finger was in a jar of alcohol at home and accepting visitors. That Garcia kid surely had a twisted sense of humor.

Although Menlo Park was a placid suburb seemingly ideal for raising a family, Garcia's life was again destined to be unsettled. In 1957 the family returned to San Francisco, where Jerry attended a much rougher school and had to, in his later words, become "a hoodlum . . . otherwise you walked down the street and somebody beats you up." The Garcias relocated once more to Cazadero, several hours northwest of the city in Sonoma County. (Once a week Garcia, whose artwork was beginning to blossom as well, also attended the California School of Fine Arts.) By then Tiff was gone; an army recruiter who'd popped into Ruth's bar convinced her that her oldest would be better off if he signed up, which led Tiff into the Marine Corps.

Starting in the middle school where they met, Garcia and Grant increasingly pushed the boundaries of what was acceptable. Jumping the fence at the Golden State Dairy and purloining chocolate milk and ice cream from the trucks in the early morning hours was one thing—"no fingerprints, no breaking locks, no damage," Grant still boasts—but their adventures soon turned more mind expanding. Garcia began bringing around pills. "He would say, 'Look at this, man!'" Grant says. "He'd have ten or twelve different-colored pills in his hand. We'd take 'em and drop 'em." Garcia never said where the pills came from, although other kids were known to sneak into their family's bathrooms and grab their parents' prescriptions. After the Garcia bar would close for the night the two boys had one job to attend to: pouring whatever was left in all the bottles into one jug, which they would then guzzle down. (Garcia later developed an aversion to alcohol, and it's easy to imagine it starting with those concoctions.) Later the two friends also shared their first joint—to Garcia, a far more immediately appealing high.

An enticing high of a different sort was beckoning. In eighth grade Garcia had taken a stab at playing saxophone, perhaps as a way to continue his father's legacy, but his partially missing middle finger made it tricky to play. Another instrument, and another genre, was beckoning. Garcia would long boast that for his fifteenth birthday his mother had given him an accordion, which he almost immediately traded in at a pawn shop for his first electric guitar, spending the following months figuring out how to play it. The timing was profound. Rock 'n' roll was now a few years old and clearly wasn't fading away: in 1957 Garcia could turn on a radio at any moment and hear the Everly Brothers' "Bye Bye Love" and "Wake Up, Little Susie," Elvis's "All Shook Up," Fats Domino's "I'm Walkin'," and Chuck Berry's "School Day."

Garcia was discovering his type of friends and his type of musical expression, but in one area at least, he didn't feel especially comfortable. Every so often a bunch of the kids would head to Playland, the waterfront amusement park in the Richmond district of San Francisco. They'd play arcade games and eat pie, but Garcia's mood would change slightly when they approached the water. "He'd get little twitches about it," Grant says. "He was always kind of weird when we went out to the beach." Garcia never said why, but friends assumed the water triggered memories of his father's death and the hole it left in him.

■   ◆   ■

Around 5 p.m. Garcia and Meier arrived at their possibly final destination. The field before them was one of gently waving golden grass, black oak trees, and nothing in sight: not the Chateau, not the roads, not the thriving Stanford campus sprawled out below them. There was no sign of Menlo Park, a town only thirty-five years old, nor of Palo Alto, which had arisen even earlier as a village for Stanford faculty. Before World War II Palo Alto had been home to only about seventeen thousand people; that number had now more than tripled, to fifty-five thousand, and the area had made way for a shopping center, an industrial park, and two thousand mass-produced homes. Subdivisions began taking over empty fields, and roughly seventy thousand cars entered and left the town every day. Yet Palo Alto also retained its only-in-California lure. When Garcia's future partner Mountain Girl arrived the following summer, her earliest memories would be riding her bike and seeing oranges, apples, walnuts, and peaches lying on the sidewalks after falling off trees. Palm trees loomed over other houses. It felt like paradise, especially because it barely seemed to rain.

Settling onto the grass, Garcia and Meier talked and cried a bit, then began singing. The song was "Go Down, Old Hannah," an African American prison work song recorded by Lead Belly, among others. (During this time Garcia had discovered the Folkways label, and one of its collections included a version of the song sung by actual Texas inmates.) In its original form the song was the inmates' way of ending the day; "Hannah" was the sun. But tonight, on this hill and in this situation, the lyric—"if you rise in the morning, well, well, well / Bring judgment for sure"—took on a far more fraught context. "We were trying to hasten the sun setting so the day would come to an end," Meier says. "We thought that if we got through the day, things would be okay—it wouldn't be the end of the world. If we got through this particular twenty-four hours of saber rattling with the Soviet Union, we would all survive." So they sang to Hannah, over and over.

Garcia had arrived in the Peninsula early the previous year after tackling the unlikeliest of jobs. After dropping out of high school, he told Tiff he was planning to follow him into the service. Tiff tried to talk his brother out of it, feeling it wouldn't be a good match, but it didn't work: "He wanted to get away from his mom and stepfather, I think," Tiff says. (According to Blair Jackson's *Garcia: An American Life*, Jerry also stole his mother's car, paving the way for his stint in the army.) Other friends think it may have been a way for Garcia to drum up some money, and Garcia himself later said it was simply an alternative to college or staying with his family. Whatever the motivation, Garcia found himself at Fort Ord in Monterey in the spring of 1960. "If you were rich, you went to West Point," says Grant. "If you were poor, you went to Monterey." Visiting him at Fort Ord, Grant was struck by Garcia's shaved head and khakis, but the sight didn't last long. Garcia's stint, which also included an assignment at a fort in the Presidio area, lasted all of eight months. After spending too much time with a friend who was considering suicide in San Francisco, Garcia was declared AWOL (one of several times this occurred) and was drummed out of the service at year's end.

As 1961 began, Garcia had no job, no prospects, and few instruments, but at least he found a thriving community to welcome him when he followed friends down to the Peninsula. Stanford, which had opened in the late 1800s, had established itself as a leading hub for scientific research and intellectual thought; just as Garcia arrived, the school built a $1.2 million medical lab. The area was crammed with students, academics, and the children of professors along with the attendant bo-hemians, artists, and liberal thinkers. With its coffeehouses and book stores, Palo Alto held an ambrosial lure to those who felt they didn't fit in with the rest of the country or their own households. Garcia began spending time at Kepler's (in its original location in Menlo Park—a second Kepler's opened in Palo Alto in 1962) or St. Michael's Alley, the high-ceilinged coffeehouse known for its Danish open-faced sand-wiches, wine, and beer. That space also became known for Joan Baez, the unswervingly pure-voiced teenager who played there when she was a high school student in Palo Alto before her family moved east in 1958.

From almost the moment he arrived in the area Garcia befriended similarly offbeat characters, sometimes at Kepler's. One was Trist, and another was Paul Speegle, a high school friend of Barbara Meier's who would prance around school in a cape just, in her words, to "outrage the straights." The three men, along with Lee Adams, an African Ameri-can who worked at the Chateau, were driving in the area on the night of February 1961 when the car, going far over the speed limit, hit a tricky curve and crashed. Speegle was instantly killed; the other three sustained a range of injuries, with Garcia, violently ejected from the car, winding up with a broken collar bone and other wounds. Although Garcia wasn't as close to Speegle as he was to his own father, it was yet another example of the way lives could change, dramatically, on a dime. "It set Jerry back on his heels," says Grant. "It brought the reality of, 'Oh, shit, you can die.' Until it happens to someone close to you, it's just something that happens to others. That's a hell of a reality sandwich, a big bite."

At the same time, a replacement of sorts for Speegle appeared in their lives. At a local production of *Damn Yankees* Garcia's girlfriend of the moment was working the lights and introduced him to one of her exes, Robert Hunter, a nineteen-year-old with horn-rimmed glasses and a clenched grin. A few nights later Hunter wandered into St. Michael's, looking for someone to hang with, and ran into Garcia again. Hunter, who'd lived everywhere from the West Coast to Connecticut, had in a way lost his own father too. Born Robert Burns in June 1941, Hunter had suffered through the breakup of his parents when he was young, which resulted in him spending time (being "boarded out," as the phrase went at the time) with families between the ages of nine and eleven. His mother eventually remarried, and his new stepfather was a national sales manager for the college division of McGraw-Hill as well as an editor at Harcourt. Growing up in different locales—from Palo Alto to Connecticut—made him feel like "always the new kid in school."

Despite their differences in family backgrounds and schooling (Hunter had logged some time at college at the University of Connecticut), Hunter and Garcia were natural allies. At Kepler's, the Chateau, or other local digs, they could be seen playing guitars together, singing Weavers' songs, riffing on *Finnegans Wake*, and chewing over whatever else they were reading and devouring at the time. "Hunter was often bummed," Meier says. "He had some sense of things being tragic. He never seemed all that happy except when he was singing—then out came this rousing, exuberant voice." He and Garcia's respective cars were parked next to each other at one point, and each slept in his own vehicle and lived off whatever food they could scrounge up (sometimes from female students at Stanford, whom Garcia would charm into nabbing grub from the cafeteria). Before long they'd even formed a loose duo, Bob and Jerry, and performed at Stanford and Meier's sixteenth birthday party, right after she'd met Garcia. As her parents cooked a barbeque, Garcia and Hunter, along with a slew of friends who all seemed to have beards, strummed and sang "Michael, Row the Boat Ashore" and other summer-camp favorites.

The move to folk music was a natural one; even though groups like the Kingston Trio were amassing hit singles and earning a small fortune on tour, the music represented everything seemingly authentic at the moment, the antidote to the commercial culture. The year 1962 was far from barren for earthy early rock 'n' roll; Dion's "The Wanderer," Little Eva's "The Loco-Motion," and Booker T. and the MG's "Green Onions" shook up the radio, but the music felt at an impasse, and schlock like Bobby Vinton's "Roses Are Red (My Love)" continued to dominate the airwaves. The high school days when Garcia would play intermittently with a band called the Chords must have felt even farther away in light of how rock 'n' roll had faltered. It wasn't uncommon to see Garcia walking around with a banjo or with one of the two guitars Meier had bought for him. A few months before the Cuban Missile Crisis he'd been introduced to the banjo by another member of the scene, Marshall Leicester, a sophomore at Yale who'd known Garcia at school in Menlo Park and reconnected with him in the Palo Alto area in the summer of 1961.

Folk music also led Garcia to the next, even purer form of acoustic music, bluegrass and string bands. Thanks to Leicester, Garcia had become fascinated with the banjo, playing on it for hours at a time at the Chateau, Kepler's, or anywhere that would have him. "I don't know if you've spent time with someone rehearsing 'Foggy Mountain Breakdown' on a banjo for eight hours, but Jerry practiced endlessly," Meier says. "He really wanted to excel and be the best. He had tremendous personal ambition in the musical arena, and he wanted to master whatever he set out to explore. Then he would set another sight for himself. And practice another eight hours a day of new licks." It would be the first indication that making music could take priority over attending to his personal life.

Garcia's musical partners in crime—Hunter, Leicester, Nelson, and another bluegrass-obsessed local picker, Sandy Rothman—shared his passion for acoustic genres. What followed, with varying lineups, was a succession of unplugged bands with ever-changing names: the Thunder Mountain Tub Thumpers, the Sleepy Hollow Hog Stompers, the Hart Valley Drifters. Hunter logged time in some of them, but Garcia didn't consider his friend a serious enough musician and didn't think he practiced mandolin nearly enough. Before long the two had had their first major falling out. Hunter had already begun writing his first novel and was seeking his own adventures at the time. To earn extra cash he volunteered for a psychology experiment at the local veterans hospital in 1962. One week he was given LSD, followed by psilocybin the next, mescaline the third week, and all four together the last week. The military wanted to know whether people who took those drugs could be easily hypnotized—the drugs were seen as potential weapons—and Hunter only told a few people about it, including Garcia and Meier. None of them could believe he'd done such a thing: it sounded so mysterious and enticing that everyone wanted in.

The string band names may have been gags—white kids gently mocking the real string bands of the South—but the fledgling musicians took to the music with an unabashed earnestness. "It was some kind of search for authenticity, for real American music," Meier says. "That's what was at the heart of it, finding something unsullied." As one newcomer to the scene noticed, the boys looked straight and dressed the same way. The previous fall a Washington, DC–based guitarist named Jorma Kaukonen (who went by Jerry for a while) had arrived in California to attend Santa Clara College. His first night on the campus he wandered into a folk club and met Garcia and a young, throat-shredding Texas transplant named Janis Joplin, and eventually he would share the bill with one of Garcia's acoustic bands in Palo Alto. "The bluegrass guys at the time dressed nicely," Kaukonen says. "We hadn't cultivated the jeans-and-T-shirt look yet. Jerry had that bluegrass ambience of the period."

Norm van Maastricht had also arrived in the Bay Area shortly before, following his parents, who'd moved from Michigan. Considering himself a serious country-style guitar player in the vein of Chet Atkins, he wanted to meet other musicians and take lessons, and he kept hearing about a teacher who worked out of a music store in Palo Alto. The business, the Dana Morgan Music Shop, was known for its impressive, jammed-to-the-ceiling collection of acoustic instruments for sale. In one of the practice rooms in the back of the store van Maastricht finally caught up with Garcia, the first bearded person he'd ever met. Given Garcia's missing digit, van Maastricht felt a strange sensation when he shook Garcia's hand, and he also noticed Garcia liked to talk while playing his banjo, making it hard to hear him over the clatter of the instrument.

Van Maastricht became part of Garcia's inner circle of bluegrass musician friends. Every so often he'd get a call asking whether he wanted to play and would soon after find himself in a car with Garcia and whoever else constituted the band, all of them making their way to a club, house party, or anyplace that would have them. "We felt almost driven to play anytime, anywhere, with anyone," he says. "The hunger was never satisfied." By the fall of 1962 the latest lineup had dubbed itself the Hart Valley Drifters and featured Garcia, Hunter, Nelson, and van Maastricht. Practice would sometimes take place at the Chateau. Every so often the same dedication and drive Meier saw in Garcia would also arise in the band too. One day the other Drifters were yapping away about this and that, all talking at once. Garcia was increasingly irked. "Guys . . . guys . . . fellas . . . *boys*," he said, his voice growing ever so slightly more assertive each time.

"You could tell he was irritated and wanted them to shut up and get on with it, but he didn't want to say, 'Shut up and get on with it!'" van Maastricht says. "He had that low tone." Garcia's insistence helped. By the time of the Cuban Missile Crisis the Hart Valley Drifters were scheduled to play an art gallery at San Francisco State and also headline a folk festival at the College of San Mateo.

■ ◆ ■

A month before Garcia and Meier made their way up through the fields near Sand Hill Road, John Perry Barlow sat in his first day of English class at the Fountain Valley High School in Colorado Springs, Colorado. Hearing a leg thrumming behind him, he turned around and saw a classmate with nerdy black glasses, short hair, a thin face, a monobrow, and a look that was slightly cross-eyed. He seemed like a bit of an oddball, but equally strange was Barlow's initial feeling that they were kindred spirits and had known each other already.

One thing was certain: both were troublemakers who'd been shipped off to their all-boys boarding school for a reason. Barlow had been raised in Wyoming, where he was part of a Boy Scout troop whose members turned borderline delinquent when they began riding motorcycles. Because Barlow's father was a Republican state legislator who didn't want to attract that sort of attention, Barlow, an only child, was sent to Fountain Valley. There he learned that many of his fellow students, including this strange-looking one behind him, had also been kicked out of one school or another. The kid's name turned out to be Bob Weir, and as Barlow learned that same day, Weir was living right across the hall from him in one of the Fountain Valley dorms.

Weir, Barlow soon discovered, had grown up in a lovely house with a long driveway and a swimming pool in Atherton, an affluent suburb west of Palo Alto. All that were missing were his birth parents. Weir's father, a military man named John Parber who years later would wind up an Air Force colonel, had been involved with a woman in his native Tucson, Arizona; when she became pregnant she went to San Francisco and had the baby on October 16, 1947, without telling Parber. The baby would later be adopted by another military man, Frederick Weir, and his wife, Eleanor, and named Robert Hall Weir. "It was an idyllic place," recalls Matthew Kelly, an Atherton buddy who met Weir during a Halloween trick-or-treat playtime one year. "No crime. A great place to grow up." According to Bob, Frederick Weir was amiable, a "consummate gentleman" who was more than capable of holding his liquor; his son never saw his father drunk, just with "a twinkle in his eye."

Bob would be similarly civil, but something inside him was incorrigible and offbeat, perhaps the result of a spinal meningitis illness during his childhood or simply the way his brain was wired. In the fall of 1960 Weir began attending the Menlo School for Boys, a quasi-military academy where students wore gray flannel pants, blue blazers, and ties. Even in that setting Weir's head seemed to operate at a different speed from his fellow students'. In class he'd deconstruct sentences and reconstruct them backward. "He'd sit there and look off into space for a second," recalls Vance Frost, a classmate, "and you knew he was working on something. Then it would come out where the object would come first and the subject would come later. It was very unusual. I'd go, 'Wow, his mind is different.'"

Weir was also a jock, a member of the football team, as he would be at Fountain Valley. (When the football coach at the Menlo School ordered everyone to go home that night and tape their name to the backs of their helmets, Weir, in a subtly rebellious gesture, returned the next time with his name in old English calligraphy; he did the same with Frost's helmet too.) But participating in team sports was one of the few ways he would conform. If students heard about a firecracker being set off outside a classroom or a prank pulled on a teacher, they naturally assumed Weir had something to do with it, even if he only flashed a sly smile and never admitted to anything. In eighth grade a group of Menlo School boys were asked to be escorts at a debutante ball. Weir and Frost tolerated it as best they could, but during a break they skipped out a back door. Weir had girls on his mind, but in other ways: another classmate, Michael Wanger, recalls that Weir could sketch a naked woman in seconds.

Weir had started playing guitar at thirteen, and by the time he'd enrolled in Fountain Valley he, like Barlow, had immersed himself in vernacular music. The two would trade records by the Greenbriar Boys, Cisco Houston, and other authentic or semi-authentic vernacular types. Neither kid was much interested in what amounted to modern rock 'n' roll, which seemed a spent force by 1962, what with Buddy Holly dead and Elvis still getting his career back on track after serving in the army. "I was fifteen, sixteen years old at the time and very much attuned to the trends," Weir said to David Hajdu. "[Folk music] was in vogue among the artsy-fartsy kids set. There was something in there that was ringing my bells. What I had grown up thinking of as hillbilly music, it started to have some depth for me, and I could start to hear the music in it. Suddenly, it wasn't just a bunch of ignorant hillbillies playing what they could. There was some depth and expertise and stuff like that to aspire to."

Even though they were holed up in the middle of the country, far from their homes, Weir and Barlow had no interest in leaving their wild streaks behind. "It was a Godless subdivision where everyone went to sleep at ten," Barlow recalls. "There wasn't too much trouble to get into, but we managed anyway." One night the two jumped a fence, wandered out into the prairie that surrounded the school, and dug a lavish tunnel complete with underground lairs. The boys were proud of their feat, but when they found the spot, school officials were less than impressed. A biology class semi–food fight—where dead frogs, not luncheon meat, were hurled—would become legendary. Both kids were now under scrutiny. Weir was clearly a misfit, albeit a mild-mannered one. As 1962 drew to a close he just needed a better, more welcoming outlet for that sensibility.

It wasn't until he made one of his trips to Kepler's in early 1962 that Phil Lesh made the connection. Among the rows of paperbacks he'd spotted a biography of French composer Claude Debussy. With his goatee and short hair parted to the right, the man on the cover looked very much like that guy Lesh had met at the Chateau the previous fall. Lesh was neither folkie nor rocker—he'd been raised on classical music, hence his interest in the likes of Debussy—but the book jacket and the physical resemblance made Garcia seem somehow more accessible and intriguing. "It made me want to listen more closely to what Jerry was doing musically," Lesh says. "How curious is *that?* Sometimes things work that way, those kinds of associations."

Born Philip Chapman Lesh on March 15, 1940, he, like Garcia, was the child of an industrious father—in his case, Frank, who was so adept at repairing office equipment that he opened his own shop in the Bay Area. Like Garcia, young Lesh was the offspring of two working parents and spent quality time during his childhood with his grandmother. But the outward comparisons ended there. Lesh's grandmother had helped raise him on a regular diet of classical music, and before long Lesh was learning to play violin in grade school. The blond crew cut he sported during this time made him look like the band geek he inherently was, and sure enough, he landed a seat in the kids' orchestra at age ten. Compared to classical music, rock 'n' roll seemed crude and unappealing. "I detested it," Lesh says. "I thought it was totally infantile. Three chords over and over and over again. I'm coming from Beethoven and Mahler." (Talking about his early antirock prejudices in a radio interview in 1990, Lesh added, with a laugh, "I'm happy to eat those words now and forever.")

Whether it was a result of his brain, his personality, or his dismissive attitude toward rock 'n' roll, Lesh not surprisingly became a loner during his teen years. "I didn't have many friends in the fifties," he says. "I wasn't very popular at all." In a sense his best friend was music, so much so that his parents moved to Berkeley so he could attend that city's high school, which had a far better music program. By then he was specializing in trumpet. After graduating high school he enrolled in San Francisco State but left halfway through his freshman year and soon returned home. Finally, in the fall of 1958—the same time Garcia began his difficult year of tenth grade at the rough Balboa High School in San

Francisco—Lesh began classes at the College of San Mateo, which introduced him to experimental modern music, Beat writing (by way of a classmate and new friend, Bobby Peterson), and pot. Taking entrance exams for UC Berkeley in 1961, Lesh met Tom Constanten, a fellow classical music fanatic and outlier. Born in New Jersey in 1944, Constanten had relocated with his family to Las Vegas ten years later. He recalls Lesh as "strikingly blond" and similarly inclined to avoid pop music. "The music we were into was off the beaten path," Constanten says. "It was rare to find someone else who was into that. It was almost like a secret society, and we didn't know we were members until we met."

During his time at the College of San Mateo Lesh began making pilgrimages to the Palo Alto area, and like so many others, he was bewitched by Kepler's, St. Michael's Alley, and the grimier, R&B-inclined hangouts in East Palo Alto. "It was the only game in town," he said years later to writer Hajdu. "There were just all these neat people who seemed to be congregated in one place. You could go to St. Michael's Alley and play music all night long, and you only had to buy one cup of coffee. Every once in a while one of the girls would get up and dance flamenco on top of a table, and that was okay." He'd also finally developed a taste for folk music, if not outright rock 'n' roll.

By way of John "the Cool" Winter, another member of Garcia's crowd, Lesh had finally met Garcia, most likely at the Chateau. At a party at the house around the time of Lesh's twenty-second birthday someone brought along a sizable bag of weed to help him celebrate, and Lesh, Garcia, and anyone else around got blissfully stoned. "It seemed like enough to last a year at the time," Lesh recalls. "I don't think we went through all of it, but we tried." Soon after, at a party in East Palo Alto, Lesh became entranced as he watched Garcia sing and play "Matty Groves," the old English folk ballad about an affair between a lady of the manor and a servant that ends in death when the woman's husband, a lord, learns about it. "It was absolutely operatic," Lesh says. "It was a deadpan delivery and minimal guitar picking, but the whole thing was mesmerizing." Afterward, in what Lesh calls "that adolescent hyperbolic way," he told Garcia he was in the presence of greatness, and Garcia just snickered and said, "Yeah, right, man."

Given his love of classical and experimental music, not to mention his barbershop-short haircut and height (he stood over six feet tall), Lesh distinguished himself in the scene in more ways than one. He seemed to talk at a quicker pace than everyone around him. For Meier's sixteenth birthday Lesh wrote her a piece of music, a score, and told her it should be "played as fast as possible." He seemed like the last person who would connect with Garcia, but for reasons both musical and personal, Lesh felt a bond from the start. "I have to confess, I always told my parents 'Gee, I'd really love to have a brother,'" he says. "I guess I saw other families where there were two brothers. He was one of those guys you realize would be a friend for life." To Constanten, the two were "complimentary and sympathetic, like strings on a guitar. Phil and I were into avant-garde, and Jerry was into the Carter Family. We hadn't had enough of a map exposed to see where the roads would lead. But we knew there was a connection somehow."

That connection grew sturdier when, after hearing Garcia perform "Matty Groves" that night, Lesh offered to make a tape of his new friend singing that and other traditional songs. By then Lesh was volunteering as a recording engineer at KPFA, a noncommercial talk and music station funded by listeners, and he sensed Garcia would be an ideal addition to the station's folk show. After grabbing Constanten's tape deck out of the apartment they were sharing, Lesh and Garcia raced back to the party, recorded Garcia, and soon played it for Gertrude ("Gert") Chiarito, the host of KPFA's folk show, *Midnight Special*. The friendship was mutually beneficial: thanks to Lesh, Garcia had the potential to be heard by more people than ever before, even if his own career plans were still uncertain.

Lesh was soon gone from the scene; dropping out of the University of California at Berkeley, he wound up living with Constanten and his family in Las Vegas during the summer of 1962. (In between, he and Constanten signed up for composer Luciano Berio's composition class at Mills College in Oakland, which also fostered their mutual love of adventurous music.) Constanten's parents took issue with Lesh—who, by then, was letting his hair grow out—and asked him to leave, although Constanten says he never understood what happened: "They would yell at me, and I never knew what I did," he says. "It was a very old-world sort of thing." Either way, Lesh wound up taking a job at the post office in Vegas, hoping to work his way back to Palo Alto when he could.

But that night on the *Midnight Special* show Lesh didn't simply have another chance to observe Garcia's musical prowess; he also noticed the way Garcia effortlessly bantered with Chiarito, whom everyone knew was no pushover. "She had a lot of local folkies kissing her ass, and Jerry didn't do that," Lesh says. "He was just himself. I was watching him win her over instantaneously." Few others in their world, Lesh included, had those types of people skills at that point in their lives, yet Garcia already seemed to have mastered it. As Leicester would later tell Hajdu, Garcia was "a kind of natural bohemian, but he was a bohemian who knew how to find his way through the establishment. He had the ability to make people like him and get done what he wanted to do." That ability to subvert from within would become increasingly useful as the years went by.

◆ ◆ ◆

As dusk approached, Garcia and Meier sang "Go Down, Old Hannah" a few more times. Eventually the sun set, and they were still alive.

The two didn't know it at the time—in the days before the Internet and twenty-four-hour cable news, few did immediately—but Kennedy and Khrushchev had already defused the situation with Cuba. At almost the same time the couple had climbed their hill, at 8:05 p.m. Eastern time, (5:05 p.m. Pacific time) Kennedy had offered a deal to

Khrushchev: in a telegram he asserted that the Soviet Union "would agree to remove these weapons systems from Cuba under appropriate United Nations observation and supervision; and undertake, with suitable safeguards, to halt the further introduction of such weapons systems into Cuba," while the United States would vow not to invade Cuba. (The United States would also remove its missiles from Turkey.) The Peninsula hadn't been scorched by a nuclear mushroom cloud; the grass around them was still golden.

Garcia and Meier began making their way down the hill and back to their homes. When she arrived at her parents' house late that night, Meier's parents made her dinner and told her they'd been worried sick, and her mother hugged her.

For Garcia, who'd been deeply affected after reading George Orwell's *1984* in grade school, the incident was yet another reminder that the establishment, especially the government, couldn't be trusted. The mere thought that the world had almost ended over a macho showdown between two heads of state felt absurd to both him and Meier. A few years later, with the band that would finally make him more famous than he probably wanted to be, he would begin singing "Morning Dew," Bonnie Dobson's elliptical but haunting ballad about life after nuclear fallout, inspired by the novel (and movie) *On the Beach*. The song had a mournful and resigned tone to start with, even when pop star Lulu covered it later, but Garcia brought to its lyrics a palpable ache, stretching out some of the notes as if he were digging deep into that spooked side of himself and his past.

The Cuban Missile Crisis was also another reminder of the fragility and impermanence of the world. The planet hadn't ended, but just as with the death of his father and Speegle, Garcia's world could have been tossed on its head in a heartbeat. "It was the beginning of us realizing that there were forces that could whisk away the people you love and the whole freaking planet," Meier says. "With the Cold War that

became an ongoing subliminal message, which is probably one reason why Jerry never made any plans." Years later, after she had reconnected with him, Meier would wonder about the impact of that night
on Garcia's later bad habits, as well as the culture of the Grateful Dead
itself. The message couldn't have been less ambiguous: it was best to
live in the moment, do whatever one wanted, and find pleasure in it
because that moment could be taken away at any time.

The Warlocks, 1965: Garcia and McKernan (top row),
Kreutzmann, Weir, and Lesh (seated).
© HERB GREENE

CHAPTER 2

MENLO PARK, CALIFORNIA, MAY 26, 1965

It was pretty much the last place anyone expected to find a rock 'n' roll band. Jammed between local business stores on Menlo Park's main shopping drag, Magoo's was a pizza parlor, not a nightclub or bar. It didn't look all that different from the thousands that had popped up around the country after World War II, when American soldiers returning from Europe talked up the delicious bread, tomato sauce, and cheese concoctions they'd wolfed down in Italy. Most of the American pizza chains and restaurants bore a resemblance to Magoo's—long and narrow, picnic-style benches lined along the wall up front, a counter and oven to the right, florescent lighting overhead. But in a town teeming with college and high school students yearning for places to bond, Magoo's was a gathering place for the emerging tribe.

On this Wednesday night the young band making a clanging racket inside was as idiosyncratic as the setting. The lead guitarist now had a helmet head of thick, curly hair; his goatee had been banished for the time being to his bluegrass days. Hunched over a portable Vox organ was a stocky kid with an equally unkempt mop, a spotty complexion, and a truculent gaze that dared anyone to mess with him. (The hair on both looked like it had been smushed down on their heads.) The other three—the drummer, the bass player, and especially the rhythm guitarist, so young looking he could easily have been on a middle school night out—appeared straighter and not quite as grubby. The sound they were making, bouncing off Magoo's brick walls, was a clattering, exuberant, but not fully shaped mash-up of blues, jug band, rock 'n' roll, and R&B. "They were still searching for their own sound," recalls John McLaughlin, who'd taken percussion lessons from the Warlocks' drummer, Bill Kreutzmann. "I thought, 'This is weird stuff.' Most of the local bands sounded like the Beatles or the Stones. The Warlocks sounded like music from the first *Star Wars*, when Luke Skywalker walks into the bar and they're playing reverse jazz. It sounded really strange."

The first time the Warlocks had set up musical shop at Magoo's, three weeks earlier, a small group of friends had shown up along with a smattering of high school kids they'd enticed. "It wasn't too hard to get the student population to come hear music," says one of those friends, Palo Alto High School student Connie Bonner (later Bonner Mosley). "It was perfect timing: 'Come over after school to Magoo's—have a pizza!' They all came." It almost didn't matter how the band sounded; with rock 'n' roll experiencing a heady, joyful rebirth, the *idea* of the Warlocks would be enticing enough.

That first night at Magoo's, May 5, the Warlocks' lack of experience—the second guitarist, Bob Weir, had barely even held an electric guitar before—became amusingly apparent when they started playing. Some of them sat on stools, staring at each other instead of at the small crowd gathered in front of them. Bonner and her friend Sue Swanson, who'd become the band's first two loyal fans, the original Deadheads, called upon their extensive knowledge of the Beatles' stage craft and went over and offered the Warlocks advice: leave the stools, stand up, turn around, make eye contact. They were playing *rock 'n' roll* now, not bluegrass or jug-band music, and the songs required more visceral skills. The musicians, especially the lead guitarist, Weir's older buddy Garcia, seemed thankful for the suggestions. After all, what did *they* know about doing this? Tonight's show had at least one slightly wholesome touch: because it was Swanson's seventeenth birthday, her mother, much to her daughter's embarrassment, showed up with a cake.

With each of the Warlocks' weekly Wednesday shows that followed, Magoo's grew a bit more congested, the crowd eventually spilling out onto the sidewalk on Santa Cruz Avenue. (Granted, it took only a few dozen people to do that, but it certainly looked impressive to anyone passing by.) Sometimes the Warlocks played in a corner in the back; other nights, like tonight, they were jammed into a space near the front window. Earlier, the local fire marshal had dropped by and been concerned about the overflow crowd. (Although May 27 has often been cited as the day of the Warlocks' third Magoo's show, that was a Thursday, so May 26 is likely the correct date.)

Among Garcia's musician friends word had spread that he was secretly venturing into electric rock 'n' roll. Some of his bluegrass-inclined buddies were dismayed, but another acquaintance outside that circle was curious to hear the makeover. As the band played that night Phil Lesh and his girlfriend, Ruth Pakhala, walked through the front door. Lesh had tried to see the Warlocks before at Magoo's but had shown up so late that he'd only been able to join in on after-show party elsewhere. There he, Weir, and Garcia shared an ample stash of pot. Tonight, though, the couple had arrived on time.

By then a thought had been buzzing around in Garcia's brain. He knew the bass player, Dana Morgan Jr., wasn't cutting it: he was too square, too straight, too disinterested in getting stoned. The Warlocks needed someone more like them: adventurous, hard-headed, a little wild. As the band took a short break—and partook of the free beer and pizza the owners of Magoo's offered in lieu of pay—Garcia put down his guitar and made a beeline for Lesh.

■ ◆ ■

The calls from Garcia with another bluegrass gig would still come into Norm van Maastricht's parents' house. On the way to the job the players would scramble to concoct a new name: in the early months of 1963 the Hart Valley Drifters gave way to the Wildwood Boys. No matter where they were headed they found themselves in one of Hunter or Garcia's scrappy cars, which chugged and wheezed their way around the Peninsula. After one particularly bumpy ride van Maastricht told Garcia he needed better wheels, if only for his safety. "Look," Garcia told him, firmly but politely, "all I want to do is to live my own weird little life my own weird little way and play music for a living." For decades to come friends and colleagues would hear a variation on that line emerge from Garcia's mouth.

For Garcia *weird* was a compliment; by then he knew he was destined for some type of alternative lifestyle and sought out friends who'd made the same decision. Two and a half years had passed since the Cuban Missile Crisis, yet those days must have felt like another lifetime for Garcia. In the time since, one relationship had dissolved and another had begun; he'd become a husband, father, and to some degree a breadwinner. The days of the Chateau were over, at least for him, and it was now his job to put meals on the table every night. Maybe this new venture—a rock 'n' roll band—would help his fiscal issues and even be artistically fulfilling.

Within months of the Kennedy-Khrushchev standoff Garcia's personal life had been dismantled. When Barbara Meier's parents learned she'd slept with Garcia, the couple suffered a serious setback. "Everything shifted," Meier says. "Then it became very difficult and it wasn't as wonderful as it once was. I had to get these geeky guys on so-called dates so I could then go with Jerry." As much as she admired her boy-friend's musical diligence, it was also becoming tedious for Meier to sit around patiently and watch him practice banjo for hours and hours on end. By early 1963, after she'd started seeing other boys, their relation-ship had soured and burnt itself out.

Whatever mourning consumed Garcia faded quickly. He soon met Sara Ruppenthal, a striking Stanford sophomore and fellow folk music fan who, like many men and women at the time, was taken with Gar-cia's Hispanic-beatnik air. (In Lesh's memory the future couple met in a parking lot as Garcia was walking and Ruppenthal was bicycling, and he hitched a ride with her.) Almost immediately the two fell into each other's arms and then his bed in his room in a shack behind the Chateau. As Ruppenthal later told Garcia biographer Blair Jackson, Garcia called her within days of their first night together and told her, "I'm really fucked up. I need to be with you. I can't eat. I can't even play music, man!" The initial heat generated between the two became palpable in more than one way. Weeks later, hanging out with Nelson, Hunter, and van Maastricht at the Peninsula Creamery, a local diner, Garcia put both elbows on the table and said, "Well, guys, looks like I have to get married!" They were shocked and asked, "Are you kid-ding? To whom?" Garcia told them his new girlfriend was pregnant. "In those days," van Maastricht says, "you did the right thing." Garcia didn't seem distraught or freaked out by the idea of becoming a parent, and in April the couple were married in Palo Alto.

Three months before the wedding a new club, the Top of the Tan-gent, had opened in Palo Alto. Located on University Avenue near the front gates of Stanford, the Tangent was run by two local doctors who wanted to bring folk to the city on a regular basis. The space was located above the Tangent restaurant and only had enough space for about twenty tables, some of which bumped up against the stage, yet

the club, which had a beer license, was more professional than anything
else in the area. A staircase led into the middle of a low-ceilinged performance space where, "if we were lucky, there was one microphone,"
recalls Jorma Kaukonen. "But they had a PA. It was a bit more glitzy.
It was a *real* place, like one of the folk clubs in LA."

The Tangent hosted Garcia's then-current bluegrass band, the Wildwood Boys (who also played at his and Sara's wedding), and before
long the new couple were also playing together there, singing folk
songs as Garcia alternated between guitar, banjo, and other instruments. In the meantime Garcia continued jamming and performing
with one or another acoustic band, including at a folk festival in Monterey. But those shows barely paid, if at all, and to earn something close
to a living Garcia had begun teaching at the Dana Morgan Music Shop.
One of his new students was Bob Matthews, a skinny Berkeley-born
teenager whose mother, a grade-school teacher, happened to mention
to a Stanford documentarian that her son wanted to learn how to play
banjo. The filmmaker turned out to be none other than Ruppenthal,
who tipped Matthews's mother to her husband, Jerry, and his classes at
Morgan's store.

As Matthews realized, Garcia was a commanding presence and impressive musician who didn't let his students get away with slacking off.
"He had a very sinister look to him," he says. "He didn't talk a lot, but
his eyes would curse you. He'd be sitting there playing and looking to
see how you were responding to his playing." Matthews, who admittedly wasn't as devoted to the instrument as was his new teacher, only
lasted a few months: "Jerry was like, 'You don't practice, you're not
gonna learn this stuff.'"

By the end of 1963 Garcia's life had taken two different and potentially conflicting turns. His daughter with Sara, Heather, arrived in
December, and on New Year's Eve he found himself alone in a practice
room in the back of Morgan's store when Matthews and two friends

popped in. At an earlier point Matthews had introduced Garcia to one of his classmates, Bob Weir, but that moment hadn't amounted to much. Tonight's get-together would be far more memorable.

To no one's surprise, Weir had arrived back in his hometown area months before. He'd been kicked out of Fountain Valley in Colorado at the end of the 1962–1963 school year, and after summering with the Barlow family in Wyoming in the middle of 1963, he'd returned to the West Coast to continue his attempt at conforming to the educational system. His efforts weren't any more successful than they'd been in Colorado. He then attended Pacific High School, a period most distinguished by the forming of Weir's first band, a folk group called the Uncalled Four that included his former Menlo School classmate Michael Wanger on banjo. "Rock 'n' roll was pretty limp at the time," says Wanger, who recalls talking with Weir about music as the two sat side by side for yearbook photos. "The only thing happening was the Beach Boys."

The group, named by Wanger's father, landed at least one job at the Tangent, and Weir, whose fascination with folk and other vernacular forms of music was expanding, began spending time at Kepler's and St. Michael's Alley. Given Weir's previously diagnosed case of dyslexia, Kepler's was problematic: "I really couldn't read very well, so I felt a little funny in a bookstore," he recalled to writer Hajdu. St. Michael's had an added attraction: women. It was, he said, "a good place to go and meet girls—and hang out with people who were the youth intelligentsia." The Tangent also pulled in its fair share of female music fans.

That New Year's Eve at Morgan's store Garcia apparently didn't realize his prospective student wouldn't be showing up, but when it hit him, he invited Matthews, Weir, and their other friend, Rich McCauley, inside. "Jerry asked us if we played and we said, 'Yeah,' and he said, 'Well, I got the keys to the front of the store, let's grab some instruments,'" Weir has said. (In another retelling of the incident Weir thinks someone suggested, "Why don't we break into the front of the store?") For several hours they all made a carefree racket on banjos and guitars, and Garcia and Weir overcame their five-year age difference—Garcia was twenty-one, Weir all of sixteen—and connected by way of music. "It was like meeting an old friend," Weir has said. "It was like taking up a conversation we'd left off." Garcia must have been equally inspired, as he suggested they converge again the following week at the store. This time they brought along two other local friends, David Parker and a scraggly East Palo Alto blues-loving renegade named Ron McKernan, who went by the nickname Blue Ron, for his love of the blues. All of them gathered at least once more to play, this time at Parker's house.

In early 1964 Weir was enrolled in yet another school, Menlo-Atherton High School in his hometown of Atherton, and was already carrying himself like a musician. During lunchtime he could be seen toting a guitar, just like Dylan; when Bonner took guitar lessons from him at Guitars Unlimited Weir demonstrated his ability to blow smoke rings across the small room. In her world history class Swanson, a pert brunette, was yapping with a classmate about trying to get into a nearby Beatles concert—they'd just played the *Ed Sullivan Show* and had, to put it mildly, made a strong impression on the youth of America—when the boy sitting in front her turned around and said, "Well, *I* have a band."

By way of horse-riding lessons, Swanson had befriended fellow rider Wendy Weir and had heard mention of the kid others referred to as "Wendy's weird brother Bob." ("Blob Weird" was another nickname of the period.) Swanson too would also come to notice Weir's eccentricities: the way he would fill in a drawing of an airplane instead of his name on a test exam or refuse to stand up for the morning flag salute. Here he now was, sitting in front of her and knowing precisely the right way to get a girl's attention. And, it turned out, he did have a band, even if it sounded nothing remotely like the Beatles.

■ ◆ ■

Laird Grant, Garcia's partner in mischief from middle school days, was among those who wandered into Magoo's to watch the Warlocks take a crack at playing rock 'n' roll. To no one's surprise the acoustics inside a pizza parlor were pretty atrocious, and on the night Grant showed up the band was stuffed into a corner: "No stage, no nothing, flat on the ground." But he was still delighted to see Garcia making music with the keyboard player with whom Grant had already bonded over drinks in bars in East Palo Alto. Whereas once he'd been called Blue Ron, thanks to his largely great-unwashed demeanor, he was now and forever Pigpen.

Garcia and others on the Peninsula music scene wanted nothing more than to be viewed as authentic, not products of what they saw as the increasingly plastic, conformist society around them. (Garcia had a word for people in that world: "mugs.") Yet here in their midst was someone who exuded dark-end-of-the-street realness in ways they never could. Ron McKernan had been born in San Mateo on September 8, 1945, and his father, Phil, was a recording engineer and DJ at KRE, a local radio station. ("Being a DJ was a side job to being the engineer at the station," explains Phil's daughter and Ron's sister, Carol.) Thanks to his father's interest in R&B and blues and vast record collection, young Ron quickly developed a deep, profound connection with those genres. That bond was only made stronger when the family moved and Ron began attending a largely African American high school in East Palo Alto. Neither surfer nor jock, he so identified with the African American community there that, according to one friend of the time, he wore a steel-chain bracelet to make sure he never forgot about slavery.

In light of his funky hygiene habits and charming grubbiness, McKernan went from being called Blue Ron to Pigpen in honor of the unkempt character in *Peanuts*. By early 1964 Pigpen sightings were everywhere: he was spotted at Pacific High, at Kepler's, at bars, and at the Dana Morgan Music Shop, where he was a teenage janitor. At one point he took a job delivering donuts to local stores, and his routine became part of his local legend: finishing a shift at three or four in the morning, he'd cap it off by pulling out a jug of cheap wine sold in grocery stores. (Whether it was the way he looked or the way he acted, no one ever seemed to question or card him.) In the early morning hours he'd sing and play the blues on guitar and harmonica.

Despite his hardened, gruff-as-shingles exterior, Pigpen struck most of his friends as exceedingly shy. "He didn't look like he was reputable at all," says Bonner Mosley, "but he was the sweetest guy in the world." Music became his way of exorcising his demons, which would forever be mysterious to the members of the Dead. They knew little of his family or the tension between Pigpen and his father, Phil, who, they would later learn, wanted his son to take a non-arts-related career path, to become, in the father's words, a "'world renouned [*sic*] scientist.' And so I fashioned a mold for Ron that was not of his choosing, but of mine." In Phil McKernan's eyes, Pigpen felt his father didn't approve of his chosen life and so, in turn, "had to find some manner of coping with it." That coping mechanism, Phil felt, was alcohol, and it would haunt the father for years.

Pigpen and Garcia had crossed paths already; they'd both logged time in a local ad hoc rock band, the Zodiacs, in which Garcia did his best to play bass guitar. Pigpen had also taken guitar lessons with Garcia at Morgan's store, and he appreciated Garcia's knowledge of the blues. With his affinity for roots music, Pigpen was a natural for the band that began crystallizing around Garcia, Weir, Matthews, and seemingly anyone in their vicinity during the early months of 1964. For young guys who wanted to form a band whether or not they knew how to play an instrument, one option cried out: jug-band music, which was enjoying the briefest of vogues. To play this ribald younger sibling of folk music one needn't know how to play an instrument (kazoos and washboards were easy enough to master) or even the history of the music (how it originated in the South in the twenties). Here was party music: bawdy songs bashed out on everything from banjos and guitars to actual jugs. "It wasn't electric urban blues, but it was old-style urban blues," Weir recalled. "Some of the jug bands were real good. Noah Lewis, the harmonica player, was phenomenal. There hasn't been another harmonica player who could do what he could do."

After they'd bonded with Garcia at Morgan's on New Year's Eve, Weir and Matthews caught a Berkeley show by the leading jug ensemble of the moment, Jim Kweskin and the Jug Band. Both kids were so inspired that they decided they wanted to form their own combo, and the first person they told was Garcia. Now that they'd jammed with him, the two students would hitchhike over to the store on school mornings if they didn't have a first-period class. When they mentioned the jug idea Garcia, noodling as always on a banjo, looked up: "Without missing a beat, he said, 'Good—I'm in!'" Matthews recalls. Given his connections and contacts with musicians in the Palo Alto area, it was only natural for Garcia to take charge of the nascent project. Garcia would play guitar and banjo, of course, and Pigpen would handle harmonica. Parker scoured junkyards and thrift stores, eventually finding a used washboard and strapping a kazoo atop it; for a while Matthews also handled washboard and kazoo duties.

Weir, the youngest and most eager of the lot, was especially intent on having a role in the band. "He was very persistent," David Nelson, Garcia's bluegrass-band guitarist, later said to Hajdu. "He kind of barged his way into the jug band by saying, 'C'mon, I want to play in this band.' We'd say, 'Get out of here, kid.'" Almost as a way to drive him away for good, someone suggested Weir play jug. (Garcia had asked Hunter to hold down that role, but Hunter couldn't attain the right tone and opted out.) The next day Weir appeared, bringing with him a wide array of jugs, clay and plastic, and asking everyone which one had the best tone. Weir settled on an empty plastic Clorox container, an improvement over an actual clay jug. "He just kept at it and kept at it when he didn't seem to have a chance," said Nelson. "From the start it didn't seem like he knew how to do anything, but he just kept doing it. The kid had pluck." The new band began practicing in a wooden garage behind Garcia's cottage on Hober Lane, where Weir showed up one day with a pile of old jazz and ragtime records—"Look at these!" he exclaimed. Pigpen also brought along a slew of records nabbed from his father's extensive collection, including jug-band recordings from decades before.

Mother McCree's Uptown Jug Champions—the name was courtesy of Nelson, although it would change from time to time—played the first of many shows at the Tangent about three weeks after Weir and Garcia had reconnected at Dana Morgan's. "We were putting on a party, and people would dance and stuff," Weir recalled to Hajdu. "We owned the place, almost from the first night." Over the next few months and a few dozen performances the band began attracting a loyal following; a local drummer, Bill Kreutzmann, saw them at the Tangent, sitting right up against the stage and mesmerized by Garcia—"I want to follow *that* guy, forever," he said to himself. No one in the band considered jug music his first love, but it was a hoot to play, and a market existed, even in their part of the country. "As long as there was a living to be made or a buck to be made for us fledgling musicians," Weir recalled, "we were more than happy to go into it and research it and come up with the stuff."

In the spring of 1964 Mother McCree's temporarily shut down as Garcia made one last shot at fulfilling his dream of becoming a member of a renowned bluegrass band, that of mandolin legend Bill Monroe. By then the Wildwood Boys had morphed into the Black Mountain Boys, and as summer approached, Garcia and the Boys' latest guitarist, Sandy Rothman, embarked on a road trip that took them as far south as Florida and north to Massachusetts. (In the interest of avoiding any harassment in the South, a part of the country far more suspicious of beards than Palo Alto, Garcia shaved off his facial hair before he left.) He and Rothman checked out bluegrass bands at clubs and festivals and hooked up with numerous musician friends, making the trip culturally rewarding. In the end Garcia wound up driving back home to California without a job; he didn't have the confidence to apply for the gig in Monroe's group, even if it were available. But by then it almost didn't matter. Another reinvention cried out to him, one that promised far more imaginative journeys than those in bluegrass or jug bands. And perhaps it even offered the chance to make something close to a livable wage.

■　◆　■

The song list for the May 26 show at Magoo's would be lost to history, although it most likely included a Chuck Berry cover and songs any well-meaning garage band of 1965 had to learn, like Sam the Sham and the Pharaoh's deliriously silly "Wooly Bully." The song embedded most in the minds of those who were there was Slim Harpo's deep, slow, sexual blues "I'm a King Bee." In another variation on the folk boom, white kids around the country were digging into the blues, forming bands and playing their own versions of Muddy Waters and Howlin' Wolf songs. Some of those covers could be embarrassingly callow, but the Warlocks' rendition at Magoo's was on a different level, largely thanks to Pigpen, who growled it with a menacing seductiveness. "The vocal sound of that band was Pig—that's what I remember," recalls Jorma Kaukonen, who popped into Magoo's on one of those May nights and was thrilled to see his friends plugging in. "He sounded so authentic. He was an old soul. It was like, 'Man, what am I going to have to do to sound like that?'"

Having grown up listening to electric blues, Pigpen became the first member of Mother McCree's to encourage his friends to amplify. But they all felt the tug of rock 'n' roll. When Garcia went on his southern expedition, Weir filled in for his friend at the Dana Morgan Music Shop, giving guitar lessons. Spending hours in the store, amid both acoustic and amplified fretted instruments, filled the teenager's head with new, different musical visions. "All those shiny electric instruments were starting to give us the come hither," he has said. The British Invasion had arrived on American shores that year, and the Beatles were far from the only overseas band on the charts; by the fall of 1964 the Dave Clark Five's "Glad All Over" and "Catch Us If You Can," the Kinks' "You Really Got Me" and "Set Me Free," and many other punchy, charged-voltage singles had taken over American radio. "Rock 'n' roll seemed viable—it seemed less like prepackaged, marketed pap and more like there was some expansiveness to the music," Weir recalled to Hajdu. "None of us had stopped long enough to think about taking rock 'n' roll seriously until the Beatles came out, and they were downright musical." The fact that the music made girls scream wasn't lost on anyone, and neither were the rent-paying possibilities: at the Top of the Tangent, Mother McCree's Uptown Jug Champions would play three sets a night and end up with $15 dollars in each of their pockets. (A few months later in August 1965, Weir, Bonner, and Swanson jumped in Swanson's car and chased the Beatles from the airport to a local show. Encouraged by his friends, Weir tried to climb up the chain-link fence and crash the show, but he didn't make it.)

Just as jamming in Morgan's store had helped initiate their jug band, so did the store lure them into rock. Morgan's son, Dana Jr., who helped run the shop and harbored his own dreams of becoming a musician, made them an offer: if they wanted to start a rock 'n' roll band, the store would loan them instruments, as long as Dana Jr. could play bass in the group. Morgan wasn't intrinsically one of them: with his reddish-blond hair and preppy wardrobe, he looked more like a member of the neat and tidy Kingston Trio than a fledgling rocker. He didn't seem all that interested in pot. But Garcia, according to Lesh (who wasn't there at the time), saw the value in free gear and "put a good charm offensive on Dana." They now had a rehearsal space and free instruments. "What more could a boy want?" Weir told Swanson as he stood in the driveway of his family home in Atheron, leaning his new electric guitar against his equally new Fender amp.

Overnight the jug-band fever dream broke—Mother McCree's Uptown Jug Champions would give its last performances shortly into the new year, 1965—and the washboard, kazoos, and other eccentric instruments were dispatched. (Garcia would continue playing banjo, but its days too were numbered as far as playing an integral role in his music.) Garcia, Weir, Pigpen, and Morgan began congregating in the front part of the Dana Morgan Music Shop, now accompanied by yet another musical soul mate.

Of them all, Bill Kreutzmann, born May 7, 1946, had the most experience playing something close to rock 'n' roll. The son of a lawyer and a dance teacher, he had both financial and artistic impulses implanted into his brain from an early age. Like many kids, Kreutzmann began banging on whatever was around when he was a toddler, but in his case, he never stopped; by grade school he was obsessed with rhythm and drumming. When he was still in high school Kreutzmann's parents divorced, and for a time he was sent off to school in Arizona. Kreutzmann's parents hoped he would attend Stanford as they had, but the academic life wasn't Kreutzmann's destiny. "Bill was a stud," recalls John McLaughlin. "He had girls falling all over him." Kreutzmann soon had a family of his own to support: he and his equally young girlfriend, Brenda, had a daughter in the middle of 1964 and were married. Increasingly drawn to music over school, Kreutzmann took the drum seat in a local R&B cover band, the Legends, who powered many a Palo Alto party with their covers of James Brown, the Isley Brothers, and others. Although not the frontman, Kreutzmann made his presence known: McLaughlin remembers that one of the highlights of a Legends show was the way it would wrap up with an extraordinary drum solo.

Given how relatively small and insular the Palo Alto community was, it wasn't surprising that by 1964 Kreutzmann had met or played with some of the future Warlocks. He'd not only seen Mother McCree's at the Tangent but had been part of the Zodiacs with Pigpen and Garcia. (The guitarist who organized the band, Troy Weidenheimer, was partly responsible for the birth of the Dead in the way he brought those three young musicians together.) Most importantly, though, Kreutzmann could swing; having been exposed to jazz drummers, he was already remarkably accomplished for someone who was only eighteen when the new rock 'n' roll band began congregating at the music store. In fact, his playing, influenced by drumming heroes like jazzman Elvin Jones and big-band walloper Buddy Rich, was so advanced that he was already teaching drums there, another bit of common ground with Garcia.

The nascent rock 'n' roll band had equipment and a lineup of two guitars, bass, drums, and keyboard; Pigpen, who could play first-rate blues piano and gave an occasional lesson to local kids, switched to the more garage band–fashionable organ. Now they also had a space to boot: the front of the Dana Morgan Music Shop. The room was cluttered as it was; anyone walking into the store had to duck under a hanging cymbal or two and navigate around a few amplifiers. With the band set up, the room felt even smaller, and on the second day of rehearsal the musicians also had to make room for Bonner and Swanson, who immediately became the group's first cheerleaders—bringing along donuts or playing records for the band to learn and copy. They tried some of Pigpen's favorite blues songs or Rolling Stones or Everly

Brothers covers—almost everything except the Beatles. ("They were untouchable," said Weir.) The music was so loud that the instruments dangling on the walls swayed and made their own clamor.

If the nascent band had a front man, it was Pigpen; his voice was the most distinctive and guttural, and he commanded the material in ways the others couldn't yet. Without meaning to, he had antistar charisma. But Garcia remained the most assertive and was clearly in charge of the proceedings. "There's a difference between being the star of the band and being the leader," Swanson recalls. Before long they had a name, the Warlocks, probably an homage to fantasy books in vogue at the time. Soon after came their first booking, at a pizza parlor in Menlo Park. As Weir said, "And bang, we're on."

◾ ◆ ◾

Garcia wasn't alone in taking note of the gangly blond guy with the Beatle haircut who sauntered into Magoo's, buzzing off some acid he'd taken beforehand. Anyone who'd met Phil Lesh knew he was tall, but they also noticed he'd let his freak flag fly high since his days kicking around Palo Alto and the Chateau two or three years before. "That blond page-boy look was his signature—it definitely stood out," recalls Jim Cushing, a friend of Bonner's who attended two of the Magoo's shows. "If there was a crowd of people, you'd spot Phil in a heartbeat."

By his own admission, Lesh's life over the previous two and a half years had been aimless and frustrating. By the spring of 1963 he'd fled Las Vegas and his post office job. (He'd also left Constanten's family's house and was crashing with a nearby friend.) Hopping aboard a Greyhound bus, Lesh returned to Palo Alto and was able to score a room at the Chateau. Once more he was immersed in the outlier scene he'd come to love, which included attending Garcia and Sara Ruppenthal's wedding—where Lesh would see Garcia's "scuzzy beatnik friends," as he put it, wolfing down as much of the free food as possible.

But the good times, which included Lesh's stab at writing an ambitious orchestral work, ended when the owner of the Chateau announced he was selling the house. After bouncing around a few places, Lesh rented an apartment in San Francisco with Constanten, who had himself returned to the area. Lesh resumed work on his classical piece, but the fall of 1963 and most of 1964 became a lost, open-ended period for him. To support themselves, both he and Constanten took jobs with the post office, Lesh driving a delivery truck. "Those jobs weren't that hard to get," Constanten says. "We worked 6 to 10 p.m., four hours. And it paid quite well."

Another rising composer, Steve Reich, whom he'd met at Mills College, introduced Lesh to the world of the San Francisco Mime Troupe, a three-year-old hotbed of political theater and activism. Again, Lesh's world seemed to be on the verge of blossoming: he wrote a piece to be performed at a Troupe-led concert and met his soon-to-be-girlfriend, Pakhala. He'd also obtained his first-ever cube of LSD and, taking it alone in his apartment, saw "a kaleidoscope of emotional peaks," as he would later write. But again Lesh's life stalled. He realized the piece he'd written wasn't working and soon fell in with a crowd who loved to shoot speed, which Lesh himself dabbled in. "I was content to live in the moment, I guess," he says. "I didn't see any future in composing. You had to be either part of the academic scene or I didn't know what. I wasn't going to back to school; I was completely done with that."

During a break in the Warlocks' set Garcia sat Lesh down in one of Magoo's booths. Without any preamble he said, "Listen, man, I want you to play bass in this band. We have to tell this guy every note to play. I know you can do it. I know you're a musician." Lesh was stunned. The idea seemed ludicrous: Lesh didn't know how to play that instrument, had never even held one in his hands before, and hadn't played rock 'n' roll yet. But Garcia was insistent. Watching nearby, Swanson recalls "the feeling of trying to get Phil to become part of the band."

Both Swanson and Denise Kaufman—another band friend who'd graduated from an all-girls private school in Palo Alto and had seen various Warlocks play in different configurations—recall Garcia venturing to Lesh's apartment in San Francisco to make a final push for Lesh to sign up with the band. (Swanson believes she drove Garcia and then waited outside Lesh's apartment during the talk.) Lesh himself has no recall of such a meeting: "I don't remember him having to convince me to join the band," he says. But Garcia's determination to make Lesh a new Warlock was undeniable. "I remember Jerry telling me about it," says Kaufman. "It was a big deal. Jerry was a very discriminating guy, but he was excited by the level of Phil's musicianship." Lesh's lack of bar-band experience, Kaufman thinks, wouldn't have been a deterrent to Garcia. "Jerry was an out-of-the-box creative person, so what would be a left-field choice for someone else wouldn't be for him," she says. "He thought Phil would make the music more interesting. Phil had already put years into his musical development, and that was fascinating to Jerry."

Ultimately Lesh didn't need that much convincing to join the Warlocks. "That's when I realized this is what I'd been waiting for," he says. "This is why I hadn't done anything else in music. There it was— the reason I didn't go back to classical. This was my chance to play with Jerry. And it was a chance to redefine part of that music, shape it in my own image, if you will. I could bring my training and compositional sense to that level while still collaborating." Grant says he felt Lesh's joining a band gave him "a physical manifestation of what he could do musically instead of just on paper." Lesh was now a Warlock.

The timing was right. Lesh was no longer a rock hater: he'd seen the Beatles' *A Hard Day's Night* (after which he'd adopted his Fab haircut), caught a Rolling Stones show in the area, and was mesmerized after hearing Bob Dylan's "Subterranean Homesick Blues" on the radio. As with the guys playing at Magoo's, Lesh now realized rock 'n' roll had endless possibilities, and the idea of joining the array of misfits was supremely appealing as well. "To find a place where everybody seemed to be on the same wavelength—about music and about substances, if you will—it was just a revelation," he later told Hajdu. In a 1990 interview Lesh, who'd been fired from the post office in San Francisco thanks to his grown-out hair, admitted that taking up the bass was "a way to earn a living" as well.

Back at Garcia's house after the Magoo's show Lesh said, "Let's have my first lesson." After all, Garcia was a well-regarded and hip teacher, and Lesh was curious to see his technique. Once Garcia had put one-year-old Heather to bed, he grabbed a guitar and said, "Now, the bottom four strings on this guitar are tuned exactly in the same way as the bass." Lesh replied that he knew *that* already, so Garcia said, "This is your lesson. Borrow someone's guitar and start practicing those bottom four strings. That's all you have to do. Get it under your fingers before you come down." ("Phil plunked away on it, and there it was," remembers Grant of that night.) Lesh did indeed borrow a guitar from a friend, and within two weeks he and Pakhala had moved from San Francisco to Palo Alto, with Grant's help, to start what looked to be a new life. "It was seamless," Bonner Mosley says of Lesh becoming part of the Warlocks and their sensibility. "He was a friend, and everyone knew him."

The Warlocks would never again play Magoo's. By Menlo Park standards, the scene growing around them at the restaurant was becoming too boisterous. The night he finally saw the band's complete set, Lesh himself was told by the owner not to dance, and the threat of another visit by the fire marshal hung in the air.

May 26 would also be the Warlocks' final public performance with Dana Morgan Jr. Although it would remain unclear who did the actual firing (Lesh says he never met or spoke with him), the younger Morgan was soon out of the band—the first sign that Garcia, for all his casual airs, knew where he wanted his music to go and how to make hard choices. Because neither Dana Morgan Jr. nor his store-owning father was happy with the decision, the Warlocks were soon stripped of a rehearsal space and instruments. But thanks to family loans and neighboring music stores, the gear would soon be replaced. It had been a night of dreams, new connections, and pasta, in that order. Now they simply had to find someplace that would foster and tolerate them as they transformed into whatever came next.

*Rock Scully, Garcia, and Tom Wolfe in Haight
Ashbury during the Acid Test era.*
© TED STRESHINSKY / CORBIS

CHAPTER 3

PALO ALTO, CALIFORNIA, DECEMBER 18, 1965

Connie Bonner saw the look on Phil Lesh's face when she told him. He didn't seem to either believe or grasp it, and why should he? Here they were, a week before Christmas, gathered with friends, strangers, and random street people inside a large, darkened building in an industrial wasteland off Highway 101 in Palo Alto. Disembodied speaking voices were echoing around the room. A strobe light was making anyone dancing look as if they were in stop motion. People were growing spacier by the minute, especially once they began dipping their paper cups into the plastic bins filled with liquid. And now here was Bonner, along with her friend and fellow Warlocks devotee Sue Swanson, telling Lesh that George Harrison had walked through the front door.

Peering out through his waterfall of blond hair, Lesh paused for a moment to digest the news. To learn about an Acid Test was one thing; to know where it was and how to get there was another. The following week the building would officially open as the Big Beat—"the Peninsula's Most Popular Go-Go Spot," as a local newspaper ad announced. But right now it was just an empty hall that had been rented for the night by the Merry Pranksters, the festive, nonconformist freaks and creative types who'd been gathering around Ken Kesey. The fanciful Acid Test fliers, crammed with wildly varying typefaces and illustrations, listed neither date nor address, simply an exhortation to come "this Saturday night." And even if a Beatle happened to know about all this, how would he know who the Warlocks were? They'd just made their first recordings the month before, but none had been released nor might they ever be. They'd changed their name to something far more macabre than the Warlocks, but the new name turned off so many of their friends that it could have easily kept George Harrison away too.

As dubious as Bonner's sighting was, something about it was strangely plausible. As the Kesey crowd knew, almost anything could happen at an Acid Test. You never knew who'd you see there, what wired-on-*something* idea they'd have for the night, or what condition they'd be in by the time the sun rose in the morning. And as the Warlocks, now the Grateful Dead, were about to learn on this late December night, you never knew which future comrades, lovers, and inspired crazies would show up and ingratiate themselves into your world.

Try as they might, the Warlocks couldn't quite pull off the role of eager-to-please rock 'n' roll band. They were either too loud, too unattractive, or too raucous for someone or another's tastes. Herb Greene, a local photographer who would soon become one of the foremost chroniclers of the emerging Bay Area music world, was among the first to recognize the Warlocks' innate wooliness. About a month before the December Acid Test in Palo Alto they had convened for an auspicious event, their first photo shoot. Greene, who'd worked as a stage manager for the San Francisco Mime Troupe, had met Lesh through that group and would be the man behind the camera.

Cavorting and indulging in funny, Beatle-inspired faces and poses under the Golden Gate Bridge, the Warlocks tried to make like a friendly, accessible band for local teenagers. But collectively they weren't the most handsome or restrained guys on the planet. A short time later they were invited over to Greene's home to inspect the photos, and Greene would never forget the clamor as they barged in and ran up the stairs. "It was a thundering herd," he says. "They were the rudest, loudest people. Pigpen was the first one up the stairs, galloping, and he's terrifying looking." When he saw Greene, Pigpen said, "You got any *juice?*" Greene told him he had apple juice in his refrigerator, but Pigpen meant Thunderbird, the cheap white wine known as one of the best ways to get a quick buzz.

With Lesh now installed as their bass player and Garcia teaching guitar at another store now that the Dana Morgan Music Shop was no longer an option, the Warlocks had begun poking their way around the world of show business. Rock 'n' roll wasn't quite respectable—many still considered it a fad—but so many kids were forming bands and trying to write their own material that the dream of making it didn't seem that absurd, even for a months-old combo like the Warlocks. Garcia was relentless in pushing them to rehearse, including at least once in the backyard of the Swanson family house. Garcia brought his young daughter, Heather, and Kreutzmann his daughter, Stacy, and the kids cavorted in the pool. But the sound of the band practicing was so obtrusive that the neighbor next door complained that his own child couldn't take a nap. (Swanson never told her father about the Warlocks' takeover of their yard and pool cabana, which was probably for the best.) Meanwhile one friend or another, from Bob Matthews to a pal of Lesh's named Hank Harrison, took a stab at managing them and booking them into whatever venues would have them.

During the summer and into the fall of 1965 those venues mostly amounted to bars, dives, and a strip club or two, but somehow that suited the Warlocks. They weren't polished, musically or physically, and some of them still didn't know that many chords. A few weeks after Lesh had joined up with them the band was booked into Frenchy's, a teen hangout in nearby Haywood. During his school years Lesh had played trumpet and violin onstage; now he was faced with the idea of mastering a new instrument, electric bass, and shaking loose any of the classical-music formality he'd accumulated. "The only thing I can remember is how stiff I felt," he recalls of that show. "I didn't feel I had the groove. And I didn't know what the other guys were going to be doing." When the Warlocks returned for a second night they were told they'd been replaced by an accordion, bass, and clarinet trio, the polar opposite of what the Warlocks were trying to accomplish. "That was such a moment," he says. "I can't even remember what we did the first night that would have thrown up the red flag."

Whether they wanted to or not, the Warlocks threw up plenty of such flags. From Quicksilver Messenger Service to the Beau Brummels (who managed to land in the Top Twenty early in 1965 with "Laugh Laugh"), one-time folkies were plugging in around the Bay Area; another new band, Jefferson Airplane, featured Jorma Kaukonen, who'd shared the stage at the Tangent with Mother McCree's Uptown Jug Champions. Next to them, the Warlocks were motlier and, with the exception of Weir, prematurely hardened. Onstage they wore mismatched striped shirts and vests; combined with Lesh's, Garcia's, and Pigpen's mushrooms of hair, they sometimes resembled better-dressed versions of cavemen.

In September the Warlocks were awarded a genuine prize for any upcoming band: a week of gigs at the In Room, a bar in Belmont, that wound up stretching to over a month. Starting with its awkward name, the In Room was such a wrong-side-of-the-tracks place that it was actually located *near* railroad tracks. Six nights a week, with Sundays off, the Warlocks played to a small and often indifferent crowd of boozers, men and women on the prowl, and what Weir would call "wooly freaks." Attendance was low, especially at the start: Tom Constanten, Lesh's music-college and Las Vegas friend, took a weekend leave from the Air Force, where he was now serving, and realized he was one of the only people there. But the gigs amounted to extended paid wood-shedding: playing covers of songs both rock ("Gloria") and R&B ("In the Midnight Hour"), they learned how to lock in together, even how to hold their electric guitars and bass the right ways onstage. "With the Warlocks, we were just trying to work up a lot of tunes—the more tunes the better—and become a proficient rock 'n' roll band, so we could get work," Weir recalled to Hajdu. "When we got a steady gig at the In Room, practice makes perfect, I gotta tell you."

Still, the Warlocks couldn't simply grin, bob their heads, and play polite covers to whoever showed up at the In Room. Even when they launched into a rendition of a hit people would recognize, they'd forget the words or simply devise new ones on the spot: "Hey, you, get the fuck off my cow," went one of their additions to the Rolling Stones' "Get Off My Cloud." ("It was actually pretty funny," says Greene, who checked out their set one night.) On their night off they'd take acid—or, at least, Garcia, Lesh, and Weir would, as Pigpen was averse to it and Kreutz-mann was, for the time being, abstaining. By then some of the Warlocks had already tried the legal, odorless, and colorless hallucinogen discov-ered by Dr. Albert Hofmann in Switzerland about three decades before: Lesh during his pre-Warlocks days at his apartment in San Francisco, Garcia earlier in 1965 with a group that included his wife, Sara (both freaked out after they'd taken it). "LSD gave us an insight, because once you're in that state of profound disorientation, you play stuff out of mus-cle memory that you're used to playing," Weir added. "We were taking acid every week for a couple of months, and I think we learned what we were going to learn with that method in that couple of months. We learned in that time an important lesson, to try to step back from what it is you're playing—not be there, to step back and let the song be itself."

To Sam Salvo, a bartender at the In Room, it would have been best if the Warlocks had stepped as far back as possible. The band was, in his words, "getting high smoking weed"—still a fairly foreign sight in public in the middle of the sixties—and when they were high they "talked of LSD," he said. Weir would later claim he took more than enough acid—"I think I overdosed myself," he has said—right before an In Room show. He was so discombobulated that the other Warlocks kept an eye on him all night to see whether he'd make it through; somehow he did.

With or without pharmaceuticals—and most of the time they didn't play high at the In Room—the Warlocks found their music slowly edging out into another, stranger zone. To Salvo the band sounded "loud and outrageous," and he wasn't off beam. Because their repertoire was fairly limited at this time, stretching the songs out made it easier to fill up their sets, and one night they extended "In the Midnight Hour" to about forty-five minutes. The one song they wrote together during their stint at the In Room hinted at life after a cover band. A rumble-seat of a song, "Caution (Do Not Stop on Tracks)," inspired by a sign in the area, was loose and darker, driven by Pigpen's harmonica and Kreutzmann's astonishingly limber, jazz-rooted syncopation. Around this time they also began jamming on "Viola Lee Blues," a bound-for-prison jug-band song from the twenties that the Dead played with sharp, cutting chords, more a strut than a plea bargain. For Lesh, the moment the band stretched it out at a rehearsal, playing what he calls "that crazy windup," was a major musical breakthrough, hinting at what they could do.

In November they lost their gig at the In Room; the owners had had enough of them and their eccentric take on rock 'n' roll. (Garcia later told a friend that another turnoff was the arrival of an intimidating guy who told them they had to join "da union" if they wanted to keep their night job.) But beginning earlier that year they were far more welcome somewhere else in the area: Ken Kesey's house in La Honda. One or another of them had met the writer during the early Palo Alto days, when Kesey, then a Stanford graduate student, lived in a cottage on Perry Lane in the town's undersized boho section. When Lesh would party next door to Kesey's, at the home of another Stanford graduate student and professor, Vic Lovell, Kesey would "come over from next door and throw us all out," Lesh would later recall. The scene at the Chateau, where Garcia, Hunter, Lesh, and others had crashed on and off, wasn't particularly appealing to Kesey, a commanding figure whose stocky build reflected his days as a college wrestler and football player in Oregon. Since that time Kesey had become a celebrated literary hero due to the 1962 publication of his novel *One Flew Over the Cuckoo's Nest*; thanks to its success he'd earned enough to buy a home that looked like an oversized two-bedroom log cabin tucked into the redwoods near the Santa Cruz mountains.

Kesey's next novel, *Sometimes a Great Notion*, wasn't as much of a sensation as his first, but further adventures lay ahead: in 1964 he and the other members of his loose-knit, acid-enhanced gang, officially dubbed the Merry Band of Pranksters (shortened to Merry Pranksters), had driven a multicolored bus across the country, filming all the way. Their encounters with the straight world could be hilarious; once, when they pulled into a gas station, people ran out to check out the hand-painted International Harvester bus, dubbed "Furthur." The Pranksters—who counted among them Ken Babbs, a gregarious, rubber-faced writer who'd met Kesey in 1958 and had just finished a tour of duty in Vietnam—would pretend to be fictional characters, complete with made-up dialogue. The footage had the makings of a unique full-length feature film. "No one had ever done anything like that before," Babbs says, "a combination of documentary and made-up stuff. We were real serious about it."

Anyone who wanted to see bits of the unfinished movie had to show up at one of the Saturday night parties Kesey began throwing at his house. LSD was always on the menu: Kesey had his first taste of it when Stanford asked for paid volunteers to test hallucinogenics for the army, for $75 a session, at the Menlo Park Veterans Administration Hospital. A group of Hells Angels pulled into a Kesey bash for the first time that August, and partygoers routinely began staying until 4 a.m.—not the best situation for Kesey's wife, Faye, and their young children nor for Kesey, who often had to clean up for days afterward. The Pranksters needed a bigger space, and what would be seen as the first attempt at an Acid Test took place in November at Babbs's home in Soquel. Garcia, Lesh, and Weir were there, as were Allen Ginsberg and Peter Orlovsky, along with Neal Cassady, the fast-talking whirligig of a man who'd been the real-life inspiration for Dean Moriarty in Jack Kerouac's *On the Road*. With his waist-long hair, Orlovsky looked so foreign to them that Swanson, who also partook, asked him what happened if we went to a shoe store—meaning how would regular people deal with him. "He just looked at me like, 'Who is this kid?'" she recalls. Lesh, tripping hard, bashed away on Kesey's guitar. (According to Dead historian Dennis McNally's *A Long Strange Trip*, Orlovsky, Ginsberg's lifelong lover, would forever be envious of Weir after Weir sat next to Ginsberg that night.)

When the Pranksters still couldn't find a hall to rent, a second, larger gathering was firmed up at the San Jose home of a local African American legend with the politically incorrect nickname Big Nig. There the Warlocks, some of whom had met with Kesey right after the party at Babbs's house and asked to play, set up in a large bay window; Babbs would always remember how heavy Pigpen's organ was and how difficult it was to haul it through the front door of the house. Tripping and listening to rock 'n' roll were two of the basic tenets of an Acid Test, but so was a type of underground marketing. When it came to the Pranksters' still-uncompleted road-trip movie, reality set in. "We thought, maybe it wasn't going to come out in theaters as a big two-hour movie," Babbs says. Instead of attempting to sell it to a Hollywood studio, maybe they could rent out spaces and show the footage in the middle of Acid Tests.

Parts of the movie were likely shown at the next Acid Test, on December 11 in a lodge at Muir Beach, a cove just south of Muir Woods. Then another Prankster cohort, Page Browning, heard about a nightclub in Palo Alto set to open just before Christmas that would be empty the night of Saturday, December 18. The owner, an area restaurateur named Yvonne Modica, was fifty-one years old but very young at heart, and she agreed to rent the space to Kesey and the Pranksters for a small fee. As with the cabin at Muir Beach, the Pranksters made sure to avoid telling Modica exactly what was planned—what happened at the Acid Tests would stay at the Acid Tests. But everyone knew intrinsically that the one local band bold enough to brave it all—and play music that would somehow fit in with the proceedings—was the Warlocks. Once more they crammed into Kreutzmann's station wagon, the band's transportation mode of necessity, and headed for a gig not too far from Magoo's.

Lesh had invited his striking new female acquaintance, Florence Nathan (later rechristened Rosie McGee), who agreed to meet him there. Driving to the address on the far side of town, McGee arrived at a wide, squat A-frame building that, she recalls, looked like "one of those strip clubs in the nasty part of town." The building was so ordinary it was hard to tell what might be happening inside. "It could have been anything," she says, "and anything could be going on in there." She parked and ventured inside.

■　◆　■

Before the paying customers began arriving at the Big Beat, the Acid Test needed to be set up, and Mountain Girl was happy to volunteer. Having flown back to the East Coast to visit her parents for Thanksgiving, she'd missed the previous Acid Test. But now she was back in the

Peninsula and ready to serve in Kesey's army. The place would be filled with tape recorders, movie projectors, and other electronics gear, and Mountain Girl, who was learning how to edit and archive film, signed up for the task. Given all the equipment she'd have to oversee, she only took one sip of the acid-dosed Kool-Aid that would be distributed for the night. There was work to do, and she needed to be as straight and proactive as possible.

Born Carolyn Adams in May 1946 and raised in Poughkeepsie, New York, Mountain Girl was made to be a Prankster. Weeks before her high school graduation she'd been kicked out of school for venturing into the boys' locker room to sneak a peek at the mysterious new Nautilus machine installed there. "I had never seen anything like it," she says. "I had no idea what it was. It looked like an alien machine from outer space." She popped into the locker area for less than a minute, but a janitor saw her and reported her, and she was out. ("They had been waiting for something," she says, given her past indiscretions at school.) Her older brother, a graduate student at Stanford, invited her to fly out and live with him, and Adams arrived in Palo Alto in the summer of 1963. By September, at age seventeen, she'd found a job at Stanford's organic chemistry lab and begun killing time at the local coffeehouses and clubs like St. Michael's Alley and the Tangent—the same places as Garcia and his gang, although their paths had yet to cross.

At St. Michael's Alley Adams met Cassady; the Furthur bus had just arrived back in town, and Cassady was in search of Benzedrine. "You want to go for a ride?" he asked her, and Adams, no longer working at the lab and dealing with what she calls "some personal struggles" that included breaking up with her boyfriend, went along, saying, "What the hell." With his brain-on-overdrive charm, Cassady was hard to turn down. At dawn the two wound up at Kesey's place, the iconic Furthur bus parked in the driveway and Kesey hard at work on its wiring. Adams was immediately smitten with the bus. Having been a monitor in grade school, she was familiar with school transportation, and this overhauled vehicle, outfitted with bunks by the previous owner, was "the most fascinating object I'd ever seen," she says. She spent several hours examining it and all its finger-painted characters and symbols.

Tall, strapping, outgoing, and headstrong—or, in the words of Tom Wolfe in *The Electric Kool-Aid Acid Test*, "big . . . and loud and sloppy"—Adams had a warm, earthy aura and easily ingratiated herself into the Merry Pranksters' world. Soon she was helping catalog the seemingly endless amount of film shot on the Furthur bus trip. (She was less than taken with Big Nig's nickname at the second Acid Test: "I could never say that name. The guy might have called himself that, but Kesey had a conservative streak.") She lived here and there—in a tent in the area, on the boat of another Prankster, Mike Hagen, even briefly squatting in a house in La Honda. When Cassady found out her name was Carolyn, also his wife's name, he stopped hitting on Adams, but she wouldn't be Carolyn for long. One day she visited Hagen in the ramshackle home he called the Screw Shack. Asking her where she lived, she pointed up to the mountain, where she was crashing in a cabin. "Oh, so you're *Mountain Girl*," he said. Adams wasn't thrilled with the name—"oh, great," she thought to herself—but it stuck, and from then on she would be Mountain Girl, or MG to her friends.

Showing their movie was one of the Pranksters' goals for the Acid Tests, but they also wanted to transform the parties into a type of living, breathing, heaving performance art. At the Big Beat they'd be placing microphones on the floor and encouraging everyone to walk up to them and scream or talk into the mics. The recordings would then be broadcast during the evening, and part of Mountain Girl's job that night would be to continually circle around the room, setting up the projectors, tape decks, and microphones, using masking tape and glue to repair them if they broke down. In what Mountain Girl called "a gift from the gods," her brother hauled in a strobe light on loan from

Stanford. Acid Test cards—which asked those who entered to write down their address, eye and hair color, and weight—were also printed up and handed out.

Last but extremely far from least were the small buckets the size of household waste-paper baskets, each containing Kool-Aid dosed with LSD. Kesey would long brag about all the acid he purloined from the VA hospital during his stint there; he said he snatched it right out of a desk. But Babbs would also say the acid at the Tests didn't come from the Pranksters. According to others, it arrived by way of people with connections at Stanford who'd obtained some of Dr. Hofmann's stash. Mountain Girl also heard some of it came to the school by way of the CIA: word had it that the government had shipped the drug to hookers in San Francisco for testing and, in some way, for spying on business-men who were availing themselves of the prostitutes.

When Mountain Girl first saw Garcia hanging around Kesey's place in La Honda, she immediately recognized him from around town. She'd seen him at the Tangent; hearing someone play banjo as she bi-cycled past, she parked her bike, went upstairs to the second-floor per-formance space, and came across a hairy guy diligently working on what sounded like a complicated banjo tune. He was clearly diligent, playing the melody over and over, but he was also imposing in the same way others felt about him—he was, she recalls, "scowling horribly." A few weeks later she returned to the Tangent—or possibly stopped into another area spot—to catch a set by Mother McCree's Uptown Jug Champions. And there he was again, this time part of that ragtag jug-band ensemble, all of them playing, singing, and joking onstage. She found the group highly entertaining—it took her back to her own folk-singing days during high school on the other side the country—but didn't introduce herself to him or anyone else in the band.

To Mountain Girl the Warlocks always seemed game when it came to adventures with Kesey. They'd arrive in time to help everyone set up the Acid Tests, bringing along their own, better gear, as the Pranksters' speakers and equipment weren't up to snuff for a rock 'n' roll band. Along with everyone else on the scene, she'd also heard that the Warlocks were now going by a very different name, thanks in part to their first shot at the record business.

For a few hours on November 3, about a month before the Big Beat Acid Test, the Warlocks had auditioned for Autumn Records, the company co-run by rotund and influential San Francisco DJ Tom Donahue. At Golden State Recorders in San Francisco they put their music on tape for perhaps the first time. The tape revealed how much the Warlocks were still in the midst of figuring out who they were and how they should sound. On two songs—a cover of Gordon Lightfoot's "Early Morning Rain," with a lead vocal by Lesh, and a group-written ballad, "The Only Time Is Now"—they made like a proficient folk-rock band, even down to the use of a de rigueur tambourine. On "Mindbender" and "Can't Come Down" they showed how much they could be a conventional organ-driven garage rock band. Their sense of dynamics was already evident in the way they stripped down and then built up their rhythms toward the end of "Early Morning Rain." "We knew instinctively that with all this stuff converging it would take some time to sort it out," Weir told Hajdu, "but once we started getting stuff sorted out, it would be meaningful—meaningful to us and we hoped meaningful to others." But on those and other songs, like the traditional "I Know You Rider," the guitars were timid and the harmonies underdeveloped; Garcia's attempt at a solo in "Mindbender" was halting. As Paul Curcio of the Mojo Men, who was at the session, recalls, "They came in and scared the hell out of everyone. No one had ever seen a band that grungy."

They didn't get a record deal—the label wound up passing—but one career-altering change did emerge from it all. Flipping through vinyl at a record store in town, Lesh had come across a 45-rpm single credited to the Warlocks, so a new name was needed, fast. At Autumn, they dubbed themselves the Emergency Crew. Even they must have sensed what a terrible band name *that* was, as a little over a week later the band, along with friends Swanson, Bonner, Matthews, and Grant, congregated at Lesh's apartment to finalize a new one. After Garcia (and maybe others) had smoked DMT, a hallucinogenic far stronger than LSD, Lesh began flipping through his copy of *Bartlett's Quotations* for inspiration. A slew of silly names were tossed out, none deemed acceptable. Finally, according to Matthews, Garcia said, "We aren't able to find a name, so maybe a name will find us." With that he flipped open a copy of a Funk & Wagnalls dictionary on a book stand, ran his finger down the page, stopped and read it. And there it was, "The Grateful Dead," a folk tale about a heroic figure who encounters people "refusing to bury the corpse of a man who had died without paying his debts." After giving "his last penny" to them so that the corpse can be properly disposed of, the hero leaves and later meets a fellow traveler who comes to his aid—and who winds up being the ghost or reanimated body the hero had saved.

The story was appropriately creepy, as much in the tradition of Rod Serling's *The Twilight Zone* as one of the death-haunted Child folk ballads of the 1800s that Garcia loved so much. But for a band that would never be terribly genteel with each other, the name was fitting, and to Garcia, everything else on the page disappeared in favor of what he called "a stunning combination of words." From the tone in Garcia's voice, Lesh sensed his friend loved the name and bounced up and down in agreement. "I was so excited," he says. "It had so much resonance." Reactions from everyone else in the room were varied: "We all looked at each other and said, 'How morbid,'" recalls Matthews. Weir and Pigpen were particularly unimpressed, but according to Lesh, their opinions took a backseat to his and Garcia's. "We just went ahead and said, 'Sorry, guys, but this is it,'" Lesh says. "At least *I* did. I went ahead like it was an accomplished fact, and I just kept calling us the Grateful Dead. It just became our name."

When Mountain Girl heard about the change she too was taken aback. "I said, 'The Grateful *Dead*—what kind of a name is *that?*'" she recalls. "I thought, 'That's not very attractive!' But 'The Warlocks' wasn't very attractive either." As the Warlocks began arriving at the Big Beat she saw that the name wasn't the only alteration. She'd seen them at the party at Big Nig's house, but tonight she was able to better focus on them and notice how different they both sounded and looked compared to the Mother McCree's era. She took note of the new drummer and the new bass player, how impossibly young Weir looked, how long Pigpen's hair was, and how wild Garcia's was. (Garcia would later recall they wore loud-colored shirts and pants.) It was, she says, "a complete transformation." And she had to admit that, in their way, they were pretty cute.

The feeling was apparently mutual on Garcia's part. One day at Kesey's La Honda home Garcia was hanging with Denise Kaufman, now one of the female Pranksters, nicknamed Mary Microgram. Although Garcia was married, Kaufman couldn't help but notice how Mountain Girl grabbed his attention when she walked by. "I'd give up music to be with Mountain Girl," Garcia said. As Kaufman says, "On a deep psychic level I could see him totally connecting."

■ ◆ ■

As Bonner soon realized, George Harrison had just walked through the front door of the Big Beat to see her friends' band, and Lesh went back to playing. But there was no denying that the guy who'd wandered in sported a variation on a Beatle haircut—long and straight, with bangs—and the same sharp sense of fashion. Walking over to Bonner and Swanson, he said, "Do you know these guys? Will you introduce me?" Swanson said sure, when the time came.

Only twenty-four, Rock Scully had already lived a multinational, psychedelicized life. Born in Seattle and named after his grandfather, young Rock had at age seven moved with his mother, Jane, to Chicago, where his stepfather, left-leaning newspaper columnist and author Milton Mayer, worked and wrote. The couple wound up dragging Rock along with them on transcontinental trips to tape interviews for the radio show *Voices of Europe*. (Jane Scully, a civil libertarian herself, coproduced the show with her husband.) During his high school and college years Rock bounced back and forth between schools in Europe (Germany and Switzerland) and the States. Between his parents' progressive views and his own experience in Germany, where he saw the landscape scars of World War II, he became an avid peace activist—and happy tripper. In school in Switzerland he placed a small amount of mescaline sulfate on his tongue and began experiencing less-than-normal sensations. "I'd bend my arm and hear my shirt," he says. "It was so loud it startled me."

Eventually making his way back to California, Scully settled into San Francisco State, where he considering pursuing the academic life while getting his graduate degree, but the entertainment world tugged at him. In college in Europe he'd met a student whose parents owned a nightclub, and back home he'd worked as an usher at the Monterey Jazz Festival. By 1964 he'd grown out his hair and was making a living selling pot and helping out the Charlatans, a pioneering psychedelic-folk band that came together a year before the Warlocks. By the time Scully arrived at the Big Beat he'd also inherited the Charlatans' fashion sense, a blend of Victorian and Old West couture.

Scully almost hadn't made it to Palo Alto. When he heard who was playing he grumbled that he'd already seen the Warlocks, although exactly when he had would be up for debate decades later. It's possible Scully first caught them at a benefit for the San Francisco Mime Troupe eight days before the Big Beat. Other possibilities—or reports of him seeing the band when not totally stoned—place it after the Big Beat. In some tellings Scully saw the band at the Acid Test at the Fillmore on January 8, the same night he promoted a Family Dog show at California Hall featuring the Jefferson Airplane and the Charlatans. As many would point out, Scully's memory banks could be problematic, but Scully would always insist he was at the Big Beat, and several witnesses place him there as well.

Whatever the case, the Warlocks hadn't initially wowed Scully, so when he heard they were playing an Acid Test at a space in Palo Alto, he wasn't inclined to haul down from his apartment in San Francisco on a Saturday night. But a friend of his insisted, telling Scully they needed a manager. When Scully countered that he could promote their shows, the friend replied, "No, you don't want to be a promoter—promoters steal from bands and lie to them! You don't want to do that to musicians. You want to be on their side." Eventually Scully wound up inside the mysterious strip mall–like structure on the outskirts of Palo Alto, all thanks to his friend Owsley's advice.

Few would doubt Owsley Stanley's powers of persuasion, his ability to convince anyone in his vicinity to accompany him on whatever mission he was on. Small but well built, a sprout of curls atop his head, Stanley—or Owsley, as everyone called him—cultivated an air of gnomish mystery. His given name was a tribute to the middle name of his grandfather, A. O. Stanley, who'd been elected governor of Kentucky in 1915 and then became a US senator ten years later. (Once, as senator, Stanley heard that a judge who'd been protecting an accused black man was being threatened by a mob; leaving a legislative session, he took a train to the town and told the rabble they'd have to hang him first.) Owsley attended public high school in Virginia. His nickname, Bear, derived from his excessive body hair. A gadgets freak from an early age, Owsley had taken a stab at engineering school before signing up for the Air Force; that stint was followed by jobs at electronic companies and at TV and radio stations. Shortly after the Cuban Missile Crisis he'd moved to Berkeley, where he discovered LSD and decided to make his own. With a fellow student and future lover, he began making speed in order to raise the cash to make LSD. By 1965 a good-sized number of capsules of his stash were available for consumption; one ended up on the tongue of none other than Kesey, who became an instant devotee and made Owsley's LSD part of his Acid Tests.

Mountain Girl's early memories of Owsley would involve, she says, "his little leather hat and his permed hair, and he reeked of patchouli." Chemistry was only one of Owsley's obsessions; women were another. As Scully observed early on, Owsley was also an incessant flirt. "At these dance concerts he'd corner girls and say, 'Hi, I'm Owsley—do you know who I am?'" he recalls. "He had that wizard thing about him. He wasn't shy about introducing himself. And if they didn't know who he was, he would tell them." His other infatuation was sound that was as pure as possible, especially at a time when "PA systems" at concerts were practically a joke; thanks to the absence of monitors, bands couldn't even hear themselves sing. "He said he'd done acid one time and *saw* sound," says Sam Cutler, who met Owsley years later. "He saw what sound was doing, and it kind of revolutionized his whole take on what should be done with it. When the Bear got interested in something, he was absolutely relentless."

Now thirty, Owsley had arrived in the Dead universe by way of one of Kesey's house parties; he'd then attended the Acid Test a week prior to Palo Alto in the lodge in Muir Beach. ("Find It, Fool!" read the poster, again failing to give a location.) As auspicious debuts in the Dead world went, few would top Owsley's night at Muir Beach. As the Dead were playing he began freaking out from a combination of the music—Garcia's guitar in particular, which he found monstrously frightening in his state of mind—and the acid he'd taken.

Discombobulated, Owsley jumped into his car and drove into a ditch, and a friend dragged him out to safety.

When Owsley and Lesh eventually met, Lesh was instantly intrigued. "He just looked like a man who knew something I wanted to know," he says. "His reputation had preceded him, as had his product. We'd had occasion to try his product." (Lesh's personal favorite of Owsley's stash was White Lightning: "It was what they said it was—it opened you right up, and you could see how everything fit together, how all the colors fit together.") The two became immediate cronies in sonic quality and psychedelics. Lesh mentioned to him that the band needed a manager and that Owsley could be that person. Owsley immediately rejected the idea, but the job of sound man, another opening in the Dead world, appealed to him. Owsley didn't know any rock 'n' roll managers, but he knew of Scully from his work with the Family Dog, the loose-knit coalition putting on rock 'n' roll dance concerts around town, and soon tracked Scully down at his home.

Scully would have vivid memories of driving down to the Big Beat with Owsley in the latter's mini sports car. Owsley himself would say in interviews that he hadn't attended the December 18 Acid Test, and more people remember Scully there than Owsley. Whatever happened exactly, Scully arrived with a mission: to see the Warlocks—now named the Grateful Dead—without being as stoned as when he'd caught them the first time. To ensure he had a few brain cells for the night, he only took half a tab of Owsley acid.

■ ◆ ■

Ed Levin, who drummed in a local band called the Vipers and had popped into the Big Beat, heard what he called "weird amplified voices" all around him: "Where is Pigpen?" they said, over and over. The Dead couldn't begin playing until the man who sang many of their songs could be found, and eventually he straggled in from the parking lot. Onstage the night didn't grow any easier for Pigpen. "It wasn't a job, ya dig?" Garcia would later say. "It was the Acid Test." For Pigpen, who didn't take acid, the night could still be challenging. Thanks to the strobe lighting, he could barely see the keys on his organ.

That wouldn't be the only distraction as the Dead began playing. Glancing around the space, Garcia saw Kesey writing messages that were then projected onto a wall. Looking closer, he realized Kesey was writing about what he was witnessing in that moment around him. Meanwhile a voice booming over the sound system chronicled every move Kesey was making. At another point the Pranksters took up positions behind their gear at the other end of the room and began bashing away on their own version of music. Babbs had played trombone in high school, but that training was about as close as the Pranksters came to actual musicianship; with Kesey on guitar and Paula Sundsten (also known as "Gretchen Fetchin'") on keyboard, their half-musical commotion was so ramshackle, it made the Dead sound like a tight, professional R&B and blues cover band.

The night was quickly becoming both musical and sensory overload. Everyone who walked in and paid the $1 admission was given a paper cup for continuing dips into the dosed liquid. "Don't drink the Kool-Aid," people nearby were saying cheekily. (When he heard about these nights later, Weir's boarding school friend John Perry Barlow was appalled: "What we heard was that it sounded like drug abuse," he says. "Mixing up a bathtub full of Kool-Aid and serving it to anyone who wanted it, and they could come back for seconds? Crazy.") If the music wasn't interesting, anyone could walk over to one of the microphones set up around the room and talk, scream, or babble into it. "We didn't all hold hands and close our eyes and do those things," says Babbs. "We'd participate."

When the music or other activities halted, everyone was free to watch a ten-minute slide-show presentation, "America Needs Indians," compiled by Stewart Brand, a twenty-seven-year-old ex-army officer. (Not long after, he became best known as the author of the *Whole Earth Catalog*.) A former resident of Perry Lane in Palo Alto while studying at Stanford, Brand served two years active duty before immersing himself in photography, Native American research, and environmental pursuits. Tapping into the country's slowly emerging interest in Native American history, Brand's presentation combined photographs he'd taken on reservations with historical shots of Native Americans. That night his slide show was greeted with what he calls "a mixture of mild enthusiasm and indifference." If interest in that wore off, people could watch Neal Cassady and his hammers in the middle of the floor. Looking for something to do while he talked, the ambidextrous Cassady, whose sinewy torso could gyrate like a spinning top, had developed a knack for flipping and catching a tiny sledgehammer using both hands and balancing the hammer on the tip of his finger. To Scully, watching on the sidelines, it was "the most bizarre thing" but nonetheless captivating.

At various times that night footage of the Pranksters' bus trip was screened on a wall. On another Babbs showed *The Frogman Prince*, his homemade take on a monster movie inspired by both his time in the army and the sight of divers in California waters. Set to Del Shannon's "Keep Searchin'," the odd little movie featured a military frogman in a wetsuit and mask emerging from the water, meeting a lovely surfer girl, and kissing her; shedding his wetsuit, he turned into a handsome sort of prince. The mini-movie had little connection with anything else taking place inside the Big Beat, but distractions were as much a part of the experience as the Test itself. "It got pretty boring after a while," Brand says, "and then what do you do to relieve the boredom?" Roy Sebern, the artist who'd painted "Furthur" on Kesey's bus, ran into the men's room, grabbed a batch of paper towels, tore them up, and tossed them into the strobe, resulting in what Brand recalls as "this amazing blizzard snowstorm effect." People gathered around and sat in a circle and watched it; it was as entrancing as anything else they witnessed that evening.

In that context the Dead were far from the main attraction, which may have been for the best. Kaufman, who partook of the evening, remembers them playing a soulful set that included "In the Midnight Hour," a staple of the Warlocks' bar repertoire. To Scully they were "sloppy as hell. They'd get into a blues song and stay in the blues groove forever." Still, Scully found them hard to dismiss; they were charismatic in an antistar way, and every so often the music would take shape: Garcia's guitar would emit some strange, exciting sound, or what Scully calls "something cohesive" would emanate from the whole band. The music felt tight one moment, loose the next—not ideal for a record company, perhaps, but perfect for the context of the night. "You couldn't put your finger on it, but it was different from what was going on at the time," says Babbs. "They'd play for however long, and the songs were long. A lot of it was made up on the spot, and that was the beauty of it. They were perfect."

Whether the music had a steady, tick-tock consistency or not, some of the hundred or so people roaming around inside the Big Beat were dancing. One was Lesh's new female friend, Rosie McGee. Born in Paris, McGee had relocated with her family to San Francisco when she was young. By the strangest of coincidences, she'd been working as a secretary at Autumn Records the day the Dead had their audition, although she barely remembered them, given how quickly the recording had gone down. Always a stylish dresser, she'd been sent home one day from her job in an ad agency when she wore knee-high go-go boots to work; her bosses deemed it unprofessional attire. In contrast, the world of the Dead and the Acid Tests offered her a sense of liberation and community.

Before she'd left for the Big Beat, McGee made Lesh promise to stay with her all night; she didn't want to be left to her own stoned devices, and he agreed. Certainly Lesh was unlike anyone McGee had known. In honor of the stick figure created by the advertising world to market the electricity industry, he'd been dubbed Reddy Kilowatt, and to McGee the nickname more than fit Lesh. With his jittery energy, he walked in a staccato manner (years later she'd be reminded of him when watching Kramer on *Seinfeld*), and he didn't seem to climb out of her car so much as jump out of it. "He was very electric, very kinetic, like he'd stuck his finger in a socket sometimes," she says. "He was not a laid-back kind of guy. He was always jumping up, that live-wire stuff."

By comparison, Garcia struck her as laid back and slower moving, yet the two men seemed to complement each other. More than once McGee saw Lesh and Garcia huddle and plunge into deep conversations about an arcane music topic, leaving everyone around them puzzled. "Everyone else would think, 'What the hell are they talking about?'" McGee says. "But they would really be into some sort of exploratory discussion. They were both fearless, and it was all just one big experiment."

◾ ◆ ◾

For the Dead that night momentous things would occur even when they weren't playing. At one point in the evening they took a break—whatever that meant in the context of an Acid Test, which never had anything resembling a schedule—and made their way to the bar. With that Scully made his move, walking over and introducing himself. He said their mutual acquaintance Owsley had suggested he become their manager. They responded with varying degrees of skepticism and bemusement—"smart-alecky," Scully says—but Garcia shook Scully's hand in what struck Scully as a genuine way. The surly looking organist, whom Scully soon learned was nicknamed Pigpen, told Scully he thought "Rock" was a "cool handle." Nothing would be firmly decided on for a few months, but the basis of a working relationship was struck.

During one of the night's breaks Garcia went outside with Kaufman for a time out from the craziness inside. Soon after, the police arrived. Because Kesey had been busted for pot at La Honda the previous April, no one wanted to attract any unwarranted attention. According to Mountain Girl, the Kool-Aid being dispensed was intentionally low dose. "We weren't trying to create too big of a stir," she says. "You had to drink five or six cups to really launch."

Garcia and Kaufman watched as the squad car pulled into the Big Beat parking lot and a policeman stepped out and headed their way. "You could tell he was walking over with an attitude," Kaufman says. "He had a serious law-enforcement vibe."

Anyone else might have acted uptight or defensive, but Garcia radiated the opposite attitude; the people-handling skills he'd learned—perhaps from watching his mother working at her bar—rose to the fore. As Kaufman watched, Garcia charmed the cop in only a few sentences, and the officer, suddenly less agro than he'd first been, simply said, "Uh, okay," returned to his car and drove away. Reflecting back on Garcia's modus operandi, Kaufman says, "It was like watching someone do this beautiful martial-arts move where someone comes in with an energy and you dance with it and turn it around and off it goes." When the cop drove off, all Kaufman could say to Garcia was, "How did you *do* that?"

Garcia had one last, enduring gesture. As the cop was leaving, Garcia took off the hat he was wearing and genially said, "Trips, captain," which Kaufman interpreted as shorthand for "Have a good trip." (According to Kaufman, the often-reported legend in which Garcia said "Tips, captain"—meaning a tip of the hat—is incorrect.) Back inside the Big Beat, Kaufman relayed the story to Kesey, who so loved Garcia's comment that he flipped the words around and came up with Garcia's new nom de Prankster, Captain Trips. (Everyone had a nickname: Babbs, for instance, was "Intrepid Traveler.") In the course of two breaks the Dead had a potential manager and a nickname for one of their front men.

■ ◆ ■

As dawn approached, the Acid Test at the Big Beat began gravitating back down to earth. The Warlocks and the Pranksters started packing their instruments, movie projectors, strobe lighting, and whatever else they'd each dragged along. Everyone, even those still flying on the unorthodox Kool-Aid, straggled into the chilly night to make their way back home.

The Acid Tests had few rules, but one of them decreed that everyone had to stay put until the Test ended in the early morning hours. Prolonging the communal group vibe was one reason—it was comforting to find so many similarly minded oddballs in the Palo Alto area—but personal safety was equally tantamount. "It was not good to be high and out wandering by yourself," says Babbs. "You wanted to stay in the scene where it was safe, with the people who were with you." In her car, McGee, along with Lesh, both still tripping, turned on the heater and watched the ice crystals on the windshield melt—which, in their state, seemed like the most mesmerizing thing they'd ever seen.

The Acid Test at the Big Beat would be neither the last nor largest of those gatherings. In the months ahead others would be held in San Francisco, Portland, and down in Los Angeles. The setups would be similar. Once sound systems, projectors, microphones, and whatever else were installed, everyone was told to leave the building, re-enter, and pay the admission. Each Acid Test would add its own lore and yarns to the legend: dazed Testers wandering out into the streets of LA, huge garbage cans filled with dosed Kool-Aid, Lesh and Owsley conspiring about sound systems, Garcia and Mountain Girl sweeping up, Pigpen uncharacteristically asking Swanson to dance. Delays would be added to the tape recorders to make people's recorded voices reverberate more around the rooms. In late January 1966 about ten thousand people would gravitate to the Trips Festival, a three-day-long, acid-driven freak-out at San Francisco's Longshoremen's Hall that presented some of the Big Beat contingent—the Pranksters, the Dead—along with poets, dancers, and Big Brother and the Holding Company, pre-Janis Joplin. No one, least of all anyone in the mainstream media, had witnessed anything like it. Far more than any of the earlier Acid Tests, the Trips Festival confirmed the existence of a growing movement. "In the Peninsula the people interested in something like that would be a few dozen or people who knew each other," says Brand, who co-organized the Trips Festival. "But no one knew there were thousands of hippies."

Compared to that gathering, the Big Beat Acid Test felt more like a test run than a major happening. "It was lighthearted fun that night," Mountain Girl recalls. "Nothing too heavy happened." She was right— no arrests, no overdoses, no violence, no calamities—but something did take place that night, a coming-together of disparate people, media, and chemicals that signaled a series of new beginnings for the Dead. By the time many of the band members drove off in Kreutzmann's station wagon, other aspects of their world had begun taking shape. They'd met not only their future manager but in the house were two women who'd play leading roles in their lives, McGee and Mountain Girl. (When McGee arrived at Lesh's home she discovered he had a girlfriend—who didn't seem to remotely mind when McGee and Lesh kept walking into their own private back room.) Other attendees included Hugh Romney, the activist, satirist, and counterculture clown known as Wavy Gravy, and Annette Flowers, who would later work for the Dead's publishing company.

The Acid Tests were also where the Dead began finding their collective musical voice. They'd already begun reaching for the outer limits at bars like the In Room, but those gigs were straight-laced compared to the ones at the Acid Tests, where a song could last five minutes or fifty. Neither traditional rock 'n' roll nor copy-cat blues or R&B, the sound was morphing into a mélange of it all, heavily dosed with free-form improvising. "We played with a certain kind of freedom you rarely get as a musician," Garcia later told TV interviewer Tom Snyder about the Acid Test experiences. If Owsley was indeed at the Big Beat, as Scully recalls, they also spent additional quality time with the mad genius who would make a body-slam impact on their sound, finances, and sensibility. "He kept talking to me about how the better sound was low impedance," Lesh says of conversations the two had at one Acid Test. "While we were waiting to start playing, it was all very loose. We were all peaking and ready to play. Bear and Tim Scully [Owsley's electronics-whiz friend] are down there on their hands and knees soldering a box to make it work with the system. It was like a bunch of guys watching someone work on a car." When the system finally was up and blasting, Lesh was impressed with the bass, but the Dead only played for a few minutes and then, according to Lesh, Garcia "decided he wanted to go do something" and they stopped. But within a few months they would be playing through Owsley's sound system.

"Can *YOU* Pass the Acid Test?" read the fliers passed around by the Pranksters. Whether the locale was Muir Beach, Palo Alto, or southern California, the Acid Tests *were* endurance tests of sorts: if you were strong, wily, and open-minded enough, you could make it to dawn. ("It was pretty scary if you weren't expecting any of that stuff," says Tim Scully, unrelated to Rock, who helped Owsley by building a mixing board, finding speakers, and ensuring the Dead's instruments didn't emit odious hums and noises.) The same mentality would now extend to the Dead. Theirs was an increasingly demanding world, one that would take stamina, thick skin, and the proper constitution to survive. "The Acid Test was the prototype for our whole basic trip," Garcia later told *Rolling Stone*'s Jann Wenner. He was right, and in more ways than he probably foresaw.

*Weir (alongside Rosie McGee, with Toni Kaufman and
Danny Rifkin behind them) during the bust at 710.*
PHOTO: BARNEY PETERSON / *SAN FRANCISCO CHRONICLE* / POLARIS

CHAPTER 4

SAN FRANCISCO, OCTOBER 2, 1967

Mountain Girl didn't give it a second or even third thought when the visitor—let's call him Snitch—unexpectedly appeared at the front door of 710 Ashbury. Plenty of people, friends and otherwise, had scaled the dozen steps that led to the front door of the Victorian rowhouse in Haight Ashbury. Two years before, college students who'd rented rooms there were trudging up and down with their backpacks. Ever since the Dead had settled into the building in what amounted to a less-than-hostile takeover, Mountain Girl, her long hair now in a short, boyish bob, was more likely to greet local musicians, various Pranksters, and the band's assorted girlfriends, childhood pals, and business associates. Some might stay a few hours, some a few days; most would make their way there by hitting the intersection of Haight and Ashbury before striding up the sloping Ashbury Street and arriving at the house with the bay window.

Today's visitor, Snitch, small and curly haired, was an acquaintance of the band's from the area. In what was another commonplace request at 710, Snitch asked Mountain Girl whether she had any weed, and she didn't vacillate. "There's some funky pot in the colander in the kitchen," she told him. As she would later recall, "I would do that for practically anybody I knew." She didn't know Snitch that well, but she accepted him along with others who straggled into what had become the Dead's combination home, clubhouse, and business office.

The house at 710 wasn't their first attempt at group living. Less than two months after the last attendees had drifted off into the daylight hours after the Acid Test at the Big Beat nightclub, the Dead and their extended posse had decamped to Los Angeles. Rock Scully was now their comanager along with Scully's friend and neighbor Danny Rifkin, and both felt the Dead needed time to work on original material, and Los Angeles in early 1966—home to the Byrds, the Turtles, Sonny and Cher, and many others—was a throbbing heart of the music business. "We needed more songs and needed to get tight," says Scully. "We wanted to go back to San Francisco with more songs."

With the help of the Pranksters, already ensconced in the area, the Dead and their growing family found a home on the outskirts of Watts. (According to Babbs, the Dead and the Pranksters first shared a house in LA, but it was so packed with people that the Dead got their own place.) Tim Scully, who came along with them, remembers the pink-painted house as once home to a bishop or priest, down to its confessional booth in the living room. Next door was a brothel, and many would later recall the sight of pot growing outside between the whorehouse and the Dead's house, thanks to customers who tossed seeds out the window of the brothel. Mountain Girl also feels another reason the Dead headed south was to deal with their growing following, even at this early stage. "They were already beginning to attract serious fans, both good and bad, but they hadn't thought about how they were going to handle people paying attention to them offstage," she says. "I got the sense they were trying to protect their privacy down there."

Over the course of roughly two months and several Acid Tests in the LA area, the Dead practiced in their temporary living room. (Not surprisingly, neighbors would sometimes call the cops to complain about the noise.) They learned they could live together in the same house, even if it meant adhering to the all-meat diet that the proudly eccentric Owsley imposed on everyone else. Anyone peering into the refrigerator would be greeted with the sight of slabs of raw beef. Some were disgusted; others didn't seem to mind. "It got a little old after a while," says Lesh, "but I had gone through a period where I hadn't had a lot of meat to eat, so I was happy to have it." The women in the house didn't seem as enamored of Owsley as some of the Dead were, but no one had a choice when it came to coping with Owsley's eccentricities: he actively supported and financed the band, "buying and renting equipment as needed and paying for groceries," says Tim Scully. Scully also lived in the house, along with various Dead girlfriends and a friend from the Dead's Palo Alto early days, Don Douglas.

At first Owsley refrained from manufacturing acid in the house, although there was still plenty around; about once a week, according to Douglas, everyone took Owsley's product en masse. Weir had been irked one night when Owsley exclaimed, "Well, we're surely doing the devil's work here!" Weir had to admit that between the chemicals and the loose social arrangements, one had to have a fairly liberal brain to accept it all, but he didn't fully agree with the devil remark, and he rarely ventured upstairs to Owsley's lair on the third floor. "Every now and then I'd go up and talk to him about this or that," he told *Rolling Stone* in 2011, "but we spent most of the time on the bottom floor rehearsing or hanging. I know he was making stuff and cranking it out, but I don't know where the apparatus was."

Their journey to Los Angeles puttered out for several reasons, one of them financial. Owsley soon ran out of money, and according to Tim Scully, Owsley and his cohorts took some of the leftover crystal LSD from a previous lab and sold it. (Lesh would often imagine the dust from Owsley's hand-pressed Blue Cheer acid drifting down through the ceiling and infusing the music they were making in the living room.) Although the Dead managed to play a few shows in town, locals didn't know what to make of them, as Bonner learned when she pitched in posting fliers for the LA Acid Tests. As she recalls, "People would say, 'What is that—Grateful Dead? That's disturbing!'"

By April, they'd flown back to the Bay Area and, with the help of McGee, relocated en masse to a rented house called Rancho Olompali in Marin County. For six weeks they lived the alternative lifestyle— ingesting acid, taking advantage of the swimming pool, and throwing communal parties. One day their folk-scene friend Jorma Kaukonen, now with Jefferson Airplane, was sitting around with Garcia and another pal, Janis Joplin. "We're gonna be archetypes," Garcia told Kaukonen, who found it startling that someone would say that so early in his career; the Dead hadn't even made a record yet.

For Douglas one memory from the Los Angeles trip would always linger. One night a bunch of them gathered around a Ouija board, and one of the directives spelled out the message that they'd be leaving the stage on July 9. "Everybody seemed to think it meant July 9, 1966," says Douglas, "and by 'leaves the stage,' we thought the group-high thing, like lifting off the stage." No one thought much of it, especially because they were heading back home to see what the Bay Area now had to offer them.

◆ ◆ ◆

The sights and sounds of Pigpen alone were enough to help them secure what would become their grandest experiment in all-for-one living. It began with Danny Rifkin, a transplanted New Yorker working as a building super at 710 Ashbury after a brief student career at Berkeley. For him 710 was a college rooming house, but one of his renters was Rock Scully. Because people in town associated the Haight with the crumbling Fillmore district nearby, the area, home to artists and African Americans, was, Scully says, "the best deal in town." After he'd moved into the building, Scully hit upon the idea of having his new clients, the Dead, relocate to 710 as well. Though he was far from a nondabbler, Rifkin wasn't overjoyed at the thought of scruffy, revenue-challenged, LSD-imbibing musicians moving into a house for which he was responsible. Eventually he agreed only if Scully became the superintendent and had his name replace Rifkin's on the lease. Given the relative freedom they'd had at Olompali, few thought anything could go wrong, and Scully's name was now attached to the paperwork for running the building.

One by one during the fall of 1966 the Dead made their way into 710, and the tenants already there began packing up and leaving. Rattled by the sight of the stout, seemingly gruff Pigpen and the sound of his blues records and guitar playing in the back room, they individually decided it was time to leave. ("Unbeknownst to him, Pig was a big help," chuckles Scully.) Wherever anyone could find space, they took it. Garcia, Lesh, and McGee, now Lesh's girlfriend, settled in upstairs, with Scully in a room next to theirs. Rifkin installed himself in the garage apartment, complete with antique lighting from the days when that part of the 1890s house was a horse stable. Weir settled into the living room, which doubled as an office. Sue Swanson, Weir's friend from high school, crashed sometimes as well. "As people would move out of the rooms, some of us would move in," Lesh recalled. "We just weaseled our way in and eventually took over."

Given that the front door was never locked, plenty of other friends made their way into 710 too. ("We'd argue about how many friends could spend the night," Mountain Girl recalls. "There was no place to sleep.") One day it was Betty Cantor, a teenager with long, sandy-colored hair who hailed from Martinez, northeast of Berkeley. In love with the new rock 'n' roll and the culture rising up around it, Cantor had put up posters and worked the concession stand at the Avalon and already had a fine-tuned set of ears for music and sound reproduction.

(Later she worked at the Family Dog in Denver after meeting promoter Chet Helms at the Avalon.) In a nearby park, she found herself at 710; one of her friends knew Rock Scully's brother. As she walked up the front steps, out came Weir, who held the door open while holding a guitar, extending his arm and exclaiming, "Come on in!" It was an especially vivid memory; Weir had, she recalls, "hair down to here and big doe eyes."

During his own initial visit to 710, about a year after the Dead had moved in, John Perry Barlow wandered upstairs and found Weir lying on a couch. Although Weir's eyes were open, he seemed to be asleep, Barlow recalls. Next to Weir, shirtless and high on speed, was none other than Neal Cassady, listening to jazz with headphones and scat-singing along with the music as he danced around the couch. (To Barlow it almost seemed as if Weir was conjuring Cassady up from his imagination.) For Weir at least, the disorder of 710 was initially constructive. "It reinforced how to operate in a profound state of flux and chaos," he told writer David Hajdu. "Haight-Ashbury offered that in copious servings. When we put our instruments down, we still lived in chaos. Our entire lives were about sorting our way through chaos and making little pockets of, I won't call it order, but little pockets where we could function, and that's what we ended up doing in our sets too. You know, life imitates art, art imitates life. There was no separation between living and playing for us."

A more frequent guest at 710 was Laird Grant, Garcia's carousing buddy. By 1967 Grant had logged time as the band's first roadie, driving them to bar gigs and helping them set up their sometimes screeching sound systems and instruments. With his scraggly beard and rugged looks, Grant looked the part of a hardened laborer for the Dead, and he had a new nickname to match: to help deflect the wind when he rode his motorcycle, he'd taken to wearing a hat made out of the bottom of a leather purse and folded up Robin Hood–style. "You look like a

Barney!" Pigpen chortled when saw Laird wearing it, and Grant was Barney forever after.

Grant's brief stint with the band ended at the Monterey Pop Festival, a multi-act gathering in June 1967 that found the Dead on a bill that included Simon and Garfunkel, the Byrds, the Jimi Hendrix Experience, the Who, the Mamas and the Papas, and Otis Redding. Along with other San Francisco bands, the Dead had to be talked into appearing at the festival, especially because it was run by John Phillips of the Mamas and the Papas and their label head, Lou Adler, both LA pop kingpins who represented everything San Francisco rockers were against. (Scott McKenzie's comely if hokey summertime hit, "San Francisco [Be Sure to Wear Flowers in Your Hair]," was written by his friend Phillips.) At a meeting at the Fairmont Hotel in San Francisco Phillips and Adler tried to make their case to the local musicians, and for a while relations almost went south. "It was that kind of volatile situation," admits Adler. But thanks to the intervention of Ralph J. Gleason, the well-regarded *San Francisco Chronicle* music columnist who wrote favorably about the new Bay Area rock in spite of his inclination toward jazz, the Dead agreed and wound up playing a respectable but far from show-stopping set between career-defining performances by the Who and Jimi Hendrix. Averse to playing too many industry games, they refused to allow their footage to be used in the eventual documentary about the festival. Adler says the Dead did leave with a prize, though: they wound up carting some of the festival's amps back to their home base. "When I asked for the amps," Adler says, "Rock Scully said, 'Why don't you come up here and get 'em? And be sure to wear flowers in your hair.'"

After seeing Hendrix light his guitar on fire, Grant looked at Garcia and said, "This ain't fun anymore, man—this is a job." Garcia just shrugged and told his friend, "Bon voyage," and Grant was gone the next day. Although he always enjoyed hanging with Garcia and the other members of the Dead, Grant had reasons for leaving the band and the area. To him the situation at 710, especially the out-front pot smoking, was begging for trouble, and given that he'd already logged time behind bars, he wanted nothing to do with a situation that could send him back there. "The philosophy and the freedom of doing things that we set out to do—they were definitely going to have a thumb put on them," he says. "And I didn't want to be anywhere near that. I knew what was gonna go down." Grant jumped onto his bike and rode off to New Mexico before something "strange," as he calls it, could happen.

■ ◆ ■

On this October morning—and nearly every other one—music crept up on 710 early. As always it would start with Garcia, who would rise at dawn and immediately start practicing scales. By now his hair was long and thick, falling on either side of his head and separated in the middle, deflecting attention from his small chin. To Grant, Garcia's musical discipline had its roots in his friend's brief stint in the army seven years before. "After the army he was a little more disciplined," Grant says. "Prior to that it was, 'Oh, well, the sun's up.'" Mountain Girl knew Garcia was talented from the first time she saw him practicing banjo in Palo Alto, but living with him brought his focus into sharp relief. "It took me a while to find out what an obsessive person he was," she says. "Rehearsing constantly and talking and smoking and practicing." The two would watch Jefferson Airplane's Paul Kantner drive by in his Mercedes and want to scream "sell out!" But at the same time, they were envious of the Airplane's burgeoning fame.

Creatively, the eighteen months since the heyday of the Acid Tests had been a relentless parade of practicing, getting high, scrounging for money, and watching Scully and Rifkin scrounge for gigs and in general attempt to transform the Grateful Dead into a professional enterprise. To Mountain Girl and others, Scully and Rifkin clearly wanted the Dead to make it even as both were learning how to be managers, but Garcia himself was becoming increasingly proud of the band's abilities. On January 11, 1967, he wrote to a fan who'd sent a letter to him at 710; in it, he summed up each band member's strengths. Weir was "a hard-working young musician with fantastically good time," and Garcia described himself as having "spent three years as a bluegrass banjo player. Switched back to electric guitar when the band formed." Most of their songs were "traditional," but he added, "We write our own melodies." He admitted that Lesh had only been playing bass for a year and a half but that he had "absolute pitch." In an early indication of the direct level of communications that would exist between the Dead and their fans, Garcia criticized the band's earlier show in Sacramento, calling it "far below standard," then signed off, "Captain Trips."

In the middle of 1966 they assembled at yet another studio in San Francisco to cut a single for an indie label, Scorpio, and the time they'd spent wood-shedding in Los Angeles announced itself: Pigpen's roughhouse voice and stabbing organ were both stronger, dominating their makeover of the twenties blues song "Stealin'," and Garcia's extended lead on the group-written "You Don't Have to Ask" showed signs of pushing the boundaries of the traditional guitar solo. They attempted "I Know You Rider" once more, but with a telling change; in a sign of another future direction, the merest hint of a country lick popped up in Garcia's lead. As with their Autumn Records session the previous fall, though, the recordings still felt embryonic, and only a limited number of copies of a single—"Stealin'" backed with "Don't Ease Me In"— were released in August.

The Dead had little time to be discouraged—their lives and career would, in fact, change for the better that same month. At the urging of DJ Tom Donahue, Joe Smith, who ran Warner Brothers Records, flew up from Los Angeles to check out the band at the Avalon Ballroom. Having come straight from dinner, neither Smith, in a suit, nor his wife,

Donnie, in pearls, were sartorially fit for what they were about to see. "No one my age had ever seen anything like that," Smith recalls of the music and the fans who sprawled out over the ballroom. "People painting bodies and lying on the floor and smoking, and of course the light shows." The band was playing, as Smith recalls caustically, "one of their forty-minute drone sets." The label head was even less enchanted when a guy in the crowd asked his wife to dance: "I said, 'Oh no, no, no,' and I sat her down with a security guy."

Despite his reservations about the band, its approach, and the people they attracted, Smith knew a mushrooming market when he saw it. Warner Brothers and its sister label Reprise, launched earlier by Frank Sinatra, were far from in vogue and needed desperately to catch up. Smith met with Scully, Rifkin, and their newly enlisted lawyer, Brian Rohan, promising them specialized marketing, as if they were a country act—"and they bought it," Smith says. In the fall a deal was hammered out, giving the band a $10,000 advance and ownership of their song publishing. Scully also negotiated what were called jazz rates—getting paid by the length of the song, not the number of songs on an album—which he'd learned from getting to know musicians like Dave Brubeck and Paul Desmond while working as an usher at the Monterey Jazz Festival.

The signing was the culmination of an astonishing nine months in which the Dead had progressed from being the Acid Test house band with hardly any original material and a sound very much in flux to a tighter rock band with a contract at the record company that was home to Frank Sinatra and Peter, Paul & Mary. As Smith admits, the arrangement benefited the label just as much. "That was one of the two or three most important signings in all those years," he says. "It changed the nature and opinion of the record company. We were out in front. It was important to indicate we were more than Dean Martin and Sinatra—that we were hip."

In January 1967 the Dead returned to Los Angeles, but under more welcoming circumstances than the year before. The making of their introductory album was scheduled for RCA Studios, where Garcia had helped out the Airplane on their breakthrough, *Surrealistic Pillow.* They hardly got off to a promising start, though: just before they flew down, Garcia stepped on a nail and had to spend part of the time on the plane and in the studio in a wheelchair. The producer assigned to the task, Dave Hassinger, had an impressive résumé—he'd worked with the Airplane, the Rolling Stones, and others—but the Dead soon realized they wouldn't have quite the creative control Warners had promised them. "It wasn't exactly a fun trip," says Mountain Girl. "The expectations were so widely different. The band wanted to be in-your-face outrageous, and the producer wanted pop that would sell—and who could blame him? There was more discussion than recording. It was pretty uncomfortable."

To the band's consternation, guitar solos were edited, and other songs were trimmed; Mountain Girl witnessed more than a few people in the band walking out of the studio in disgust. It didn't help that band members popped Ritalin and possibly diet pills, according to one source. Speaking to *Rolling Stone* writer Michael Lydon about it two years later, Garcia remained philosophical about the sessions: "At the time it was unreasonable to do what we do, which would have been one LP, two songs or one song," he said. "Nobody would have gone for it. So we made the first record of songs we did."

Despite their frustrations, they managed in just under a week to record and mix a full album that took listeners on an abbreviated but still enlightening trip through their past and into the present. The songs ranged from their Mother McCree repertoire (Jesse Fuller's "Beat It on Down the Line") to tracks that recalled their primordial days as a garage band ("Cream Puff War"), the latter driven by Pigpen's amusement-park organ. There were blues ("Good Morning Little

School Girl") and folk rock ("Cold Rain and Snow," which found their group harmonies more amply developed). From the drugs they took or the tension between band and producer—or all of the above—the songs had a brittle, jittery energy, as if the Dead were hurtling through their repertoire as quickly as possible. Pigpen's soul-vamping finale for "Good Morning Little School Girl" leapt out, but it was their charged version of "Viola Lee Blues" that hinted at their future. More freeform and less constrained than the other songs on the album—it ran nine minutes long— it had a swirling, psychotic-breakdown midsection that took its cues from their Acid Test days. "The Golden Road (to Unlimited Devotion)," recorded later in San Francisco when it was clear they needed something approaching a single, was twisted-kicks garage rock with crackling Kreutzmann drums and a sing-along chorus that made a concession to a hook.

As soon as Warner Brothers released the album, *The Grateful Dead*, in March, the band made it clear that compromise wouldn't be a regular part of their relationship with the label. Smith, label ad-copy writer Stan Cornyn, and other executives at the company flew up for a long-infamous launch party at Fugazi Hall in the North Beach section of San Francisco. Cornyn walked in to encounter what seemed like a giant tub in the middle of the room, filled with dry ice, water, and half-naked women. "I wasn't prepared for it, and Joe wasn't prepared for it," he recalls. Smith made a toast: "I wanted to say something like, 'We at Warner Brothers want to welcome the Grateful Dead to the world,' and Rock or Jerry said, 'We want to introduce *Warner Brothers* to the world.'" Everyone laughed, and in late May Warners ponied up enough money to send the band on its first-ever trip to New York, which included shows at the Central Park Bandshell and the Stony Brook campus.

During that trip they settled into Café au Go Go, the hot-spot club on Bleecker Street in Greenwich Village, for over a week's worth of shows. Despite its hokey name, the Au Go Go was one of the jewels of the Village; in the previous months it had hosted Jefferson Airplane, Richie Havens, Tim Buckley, and the Mothers of Invention (at a small theater upstairs from the club). In the audience to see the Dead one of their nights was Barlow, who by then had moved east and was studying at nearby Wesleyan in Connecticut. Although Barlow and Weir had communicated by mail for a while after their boarding-school days in Colorado, Barlow had lost touch with his friend and only heard later that Weir was in a band called the Grateful Dead.

Now, three years after last seeing each other at school and in Wyoming, Barlow was confronted with a very different Weir at the Au Go Go. The short-haired, somewhat stocky football player of school days had been replaced with a nineteen-year-old who had what Barlow calls a "thousand-yard stare" and longer hair than he'd ever seen on a man. Weir also seemed barely verbal. "He was completely different," says Barlow, who didn't know at the time that Weir had been off acid for nearly a year. "He seemed like a complete space cadet." But given the new direction Weir seemed to have in life, none of those new attributes necessarily seemed like setbacks.

■ ◆ ■

With Snitch trailing her, Mountain Girl made her way to the kitchen of 710, which was painted in green and orange colors that lent it the feel of a pumpkin and avocado patch. As she watched, he grabbed some of the newly strained pot from a colander on the counter (other times they kept it in an empty aluminum pie pan). The colander was the same appliance everyone used to wash their lettuce, and it did double duty of filtering out the seeds from mangy piles of weed. Mountain Girl watched as Snitch rolled a few joints for himself. She didn't need to reach up to one of the highest shelves in the kitchen cabinet, where, wrapped in waxy cellophane paper, was a squat brick of pot, one of its corners torn off to make the latest batch. The brick looked as if someone had simply yanked the plant out of the ground and crushed it down into a few pounds, seeds, stems, and dirt included.

As Snitch went about his rolling business, Mountain Girl paid only perfunctory notice. She had other things on her mind. That afternoon she and Garcia were planning to take a day trip to a clothing store in Sausalito to buy ribbons; she'd use them to decorate a black velvet shirt for her boyfriend.

In what felt like destiny, Garcia and Mountain Girl had hooked up in the fall of 1966. When Kesey had fled to Mexico earlier that year to avoid jail time for his pot busts, Mountain Girl and other Pranksters followed him down, and they all lived on the beach at Manzanillo Bay for a few months. (During that time Mountain Girl became pregnant with Kesey's daughter, whom they named Sunshine; according to Mountain Girl, Kesey's wife, Faye, who was also in Mexico, was accepting of the situation: "She was a kind and forgiving person.") Everyone but Kesey had to return when their visas ran out, and with that, says Mountain Girl, came "the end of the whole Pranksters trip." Taking Sunshine with her, she moved back in with her brother in San Francisco, and shortly thereafter she and Garcia became inseparable. By then Garcia's marriage to Sara Ruppenthal was on its last legs, and Sara's one visit to 710 didn't portend a future for them: as she told Garcia biographer Blair Jackson, "It didn't exactly feel 'family friendly' to me."

Garcia had another short-lived girlfriend when he moved into 710; as McGee recalls, "Jerry went through women until Mountain Girl showed up." But he and Mountain Girl did seem destined to be a couple. For their first date the couple went Christmas shopping. From a love of pot and psychedelics to the fact that both were young parents, Garcia and Mountain Girl shared many traits. "He had determination and willingness to jump into anything at any time," she says. "He had extra aliveness. He was not disconnected, ever. The young Jerry was such a character." To Grant, the ties between his old friend and Mountain Girl was obvious. She liked to be in charge. (During the Trips Festival Stewart Brand watched as Mountain Girl, trying to organize workers who were getting high on nitrous, put her hand on the valve and shut it off.) And at that point in his life Garcia didn't mind women overseeing him. "Jerry was always one of those guys who drew women to him because he seemed needy," Grant says. "He never took care of his own shit, and he needed someone else to do that, like, 'Help me, be my old lady.'"

As free as he wanted his relationship with Mountain Girl to be, though, Garcia still flashed a deeply jealous streak. During one New Jersey trip Barlow had driven them to a Guild guitar factory, Garcia and Mountain Girl in the backseat of his Chevy. At one point Barlow looked in the rearview mirror and had a moment of eye contact with his female passenger. Garcia caught it and subtly made his displeasure known to Barlow. "He was very territorial," says Barlow. "He didn't want anyone looking at his woman that way." Mountain Girl noticed that Garcia would get angry if he saw her talking with other men, even those in the Dead, which to her reflected his roots as a "street guy" from outside San Francisco.

For Mountain Girl life in the Dead household at 710 meant a degree of readjustment. When she was part of the Kesey posse she was not just a free spirit but someone who worked on recording and editing tapes; she didn't just have gumption but a job. She longed to have a similar role with the Dead, but it wasn't to be. The house was filled with female friends, including Pigpen's beloved African American girlfriend, Veronica Barnard, who hailed from nearby Vallejo. Their jobs were to clean the house, including its one and a half bathrooms, and cook the meals, such as Grant's mouth-watering rice and beans. Mountain Girl and the other women tried to organize a 710-wide cleaning day on Saturdays, but the concept didn't go over well with the men. She also had to take care of Sunshine because she couldn't afford a babysitter and was tasked with collecting $15 a week from everyone in the house to take down to Haight Street for food.

The scenario was oddly retro—the bread winners and the stay-at-home moms and girlfriends—but no one seemed to object. "We just hung out together and cracked jokes and watched TV," Lesh said to David Hajdu. "The women did the cooking and cleaning. All we had to do was get high and play music. It was like paradise." Mountain Girl accepted her newfound role as, in her words, "a solid citizen" to keep the house running. "It was *very* traditional," says Swanson. "We were right on the cusp of [women's lib]. Me personally, I always thought, 'Whatever I could do to help was good.'"

Of the men Weir was the only one who didn't need help with the meals. After giving up LSD the year before (he'd had his mind blown one too many times), he went macrobiotic. Regularly preparing brown paste out of rice, he cooked for what seemed like endless hours and then ate it very slowly, chewing each bite dozens of times. Fellow 710 residents would walk into the kitchen and find him cooking seaweed on the stove. For years afterward the other Dead members would kid Weir about that part of his life. But at least Weir worked hard on healthy habits at that point. Orange juice was a staple of the refrigerator at 710; with all the smoke in the house and trips to equally smoky clubs, everyone was getting sick faster than ever before.

Having finished rolling his joints, Snitch paused. On the way out he turned and asked whether Mountain Girl and Garcia would be around later, and Mountain Girl mentioned they had planned a trip out of town, to Sausalito. Snitch asked when they were leaving, and she told him in a few hours, around 1 p.m. When she later thought back to his questions, she had to wonder why he asked for all those details. Maybe he was being thoughtful, or maybe he was simply afraid of her and Garcia. Given what was about to happen, she later wondered whether he was actually being considerate.

■ ◆ ■

Pigpen was in the john and Weir was upstairs practicing yoga when the pounding at the door began around 3 p.m. In the living room Bob Matthews, who'd become the band's electronics expert (hence his nickname "Knobs"), had just cracked open a box of new speakers when he looked up and saw them: five agents from the California State Bureau of Narcotics Enforcement, along with two city inspectors, barging into 710. "Well, what do we have *here?*" one of them said to Matthews, peering into his cardboard box. Rifkin was returning to the house from an errand when he saw a man in a suit who growled, "So, you're Rifkin."

Leading the charge was Matthew O'Connor, head of the Northern Californian division of the state's narcotics bureau, a fervent antipot crusader who two months before had told a group at the Hibernian Newman Club that pot was a "dangerous, unpredictable substance" and that he wanted possession to remain a felony, not a misdemeanor. Right behind him at 710 was Jerry (short for Gerrit) Van Raam, a seven-year veteran of the department who'd resigned as a cop after being charged with beating a boy outside a deli. (Van Raam claimed the kid was trying to steal change from him.) Two days after turning in his badge Van Raam was sworn in as a member of the narcotics bureau. On a mission to rid the Haight of illicit drugs, they first hit houses on Haight and Divisadero Streets, but according to O'Connor, 710 kept coming up as what he called "a supply source."

Sue Swanson was next. Earlier that day she'd been at 710 and had walked down to Haight Street—everyone pounded the pavement because no one at the building had a car—to buy a carton of ice cream. Walking up the stairs of 710 she noticed the door was uncharacteristically locked; on the other side stood an older man in a suit and tie, who opened the door and asked, "Do you live here?" Later Swanson realized she should have said no and walked back down the steps.

Instead, in a moment of bravado, she snapped, "And who are *you?*" The man pulled her inside and escorted her into the kitchen, where she saw Rifkin, Weir, Pigpen, and Matthews, among others, all sitting silently. Around them everyone could hear men clomping up and down the stairs, pulling open file cabinet drawers, and talking.

Next up the front steps was Scully, equally confounded by the sight of a locked front door. At first he thought it meant the band was doing an interview; such requests were coming in more frequently now that they had made an album. But when he saw the same suited officer, Scully realized something more ominous was taking place. When he told them his name, the police recognized it—it was on the lease—and gruffly informed him of the reason for their visit. "What—is someone smoking marijuana?" Scully replied faux innocently, but no one bought it, and he too was hauled into the kitchen.

The cops thought they had them all until they saw McGee coming toward the entrance. Lesh and McGee had only briefly lived at 710 in the same room as Garcia and a girlfriend. The two couples (and Garcia's waking-the-dead snoring) were separated only by a thin Chinese screen, which McGee says was "not acceptable." Within a few weeks she, Lesh, and Kreutzmann had found a place together a few blocks away on Belvedere Street. "I just wanted a change of scene," says Lesh. "It wasn't like in '66 when we were all living together. It just changed in some unidentifiable way that made me think, 'This part of it is over.' Everybody had girlfriends, and there were too many people in the house and not enough room for your own personal space."

Because her mail was still being sent to 710, McGee was stopping by the house that day to grab it. On her way up the front steps she saw Swanson, frantically waving to her to go back, but before McGee knew what was happening, she too was asked whether she lived there and then found herself in the kitchen.

As police stood guard, everyone in the pantry was eerily quiet, either silently stewing or simply stunned. McGee was possibly the most anxious: leaning over to Swanson, she whispered that she had a ball of hash in her purse, tucked under her poncho. Swanson said nothing, and they continued listening to the police trample through the building, until Swanson finally said, "Let's get some ice cream." Because the cop in the room had his back to them, Swanson and McGee cracked open the freezer, pulled out the dessert, and quickly crumbled McGee's hash into bowls with the ice cream. They were careful not to open the nearby pantry with the gnarly brick of pot. McGee decided to eat the evidence and dug into the ice cream, which tasted like it was sprinkled with grains of dirt.

Finally, after what seemed like hours, it was time to head to police headquarters. In boy-girl pairs, the busted—Weir, Pigpen, Scully, Rifkin, McGee, Barnard, Matthews, Swanson, and Christine Bennett, girlfriend of the band's new sound man, Dan Healy—were handcuffed and marched down the steps of 710 as photographers, alerted to the raid by police, snapped away. From Weir's long, girlish mane to Rifkin's mushroom head of hair to Pigpen's untucked shirt and headband, they looked more like scraggly bohos than menaces to society, and Weir, cuffed to McGee, waved flamboyantly to the crowd. ("As they say, just spell the name right," Weir has joked of the bust.) As Scully and Swanson made their way out, Swanson's small hand kept sliding in and out of the cuffs, and Scully scolded her, "Just keep your hand in there! Don't get me in trouble!" Before long they were all sitting crammed into a paddy wagon and were on their way to the police headquarters in the Market District. (For unexplained reasons, five other people in the house—a girl of thirteen and what were later described as "a young man and three other girls"—were set free; Bennett, who was underage, was sent to juvenile hall.)

The shopping trip to Sausalito over, Garcia and Mountain Girl were walking up Ashbury when they heard Marilyn Harris, a neighbor living across the street, summoning them up to her apartment. From the vantage point of her window they watched as their friends were marched down the front steps of 710 and into the wagon. Having been busted before, Mountain Girl wasn't overly rattled, but it was still disturbing to see their friends, especially dope-averse Pigpen, in the hands of the law. "Oh shit, oh shit," was all she and Garcia could say to one another. They didn't have to say much more.

■　◆　■

Lesh, Kreutzmann, and their new roommate, a drummer named Mickey Hart, were preparing an early dinner at 17 Belvedere Street when the phone rang. On the line was Mountain Girl, telling Hart a bust was going down at 710 and that none of them should drop by. "She said, 'Don't come over,'" Hart recalls. "'*Don't come over?*' She said it real quick." Lesh would remember picking up the phone, hearing the news, and immediately redialing the house number to confirm what was happening; when a "very serious, unknown, masculine voice" answered, Lesh received his answer and hung up. The news was out, and Hart found himself in yet another alien situation with a band he'd only just joined.

Hart's initiation into the fold had been typically loose and laissez-faire. On a night in late September 1967 he'd wandered into the Straight Theater, where it was immediately clear the name was something of a joke (as was the billing on the marquee, which called the event a dance class). Decades earlier the Straight had been the Haight Theater, a movie house on the corner of Haight and Cole streets, but only the shell of the old structure remained. The first two dozen rows of seats on the main floor had been ripped out, a wooden dance floor was installed in their place, and all around Hart were bodies—some dancing, others intermingled. The overwhelming aroma of freshly lit joints wafted over it all. (The show had been billed as a "school of dance" event to avoid having to land a permit for a concert.) Hart made his way to the stage, where his new friend Kreutzmann was playing with his band, the Grateful Dead.

The two drummers had met shortly before, introduced to each other at a Count Basie show—possibly at the Fillmore in August 1967—by someone neither of them knew. (Decades later they would still puzzle at that mysterious stranger who altered both of their lives before disappearing into the night.) Hart and Kreutzmann had different personalities. Hart was brash, wiry, and proactive, with a goatee that gave him the look of a freshly arrived Eastern European immigrant. Kreutzmann was taller, laconic, and laid back, with a page-boy haircut and a grin that always seemed as if he were pulling a practical joke. Yet they shared a love of banging on things, and that first night they ran together around the streets of the Haight, making a percussion racket on anything in sight. "We took two pairs of drumsticks and played the whole city—cars, bumpers, street signs, trash cans," Hart says. "We were yakking and laughing." Afterward Kreutzmann invited Hart to jam with his band at a garage rehearsal space, but he never gave Hart the exact address, leaving Hart to wander the neighborhood in vain before heading back to home and work.

Work was Hart Music, an instrument store in a San Francisco suburb run by his father, Lenny. The Harts originally hailed from Brooklyn, and Mickey would long remember his grandmother's minuscule backyard, what he called "sacred space—because there wasn't that much space in Brooklyn." Lenny, who'd won a drum championship at the 1939 New York's World Fair, had left his wife and their son—born Michael Steven Hartman on September 11, 1943—during his son's formative years, after which Mickey became obsessed with drumming himself. After high school and during a stint in the Air Force, he learned his father was in California and tracked Lenny down after his Air Force days were over; by then Lenny was running the instrument store, and Mickey went to work for him. (Coincidentally, Hart had met Connie Bonner about two years before, when she and some friends stopped by his place, but the Dead were still in their gestation years.)

In the relatively tight San Francisco music scene of the time Hart had heard about the Dead but hadn't heard them, and he wasn't sure what to make of them at first at the Straight Theater. As he watched from close to the stage, the music was overpoweringly loud and deafening— "cacophonous," he would later call it, "this amazing wall of sound swirling around." The rumble of Lesh's bass and a bit of Garcia's guitar rose up through the murk, but little else did; he couldn't hear the other guitarist at all, never mind the guy behind the organ. It didn't sound like anything typically rock 'n' roll except in its volume, which seemed to overtake the entire theater.

Between sets Hart reacquainted himself with Kreutzmann, who immediately asked his fellow drummer to sit in. Jumping into Kreutzmann's Mustang, they found a kit and made it back to the Straight in time for the second set. They all launched into "Alligator," a loose, newly written boogie that featured Pigpen's voice and allowed for endless improvisation. No matter what Hart was playing, it all seemed like one very long song, tribal and amorphous, firm but nebulous. "It started up," Hart recalls, "and I was holding on for dear life." The people splayed about the Straight didn't seem to notice there was another musician onstage, and they didn't seem to care whether he knew the song or not; they were too busy screwing, dancing, or both. Dust drifted down from the ceiling, intermingling with the strobe lights and casting surreal shadows across the whole scene. The whole scenario struck Hart as a throwback to Dionysian times.

Finally, after what seemed like a few lifetimes, the music wrapped itself up. No one applauded, and Hart wasn't sure whether the audience was preparing to boo or throw things at them. Instead, what he heard was the sound of people breathlessly exclaiming, "Aaah!" (Even their reactions to the music weren't conventional.) Garcia turned to everyone and said, with a smile, "We could take this around the world, man."

They didn't immediately know it, but they had just found the final element to their sound and identity. Lesh wasn't interested in playing conventional bass lines, so the music lacked a bottom end that kept it tethered to the ground. But two drummers would finally help anchor their arrangements. The drums made the songs feel more expansive, grander, and more rubbery—in a strange way, more limber with two percussionists potentially colliding. "Right away, it became obvious that two drummers would really help matters," Scully recalls. Kreutzmann seemed interested in adding another drummer, but, like Scully, he had financial concerns: How were they going to be able to afford it? Despite his encouraging remark to Hart onstage at the Straight, Garcia was initially reluctant to hire Hart, telling Mountain Girl that Hart's kit would take up too much space on stage and leave Garcia less room to move around. "But you can't hear what it's like in the hall," she told him.

Hart quit his job at Hart Music, without even telling is father at first, and moved into 17 Belvedere Street, where for a while he slept underneath a set of stairs. Almost immediately rumors began drifting back to 710 that the new member was hypnotizing Kreutzmann. They were partly right: in order to help the two men play in sync, a doctor friend had suggested a mild form of hypnosis. "Bill and I were using it in our practicing in order to get coordination and be able to practice for long periods of time," Hart says. "At that point only James Brown had two drummers. Owsley said, 'Why don't you do that to play like one?' It was like training: we're going to play for five hours, but it will seem like twenty-four, and we're not going to get tired. You play with your right hand and I'll play with the left hand. We split the body up like that. It was one of the things that really created a bond with me and Bill." Word filtered back to 710 that they'd also tried to hypnotize Pigpen, who ended up walking through a door instead. "Mickey had a bumpy entry into our world," says Mountain Girl. "There was quite a lot of discussion about whether he had hypnotized Bill into letting him join the band—that maybe it was a trick. Mickey said nothing like that ever happened, but I don't think any of us really believed it."

In the end the music—and the fire blazing within them to improve and expand on it—won out, and Hart became a member of the Dead. In time his hustling quality and energy appealed to Garcia, who was equally driven but more passive about success. "They wanted to be a big-time rock band, and they had serious competition from bands like Cream," says Mountain Girl. "And they felt they needed a bigger sound to get bigger." To the thrill of some and the uncertainty of others, the Dead were now six.

■　◆　■

At the police station the arrested suspects arrived, took seats on benches, and waited for their paperwork to be processed and for their legal team to arrive. Her hash high having kicked in, McGee had to be propped up between Swanson and Grant. "I was melting onto the floor, and they were holding me up," McGee says. "It was probably a near-lethal dose of hash. To this day I don't eat vanilla ice cream." O'Connor and the other lawmen presented their case—boasting to the press that they'd confiscated "over a pound of marijuana and hash"—and that they were "processing some marijuana in the kitchen." (In that regard he was right.) Not all of them knew who they'd arrested: "Hey, have you guys heard of a group called the Grateful Dead?" asked one of the sergeants when he returned home that night to his family.

In a sense their time at Olompali had been a pyrrhic victory; it made them seem as if they could live in whatever way they wanted. "We were living in a bubble," admits Swanson. "We were all into flaunting the life we'd grown up in. We felt untouchable in a way." But the word was out on them even outside the city. The previous summer Weir's Menlo School for Boys classmate Michael Wanger heard that a nearby band called the Warlocks had changed their name to the Grateful Dead, but he didn't know Weir and Garcia were members until someone filled him in. Although he'd lost touch with Weir, Wanger still went to see the Dead, largely because of a warning he'd heard from a friend: "If you want to see them, better see 'em fast because they're way involved in the drug scene and they're going to be arrested soon."

At the police station Pigpen was particularly rattled. "What are they gonna do—are we gonna have to go to jail?" he lamented to Scully, who told him to cool it and said they'd be out on bail soon enough. Ironically, it would be Pigpen's face that would be plastered on the front page of the next day's *San Francisco Chronicle*. Pigpen was still more of a drinker than a doper. He seemed to spend much of his time in his room, playing blues records and harmonica, only drinking late at night, out of sight of the others in the house. On the road he and Grant would usually be paired off as roommates because, Grant says, "we both stank of alcohol." Together they'd drink a quart of 100-proof Southern Comfort every day, but Pigpen generally steered away from pot. (Grant would also watch as one lovely or another would brush out Pigpen's long hair with his whale-bone brush.) But as the jail incident revealed, Pigpen was also easily spooked. During the Dead's earlier trip to New York all the traffic rattled him, especially when he found himself in a truck speeding up to Central Park, and bees rattled him too. During their time in Los Angeles he and Swanson shared a room, platonically, and Pigpen lulled her to sleep in her own bed by reciting recordings of Lord Buckley, the quasi-beat, boho-spewing comedian and monologist.

Back on Ashbury Street, the press and media now dispersed and onto their next assignments, Garcia and Mountain Girl made the decision to venture across to their home. To make sure all was clear, they called first; when no one answered they crossed the street and made their way into 710. The place was eerily quiet, and Mountain Girl rushed into the kitchen to see if the colander with pot was gone. Not surprisingly, it was, but to their shock, the brick of wrapped pot in the cabinet was untouched. All seemed intact, but not enough to make them want to stay much longer; after forty-five minutes Garcia and Mountain Girl left their home, unsure of its—and their—future.

■ ◆ ■

By the time everyone was booked—for either drug possession or a charge related to it—six hours had passed and night had fallen. By chance Rohan and a fellow lawyer, Michael Stepanian, had a make-shift office at 710 for HALO (Haight Ashbury Legal Organization), which came to the aid of runaways, drug bustees, and other in-need local clients. Their secretary, Antoinette "Toni" Kaufman, was also arrested in the bust. Police found pot in the couch in their office but only dusted their file cabinets. At the police station Stepanian was im-pressed with the proactive attitude of those who'd just been arrested: they announced they'd stand together and not blame anyone else for what had happened. "They said, 'We're going to get through this case, we're going to have some fun, but we're not going to act like jerks,'" Stepanian recalls. "And I said, 'Fine, that's a great attitude.' There was no panic."

At Barrish Bail Bonds, right across from the San Francisco Hall of Justice, owner Jerry Barrish, who had a reputation for coming to the aid of antiwar protestors, students, and the underground, gave them $500 each for their bail and didn't demand immediate repayment. Later they learned more about what had happened: Snitch had been threatened by police for alleged offenses if he didn't cooperate with them, and he had little choice but to turn them in. Soon after Mountain Girl handed him the pot, he turned it over to the authorities. For decades after, Weir would have the feeling that the band had been set up, the pot planted.

Those who were already living or crashing at 710, like Rifkin, Swan-son, and Weir, made their way back to the building. "It was odd," says Swanson. "It was like coming home after your house had been robbed." Again they congregated in the kitchen, and the first order of business was disposing of the craggy brick of pot still partially tucked away in the kitchen cabinet. "We got that out of the house immediately," says Mountain Girl. "There was a great cleanout." One rumor had it that it was transported across the street to the neighboring apartment where Garcia and Mountain Girl had holed up during the raid; at the very least it was out of their home in case the police returned.

In the hours and days that followed, everyone attempted to resume as normal a life as possible, but a lingering sense of paranoia and apprehension settled over the building for the first time. The vibe, as Mountain Girl recalls it, was "a lot more edgy. It was, 'Cool it for a while.'" They didn't *quit* smoking, of course; they simply reverted to doing it in the upstairs parlor, out of street-level sight, not leaving any extra pot or roach clips lying around. "Before that, we had joints hanging out of our mouths all day long," says Scully. "They'd go out like a stogie and just hang there. But we got a lot more careful."

■ ◆ ■

When the raid was in progress someone had tipped the nearby offices of a new magazine about to launch, *Rolling Stone*. Jann Wenner, the twenty-one-year-old who was its founding editor, had his own personal history with the Dead. He'd dropped by one of the Acid Tests—watching them play in the large bay window at Big Nig's house—and had written about the Trips Festival in his column for UC Berkeley's student newspaper, *The Daily Californian*. Wenner had loved the Dead's first album; in Swanson's memory Warner Brothers sent out a copy of *Rolling Stone*'s imminent first issue to everyone in the band's fan club.

When Wenner heard about the arrests he immediately dispatched his chief photographer, Baron Wolman, to shoot the band and friends at the bail bonds office. Although he knew it was a major story, for both the city and the local music community, Wenner scoffed at the raid itself. "It was more like the Keystone Kops raiding the Dead," he says. "The Dead were just laughing about it."

The arrests and their lingering, sour aftertaste didn't drive them out of the Haight immediately, but it was the most distressingly apparent sign that the neighborhood—and their time in it—was coming to an end only about a year after they'd all moved into 710. "It was one more stick on the bonfire that was consuming the Haight," says Mountain Girl of the bust. "It was making it less than fun. Jerry and I both felt pretty uncomfortable being there." The Summer of Love media hype had been eye-rolling enough, as were bad-trip faux-psychedelic pop hits like the Strawberry Alarm Clock's "Incense and Peppermints." (Granted, the Strawberry Alarm Clock wasn't that different from the alternate names the Dead had kicked around before stumbling upon their ultimate moniker.) The sightseeing buses that began driving though the Haight were amusing at first. The Dead and their camp made absurd fun out of the tourists gaping at their home: Pigpen mooned one bus, and at the band's urging during a visit Warner's Joe Smith ran up to the top of the street and whistled when a bus approached so that everyone at 710 could hide, depriving bus riders of any sightings.

The bust was far from such goofy fun; instead, it was proof that the eyes of part of the world were now upon them. "It was a reminder that what you did was illegal in nature and there were consequences involved in that," says Jefferson Airplane's Jack Casady, who rolled the joints at a 710 Thanksgiving dinner in 1966. It was also another sign that a darker side of the Haight was revealing itself. Runaways were showing up more regularly, people were tripping and stepping out of top-floor apartments and splattering themselves on to the sidewalks, and harder drugs were dirtying up the neighborhood. The latter problem was more than reinforced to the Dead when they learned of the murder of William Thomas, an African American drug dealer known as Superspade. Scully had known Superspade even before he'd met the Dead. (Scully himself would sell hash periodically to help pay the rent, both at 710 and the house he previously lived in.) With his flamboyant wardrobe, Superspade was one of many local characters, but two months before the bust at 710 his body was found shot, stabbed, and stuffed into a sleeping bag that was hanging off a nearby cliff. Shortly before that grisly discovery another local dealer, known as Shob, was stabbed to death a dozen times with a butcher knife, and part of his right arm was hacked off.

The Haight was on the periphery of a high-crime area, and some thought Superspade simply wasn't being discreet enough (he had a tendency to flash wads of bills in public) and had probably found himself in a turf war. Either way, his brutal killing was a sign that the dealers in the Haight had become murderously territorial, each fighting to make as much money as possible over the dazed teenagers burrowing into the Haight in the wake of the Summer of Love. "Superspade was a really calm, really nice dealer who we trusted," says Hart. "No one would want to kill him. When that happened, that put a big shock in me. The mood on the street was turning ugly. People were getting stoned for no reason and people were going because it was an 'attraction,' like Disneyland. The world was closing in on us."

They had to start thinking about leaving, and the signs were already in the air that it was happening. At Scully's invitation, Stan Cornyn of Warner Brothers had flown up from Los Angeles for a meeting at 710, and Cornyn was finally able to walk up the fabled front steps he'd been hearing about. Someone let him in, and he took a seat in the living room and waited. And waited. And waited some more. He sat taking in the sights, especially a black-and-white photo of a naked girl facing a naked boy. "Hippies—wow!" Cornyn thought. "It was so much nicer than what I was doing." But no one ever came out to talk with him, and he was eventually told that maybe they were asleep. Cornyn had no choice but to leave.

■　◆　■

Three days after the bust came one of the Dead's last great escapades at 710. At Gleason's suggestions, they held a press conference at their ransacked home. Beforehand Rifkin expressed what he wanted to say to his former UCLA classmate Harry Shearer (later an actor and comedian known for his work on *The Simpsons*, *This Is Spinal Tap*, and *Saturday Night Live*), and Shearer, who would often visit 710 on weekends, helped Rifkin write it out. Flanked by the band members, Garcia smiling gently, Rifkin called pot "the least harmful chemical used for pleasure and life enhancement," decried pot laws as "seriously out of touch with reality," and derided the media's image of the "drug-oriented hippie. The mass media created the so-called hippie scene.... The law creates a mythical danger and calls it a felony. The result is a series of lies and myths that prop each other up. Behind all the myths is the reality. The Grateful Dead are people engaged in constructive, creative effort in the musical field, and this house is where we work as well as our residence."

A bowl of whipped cream, a spoon jammed into it, was placed in front of Rifkin, but it wasn't meant for any sudden attack of the munchies. The band decided that the first reporter who asked, "How long did it take to grow your hair?" would get pied. Luckily, no one was brave enough to toss out that question, and the dessert remained untouched. Among those at the event were *Rolling Stone* photographer Baron Wolman. At thirty, Wolman was older than most of the subjects he'd begun shooting for the nascent magazine, and he never got high (he preferred the roller derby over acid). But he had a way of putting his subjects at ease (the ever-caustic Grace Slick would happily pose for him in a Girl Scout uniform), and he respected the new style of rock 'n' roll. Even with his innate bedside manner, Wolman found himself in a challenging situation at 710. He watched the press conference, and the band seemed, in his mind, "weirdly elated—they were so high, on a natural high, over the message they were giving." Because *Rolling Stone* didn't yet exist and he had no business cards, Wolman had to convince Scully, Rifkin, and the band of his legitimacy.

For his photo shoot Wolman asked for a group pose, but between their energy and agitation, it was hard to corral them all. After the conference was over the band—with Sue Swanson and Veronica Barnard yapping away in a nearby window—was asked to gather on the stoop, and Wolman sensed his one chance had arrived. Kreutzmann flashed a middle finger, and Pigpen and Garcia goofed around with an antique Winchester rifle that Scully had found on a trip to Mendocino. The gun was so broken it couldn't have fired even if it had ammo, but Wolman was still unnerved. "I was slightly worried they were going to do me bodily harm," he recalls. "Had I been close to them and part of that coterie, I would've been much more comfortable with what was going on. But I was happy to shoot them on the stoop and get the fuck out of there before I got killed."

As Wenner had predicted, the bust didn't amount to much in any legal sense of the word. In the end Scully and Matthews pled guilty to a misdemeanor charge of "maintaining a residence where marijuana was used" and were fined $200 each, while Pigpen and Weir were each fined $100 for being in a place where the drug was used. "The DA said, 'Look, how about if you guys plead to the lowest possible health and safety-code regulation it could possibly be?'" recalls Stepanian. "I said to them, 'What do you think about paying a fine?' They said, 'No jail? Fine.' Here's a hundred bucks—see ya later, good-bye." All were put on probation. It was time to leave the Haight and strike out elsewhere in search of new homes and adventures. But as their defiant pose on the stoop showed, that bust and its aftermath came with an unexpected bonus: it proved that, though they weren't above the law, they might be able to live just outside it—and endure.

Stretching out at one of many Family Dog shows.
© ROBERT ALTMAN/RETNA LTD.

CHAPTER 5

SAN FRANCISCO, NOVEMBER 2, 1969

They'd been playing the song nearly two years, and tonight it started the same as it always had. Lesh played four notes on his bass, and gentle maracas and a caressing organ began poking around him. No matter if you were in the band or in the audience, it was anyone's guess where it would go from there. Garcia's instantly recognizable pierce-the-clouds guitar began slithering its way through the swamp, playing off the introductory motif and looking for a way in. It's as if the players had each joined a conversation at a party but hadn't yet decided what to say.

The delicate musical dance, which at times sounded as if the musicians were tuning up, continued for several minutes. Then, three and a half minutes in, the organ, played by the newest addition to the now seven-man Dead, took the reins and played the melody, but not for long. Garcia jacked up his lead line, Lesh joined in with his familiar rumble, and the two instruments began circling each other like two puppies at a dog run. Finding his footing, Garcia unleashed a barrage of stinging-bee notes that all but asserted his dominance. Five minutes in, when most rock 'n' roll bands would have finished whatever they were playing, the Dead were just warming up.

■ ◆ ■

The setting for this performance was surreal but fitting. Only a few years before, the hulking building on the Great Highway, the road that ran along the western side of San Francisco, had been home to the world's largest slot-car raceway. Miniature-car freaks gathered to watch their toy autos careen along an electrical track that stretched out 220 feet. For Garcia the mere sight of Playland at the Beach, where he'd once romped as a teenager, must have brought back memories of another, different lifetime.

The model car freaks were now gone, and a different type of freak had taken their place. In 1968 promoter Chet Helms, who'd been booking some of the Dead's shows, reopened the space as a concert hall called the Family Dog on the Great Highway. He proudly called it a "musical environment sensorium," but the spirit of the previous business lived on. During its slot-car days, everyone knew where the track began and ended, but given its twists, turns, and bends, you couldn't predict what happened in between: go too fast, and your car would jump the track and wipe out. The song the Dead were now playing, three songs into the set, had its own share of lurches and potential derailments: no one ever knew how long it would last and where it would go before it ended.

"Dark Star" also embodied the mixture of creative struggles and triumphs they'd endured since the bust at 710 Ashbury. The previous two years had been unpredictable, often discombobulating—a seemingly nonstop series of growing pains. Starting with their look, so much had changed. Their previous image—be it black Beatle-style boots or page-boy haircuts with headbands—were gone, replaced by slightly shorter, scruffier almost-shags. Garcia had grown a beard that lent him the look of a kind-eyed mountain man; whether he liked it or not, it also made him the band's physical focal point. With their denim, ponchos, and cowboy hats, the Dead now looked more like a gang of bemused hippie ranchers than a blue-collar garage band. The days of communal living in the Haight were also long gone. They'd staggered their way through two more studio albums—and, along the way, clashed with their record company and producer, almost imploded as a band, and added a new member meant to compensate for what some saw as the musical shortcomings of another. They'd put themselves and everyone around them through a trial by fire that threatened to scorch everyone in its path, and yet the Dead seemingly wouldn't have it any other way.

"Dark Star" became a turning point for the Dead on several levels. Evolving right before the bust at 710 Ashbury, it marked Robert Hunter's return to Garcia's life and the world of the Dead. Tried though he had, the hypersensitive Hunter wasn't destined to be a member of the Dead (or, for that matter, any band). His earlier attempts to join Garcia's bluegrass or jug combos hadn't worked out. When he'd heard the Warlocks had changed their name to the Grateful Dead, he was somewhat appalled, thinking it was a bad name. Embarking on his own idiosyncratic journey, he'd spent time in Los Angeles, an outgrowth of his fascination with a relatively new movement called Scientology that appealed to his spiritual quest. Back in San Francisco Hunter's wanderings had also led to speed and meth—a journey so dark he had to remove himself from the scene and relocate to New Mexico. All along Hunter was writing, and one day at 710 Ashbury Garcia received a batch of lyrics in the mail, a collaborative method Hunter would adhere to for decades to come. Never one to have the patience to write his own lyrics, Garcia loved Hunter's words so much that he asked his friend whether he'd consider returning to San Francisco to become the Dead's in-house lyricist.

Like so many other aspects of the rock life the Dead were tweaking and broadening—and would continue to do so for years to come—the idea of a band member who only wrote lyrics was radical. Comanager Scully immediately had concerns: How would this upset the nitroglycerin balance in the rest of the band? How would they set up a publishing arrangement that included all of them as composers? And given that they weren't really making any money, how were they going to *feed* this new guy who was only supposed to write words for their songs? As things stood, they barely had enough income to fill their own stomachs. (At the very least, Scully didn't have to worry about putting Hunter up; there was no room at 710, so he was forced to crash elsewhere.) "Usually the arranger is the band, and that's what I suggested," says Scully. "Except we found that Jerry and Hunter got so prolific off the bat we had to make a separate arrangement. It wasn't fair to include four other guys in there as arrangers when Jerry came up with the tune and Hunter came up with the lyrics. That's when it got very complicated. I was working at the time with a number of tricky relationships."

Yet the advantages of having Hunter at their disposal became immediately clear. After hitchhiking his way back to San Francisco, with a lengthy stop along the way in Colorado, Hunter—in one of the Dead's most enduring and mythical stories—found himself listening to the Dead practice for a show at a dance hall in the small nearby town of Rio Nido and scribbled down a verse inspired by T.S. Eliot. Later, sitting on a bench in the Panhandle section of San Francisco, he continued working on the lyric, which proved a game-changer for him and the band. "I remember Hunter bringing it to us at 710 and me going, 'Whoa, where's *this* gonna go?'" says Scully of watching Hunter and Garcia piece it together. "I'm looking over their shoulder and going, 'Oh my God—what kind of freak stuff is *this?*'" The song had verses and a chorus, but the similarity to conventional rock 'n' roll ended there. Like the melody that was developing around it, it was spacey and spacious, meandering and lovely, so open-ended it could go anywhere—much like the elliptical lyrics themselves. Called "Dark Star," the song was recorded in a studio and released as a single in 1968, but the record, barely three minutes long, was like a charcoal sketch of a painting that wasn't yet finished.

"Dark Star" was one of a handful of songs Garcia and Hunter began writing during this period. Having entertained visions of becoming a novelist, Hunter now realized he'd found both a direction for his life and an outlet for his lofty literary goals. "You'd see Hunter standing over in the corner," Hart recalls. "He had this little dance he'd do. He had one foot off the ground, and he'd be writing in his notebooks. He was communing with the music. And all of a sudden we had *songs*." About a week after the Family Dog on the Great Highway gig they would release a two-record set of live performances, *Live/Dead*, that would include two of those collaborations—"Dark Star" and "St. Stephen"—in drawn-out, largely improvised renditions that made the studio takes seem precise and already outdated. "We'd leave the songs behind and go into a different place," says Hart of this period. "Sometimes we might come back to that place and sometimes we might not. We rarely talked about it. It just happened."

It was happening again tonight. Seven minutes into "Dark Star," they still seemed to be working their way toward *something*, Garcia's dots-and-dashes notes as much Morse code as rock 'n' roll. Finally, around nine and a half minutes in, Garcia began to sing. His voice pushed into an upper register, as if he were trying to match the sweetened tone of his guitar. They'd reached one mountain; now it was time to scale a few more.

■ ◆ ▲

In the months after the bust at 710 Ashbury, fleeing the Haight became as pressing as earning a living. "Behind all the publicity and all that shit, the tourists started coming and the out-of-town kids and all that kind of stuff," Garcia bemoaned to *Rolling Stone* writer Michael Lydon a short time later. "And pretty soon there was a big traffic problem on the street. And all of a sudden it was a political trip. And who needs it?" He added that most of his friends were heading out of town anyway, and, in a comment that would presage the band's future, he said their community "is larger than Haight Ashbury."

All signs pointed to the six hundred square miles on the other side of the Golden Gate Bridge known as Marin County. History itself was a lure: named after a chief of the Licatiut Native American tribe who'd long ago vanquished the Spanish, the area had defiance in its blood. One of the earliest histories of Marin, written in 1880, described it as "one interminable mass of hills of varying altitude," culminating in the three-thousand-foot-high glory of Mount Tamalpais. The area implied space, privacy, somewhat warmer weather, and distance from San Francisco cops, all of which appealed to the Dead and their community at that moment. "Some friends came in one day, and they were always in shorts and T-shirts, and we were always in sweaters," says Bill "Kidd" Candelario, who'd become part of the Dead's crew the year before. "We were like, 'Where you guys from?' and they said, 'We're from Marin.' The next week we drove up, and after that we were always there."

Garcia and Mountain Girl were among the first to kiss the Haight good-bye, landing an apartment in another part of town before heading north. Eventually almost everyone else rented houses or semi-abandoned ranches in the Marin area: Lesh and his girlfriend, Rosie McGee, in what Lesh calls a "little shack" in Fairfax, and Kreutzmann and his girlfriend, Susila, in Novato. Weir, Hart, Hart's girlfriend (but not wife) Frankie, and 710 regular Sue Swanson initially shared a house in Novato, but by early 1969 Hart had settled into his own Novato ranch, the one sometimes called Hart's Delight, and Garcia and Mountain Girl had taken root in their home in Larkspur. Only Pigpen stayed behind in San Francisco, almost as if he were subconsciously hoping the scene—and the music the band was playing—would remain the way it was, untouched by the Dead's growing improvisational fervor and the psychedelics Pigpen himself disdained. Eventually he too gave in to the Marin scene, finding a place in Novato to live with his girlfriend, Veronica. Even then his life didn't get any easier: in 1968 Veronica (also known as Vee) had a stroke. Desperate to find someone who would help, Pigpen called around looking for Scully, and Sue Swanson wound up taking the call. "Please, pray for Veronica," he told Swanson, and the worry in his voice and his use of "pray"—"not a word we used much," she recalls—was downright terrifying. It was one of the few moments anyone recalled when he seemed so vulnerable.

Frankie Hart, a petite but feisty new addition to the Dead family, was the type of free but strong-willed spirit now regularly winding up in their community. Born Judy Louise Doop, she told Dead biographer Dennis McNally that she'd been adopted not once but three times, and strangely enough, the last family to do so had been named Hart. Growing up in San Luis Obispo, she'd won a dance contest in high school and eventually made her way to New York, go-go dancing (with clothes, she proudly pointed out later) at clubs like the Peppermint Lounge; she also began dating a member of the Rascals, New York's preeminent white R&B band. Small and lithe, with a slender dancer's body, Frankie first saw the Dead play at the Electric Circus in New York. Although she hadn't been initially impressed with their music, she was captivated by Hart. The attraction being mutual, he invited her to their next show, in Virginia ("drop out or drop in," he told her), and she followed them back to San Francisco. She'd already been married—to a singer and pianist named Charlie Azzara—but after their divorce she'd gone back to calling herself "Frankie Hart" when she applied for a cabaret license to be a dancer. Admittedly impulsive, she left Hart for a period, moved to Oregon, and landed a job in the Beatles' Apple headquarters in London by way of their California-based publicist, Derek Taylor. There she took George Harrison's phone messages and heard plenty of gossip about the increasing friction between the Beatles.

By late 1969 Frankie and Weir had hooked up once she heard he was available. Her first-ever nude bathing took place with him when the band played a discombobulated, wiring-challenged set at Wood-stock that August (one that, as with Monterey Pop, wouldn't end up in the film of the event). Some of the women in the Dead scene didn't know what to make of Frankie at first. "She was a mysterious gal," says Mountain Girl. "Nobody could quite figure her out. She was able to move through social situations with a lot of grace without revealing much about herself." Still, the consensus was that she became a stabi-lizing influence on Weir. "She was good for Bobby in a lot of ways," says Swanson. "He was going through that period when he was doing his macrobiotic, when he was pretty spacey because of the diet. She brought him out of that and brought him back." In due time a British tie-dye artist, Courtenay Pollock, made his way to the West Coast and moved into the ranch dubbed Rukka Rukka at Frankie and Weir's invi-tation. With her ever-present nose ring, Frankie was, to Pollock, "hip, cool, and connected"; she not only helped install him as the Dead's official tie-dye artist (his creations would soon grace the front of their amplifiers) but introduced him to other nearby bands.

In late 1967, shortly before the treks north began, the Dead started the process of making a second album, once again in Los Angeles. This time, though, the music wasn't coming together as fast as it had on *The Grateful Dead*. The songs were freakier, weirder, and at times more mannered than those on the first album, and not surprisingly, the initial sessions, again with producer Dave Hassinger, yielded "only fragments," says Lesh, who openly pressed for more and more console-blowing experimentation. Helping his cause was his former roommate and music-college pal Tom Constanten. Although he'd joined the Air

Force in 1965, Constanten never lost interest in music, and after being sent tapes of the Dead's new songs, he used a furlough break to drive to LA from Las Vegas, where he was stationed. "They wanted my bizarre avant-garde stuff," Constanten says, and he was more than happy to oblige. In the studio, as Hassigner watched, Constanten—or TC, as he came to be known—would insert small 10-cent coins from the Netherlands into the strings of a piano to attain a cowbell-like sound or put a gyroscope on the piano to make a clattering noise.

Work eventually shifted to a studio in New York, which famously proved to be Hassinger's last stand. The producer grew particularly agitated when it came to the band's vocals, which rarely achieved pitch perfection. "Nobody could sing the thing," Hassinger told Garcia biographer Blair Jackson. "And at that point they were experimenting too much in my opinion. They didn't know what the hell they were looking for." When Weir suggested they try to imitate the sound of "heavy air," Hassinger had finally had enough. As Lesh recalls with a laugh, "Hassinger literally threw up his hands and walked out, mumbling." Adds Constanten, "Hassinger was proud of the recordings he'd made [with other bands], which were very doctrinaire. These were not like that. He had the same mentality as Joe Smith, that we were uncivilized, unwashed ruffians."

The incident wasn't so amusing to Warner Brothers, especially when Hassinger called label head Smith to tell him he didn't want anything more to do with the Dead after spending plentiful (and plenty unproductive) amounts of studio time on the new record. "It was terrible—they were so undisciplined," says Smith, who was already experiencing buyer's remorse a year after signing the band. "You're in the studio and the clock's running. If you want to do this at home, go home and fuck around. But don't do this at a recording session with all the equipment and engineers." Smith was so exasperated that he did something he'd never done up to that point in his career: he wrote a letter to the band expressing his outrage about what he called their "lack of professionalism." "Your group has many problems," he wrote. In the letter, addressed to Rifkin and sent to 710 Ashbury, Smith was particularly displeased with Lesh: "It's apparent that nobody in your organization has enough influence over Phil Lesh to evoke anything resembling normal behavior. You are now branded as an undesirable group in almost every recording studio in Los Angeles. . . . You guys ran through engineers like a steamroller." The group responded by scrawling "Fuck You" over the first page of the letter, which irked Smith even more.

The Dead were now without a producer and had only portions of an album, but from the near debacle came inspiration. They resumed work with a fresh and knottier twist: "The idea dawned on us: 'Well, are we a live band or not?'" Lesh recalls. "'Let's take live footage and mix it and fuse with those studio sessions and create a tapestry or collage.' Which was so ideal, so avant-garde." The resulting album would blend live and studio recordings within the same song—especially "Alligator," where the sound of Pigpen onstage, urging the audience to dance, would be combined with studio takes.

Anthem of the Sun, as the album was called, shaped up to be one of the strangest and most singular rock albums of the time, a swirling, in-and-out-of-focus tapestry that would be the closest the band ever came to capturing its early, feed-your-head live shows in a studio. Guitars evoked Renaissance fairs or wrapped themselves around songs like snakes. Tempos shifted. Moments of languid beauty would collide with snippets of squalor, including noises that evoked the sound of car engines turning over. ("New Potato Caboose," home to the latter sounds, was also the only time Constanten would remember sharing an organ with Pigpen in the studio: TC played the high notes, Pigpen the lower ones.) Few albums of the time would dare open with a seven-minute-long track like "That's It for the Other One," a group collaboration that incorporated lead vocals from both Garcia and Weir and lyrics that referenced Neal Cassady and an exotic woman Weir had bedded. The song was an example of the collaborative spirit that ran through the album, with Garcia even writing some lyrics. "None of the songs were written completely solo," says Lesh. "That was a true collaboration in every sense. I never had as much fun in the studio as I did on that one. Everything just happened at the right time." It would remain Lesh's favorite Dead album.

Even though they eventually finished the album, releasing it in July 1968, drama was never terribly far away. Warner Brothers' Cornyn recalls a meeting with the band during the Los Angeles sessions at which some of them complained about one of their two drummers. When Cornyn said, "Well, we've got a lot of drummers here in this town," the band simply stared at him with no response. He wasn't sure whether they were just airing their differences or thought he was asking something preposterous.

One of the first signs that the Dead's world was becoming a tribal survival course came during the New York sessions for *Anthem of the Sun*. Bob Matthews, whose expertise with recording gear had given him a vital role in the organization, openly expressed his unhappiness about working with Hart, refusing to set up his drums one day. "I didn't think he belonged in the band," Matthews says. "Billy is a phenomenal drummer. He's more than one drummer. So I was making a statement I had no right to make. Phil said to me, 'Bob, what's going on? We're asking you to set this guy up.' And I said, 'No, I can't do it, man—I feel very strongly about this.'" The band had no choice but to fire Matthews and send him on a plane back to the Bay Area. In their pursuit of the best possible music, the fuzzy community atmosphere would only go so far.

■　◆　■

It didn't take long for Garcia to finish singing the first verse of "Dark Star," but words weren't the point. As they arrived at the eleventh minute, the instrumental interplay again took over, with Lesh's bass now wrestling for control of the song. In the way Garcia would take command but then retreat back into the song's haze, "Dark Star" spoke volumes of the band's peculiar dynamic, the way Garcia didn't always want to lead. But Lesh wouldn't be steering "Dark Star" for long. In fact, no one would. Moments later the song essentially crumbled to nothing and the instruments largely dropped out, leaving little but an increasingly diminishing hum of feedback and then, finally, silence. At twelve minutes all that could be heard were dribs and drabs of organ and a dollop of bass. The music was no longer jazz or rock but a variation of new-music minimalism, to the point where, at twelve minutes and forty-five seconds, no one was playing at all.

Eventually the organ—manned by Constanten, now a full-on member of the band—began stirring, like a vampire from a coffin, soon joined by Garcia's counterpoint guitar. The tone shifted from the languorous beauty of the introduction and the deadening tones of the midsection to music that hinted at horror-film soundtracks, building to a crescendo coupled, at fourteen minutes, with splashes of cymbals and elbow-nudging percussion. Garcia's and Weir's guitars locked in together, Garcia zipping up and down the fret board as if playing scales (something he would do almost every night before shows, even arriving at the venues early to work on his fingering). Kreutzmann and Hart began thumping and pounding more, with cymbals or sticks. Everyone was finally together, but the music itself was in freefall. The original melody had long been annihilated, sacrificed at the altar of wherever they were going with their instruments that night.

Many times during the last two years the transition from R&B and blues covers and zippy originals like "The Golden Road (to Unlimited Devotion)" to their on-the-fly jams was easier for some in the band than for others. By the middle of 1968 Pigpen, the most traditionally minded musician of the bunch, was already grappling with the band's increasingly improvisational focus, and Weir's guitar chops were uneven and still a work in progress. For Garcia and Lesh the situation was growing increasingly frustrating, exacerbated by the drawn-out recording of *Anthem of the Sun* that put everyone's skills under a powerful microscope. "Jerry said he was mad at Bob and Pig," Scully recalls of the early months of 1968, after *Anthem of the Sun* had been wrapped up. "Danny and I decided to ignore it. They didn't know what they were talking about."

But the interpersonal relationships within the band were becoming tangled. Lesh could be particularly assertive and edgy in his drive for perfection, to the point where the band sat him down one day and told him to pull back on his grousing. (Lesh and Weir had a complex rapport, starting with their differences in age—Lesh was a seasoned twenty-eight, Weir still an impressionable twenty—and widely varying musical abilities at the time.) Lesh's approach to bass also required the other players to compensate for the lack of solid bottom. "Phil wasn't fulfilling the role of a standard bass player," says Hart. "He was putting the one on the sixteenth note *off* the beat, instead of putting it on the beat where we could get into a groove, so Bill and I had a rhythmic problem with Phil. He was taking his liberties, and we had to concentrate on keeping it together. There were all these interrelated musical things that were rising because we were into new musical space. It was the growing pains of us becoming the Dead."

Garcia and Weir still had the same dynamic—older brother and younger sibling—and the way Garcia kept an eye on Weir struck many in the Dead world as a rare instance of Garcia willing to be in charge of anything or anyone. In the pre–710 Ashbury days Garcia always tried to make sure Weir got home on time, especially when he was still living with his rock-wary parents in Atherton. Still, Garcia could be exasperated by Weir's inability to play a steady rhythm, an outgrowth of Weir's budding interest in staking his own ground. (Contrary to rumor, he'd never officially taken lessons with Garcia, and for a reason: "If we were going to be working together, I needed to carve out another path," he later said.) At home Mountain Girl would listen to Garcia vent. "There was a lot of frustration with each other at the way some people would pick up material and execute it well, what the perceived level of commitment was," she recalls. "Jerry would get impatient with [Weir and Pigpen], that they were behind where he wanted to go. People wanted to be successful faster than success came to meet them, and everyone wanted to blame somebody else." Hart blames Weir's musical formlessness at the time on the youngest member's macrobiotic diet, and to Hart, Pigpen only seemed to want to play shuffles and "wasn't really participating or showing up." At a rehearsal as early as 1966 Kreutzmann openly complained about Weir's "asshole guitar."

By the summer of 1968 Weir and Pigpen were squarely in the bull's eye. "It was me who encouraged Jerry to think about those issues," Lesh admits. "I was more frustrated than him at first. Maybe he wasn't listening in the same way I was." Finally Scully heard from Lesh and Garcia that a meeting needed to be called, either to fire Weir and Pigpen outright or at least give them a warning. "I was asked to deliver the news," Scully says. "I said, 'Are you kidding?' It was the upshot of everybody's frustration over the recording process and what we were going to put on these next albums." With Owsley along to record the proceedings, the band congregated at the new Potrero Theatre, a shuttered movie theater now being used as the band's rehearsal space.

Gathering the entire band together, Scully, Lesh, and Garcia hardly minced words when it came to letting Weir and Pigpen know how they felt about their inabilities to improvise coherently. "It seems like the music is being carried to a certain level, then staying there," Scully told them (in comments quoted in McNally's *A Long Strange Trip*). "It never gets any better. Matter of fact, it begins to get worse."

"So after this weekend we decided that's the end of that—no more," said Garcia.

After Weir tried to defend himself ("I'm losing control of words here"), Garcia said, "Here's where it's at, man. You guys know that the gigs haven't been any fun, it hasn't been no good playing it, it's because we're at different levels of playing. . . . We're just not playing together." Lesh added, pointedly, "All four of us don't want to work that way." Looking back on the meeting, Hart recalls, "It was sad to see that, but Phil had a point."

Whether the two musicians were actually canned or not would remain a topic for debate for years to come. "Bob thought he was fired," says John Perry Barlow. "In those days he wasn't getting a lot of generosity or respect. It was a fit of pique over how spacey he was. Bob meant well, but he could be very frustrating." Lesh contends that the point was not firing but asserting to Pigpen and Weir that the other four were setting off on their own course for a while. "I've heard that Bob thought he was fired," he says. "But the way we left it was, 'The four of us are going to try this.' It wasn't, 'If you guys don't get your shit together, we're going to do this ourselves.' It was, 'We're going to try it. But you guys have to know the reason we're doing that is that we feel you're not on the same page as us.'" Weir himself would later say he did think he'd been canned.

To those who knew or worked for the Dead the situation seemed surreal. "It was horrible, like firing your mom and dad," says Connie Bonner, who had taken up with (and later married) Bob Mosley of another first-rate San Francisco band, Moby Grape. "It was wrong on so many levels." But it was done, to some degree. In the aftermath of the meeting Garcia, Lesh, Hart, and Kreutzmann played a few gigs as Mickey and the Hartbeats, a dreadful name that didn't bode well for their music. (They were, in essence, a power trio with two drummers.) "It sucked," Lesh says. "It was nowhere. So the next time we all got together to play, it was the whole Grateful Dead, and it was like nothing had changed. In order to have the magic happen, we needed everybody. We couldn't make it happen without them. That's what we needed to know. Now we can go back and work with these guys."

All of a sudden Weir and Pigpen were back in the fold, and the Dead regrouped for more rehearsing. (Trixie Garcia, Garcia and Mountain Girl's second daughter, would later say that Weir's dreamboat looks helped save him during times like this—her father knew the Dead needed at least one good-looking member to make sure girls were in the audience.) During one get-together that fall Weir began leading the charge and, once again, fumbled the ball. "Bob, when you do that, we'll do *that*," he was told, and Weir, again, didn't quite do what was asked. "Someone really got on him and made him feel really bad," Hart says. "But then we looked at each other and said, 'We can't blame anybody anymore. We can't be a band like this.' Then no one criticized anyone after that. We tried not to talk about it too much." They could make mistakes and move on. The new music had almost wrecked them, but it might have saved them too.

As the seventeenth minute of "Dark Star" arrived, they began converging, even if each man sounded as if he were playing a different part of a different song. Garcia reinserted a tease of the original melody but just as quickly discharged a biting solo, as if reluctantly declaring his leadership of the band. A wash of organ rose up with him. Two minutes later all the instruments united into a swirling orgy of sound, Lesh's bass and Kreutzmann's drums making a pounding, rattling tumult. About twenty minutes in, a hint of a standard rock 'n' roll riff emerged from the maelstrom, and Garcia interjected the merest suggestion of a country lick, reflecting his increasing interest in the genre during this period. But those too were short-lived. A minute later the Dead had again powered up into a collective fury, this time unlike anything they'd played during the previous twenty-one minutes. "Dark Star" was now almost a completely different song than the one they'd started earlier—less celestial and elegant, more charged and riled up.

The organ that swelled up and around the song was the handiwork of the first major lineup addition to the Dead since Lesh had replaced Dana Morgan Jr. Now that he'd parted ways with the military, Constanten graduated from album contributor to full-time member. "It was always assumed that if I hadn't been sucked away by the Air Force," he says, "I would have been there in the beginning." In some ways Constanten seemed like the least likely man to sign aboard. With his handlebar mustache, he looked more like a nineteenth-century detective—a descendant of Billy the Kid's nemesis Pat Garrett—than a rock 'n' roller. Constanten stood apart from the Dead in other ways as well. Like Hunter before, he'd become a Scientologist, but unlike Hunter, who'd left it behind, Constanten was still part of that group. Due to his beliefs, Constanten refrained from nitrous and even aspirin.

But during a period when the Dead were anxious to steer their music into unknown musical galaxies, Constanten, adept at everything from piano and organ to harpsichord, represented forward thinking. It's easy to see why Lesh would want his friend and ally in experimentation in the band, and no doubt the August confrontation with Weir and Pigpen helped Constanten's cause. "TC was our life jacket in case Pigpen wasn't able to play anymore," says Scully, "and to bridge keyboards with the new material." Constanten says the invitation ultimately came from Garcia: "It was Jerry's call," he says. "Jerry came to me and said, 'I think we can use you.' And if the invitation came from him, it was settled as far as everyone else in the band was concerned."

Starting with his first show with the Dead in late 1968, Constanten would take over the organ for certain songs while Pigpen sang. With that change, Lesh was now costeering the band with Garcia, who didn't seem to argue about it. Neither did Pigpen, who was relegated to thumping on a conga or walking offstage entirely during the sets. (In a sign of cooperation, though, he and Constanten did share a house in Novato, playing long games of chess together.) Gone were the days when Pigpen commandeered the stage for long stretches; during the Lenny Hart period Pigpen's organ had been confiscated for lack of payment, a move as symbolic of Pigpen's status in the band as of Hart's financial shenanigans.

Shortly before Constanten became the seventh member of the Dead they had commenced work on their third album. Named after a palindrome created by artist Rick Griffin, one of the stable of illustrators and artists accumulating around the Dead and the San Francisco scene (the supremely talented Stanley Mouse and Alton Kelley were others), *Aoxomoxoa* took yet another stylistic left turn. By now Garcia and Hunter were on a major collaborative roll, and their songs—"Mountains of the Moon," "Dupree's Diamond Blues," and "Cosmic Charlie" among them—took the band in another direction. The blend of Garcia's often folk-rooted melodies with Hunter's vibrant lyrics—loaded up with references to scenic vistas and eccentric characters—made for songs that felt like artifacts unearthed from a fictional psychedelic Old West. The results could be exquisite: played live in the studio by Garcia, Lesh, Weir, and Constanten, "Mountains of the Moon" had a refined beauty and delicacy they hadn't approached before, and "St. Stephen" and "China Cat Sunflower" felt like instant standards, the latter becoming one of their most recognizable opening licks.

Maybe it was the nitrous in the studio or the STP and mescaline that Hart recalls made for "very high sessions." For whatever reason, the production sometimes strained too hard to match the whimsy and vividness of Hunter's words. With its calliope organ and jaunty mood, "Dupree's Diamond Blues" felt contrived, and Garcia's drowning-man vocal effects on "Rosemary" and the falsetto moments on "Doin' That Rag" added unnecessary layers of gimmickry. Even "St. Stephen" had overly twee moments. At times the album was less like a move forward than a leap back to Mother McCree's Uptown Jug Champions, but with a larger production budget. As the sessions dragged on over a period of months, the cost swelled to nearly $200,000, an exorbitant price during that era. (The fees didn't end either: after the album was released, Pacific Recording, where the album was cut, sued the Dead for $120,750, claiming the band had promised to list Pacific in the credits in exchange for a 20 percent discount on recording costs. When *Aoxomoxoa* arrived, the name "Pacific" was nowhere to be seen on the record; Scully later said it was intentional. The case had gone to trial and the studio won, but Garcia, under oath, was so articulate about the complexities of multitrack recording that the judge complimented him and called him a good witness.)

In the meantime they knocked out an entire other album that only demonstrated how comfortable they were onstage compared to being in an impersonal recording studio. Something unusual was starting to kick in with the Dead that rarely happened with other rock 'n' rollers: to develop the songs they needed to shape them onstage, complete with audience feedback. The material had to be painstakingly *nurtured*, not written and banged out in a studio, and nothing proved that approach better than their live tapes. When the band played the Fillmore West and the Avalon Ballroom in the early months of 1969, Bob Matthews and Betty Cantor put the shows on tape. (Also pitching in were Owsley and Ron Wickersham, an engineer at Ampex who'd met the band during the recording of *Aoxomoxoa* and went on to work at Pacific Recording, where the album was cut. Eventually he would hook up with Owsley's 1969 startup company Alembic to make instruments and gear.) Matthews and Cantor then compiled the tapes into the Dead's first live album. "We did it as a fluke, and we liked it," Cantor-Jackson says. "Bob and I went into the studio and mixed it and offered it up to the band. They had this contract with how any albums they had to turn in to the label, and we said, 'Let's give them this one—and it didn't cost you a damn dime!'" According to Scully, Garcia, who was starting to feel the pressure of fulfilling their Warner Brothers contract, was more

than open to the Cantor-Matthews idea, and when the engineers presented copies of the proposed album to the band, the Dead signed off
on what became *Live/Dead*.

In rock 'n' roll, concert albums were still relatively rare, and *Live/
Dead* felt particularly risky given the Dead's previous track record (low
album sales) and its double-album length. But the gambit worked on
several levels. Just like the studio albums that preceded it, *Live/Dead*
didn't crack the Top Forty, but it accomplished something the other
records hadn't. An overdub-free vérité snapshot of their concerts, it
finally captured the band at its most vibrant and exploratory. "Dark
Star," which took up all of side one, left the obscure single version in
the distant dust, and "St. Stephen," shorn of its production gimmicks,
was more direct and euphoric; Garcia's guitar bore into it in ways it
hadn't on the *Aoxomoxoa* rendition. On a version of "Turn on Your
Love Light," Pipgen's essence was captured in all its biker-preacher
glory, while "Death Don't Have No Mercy" was chilling and devastating. "Feedback" was just that—nearly eight minutes of sonic crunch,
whistles, and imitation whale sounds that spoke as much to their essence as did the half-minute group-song benediction, the traditional
"And We Bid You Goodnight."

Live/Dead helped their relationship with Warner Brothers, but just
barely. When Scully and band lawyer Brian Rohan journeyed to LA
to visit Joe Smith at the label's Burbank offices to ask for more cash
for *Aoxomoxoa*, Smith finally had his chance to vent his irritation with
them in person. "I was *seething*," Smith recalls. "I said, 'You sons of
bitches—you're supposed to be able to control what's going on up
there! Get out of my office!'" Smith wound up chasing them down the
street after they'd walked out. "I said, 'Don't come back here!' I was
feisty." But the cost-efficient *Live/Dead* placated Warners, who were
able to sell the double album for a slightly higher list price than a standard LP. The resulting sales of the album, released in November 1969,

helped wipe away some of the debt incurred by *Aoxomoxoa*, which had come out only five months before. *Live/Dead* didn't make Smith any less wary of the band members, though; he continued to decline any beverage the group offered him, wary of being dosed.

The most important healing might have been within the band itself. Coming on the heels of a fractious year, the album, according to Scully, also served to remind the group that everyone had something to offer. "*Live/Dead* got everybody to realize," he says, "how special the band was and how great they were." After the turmoil of 1968 the Dead needed such affirmation.

■ ◆ ■

As a new decade loomed, the Dead weren't merely coping with internal friction and record-company collisions; in their own vicinity the business of rock 'n' roll was intensifying. Helms, the promoter of the Family Dog on the Great Highway, felt like a kindred spirit in many ways. Long haired, bearded, and taken to wearing sandals, Helms had relocated from Texas to the Bay Area in the early sixties and, once there, championed local musicians like the Dead (and his Texas friend Janis Joplin). Helms was now running the Family Dog, a loose-knit group whose goals—part commune, part rock-show production company—embodied the growing duality of the scene.

Locally Helms's rival was Bill Graham, who would never be mistaken for a hippie. Graham's life story made even Garcia's or Pigpen's feel cushy. Born in Germany, where his mother was gassed to death during World War II, he'd had to flee to France; at age ten, thanks to help from the Red Cross, he was on a boat bound for the States. Raised by a family in the Bronx, he served in the Korean War and, after taking a stab at an acting career, relocated to the Bay Area, where he began working for the San Francisco Mime Troupe and with the Dead at the Trips Festival. Graham had been appalled when the Warlocks changed their name to the Grateful Dead, and he and the band had been engaging in a particularly intricate dance. Graham was bullheaded, uncompromising, and driven, words that could also be used to describe the collective Dead. Determined that bands at his shows hit the stage on time, Graham could often be seen walking around backstage with a clipboard. The Dead, meanwhile, kept trying to dose him, even recruiting some of their so-called old ladies to put acid on their lips and kiss him. (Ever vigilant, Graham told them to kiss his hair instead, but he was eventually done in by a loaded soda can.)

Helms and Graham had produced shows together at the Fillmore Auditorium, home to an Acid Test and benefits for the Mime Troupe, but they'd had a falling-out over what Helms would call a "breach of faith" involving a booking for the Paul Butterfield Blues Band. Helms began presenting bands, including the Dead, at the Avalon Ballroom, while Graham booked the Dead at, ironically, a space they'd tried running themselves. By 1968 the Dead had already grown so wary of promoters that they made their stab at running their own enterprise. For roughly the first half of the year the band—in a business partnership with their peers and friends in the local rock 'n' roll community, Quicksilver Messenger Service and Jefferson Airplane—had taken over and rented out a two-thousand-seat theater in the downtown San Francisco area. Although the Carousel Ballroom was the Dead's personal sandbox, the enterprise wasn't built on particularly solid ground. When it came to booking bands, they couldn't compete with the likes of Helms and Graham, and thanks to a lease agreement that McGee calls "unworkable" ($15,000 a month), the Carousel ran aground soon after it opened. To the Dead's initial irritation, Graham, who was in search of a new space anyway, took it over and eventually rechristened it the Fillmore West. When Helms lost some of his permits for the Avalon in late 1968, he shifted his operation to the former Playland at the Beach, renaming it the Family Dog on the Great Highway.

As much as the Dead liked Helms (and the Avalon, which was funkier and felt far less formal than the Fillmore Auditorium), the promoter wasn't always able to pay them on time. Ultimately the Dead had to admit Graham knew how to put on a show (and reward them financially for it), and eventually they too were working for him at the Fillmore West. For a series of shows there in June 1969 they were paid $5,000. The same month they played Graham's sibling theater in New York, the Fillmore East, and walked away with $7,500. The Dead often exasperated Graham by not always welcoming him as a member of the family, but the band was also pragmatic. "They were smart enough to know that you use what you need from whomever is offering it," says Kip Cohen, who managed the Fillmore East. "You don't have to hang out with them."

The Carousel might have been a bust, but it did yield one useful outcome: thanks to the operation's do-it-yourself ambience, many of their friends and coworkers pitched in, and the sight of everyone from Matthews and Cantor to McGee and Frankie helping with the sound system and concessions lent an air of community to the operation. That blueprint would stay with them for the rest of their career. Lenny Hart, Mickey's oddball father, was now running the operation in his strange, somewhat disorganized way. As a result, Jonathan Riester, a road manager they trusted, had left, and taking over that role was Jon McIntire, a refined and diplomatic Illinois native who'd attended college in San Francisco and had first become part of the Dead's circle while working at the Carousel. Starting with his musical tastes (childhood memories of listening to his mother play Chopin on the piano at home), the blond, finely dressed McIntire was as cultivated and diplomatic as Lenny Hart was larger than life and untidy. (Rock Scully was still helping to run the operation as well.)

Although Laird Grant had long ceased being their roadie, plenty of others were willing to lug around instruments and amplifiers for the

Dead for minimal pay, if any at all. By the fall of 1969 the Dead had the core members of the road crew that would largely stick with them for the next three decades. Shurtliff, a Kesey associate who hailed from Montana and Oregon, had been among the first to sign up. Called Ram Rod (after cracking "I am Ramon Rodriguez Rodriguez" when the Pranksters needed someone to "ramrod" people into a car), Shurtliff wasn't physically imposing—he was muscular but of medium height and build—and was a man of extremely few words. Another Oregonian, Donald Rex Jackson, stood over six feet tall, his tree-branch-long arms extending out from broad shoulders, his mustache and shoulder-length hair lending him a Marin-cowboy air.

Joining up with them at the Carousel was Bill Candelario, the Oakland-born son of a welder who'd lived in nearby Alameda until he was a teenager. Acerbic and swarthy, Candelario was the sort of ready-for-anything outsider always attracted to the Dead. By 1967 Candelario was prowling Berkeley. Soon he found himself hanging around—and working at—the Carousel, helping Jackson and Ram Rod haul in equipment; the welding skills learned from his father came in handy as well. "We did whatever you could do," Candelario (soon nicknamed Kidd) says. "Whatever was going on, you just jumped in and helped. I was doing everything I could, like helping Ram Rod and Jackson load in up three flights of stairs, no elevator." As they all learned, working for the Dead could be grueling, back-breaking labor, but there were few places they'd rather be, and the perks of drugs and women were unlike anything they'd seen before.

The rituals were manifold. When Sam Cutler later took over as their tour manager they'd converge in the dressing room and share a few joints. Back in their hotel rooms after shows another part of the ceremony began. Piling in, they'd play back the tapes of the night's show—recordings supplied by none other than Owsley himself, who by now had left and returned to the Dead fold after an uneven ride of his own over the last three years.

The Dead and Owsley had fallen out in the middle of 1966. "My memories are that the band was uncomfortable with having us too involved with them while actively making acid," says Tim Scully, "while [Stanley] remembers the parting being more over equipment. Both were probably factors." In December 1967, just two months after the 710 bust, Owsley had been arrested when police found him with LSD as well as STP, and he was charged with conspiracy to manufacture and sell illegal drugs, since LSD was now illicit. Stanley coughed up the money for bail, but as his case dragged on in the California courts, he rejoined the band, recording their shows at the Carousel Ballroom after Dan Healy, their soundman, temporarily departed. In search of audio vérité, Stanley wanted to reproduce the sound, the *experience*, of whomever was playing at the theater. Rather than electronically alter the sound by using equalizers, he'd reposition or change microphones in order to achieve what he considered the purest, least electronically tainted recordings.

When the Carousel went under, Owsley began joining them on the road, mixing their sound and taping their shows. To maintain his anonymity, especially now that he was on bail, he resurrected his childhood nickname, Bear. Whenever the band had technical issues onstage they'd normally yell out "Owsley!" resulting in a room full of people turning around and staring at him. Using "Bear" ensured no one would spot him. He also refrained from having his picture taken because, as Hart says, "He was down by law, against the law at the time."

To the band's frequent vexation or amusement, Owsley was a far from standard soundman. Sometimes he'd mix the sound right onstage, standing amid the Dead as they played. During one show at Winterland, a vintage San Francisco ice-skating rink Graham also began using for concerts, everyone had left the venue except Hart and Graham—or so those two had thought. Hearing someone sobbing somewhere in the empty venue, Hart and Graham made their way back onto the stage, where they found Owsley talking to the amps as if they were living creatures. "He was saying things like, 'I love you and you love me, and how could you fail me?'" Hart recalls. "He was addressing these electronics as if they were a person." At first Hart and Graham couldn't help but chuckle between themselves at the sight, but they soon realized how serious Owsley was. "He cared so much for it," Hart says. "He was so into it." They both stopped laughing.

Whether they were amused or frustrated by him, no one could deny Owsley was one of them, and not simply because of their shared lust for psychedelics. Like the Dead, Owsley wanted to do things his way, on his schedule, and with total control. (And like the Dead, he also rubbed some people, both inside and outside the Dead world, the wrongest of ways.) Owsley was now as much a part of their mythology as their lengthy jams, Garcia's newly bushy beard, or the group-bonding photo on the back of *Aoxomoxoa*, taken by Thomas Weir (no relation to Bob) at Olompali. (Contrary to later rumor, future rocker Courtney Love was not among those photographed.) Yet Owsley's most enduring legacy during this period were a logo and his tapes. Because the Dead had begun playing many festivals—after Monterey Pop and Woodstock, multiday gatherings of bands and freaks were popping up around the country—the road crew needed help distinguishing the Dead's gear from everyone else's backstage. During a drive Owsley saw a street sign—"a circle with a white bar across it," he would later write—and thought a lightning bolt instead of a white bar would stand out. With the help of artist Bob Thomas, what emerged was a skull with a bolt inside it—"electricity, lightning, sparks," as the US Trademark Office filing read—that was first used in August 1969 (but not trademarked until seven years later).

Dating back to his earliest association with them, Owsley had also convinced the Dead to tape their shows. The recordings weren't intended merely for historical archiving: they were a form of self-examination, a way for the band to take a careful look at what they'd done correctly or incorrectly over the course of each show. "It was, 'Hey, dude, you wanna play X, Y, or Z here instead of A, B, and C?'" Lesh recalls. "Our music demanded that, and the Bear saw that and made sure we understood how it was necessary. Sure enough, it was very fruitful during the first five or ten years we were doing that."

Fruitful, but also occasionally brutal. In another groundbreaking move the Dead never played quite the same set—or played it the same way—twice. The results could be transcendent or at times chaotic. "Jerry would rush, and things would pick up when Jerry played fast," Rock Scully says. "Phil would often turn his back on the audience and be so disgusted that things hadn't gone his way. Jerry would yell to Bob, 'Keep it simple—you're losing them! There's value in the silences!' Jerry's rushing, Phil's not always keeping that bottom bass happening, leaving it up to Billy's foot. It all mixed together into a great series of near catastrophes."

Listening back collectively to the recordings after shows, the band would assess those recordings and try to learn from them. "We used to sit and listen to everything we did and kick it around," Weir explained to *Rolling Stone* after Owsley's death in 2011, "and say, 'I'm not gonna do that—that didn't work,' or 'You hear that accident in there? Let's make something from that.' That came from his tapes. We questioned everything *we* did. He instilled or reinforced in us quality consciousness. If you're going to do something, you have to absolutely achieve excellence and set your internal compass toward excellence and go for that, because nothing else matters." The process, though, could be rough. "There was always something somebody complained about," Constanten remembers. Even the people who taped the shows—which, starting in 1970, included Candelario—weren't spared. "After the show everyone piled into your room," says Candelario. "All the band members and road crew, everyone smoking and drinking beer, and you'd better damn well have recorded everyone's part or else they'd complain about you. They were discussing the music and chord changes, and they'd bring out that someone wasn't playing the part and put the blame on you, that you hadn't recorded it. You were always under the gun."

As Lesh learned during this time, that sense of impatience and perfectionism, much of it coming from Garcia, could also rear its head while they were playing. At a Carousel Ballroom show in early 1968 Lesh was still so rattled by the passing of Neal Cassady—who'd been found near death beside some railroad tracks in Mexico, apparently after he'd attended a particularly wild party, and passed away soon after—that his playing stumbled and stopped, and he caught sight of Garcia staring harshly at him. After the show Garcia expressed his unhappiness even further by either knocking Lesh down or shoving him hard. "That was almost funny," Lesh recalls. "It wasn't threatening. I knew that he never did shit like that, and we were all chemically altered at the time. I knew the next time I'd see him he'd be apologetic, and he was." (McIntire would later remark how genuinely startling it would be when Garcia's temper would flare up from time to time.)

The exchange between Lesh and Garcia was more physical than most encounters between the Dead, but moments like those were now part of the band's gestalt. For every moment of shared group bliss, musically or chemically, came one of tough self-analysis. As long as it paid off—if the musical peaks were reached—then the hardships were worth it.

At early shows like that, friends like Vicki Jensen would take in the full exploratory power of the Dead. "A piece of their music would take you on a journey, with each musician creating a variety of threads that would magically weave together in sound and movement that would take your breath away in total awe," she says. "I'd look around at everyone else standing behind the amps with me and the audience, and I could see everyone was totally synced. I would see the musicians' faces, and I could see they were so completely loving what was happening in each moment. And as all the sounds came back together for that piece of music's finale that made your soul feel as if it had come home—and looking at their faces and the surrounding energy still crackling from what had just been played—I could see that they were as amazed by what they had created as we who got to hear it."

Twenty-five minutes into what would become one of the longest-ever renditions of "Dark Star," the music began to calm down, like a rain shower that followed a hurricane. Kreutzmann and Hart put a damper on the beats, Constanten soothed his organ, and Garcia took a breather from his frenetic freeboard thrashing. Just over a minute later Lesh resurrected the long-vanquished "Dark Star" opening notes, and the rest of the Dead took that as a cue to return to the song's central motif. Twenty eight minutes in, Garcia began singing again, and an island of calm returned. With that the song took a graceful bow and came to a close. In the last few moments of "Dark Star" they made peace with the song and with themselves—knowing full well that the tumult could all start up again at any moment, and probably would.

Pigpen on the Europe '72 tour bus, Copenhagen.
PHOTO: JAN PERSSON/REDFERNS/GETTY IMAGES

CHAPTER 6

LONDON,
MAY 25 AND 26, 1972

On the other side of the thick steel door came a loud voice barking out
a concise, unmistakable command: "Back *off!*"

The drunken or stoned kids who'd been banging on the back door
of the Lyceum Theatre in London were about to learn an important
lesson. They should have known the area around the stage at any Dead
show was, in tour manager Sam Cutler's phrase, "sacred space," and
they should have known better than mess with the Dead's formidable
crew. But they hadn't been aware of any of those tenets, and just as in
the other European countries that spring of 1972, they were about to
receive a lesson in when one did and didn't mess with the Dead.

Although the Dead were fifty-three hundred miles from home, one
aspect of their world remained the same: Betty Cantor was recording
their shows and making sure every note of every performance was
skillfully preserved on tape. This time she was in a truck behind the Lyceum, a ballroom that dated back to the previous century. Tucked away
on the north side of the Thames near Covent Garden, the Lyceum was
past its expiration date, but the white columns at its entrance and the

dance floor in front of the stage were reminders that it had once been a swanky dance hall. (Cutler recalls the walls looking like "all gold leaf and crumbly wallpaper.") Not that Cantor could see much of the hall or its surrounding neighborhood. In order to record the Dead's first-ever tour of Europe, the band had rented a truck and converted it into a mobile recording studio, and Cantor had to squeeze into its cramped space and supervise the recordings with the help of her colleagues Jim Furman and Dennis "Wiz" Leonard.

The tour was almost over—only one more show remained before they'd all fly back home—so the night should have been relaxing. But then came the clamor, the shouting, and especially the banging. Something was slamming into the truck, and Cantor was reeling. "What the *hell?*" she thought. It was, she says, "like being inside a bell when it gets banged on." The sound was so rattling she was afraid to open the door and look outside, and all she could do was call her fellow crew members from inside the truck with a simple message: "Something's going on!"

Buddy Cage had seen it coming. The Dead's opening act at the Lyceum was the New Riders of the Purple Sage, which had started in 1969 as a Dead spin-off when Garcia and singer-guitarist John "Marmaduke" Dawson, an old friend from the Palo Alto days, had formed an ad hoc band built around Dawson's hippie-country songs. Unable to dedicate himself fully to both bands and aware of his limitations as a pedal steel player, Garcia had recommended Cage for the slot during the multiband 1970 Festival Express tour of Canada (Cage was a member of the Canadian folk singing duo Ian and Sylvia's band at the time). "He said, 'I stink—P.U.,'" Cage recalls. "'You gotta be the guy to take it.'" Thanks to a contract with Columbia, the New Riders, which also featured another longtime Garcia pal, David Nelson, on lead guitar, were now their own men, playing stoner Bakersfield country rock that had a growing cult following.

As the Dead played on at this penultimate night at the Lyceum, Cage seated himself on a set of stairs in full view of back doors—each the size of a bay window—that opened to the area behind the theater. He'd already seen the ushers escort four or five rowdies out of the theater, and now he, like Cantor, was hearing them trying to make their way back in—screaming, pounding on the door, and taking their anger out on the Dead's truck. Cage wasn't the only one to hear them; soon enough so did Rex Jackson.

In the four years since he'd driven down from Oregon, Jackson had become an integral part of the Dead's crew. He'd shared a house with Cutler; fathered a child with a new member of their community, Eileen Law (a daughter named Cassidy); and commanded the respect of his fellow crew members. When Jackson wanted to put an end to any trouble in the Dead world, be it in the crowd or backstage, all that was necessary was a simple gesture. "He'd poke one finger into the solar plexus, and they'd know, 'Okay, I'd better not take this any further or my ass is grass,'" Cantor-Jackson says. "He was very intimidating on that level." Tonight, though, one finger alone wouldn't do the trick. With both the show and the truck in danger, Jackson took a moment to size things up: he looked up at the doors and the cables that held them in place, rubbed his hands together, and proceeded to lift one of the massive doors right off the cables. As Cage recalls, he was "like a big steed, but far more agile."

Moving that part of the door to the next section, Jackson created a portal to the outside. Seeing this hairy mountain of a man before them, the Brits were momentarily stunned—*what kind of creature was this?*, they surely thought—and barely had time to absorb what was happening before Jackson dispensed with them. Precisely what happened remains unclear. Cage says he punched the kids out one by one, leaving them sprawled on the ground; Steve Parish, then into his second year as part of the crew, remembers the gesture being more intimidation than anything physical. ("Jackson yelled at them, and they ran down an alley," he says. "There was a rowdy scene, but he didn't hurt anybody.") But no one doubts that, after ten or fifteen minutes, the hooligans were no longer an issue. Jackson was, in Cantor-Jackson's words, "my hero," and Cutler says it was another example of Europeans encountering what he calls the Dead's "California western robustness." Dozens of feet away the Dead continued playing, oblivious to what had happened.

No one intended it that way, but the brawl, hellacious or not, was a symbolic final exclamation mark. The Dead's nights at the Lyceum were the end of a trip that demonstrated the musical might of the band to those outside the States; shored up their new, revised lineup; and cemented the power and authority of their crew. But it was also a trip that would forever rattle their original lineup and more than few personal relationships. The Dead who would board planes to return to Marin County not long after the last notes at the Lyceum faded would emerge from it all a very different band, in ways both settled and unsettling.

"We'll be with you just as soon as Pig finishes polishing his organ," Weir addressed the crowd the following night, their last of four at the Lyceum. By 1972 little about a Dead show was predictable, but one aspect remained constant: the band members rarely, if ever, addressed the audience. The fans wouldn't hear any witty banter or rehearsed repartee. At the Lyceum those who sat at tables by the bar or were able to walk right up to the front of the theater—very possible because the show wasn't quite sold out—could focus on the unique sight of the Dead at that time: Garcia's dark, full-bodied beard; Weir's waist-length ponytail; and the white sheet with the skull-and-roses logo draped over the front of Pigpen's organ. The lack of chatter only added to their mystique, making them seem more enigmatic. The most anyone could expect were a few dryly delivered, slightly halting remarks from Weir—although tonight's, about Pigpen's organ, was more meaningful than the several hundred in the Lyceum knew.

By the time the Dead had arrived in Europe almost two months before, no one could ignore the fact that Pigpen wasn't the same man he'd once been. The husky, head-banded kid from East Palo Alto was now an emaciated twenty-six-year-old with a narrow, triangular face that made his ears stick out more. Even his ever-present cowboy hat looked haggard. His arms were so thin that Kreutzmann's wife, Susila, part of the contingent of friends and family that accompanied the Dead across the ocean, could put her entire hand around one wrist.

As far back as the 710 Ashbury days Pigpen had been feeling out of sync as the band's music morphed and expanded, pushing beyond the boundaries of the blues and R&B. After shows Rock Scully would watch as Garcia would put his arm around a disconsolate Pigpen and say, "Pig, I know we lost ya, but here's what you can do," after which the two men would hunker down in the kitchen and talk. "There wasn't room for the stuff he did when they were doing 'Dark Star,'" Mountain Girl says. "He had to learn organ parts he didn't really want to play. He wanted to get back to doing 'Smokestack Lightning' and 'King Bee.' He was kind of grumpy about it."

Thanks to its folksier, more approachable songs, *Workingman's Dead* had become their best-selling album: hopping onto an elevator with the band while they were on the road that spring, Scully told everyone, to their shock, that the record was number twenty-seven on the *Billboard* album chart, marking the first time they'd cracked the Top Forty. Now, mere months after they'd finished it in 1970, they were preparing to record yet another set of new songs. Garcia and Hunter were still on a music-and-lyrics binge: alone in a London hotel room before the sessions began, only a batch of parchment paper at his disposal, Hunter dashed off lyrics to several new songs, including "Ripple" and "Brokedown Palace." He and Garcia already had "Friend of the Devil"—more wild dogs, more running away, this time set to a folkish melody (co-written with John Dawson) that sounded timeless—and "Candyman," the tale of a seductive bogeyman that had a slinky and subtly gripping melody. With Hunter, Weir, never the most prolific of writers, had penned what could be interpreted as his jubilant ode to Frankie, "Sugar Magnolia." Lesh gave Hunter a tape with a melody and a precise vocal line, and Hunter wrote an elegiac, moving lyric ("Box of Rain") about Lesh's father, who had been diagnosed with prostate cancer and would soon pass away. The collaborative spirit extended to the moment Hunter, Garcia, Lesh, and Weir sat around a pool in Florida during one road trip. Hunter pulled out "Truckin,'" a lyric he'd been working on for months, inspired by their bust in New Orleans. Their guitars in grabbing distance, Garcia, Lesh, and Weir set it to music in about a half-hour.

To put these songs on tape, the Dead assembled in yet another new-to-them studio, Wally Heider's in the Tenderloin district of San Francisco. Having worked with the Jefferson Airplane and Crosby, Stills, Nash & Young, all friends or peers of the Dead, the assigned engineer, Stephen Barncard, had heard stories about the Dead at work, the legends of "heavy air" and similar head-scratching requests. Barncard steeled himself, but the Dead who showed up were rehearsed and professional, ready to work. "No nitrous, nothing whatever except a little weed," Barncard says. "Not even much of that. They must have taken the pledge or something."

Working more efficiently than ever, the Dead cut two or three tracks a day. The songs on the landmark album that came to be called *American Beauty*—which would be released in November 1970, only five months after its predecessor—retained the melodic Americana of *Workingman's Dead* but were slightly more produced and arranged. To ensure "Box of Rain" stood apart, Lesh told Garcia he didn't want it to sound like the Dead. Lesh, who would be singing lead on an album for the first time, asked Garcia not to play guitar, perhaps pedal steel; Garcia declined and opted for piano, with Lesh on acoustic guitar, not bass. (David Nelson and Dave Torbert of the New Riders filled out the arrangement.) The switch paid off: "Box of Rain," robust and earthy, with sunny harmonies from Lesh, Weir, and Garcia, was one of the most heart-warming songs the band would ever commit to tape.

Noticeably absent from the sessions, though, were several key players in the Dead. By mutual decision, Constanten had parted ways with the band early in the year. Often unable to hear himself on stage, still a practicing Scientologist who avoided hallucinogenics, Constanten had never completely fit in with the Dead. Early in 1970 Constanten was out, prompted also by an offer to write music for an off-Broadway show in New York.

Far more dramatic, at least in terms of the circumstances, was Hart's estrangement from the band. Soon after the completion of *Workingman's Dead* everyone learned that the rumors about Lenny Hart were true. As it turned out, he hadn't been forthright about their finances. Although the band had assumed he was socking away the cash to pay taxes, Hart was actually investing it in shady companies; then he'd run off with advance money given to him by Warner Brothers. When confronted by the band, Hart promised to pay back $70,000; he gave them one-seventh of that and left, taking whatever they had in their bank accounts to boot. ("They were like, 'Oh, man, Lenny's karma will get him,'" says Cutler. "Yeah, right. Smoke *another* joint.")

Mountain Girl remembers Hart personally delivering the news of Lenny's deception to her and Garcia at their house in Larkspur. "He came around in a terrible state of apology and depression and said that leaving the band was the only thing for him to do," she says. "He was so ashamed and humiliated." Hart never officially signed paperwork to resign from the Dead, but no one in the band reached out to him either. "No one said anything," Hart says. "I never said anything to them. It was one of those understood things." With his new girlfriend, New York socialite Cookie Eisenberg, Hart began spending even more time on his funky Novato ranch, and he played only a small role in the making of *American Beauty*.

Between his father's betrayal and the rigors of being in the Dead, Hart began to collapse. "The road was hard for me," he says. "It was getting really difficult with all the drugs and stuff. I did everything everyone was doing. I didn't go off the deep end, but I tried everything." To those who visited the ranch during this period, the days of horse riding, gun shooting, and wild times suddenly evaporated. "Mickey went into a tailspin," says Swanson. "The energy around the ranch was sad and confusing." Garcia, Lesh, and Hunter were often spotted at the studio in his ranch, but the shadowy times around him would only grow darker in the years ahead. After a particularly harrowing show at the Capitol Theater in Port Chester in 1971—with a hypnotist from Long Island helping out—Hart was suddenly gone, and the Dead were now back to a one-percussionist band for the first time since the fall of 1967.

At that same series of shows Hunter announced he'd tired of trying to write songs with Weir, especially after Weir rewrote some of the lines to the party anthem "One More Saturday Night." Never happy when anyone tampered with his words, Hunter removed his name from the song and handed the collaborative reins over to John Perry Barlow, now back in Dead circles after spending time in New York working on an unfinished novel. "When Hunter turned to me and said, 'Why don't *you* write songs with him?' that was a big deal in my life," Barlow says. "My official function up to that point was Weir's best friend and someone who would carry a box here or there and drive a truck. But definitely not a hanger-on either. So that was a huge day for me."

With so much change in the air, it was perhaps too easy to overlook Pigpen's state. According to Barncard, Pigpen showed up only for one session for *American Beauty*, when he sang lead on his one prominent vocal on the album, for the funky shuffle "Operator." One of the first truly alarming signs of his health arrived a year later, in the fall of 1971, when he was rushed to Novato General Hospital with hepatitis and a perforated ulcer. Some of the Dead gave blood to help him; Pigpen's sister Carol and their mother came to visit and found him, according to Carol, "in good spirits." His father, Phil McKernan, wrote an open letter to the fans: "A couple phone calls would sure help his morale—which is just a bit low." Pigpen's friends knew little about his family back in Palo Alto and how his relationship with his father had scarred him. As Carol recalls, "We were not a family that talked about personal stuff."

Pigpen's morale wasn't at all helped when the Dead recruited a new keyboard player while he was recovering from his hospitalization. Only twenty-three, Keith Godchaux had a scraggly beard and a sweetly doleful look on his face—like Garcia, he had the feel of an old soul—yet he was so shy that his new wife, Donna Jean, had to take it upon herself to introduce the two men at one of Garcia's side gigs at the Keystone. (Garcia, addicted to his guitar, was beginning to play local club shows with his new musical friends, bass player John Kahn and keyboardist Merl Saunders.) A former studio singer in Muscle Shoals, Alabama, Donna Jean had sung backup on hits like Elvis Presley's "Suspicious Minds," R. B. Greaves's "Take a Letter, Maria," Neil Diamond's "Brother Love's Traveling Salvation Show," and Percy Sledge's "When a Man Loves a Woman." Her Presley session was among her most memorable. "My back was turned to the door when Elvis walked in, and I knew he had walked in," she told *Rolling Stone* in 2014. "He had that kind of charisma and a power about him." During the sessions Presley listened to each singer separately and critiqued each one ("it was very intense," she recalls), yet Godchaux says the singers kept their cool as much as possible. "When we were singing we were so professional—we didn't bat an eye," she said. She and the other singers only went nuts later, when they converged at a nearby International House of Pancakes, held up a Polaroid they'd taken with him, and screamed with glee for an hour.

By the early seventies, though, Donna Jean had decided to head out west; she knew she had to be part of the California music community. There she saw the Dead play at Winterland and, through mutual friends, met Keith, who'd grown up in Concord, a suburb east of San Francisco. At the Keystone Donna Jean more or less announced to Garcia that her husband would be the Dead's new pianist. "I told Jerry that Keith needed to be in the band, and I needed his home phone number," she told *Rolling Stone*, "and I got his number!" ("Donna had a lot of moxie," Mountain Girl says.) Garcia rehearsed with Keith Godchaux first, then with the entire band, and before they knew it, the Dead had a versatile pianist who could improvise, play boogie-woogie, or revel in delicate runs that would act as counterpoint to Garcia's leads. At the same time, Godchaux had a low-key personality that wouldn't upset the band's delicate balance.

When Pigpen heard the news that the Dead had a new member—not a replacement, just an addition—he didn't protest, but friends felt his disenchantment. "It was a pretty clear message to Pig," says Swanson. "It was nothing he said, but it was clear he was broken-hearted. It was just a look he had. He was being eased out, in a way." (Scully still used Pigpen's bad-boy image to the band's promotional advantage: at a convention of independent record distributors, Pigpen joined him, holding a funeral wreath that said, "Sell our records . . . or you're dead.") Whether or not it was timing—the addition of Godchaux compensating for Pigpen's increasing absence or diminished onstage aura—their music began revving up as soon as Godchaux signed up. With him they became, as Lesh later wrote, "the turbocharged turn-on-a-dime Grateful Dead that only had been hinted at before." During a series of shows at New York's Academy of Music in early 1972 they unleashed, for instance, a wild, runaway-train version of "Casey Jones."

The signs that Pigpen was unhappy were growing. During the Festival Express tour in 1970 Cutler had sat down with a lonely-looking Pigpen, who confided how isolated he felt from the rest of the band, starting with his intense dislike of pot and acid. "He just didn't like being high," Cutler recalls. "Most alcoholics don't. It shows them the true color of their walls. It's an unwelcome window into your own world. Maybe he found it difficult to perform on acid."

In June 1971 the Dead had been invited to play at a festival in Herouville, France. When the concert was rained out, the Dead threw a party of their own at the château where they were staying and took a day trip into Paris. Given her familiarity with the language, Rosie McGee—who by then had broken up with Lesh—accompanied the band and saw up-close how Pigpen had changed and how distanced he could be from his band mates. On their way to the Eiffel Tower McGee asked whether he wanted to join them. "No, I'm going to stay here at the château," he told her, and the rest of the entourage went without him. "If you're in that shape, you're on a downhill slope, but I don't think anybody knew that," McGee says. "You don't think about that stuff, and you don't think it could happen. There was a general feeling that he was going to be fine." After all, he, like most of the band, was only in his midtwenties; musically and physically, they all felt invincible.

"From a European perspective," Dead manager Jon McIntire wrote in an artfully worded letter to overseas promoters before the Dead ventured there, "the reality of the Dead may at times seem somewhat suspect." The Dead had given previous thought to touring the continent, but they'd never managed to actually do it. (They had played a festival in England in May 1970, thanks to Warner Brothers, but that show was the extent of a European "tour" that year.) This time, though, the fantasy was becoming a reality. Cutler had proven his worth within the Dead organization by landing them more gigs in the States—and doing a far better job than anyone before of handling the logistics of a tour—but a trek through Europe was his cup of particularly British tea, and he began reaching out to promoters and others with whom he'd worked while planning the Rolling Stones' European shows. "Most of the people around the Grateful Dead couldn't organize a piss in a brewery," says Cutler. "They could organize a nice party and acid trip but not a trip to Europe, so it never happened. They didn't know the logistics. You wouldn't expect them to. They were California hippies."

According to Mountain Girl, the trip was dubbed "Cutler's Folly," yet she says everyone knew it wouldn't have happened without the barking British tour promoter. "He knew the territory," she says. "He knew the music business very well. It made him terribly valuable." In the end Warner Brothers paid for the trip, providing it would result in another live album.

By the time the nearly fifty-strong Dead entourage arrived in London in April, the band was as prepared as they'd ever be to spend nearly three months away from home. The office had supplied everyone with neatly typed-out lists of hotel addresses and phone numbers, conversion tables, electricity comparisons ("Belgium—200 volts, 50 cycles"), even a list of UK shoe sizes for anyone who wanted to buy new ones on the trip. Cutler rented two trucks, one for the band's equipment and another for the recording gear and lights. Each gig would pay almost the same amount each night, $3,000, which Swanson was instructed to stash in bags in her hotel rooms until someone found the time to go to the bank.

After the bust in New Orleans two years earlier everyone had grown more paranoid about flaunting drugs in public, and they weren't about to make the same mistake in Europe as they had in the States.

According to one office employee, a "special amp" was used to hide the drugs, although Cutler would still demur about the details decades later. "Suffice it to say it wasn't on an individual person, and it got there," says Cutler. "And there wasn't any brought home. Nobody was going to spend a few months in Europe without a joint. People wanted to get high. And we were quite clever." According to Cutler, only he and Ram Rod knew exactly where the stashes were, what Cutler calls "a form of protecting people. Ignorance is bliss."

Whether it was guitars, drums, or unusual amps, the men who'd be lugging it all around had by 1972 developed into a seasoned tribe of road warriors. The original crew, men like Ram Rod, Jackson, and Candelario, had been augmented by a few other rugged Oregon guys, Joe Winslow and Clifford Dale "Sonny" Heard. (The Dead's extended band or PA crew also included Cantor, sound mixer Bob Matthews, sound man Dan Healy, lighting designer Candace Brightman, and roadie Sparky Raizene.) Several years before the trip to Europe Ram Rod, then sharing a house in Oakland with Owsley, brought around a newcomer, a tall, wise-cracking, six-foot-four New Yorker named Steve Parish who had worked his way into the crew. Following a show at the Family Dog at the Great Highway Parish and Ram Rod returned to Oakland. Parish was thrilled to finally meet the now legendary Owsley, who was reading the underground comic *Odd Bodkins* and looking at Parish with initial hostility. (Given he was out on bail, Owsley was often looking over his shoulder during this period, wary of any newcomers.) Finally Owsley gave Parish some of his acid, and together they ingested it and bonded. "That was his way of checking me out," Parish says. "In those days with the Dead you had to have a cast-iron mind and stomach. You were being tested all the time."

During their first few years on the road Dead tours were haphazardly organized. "The band would get a call and say, 'Can you make it to Florida in a day?'" Candelario says. "The shows were eight hundred miles apart. And even if we drove seventy miles an hour, we'd barely get there. One guy would drive until he couldn't stay awake, and the next guy would step up. We daisy-chained ourselves across America." For the passengers, the brutal drives were helped greatly by regular quantities of Owsley's acid, and the hard labor came with rewards: once a month each crew member would find a bag with three to four ounces of premium weed tucked inside his cubby at the Dead's office.

Around the country promoters learned to both respect and fear the crew—and to interfere at their own peril. At the first show he worked on with the band Connecticut promoter Jim Koplik was told he shouldn't drink anything backstage; he never knew if and when he would be dosed. Koplik reached for a can of Pepsi and inspected the top. Finding it untampered with, he popped it open and chugged some of it down. Within a minute he felt like he was in an elevator descending a hundred miles an hour. One of the crew had punctured the can with the tiniest of holes and dropped Owsley acid into it. "I thought I was real smart," he says, "but they figured it out." At a later show Koplik approached one of the crew onstage and introduced himself. Not believing Koplik was the promoter, the crew member picked him up and hurled him off the stage. Thanks to a recent rainfall, the grass was wet, so Koplik avoided serious injury. When Bill Graham dragged Koplik back onto the stage and verified who he was, the crewman smiled and made a joke, and Koplik knew he had to accept the situation and not protest any further. "I was really pissed at first, but I was smart," he says. "I wasn't going after that guy."

Europe presented a different set of challenges for the crew—twenty-two shows, starting at Wembley in London, followed by stops in Copenhagen, Frankfurt, Hamburg, Paris, Amsterdam, Luxembourg, Munich, and other cities before winding their way back to London on May 26 for four nights at the Lyceum. When it came time to load in, the centuries-old theaters and buildings where the band would be playing offered challenges unto themselves; sometimes the entrance to a theater might be a small alleyway. The first planned show, at the Rainbow in London, had to be hastily rescheduled when the venue closed before they arrived; fortunately the Wembley Empire Pool, the original name for what became the Wembley Arena, was available, and the band pulled in about four thousand ticket holders for each of their two shows.

From the start at Wembley the crew made its presence known to any rambunctious Brits who were looking for trouble. According to Cutler, a few dozen rowdies started getting too boisterous, and two crew members decided to fend them off (and protect the band's gear). In what looked like a bad action movie—but for real—kids would come at them, the roadies knocking them down one way or another before another wave would come. As Cutler, who was watching, recalls, "It went from skirmish to localized battle." To pacify the fans, Cutler distributed what he calls "liberal amounts of hash" to them. In Copenhagen for a TV broadcast an announcer preparing to introduce the band to the live audience decided he needed to stand atop a garbage can to be seen. To the crew's horror, he emptied the bin filled with half-empty bottles and papers right on the stage. "He turned it over and milk and orange juice and water leaked out all over our cables," Parish says. "That was disrespectful to the max, man." Parish yanked him off the garbage can just as the live broadcast began ("I didn't have to hit him—he was scared enough of me") and the show started. Inside the recording truck Cutler told the stunned director, "You can't do that, man. You do that at your own peril."

On one of the two buses that plowed through Europe—one for "bolos" and one for "bozos"—Garcia would often hang with Parish and Candelario; Parish in particular was a one-man comic relief and raconteur. Even when they weren't working the crew could raise hell to new levels. One night Cutler awoke in a brothel in Munich (or possibly Hamburg, depending on the source) and heard yelling and screaming.

Running out of his room and leaving behind his companion, he saw a naked Parish standing at the top of the stairs, holding aloft a fire extinguisher and preparing to bash in the head of the bouncer-type running toward him. (In his memoir, *Home Before Dark*, Parish recalls this incident as taking place during the band's second European tour two years later, but Cutler wasn't part of that expedition, so some confusion lingers.) "Come on, Hans, you motherfucker!" Parish yelled, promptly smashing the bouncer in the head with the extinguisher. The Dead crew ran out of the place before he'd woken up. It was, Cutler recalls, "a bit hairy."

Unintentionally the crew embodied the way the culture around the Dead had changed since the band had grown from being a local San Francisco cluster to a touring beast. Band and crew alike had to be toughened up to endure the endless road trips. Whatever cozy vibes existed in the original community—and some in it would argue there weren't many to begin with—were soon replaced by a more rugged, more aggressive atmosphere, the culture of the rock 'n' roll road, and the changeover rattled more than a few. "The more effete section of the Dead musical community would roll their eyes and sigh deeply," says Cutler. "But Bill and Jerry were used to hanging out with Hells Angels. Someone punches someone—big fucking deal." When the band was in Paris Hunter jotted down what he dubbed "The Ten Commandments of Rock 'n' Roll," a sarcastic list of the outrages and bullying he was witnessing. The list included "Suck up to the Top Cats," "Do not work for common interest, only factional interests," "Make devastating judgments on persons and situations without adequate information," and, most cutting, "Destroy yourself physically and morally and insist that all true brothers do likewise as an expression of unity."

In Paris the paper found its way tacked onto a wall backstage, and some were less than thrilled with what they read. "What the fuck *is* this?" one of the crew barked, irked by its insinuations. According to

Mountain Girl, people would add to the list, but the message was the same: far from home, the dynamics within the Dead were adapting to a new era.

■ ◆ ■

By the time they'd reached the Lyceum, nearly two months after they'd flown over, they had plenty of other tales to tell. They'd made their way around Europe by way of bus rides through the British and French countrysides and ferries to Sweden. If they'd wanted to relay any of those escapades to their audience—which, of course, they didn't—they would have had many to share. They could have talked about the night in Paris when the band was followed back to its hotel by someone Lesh recalls as "this guy in a perfectly lovely lavender jacket, complaining we didn't play for free for the people." The crew dumped some room-service chocolate ice cream on him and he went away—but probably returned, since their equipment truck couldn't start up the next morning. (They assumed he poured water or some other liquid into the tank.) Because the truck was out of commission, the gear didn't arrive at the next scheduled show, in Lille.

At the hotel Garcia suggested they tell the audience, but, never fond of confrontation, bowed out of doing it himself. Weir and Lesh decided to handle it. Soon after, Weir returned to the hotel, harried and with a big rip in his jeans: the crowd had been less than happy to hear the news, and musicians and crew alike had to dash out of a window in the dressing room. Cutler hoisted Susila Kreutzmann and Donna God-chaux, who by now had joined the band as its first female singer, out the window and into Jackson's awaiting arms.

The stories could be funny as well, like the night in one country or another when a contingent of the Dead emerged from a side street and found themselves swept into a parade. "We all stuck our heads out the window," says Cantor-Jackson. "The crowd was all pointing at us. We were probably the weirdest thing they saw. We were the best float in the parade." Or the night in Lille when Cutler was dosed and wandered off by himself into a strange nearby town. Lesh's favorite memory would be the make-up show for the cancelled performance in Lille. "A beautiful sunny day, mothers with strollers and workers taking time out for lunch, the light in France," he says. "Everything was just glowing. I'd had only one hour of sleep. But it was one of the most magical experiences of my whole life. The irony was delicious."

As their buses approached whatever country they were about to enter, a knowing cry regularly went out: "Border coming up!" Bus windows would be pushed open and several dozen hash pipes would fly out. (As a result, the crew would have another job: procuring new pipes in each new country.) Crossing from Denmark into Germany, the bus driver informed his high-as-many-kites passengers that the customs cops thought the bus "smells of hashish." They were right; they'd scored a pile of it in England. As customs inspectors boarded the vehicles, Cutler walked up and down the aisles spraying ozium (used in hospitals to instantly eradicate the odor of vomit) to disperse the smell. The customs police never found anything, largely because they failed to look behind the curtains in the windows where the hash had been stashed. Cutler did his best not to laugh or appear freaked out.

As Cutler was always reminded, something always needed to be attended to within the Dead, whether he wanted to or not. In Hamburg Cutler was talking with the head of the hotel when, outside the office window, a mirror came flying by and smashed onto the ground. They'd heard the mirror, hanging in an elevator, was the last relic from the original hotel in Berlin that had been bombed by the Americans. The manager called in Cutler: "You are animals!" he scolded. As Cutler was pulling out bills to pay for the damage, a television set came smashing down onto the ground outside the manager's office, with what Cutler recalls as "the biggest fucking bang you've ever heard." (The TV had apparently been in the room of one of the crew.) In the middle of the night the band was summarily kicked out of their hotel and forced to find another.

Along with their gear—and whatever was stashed away in it— the Dead also brought along a truckload of material written during the previous two years. By now both Weir and Garcia had made albums on their own: Weir's rushed *Ace*, finished early in 1972, featured a slew of songs he'd written with John Perry Barlow, while Garcia's *Garcia*, cut the previous summer, blended a spunky, lean set of songs with Hunter—the swinging "Deal" and "Sugaree," the doom-laden "Loser"—with a side of *musique concrete* experimentation and sound effects. "I'm doing it to be completely self-indulgent—musically," Garcia told *Rolling Stone* right before he began cutting the album. "I'm just going on a trip. I have a curiosity to see what I can do, and I've got a desire to go on trips which are too weird for me to want to put anybody else I know through. And also to pay for this house!" Garcia wasn't kidding about the latter: Warner Brothers had advanced him $20,000 for the record, and Garcia did use that cash infusion to buy a home for himself, Mountain Girl, and their two children (Annabelle and Sunshine, her daughter with Kesey) in the cozy coastal town of Stinson Beach. With only a small team—Hunter, Kreutzmann, Ram Rod, and engineers Bob Matthews and Betty Cantor—Garcia hunkered down again at Heider's San Francisco studio and banged out the album in a few weeks. To deter outsiders, a joke sign announcing "Closed Session—Anita Bryant" was taped onto the studio door. (Bryant was the fervent antigay singer, beauty-pageant winner, and orange juice spokesperson.)

Weir's *Ace*, recorded with backup from the Dead, was effectively Weir's coming-out statement as his own singer and songwriter. Thanks to a trip to Barlow's Wyoming ranch before the sessions, Weir wound up with a record's worth of songs—along with the earlier "Sugar Magnolia," the best he'd written up to that point. (The gorgeous, high-plains ache of "Looks Like Rain" would be the most openly emotional

ballad anyone in the Dead would write for some time.) A few of its
songs made their way into the European set. "Black Throated Wind"
had a humid-swamp groove inspired by Allen Toussaint (but also rem-
iniscent of Tony Joe White's "Polk Salad Annie"). The sets would also
include a few of Garcia's solo tracks along with a batch of sturdy new
Hunter and Garcia songs that picked up where the Americana feel of
the band's last two studio albums had left off. "Jack Straw," an Old
West murder tale, found Garcia and Weir swapping lead vocals; "He's
Gone" was the band's kiss-off to Lenny Hart. Steeped in alcohol and
pre–World War II America, "Brown-Eyed Women" (incorrectly
spelled "Woman" when it was first released on an eventual album,
Europe '72) had a frisky skip to it. To fans hearing them for the first
time—like young British Deadhead Alex Allen, who attended all four
nights at the Lyceum—the new songs were "a revelation."

By the time the Dead had settled into their four-night stand at the Lyceum they'd been working out the new material for at least two months.
They were exhausted but wore the songs like one of the comfortable
ponchos Garcia often donned back home. Throughout Europe and into
the Lyceum the music had a jaunty, juiced-up lightness, expansive as
rolling hills yet planted firmly on the ground. On the older songs at
the Lyceum Garcia made his guitar do whiplash spins in "Cumberland
Blues," Weir contributing what amounted to a cross between rhythm
guitar strums and finger-picking. Many examples of the glorious interplay between the musicians were heard: Lesh's deep, rumbly bass
taking over the lead from Garcia in "I Know You Rider," Godchaux
reveling in a solo in "Good Lovin'" and Garcia effortlessly picking
it up from him. In essence their instruments were having long, more
intricate conversations with each other. During "He's Gone," which
debuted in Copenhagen, the band elongated its loping groove to over
nine minutes, as if they were savoring every second of Lenny Hart's
absence from their lives.

The night at the Lyceum was filled with those sorts of small miracles, starting with Garcia's guitar: the moment notes spiraled upward in "China Cat Sunflower" or broke through the fog all mournful and bittersweet in "Morning Dew." The latter bore little resemblance to the version on their first album five years before; with almost each show it blossomed into a beautiful, enveloping church of sound, making its post-nuclear-nightmare lyrics even more potent. Still coming to terms with the hugeness of the Dead operation and sometimes struggling to hear herself over the sound system, Donna Jean Godchaux still managed to add warm harmonies to a dirge-like version of Merle Haggard's "Sing Me Back Home" that, more than ever, made the song feel like a long, slow walk to Death Row. Now alone in the rhythm department, Kreutzmann more than delivered, pushing along the songs and lending them a sinewy crackle that the dual-drum lineup didn't always have.

The previous year at Hart's ranch Hunter had heard the sound of a pump and wrote lyrics to match the rhythm. It eventually turned into what amounted to a party song, "Playing in the Band," with music largely composed by Hart with Weir. It had already appeared on the live album *Grateful Dead* the year before, and Weir had recorded it with the others on *Ace*, but in Europe it became a showcase for the band's improvisatory splendor. The song's introduction—a sweet, celestial mix of piano and guitar that, if hummed, almost sounded like something out of Aaron Copland—never changed much. At the Lyceum, once the band had dug into the first verses and chorus, the journey began. Four minutes in, the feel and groove became slower and chimier, more like the Byrds than the Dead, but that change didn't last long; a minute later Lesh's bass began playing competing notes to Garcia's guitar, giving the jam an entirely different feel. The jazz feel continued when Garcia introduced a mellower tone akin to that of guitarist Jim Hall, but that mood switched soon enough; Kreutzmann picked it up and firmed up the rhythm around the fourteen-minute mark until, finally, the song's signature chord changes returned. Throughout the performance they were exploding, prodding, pushing each other, kicking back, retreating, and moving forward. They'd taken themselves and their audience into more areas of music than most bands attempted in an entire career. When the song finally ended, at one second after eighteen minutes, they'd found a way in, out, and back to each other.

■   ◆   ▲

By the time the show was over and Cutler had stepped outside the Lyceum, midnight was becoming a hazy memory. The show should have ended long before, but no one was going to stop them or ask their crew to cut the power. "People would come on stage and say, 'The show's gotta end,' and the band would just keep playing," Cutler recalls. "You couldn't just turn the power off. It'd be a fucking brave man who tried." By then the ushers in their red-jacket tuxedos wouldn't have been able to stop them anyway; they'd been dosed too, and their shirts and jackets were long gone. So was Cutler's mother, who complained that the music was too loud and left early. (She was also baffled and confused when Cutler introduced her to Garcia, and Garcia cracked, "I didn't know you *had* a mother!") The floor was scattered with promotional goodies from booths inside the hall that Warner Brothers and Columbia, the respective labels of the Dead and the New Riders, had set up.

The Dead returned home with quality tapes of some of their finest performances and began the painstaking process of converting the recordings into an album. They probably should have made a studio album featuring the new songs. (And imagine how titanic the results would have been if the songs included the best of *Garcia*, *Ace*, and the new material played in Europe.) The year before, they'd already released a live album, *Grateful Dead*, a two-record set with two terrific new Hunter and Garcia songs, "Wharf Rat" (a gorgeous dirge about a boozer on a dock) and "Bertha" (inspired by a mechanical fan in the Dead office that would move across the floor when turned on, becoming a symbol for unwanted visitors). The album had other highlights—a swirling, potent eighteen-minute "The Other One" and a version of another jug-band favorite, "Big Railroad Blues," that had a direct, train-on-the-tracks power—but it also felt haphazard, with too many covers. But in an irony that could only happen with the Dead, the album, commonly known as "Skull and Roses" for its cover art, became their first gold-certified (five hundred thousand copies) album. The sales helped compensate for the band's initial meeting about it with Warners, in a conference room at the Burbank office, when they insisted on calling the album *Skull Fuck*. "I said, 'You worked so hard, and if we call it that, we'll only sell it in headshops, and we won't get paid for it,'" says Smith, who says he called retail stores and a district attorney to confirm that use of the "F" word on the cover would result in "arrests and all this." (Others think the band was once again testing Warner Brothers and had no genuine interest in naming the album *Skull Fuck*.)

The last show at the Lyceum would be seen as such a high point that a good chunk of the eventual three-record set, *Europe '72*, would derive from that night. But some tweaking was necessary. Their vocal harmonies weren't always in sync—at the final night at the Lyceum they were noticeably wobbly during "He's Gone"—and with Matthews and Cantor's guidance, they sang new parts for certain songs over the recorded live tracks. No one would be the wiser about the fixed vocals.

Along with the tapes the Dead also returned with more than a few cracks in their ceiling. They'd never spent so much time on the road with their extended families, and in some ways it brought them closer together. Lesh had never been especially close with Kreutzmann—the two men had very different interests, and Kreutzmann by then had two children—but the two bonded during a long, chaotic drive from Monaco to Paris. Jackson and Cantor grew even closer on the trip as well;

by then they were in love. (She and Matthews, who had become a couple years before, had broken up.)

Yet the escapade also chipped away at some of the personal relationships. The men in the Dead were unaccustomed to having their wives or girlfriends along with them on the road; generally the men hit the highway and the women stayed behind and took care of business at home. For reasons both financial and sexual, the Dead men preferred it that way. "The only way they could make money was by doing gigs, and thank goodness they all loved to play," says Cutler. "When they weren't playing, they were, 'What do you do? Stay home with the old lady?' Everyone would be home for a week or ten days and then want to go back on the road. It was more fun." As Mountain Girl says of the band's on-the-road dalliances, "They could play as much as they wanted."

With Mountain Girl, Frankie Weir, and Susila Kreutzmann along, the groupie factor was cut down considerably. But having loved ones along for that long a stretch did begin to wear on everyone. "It strained some of the marriages," says Swanson. "It was a little tough. We're creatures of habit, and the habit was that the boys club would go out on the road. All of a sudden, it's *every*-fucking-body. Some of the relationships did really well and had a great time. Others had some problems. It was a lot of together time."

Mountain Girl particularly felt the exhaustion by their last show. She'd left her daughter Sunshine with her father, Ken Kesey, in Oregon, and wasn't able to go back home a week early to see her. "By the Lyceum we were so exhausted," she says. "Jerry and I were not happy. We had been bickering ourselves. We had a couple of arguments, but we made it through." Mountain Girl grew particularly mad at Garcia when, after a propane heater in the Swiss mountains broke, Garcia playfully lit a match, risking blowing them to cinders. "He lit it and waved it around, and I said, 'God, stop that!'" she recalls. "We had a few moments like that."

The strains of the road—and the lifestyle it encouraged—also reared its burnt-out head for perhaps the first time. Cutler was so drained by the stress that he wound up in a Marin hospital with a bleeding ulcer. Yet the person who bore the brunt of the European road trip was Pigpen. On stage the band still awarded him spotlights: at the Lyceum he sang one of his own songs, "The Stranger (Two Souls in Communion)," whose lyric about getting lost on the road of life was especially poignant. (The song would only be performed live a total of twelve times.) His body was smaller, but the gravel in his voice could still be heard when they revved up a version of "Next Time You See Her." At moments like those it felt like the old days at venues like the In Room, when he was the centerpiece of the band and R&B and blues covers brought them all together.

But away from the venues the ride was far rougher for him—often literally, when it came to the troublesome combination of bumpy European roads, especially in the Alps, and rudimentary tour buses. "He probably should have never gone with us," Candelario says. "But Pigpen really suffered. The buses were cold, and he was bouncing around in them all the time. People would say, 'It's a bummer for Pig.'" But Pigpen insisted on coming—he didn't want to miss out, and he didn't want to be without his band, which would only make him feel more useless. "Pig wanted to be with his band," says Cutler. "He wanted to be happy. He was going to let these guys go on a fantastic adventure and stay home? That would have killed him quicker than the tour."

Yet he remained cut off in many ways on the trip. Some of the posse—Lesh, Scully, Candelario, McIntire—had their own rooms, but so did Pigpen, which only added to his sense of isolation from the rest of the band. When he ate, which was rarely, he munched on seeds he'd pull out from a small case he carried around. The job often fell to Cutler to watch over him, and the job could be heartbreaking. "I was making sure he had booze on that tour, and making sure he fucking ate, which he never did," Cutler says. "He was fragile and isolated. He was trying not to die." (Unlike the others in the band, Pigpen wasn't able to fix or resing his parts on *Europe '72* since he was too fragile to come into the studio.)

The show and tour officially, finally over, the Dead returned to their hotel for a closing-night party. Buddy Cage and some of the New Riders were invited along and took over part of a massive banquet table. At one point Cage looked over and saw Pigpen sitting by himself at a table in the corner. Cage didn't know Pigpen very well, but fortified with a few drinks, he went over and invited him to join the New Riders at their table. Pigpen was cordial but passed on the offer. "I really need to be here, but thanks for asking," he told Cage while nursing a drink.

Cage couldn't help but flash back to the rules Garcia had explained to him two years before, when he first met him: "He said, 'There are no rules. You can never tell another band guy what to drink or drug. Never tell another guy what to do. It'll work itself out.'" As long as Pig was still able to sit on that stage and deliver a version of his previous self, no one would trouble him. Cage returned to his table, and Pigpen stayed where he was, alone for the rest of the night.

The Wall of Sound in action, Vancouver, 1974.
© RICHARD PECHNER

CHAPTER 7

RENO, NEVADA,
MAY 12, 1974

The first sign of change was the caravan of trucks that pulled into Reno the day before. For Lesh the moment arrived when he walked onstage for a soundcheck at the University of Nevada's Mackay Stadium, a college football field that could pack in seventy-five hundred people. After strapping on his specially made quadraphonic bass, he plucked a few strings to test the levels, and out came a colossal rumble that made each note feel like the intoning voice of the Lord. The amplification was so potent that Deadheads who arrived at Mackay early and were standing near the stadium's entrance saw the water in a fountain rippling with each of Lesh's thumps. "You played one note through it, and it was like, 'Oh my God,'" Lesh says. "It was stunning how powerful and clean it was. It was a real ego-booster, I'll tell you."

The concept of massively upgrading the Dead's sound system originated with Owsley Stanley's relentless desire for sonic clarity. The Dead had already attempted stacking speakers vertically during earlier shows with Owsley; the sound would supposedly be much more coherent than if the speakers were arranged in a horizontal row on the stage.

But it wasn't enough. About six months before the Reno show, during a backstage meeting with Bob Matthews, a more precise and far more elaborate plan began to unfold. Owsley's dream called for a system that would make each instrument sound as crystal clear as a mountain stream, and the Dead now had the resources to try it. Given how many Deadheads were now showing up at gigs, enough to play larger out-door venues like Mackay, the time to do it had arrived. With Matthews, Dan Healy, and other technicians and crew all working together, the project began in all its over-the-top madness. "We were talking about the bass," Lesh says, "and Bear said the bass stack should be 20 feet high, and I said, 'Okay,' so that's how we started." As crew member Candelario recalls, "We got so big that we had to make the leap. And what does it take to move sound 350 feet? It takes a stack of speakers about 50 feet tall."

The plan ultimately called for over six hundred speakers—ranging in size from a few inches to fifteen feet tall—piled atop each other in heaven-ascending columns; each instrument had its own column. Col-lectively the setup would use over twenty-six thousand watts of power. Everyone would sing into two microphones at once: one in phase, the other canceling out leakage. The road crew would have to increase to sixteen. "There was nothing like this," says Lesh, still the one in the band closest to Owsley. "We had to invent all the technology that made the whole thing possible." No one stopped them or told them it was too ridiculous. When Sam Cutler heard about it all he could think to himself was, "Whoopie—more madness!" As Cutler recalls, "You don't think, 'I don't know about that.' You think, 'Good for them, let's go for it.'"

Even for the increasingly hard-bitten crew, some of whom had been with the Dead for seven years, the new system could bust their col-lective balls at once. They would have to build not just cabinets but platforms to hold them. Cutler would have to find a forty-foot truck with air-ride suspension to handle the delicate gear. The cabinets would have to be wrapped in straps and yanked skyward with pulleys. Sally Mann Romano, who'd befriended and worked for Jefferson Airplane (she also married Airplane drummer Spencer Dryden) before signing up for the Dead office, recalls contracts that specified four different brands of acceptable forklifts. "Nothing else would do," she says. "The wrong stage construction would have meant the stage would have fallen in and someone would have died. People had an image of the Dead as a bunch of acid-dropping navel gazers, and there was *some* of that. But we worked our asses off."

The crew would have to start at eight each morning in order to have multitiered scaffolding in place by noon. After a lunch break they'd spend all afternoon wiring the amps and installing the hundreds of homemade speaker cabinets. Scaffolding was needed to set the cabinets in place. "The idea was to give the audience the same sound the band heard onstage, with the monitor system and everything behind the band," says Parish. "Some of Bear's ideas, to bring them to reality, would just about kill you. We had to learn how to weld. It was some dangerous stuff you had to do."

The truth behind Parish's words became grindingly clear when an embryonic version of what became known as the Wall of Sound was rolled out and tested at the Boston Music Hall on November 30, 1973. One of the trucks of gear arrived late, and Candelario found himself in a unique position: dangling by wires above the audience, attempting to bolt a cluster together with a two-by-four and braces as Deadheads watched him work. "It was a real nerve-wracking performance," he says. "It was nuts—really crazy. You're right there with them. That close." Parish recalls Owsley being "out of his gourd that day. He had us tipping that thing in crazy ways. We were fighting him all day. It seemed to take years off our lives." As always the crew completed its back-breaking job, but the show didn't start until midnight.

After ongoing work by the Wall of Sound team, the system made its full public premiere at the Cow Palace in San Francisco in March 1974; it was simply too large to set up at Alembic, the company set up by former Ampex Ron Wickersham and guitar luthier Rick Turner where the band rehearsed. Garcia and Weir each had thirty cabinets; Lesh had sixteen. In this version six bass speakers were bolted through to serve as a pedestal. A cluster of speakers would dangle above Kreutzmann's kit, and the crew would have to keep tilting them until the correct angle was reached. "We attacked it like a group of killer bees," Candelario says. By then the cost had mushroomed to over $350,000, a staggering sum for the time.

Dead employees who ventured to the Cow Palace to see the towers —which looked like a skyscraper looming portentously behind the band—were taken aback by its mass. "It was, 'We bad—yes!'" says Steve Brown, a former DJ and record distribution employee who'd seen the Warlocks and served in Vietnam before working for the band. "It was like a castle behind them. Hearing different pieces of music from different sections was awesome. You could hear Phil's bass column of speakers, and the vocals were full in the middle. We thought we'd hit on something that would be a new state of the art for everybody." Another relatively new Dead employee, Andy Leonard, had caught a Dead show at Wesleyan in 1970—he and Barlow had been class-mates—and recalled them arriving looking like "a motorcycle gang who'd stolen a bus." What he saw unfolding at the Cow Palace was altogether different. Watching the road crew soldering and installing scaffolding, Leonard was reminded more of a circus than a standard rock show.

With the Cow Palace test under their belts, it was now time to cart the entire apparatus out on the road; Reno would be the first stop. As Lesh saw for himself, the monolithic structure behind him wasn't sim-ply the embodiment of Owsley's fantasy of pure sound; it was also an announcement to the world that the Dead were no longer small time; they had their own touring sound system, their own record company, and their own travel office, and they had more employees than ever. Given how many of their employees were friends, the operation was cozy in one way, a juggernaut in another. During a conversation between Garcia and *Rolling* Stone's Jann Wenner, the two leaders of their respective businesses compared notes on how many people were too many to employ and how to grow a business while retaining its closeness. "As long as you can remember everybody's name, you can do that," Garcia told Wenner, "but once you start not remembering, you gotta stop." But it was becoming harder to keep track of it all. Whether they wanted it or not, the Dead were now an industry.

■　◆　■

Fourteen months earlier the band's new era had been ushered in by a stunning loss. On March 12, 1973, members of the Dead, along with friends, lovers, and overseers, congregated at the Daphne Funeral Home, a nondescript brick building off a main street in Corte Madera. Lying in a casket, his brown cowboy hat atop his head and a wilted yellow daisy his hand, was the startlingly emaciated body of Pigpen.

For at least the previous two years everyone had sensed Pigpen's health was precarious, that his body was beginning to break down from years of drinking. They all knew he'd been indulging since his teen years (although his sister Carol doubts it began at age twelve, as others have speculated). No one thought his lifestyle was harmful or detrimental to his health; it was simply what he did, how he lived his life. In the months after the 1972 European tour ended, Pigpen moved back into his family's house near Palo Alto and later into a home in Corte Madera. By then Veronica Barnard was gone (the common feeling was that he'd sent her away because he knew he was dying), and he was living on sunflower seeds and alcohol. Sometimes he would call the Dead office or one of the wives just to have someone to talk with. Either to fulfill his artistic impulses or the contract for a Warner Brothers solo album or both, he began recording songs on a tape deck in his kitchen. Living down the road from him was Jack Casady of Jefferson Airplane and now Hot Tuna. Casady didn't know his neighbor very well, but he had a few short talks with him that intimated things weren't going well for Pigpen. "I don't think he was tremendously happy," he says. "He was watching the band move up, and he was no longer part of it. There was a lot of emotion involved."

On February 11, 1973, Pigpen rallied himself. On stationery festooned with the cover art of *Europe '72*, he penned a letter to a friend in Manhattan. "Just figured I drop you a line & let you know I'm still alive," he wrote. He said "the rest of the boys"—the Dead—would be playing on the East Coast the following month, but he wouldn't be joining them. "The Doc says I can't make it, to [*sic*] fuckin' cold anyhow. This time I got to recover *right* or else the whole trip could fall thru. So I'm coolin' and playin' it safe, can't afford to get sick again!" Flashing some of his old feistiness, he said he was looking forward to another visit to New York: "NYC does have some foxes & I'm lookin' to get me some! . . . I'll see you as soon as I make it East again."

Then on March 8 Pigpen's landlady called his sister Carol to tell her the news: her brother had been found dead on the floor of his bedroom on Corte Madera Avenue, a woodsy back road, by band accountant David Parker. Pigpen was only twenty-seven. At his dining room table McIntire took on the grim task of calling each band member and giving them the news, as Sue Swanson sat by his side, holding his hand for support. Mountain Girl had already read it in the paper and was weeping. Pigpen's official cause of death was an internal hemorrhage; an autopsy revealed that his weight had dropped from 250 pounds to 160. Somewhat confusingly, the band issued a statement attributing his death to "a massive intestinal collapse after he got home from playing our 1972 tour through Europe" and added he was under the care of specialists during the summer and fall: "Pig Pen [sic] told us last Tuesday that he felt fit enough and ready to return to his post as bluesman with the band." Condolence letters from fans arrived from as far away as Berlin and Hamburg.

Other than prerecorded organ music, no songs filled the funeral home in the chapel in Corte Madera. The two hundred mourners assembled for the traditional Roman Catholic service were evenly divided between Pigpen's family, all in suits and looking very straight, and the Dead and their extended family—a mélange of band and crew members, Hells Angels, leather jackets, and girls in belly-revealing midriffs and tie-dye. There would be no testimonials or speeches. Few in his family heard any of the classic Pig stories: the time his pressure cooker exploded and a goopy, inch-thick mix of rice and vegetables covered the walls or the time a stoned guy at one show began harassing Swanson in front of the stage, and Pig walked over and kicked him with his boot.

Following a round of Hail Marys, the priest intoned, "May he rest in peace and pass safely through the gates of death." At one point Garcia leaned over to Rock Scully and said, "Don't ever let them bury me in an open casket—this is just awful." Garcia, who avoided funerals and was visibly affected, finally rose up to walk outside, and standing near the wide, two-lane avenue in the suburban neighborhood, he was approached by several reporters. "It was a good rap," he told them. "But it was out of character. He wouldn't have wanted it this way." When it was finally over most of the entourage retreated to Weir's house in Mill Valley for a riotous wake.

About ten days later Phil McKernan, Pigpen's dad, wrote a forlorn, deeply heartfelt letter to the band, absolving them of their role in his son's declining health. The typed letter thanked the band "for what which you all gave Ron that is beyond price and of far greater value than I ever gave him when he was with us in his younger days: you gave him (or, perhaps, he found with you) something which many of us never find: a purpose and meaning for life." He told the Dead that he and Pigpen had met up ("after some years of 'second-hand' communication") and that, to his surprise, Pigpen had forgiven his father years before. From his son, Phil said that he learned about forgiveness, "bearing physical suffering and mental anguish without complaint," and "love of one's work." The fact that the father and son had grown closer, according to the letter, only made the missive more heartbreaking.

At his home studio in Novato, Hart, still in self-imposed exile (he didn't attend the funeral either), began listening to the tapes Pigpen left behind to see whether an album could be made of them. But between the sound reverberating off the kitchen tile and what Hart calls "the forty versions of 'Michael, Row the Boat Ashore,'" the tapes didn't yield much. "It was just him real drunk, having a good time," Hart says. "We all thought, 'Jesus, there could be some gems in here.' But no."

◾ ◆ ◾

The Dead rarely took the stage at the times printed on their tickets, and thanks to the Wall of Sound, Reno was no exception. An hour and a half after the supposed start time the musicians finally emerged at Mackay Stadium to take their places, looking like stick fingers compared to the colossal columns of speakers behind them. By then a wind that had been threatening to pick up all day finally kicked in, and Scully watched as one of the hanging voice clusters above Kreutzmann began to shake and sway. It took a lot to unnerve the Dead's unflappable drummer, but Kreutzmann looked up with what Scully thought was a rare concerned expression. Sharp-eyed Deadheads may have also noticed subtle changes in the band's appearance. Weir's ponytail was gone, chopped off the year before, and he'd begun dressing sharper;

that night his white flared jeans were the band's most visual component. Garcia had shaved off his beard, but Lesh now had one, which made him look older and heavier than he was.

Given the monstrous system they were taking out of the Bay Area for the first time, it was unintentionally fitting that the set began with Chuck Berry's wry travelogue "Promised Land." Instantly Lesh reveled in what he heard roaring above him. "It was a brilliant stroke," says Lesh. "The sound was absolutely clear and coherent for a quarter-mile. And *loud*." The system delivered a note fifty feet tall, which sailed over the heads of the band like a jet engine soaring overhead yet wasn't brutally deafening to the musicians.

Not everyone on stage was so taken with the Owsley towering musical inferno. The system presented a new set of challenges to Donna Jean Godchaux, who by this point had been singing with the band for two years. Her presence was still a jolt to some Deadheads: "Not everybody in the audience was used to Donna, ever," says Parish. "There were a lot of people going, 'Why is she singing?' The guys in the band liked it, though—it helped with the vocals."

But from her first appearance with them at Winterland, she had found it difficult to find the right pitch onstage with the Dead. "I was a studio singer, never singing off-key," she told *Rolling Stone*. "I was used to having headphones and being in a controlled environment. Then, all of a sudden, I went to being onstage with the Dead in Winterland. Everything was so loud onstage." At Mackay Stadium the Wall of Sound presented her with a new stage monitor system and the inability to hear herself. As a result, her singing could often be— or sound—off-key. (Only in the oddball world of the Dead could its strongest singer, the one so talented she had shared studio time with Elvis, sound out of tune.) The Wall of Sound was almost as much of a shock as the night she'd walked onstage and saw that Garcia had done away with his iconic mustache and beard, exposing a chinless, less distinct face. (Godchaux's own striking features, from her waist-long hair to her Southern-belle smile, offered fans something else to look at.)

As Donna Jean struggled to deal with the newly augmented amplification, the band dug into a set that included previews of a few new songs, "Ship of Fools" (Hunter's veiled reference to the increasingly fractious Dead scene) and "U.S. Blues," both part of an album that would be their second in a row for their own label. As early as 1969, just after the release of *Aoxomoxoa*, both band and management were starting to grow weary of Warner Brothers. Even though the label gave the Dead an almost unprecedented amount of creative leeway, especially after the disastrous collaborations with Dave Hassinger on their first two albums, the Dead weren't feeling the love for Joe Smith or his company. They went along with all of the label's creative marketing schemes, including a "Pipgen look-alike contest" in ads for their first three albums. "It was about 'pay attention to the Grateful Dead,'" says Warners' Stan Cornyn, who came up with the idea. "I thought of these weird-looking people, especially Pigpen—he was even hairier than in the picture. About a hundred people wrote in." Cornyn says the band never complained about the ad.

During this time, the Dead were already considering a switch to Columbia and its boss, Clive Davis, yet they remained with Warners, especially after Lenny Hart absconded with their funds. Their irritation with the label became the topic of ongoing conversations. "Joe [Smith] must stop holding us back," read notes from one discussion in 1971, which added that Warners should "broaden the base on [the] underground." Over the course of fifteen hand-written yellow-pad pages, the band, with Scully leading the charge, rattled off their expectations for their corporate parent. Most significantly, they wanted advances on side projects to be raised from $35,000 to $50,000, which would include a solo album by Pigpen. The band felt sales of their albums were thirty to fifty thousand copies below what they should be and groused there was "nothing new in WB approach"; the label's "response is too slow," the notes concluded.

For their part, Warner Brothers was growing tired of the Dead and its chaotic operation. "We'd run our course with them," says Smith. "They didn't want anything to do with us. They didn't want anything to do with *anybody*. They annoyed me so much. I'm seeing them sell out at concerts—why can't I get something on tape that would carry through with that?" The Dead had enhanced the label's reputation from the start, but by the time they'd packed up for the European tour in 1972, Warner/Reprise was now home to Neil Young, Van Morrison, Alice Cooper, and Black Sabbath, and it no longer needed the credibility boost provided by the Dead. Smith was also furious when Garcia released a side project—*Hooteroll?* with keyboardist Howard Wales—on another label.

When word began circulating that the Dead may want to find another home, Smith wasn't concerned. "I made no effort to hold onto them," he says. "If James Taylor had said that, I would've fought like crazy. But the Dead weren't that important to us in any way, other than they'd helped our image." The Dead's modest album sales and the fact that they hadn't yet managed a major hit single also made them feel commercially expendable. Smith had also never fully warmed to the band on a personal level. The thought of spending generous amounts of time with the Dead was about as appealing to Smith as having a scalding-hot fork jabbed into his cheek. "The Dead once asked me, 'Why don't you invite me to your house?'" he says. "I said, 'I don't want you on my *street!*'"

"Who can (on exec level) keep us informed and take our case," Scully had asked at one meeting. Although they would come to have mixed feelings about the results, neither he nor the band had to look far. They'd known Ron Rakow, a Wall Street stock trader who'd relocated to San Francisco, since the time he'd lent them money for a sound system. Rakow, who'd befriended Scully and Rifkin, had been in and around their community ever since, helping work out the deal for the short-lived Carousel Ballroom experiment (their first foray into a band-run business). A New Yorker, Rakow was the opposite of a Marin County hippie, and proudly so. "He talked a mile a minute, but he was really sharp, and he was accepted," says Vicki Jensen. "He was part of the show. Rakow was supportive of them when they had hard times, and he was magical in his own way. He spun quite a thing."

Sensing a new business opportunity, Rakow felt it was time for the Dead to take control of their music and destiny, and the answer lay in starting a record company of their own. Jefferson Airplane and the Beatles, among others, had launched their own labels, but each was distributed by another, larger company, which wouldn't be the case with the Dead. Rakow typed out his "So What" papers, outlining a strategy for the band to make and promote their own records and also making the case against Warner Brothers. As part of his research he'd dropped into a bunch of record stores in towns where the band was playing in 1972 and wrote down the quantity of Dead LPs in each. He reported back to the band that more than eighteen stores didn't have any at all. When *Time* magazine ran a story on the state and business of pop music in February 1973, Garcia, who hadn't yet officially parted ways with Warners, was quoted as saying, "I resent being just another face in a corporate personality. There isn't even a Warner 'brother' to talk to."

In the Dead's offices at Fifth and Lincoln in San Rafael, a house the band had rented several years before, Rakow's do-it-yourself idea was greeted with some wariness. Cutler was opposed. "I viewed all of it with great skepticism," he says. "Whomever had the loudest mouth and could persuade Jerry would get their hands on the wheel of the good ship Grateful Dead." McIntire was also unsure. The other members of the band were dubious or indifferent to the record company plan.

According to Lesh, no one in the band could stand the thought of dealing with all the minutiae that would be involved with any aspect of the record business.

Garcia would have little of that dissent; he was uncharacteristically irked at McIntire when he heard the manager was putting up roadblocks to the deal. Given the death of his father and its impact on his family, the idea of an in-house record company that would bond everyone together, with Rakow as requisite enforcer, appealed to Garcia. "We were so bad at business," says Hart, "and Rakow seemed to know and care and wanted to do something. Brilliant, or semibrilliant, ideas."

Rakow took Garcia to a preliminary meeting for a loan with First National Bank of Boston, which had previously invested in movie production. Both men charmed the employees. (When one of the executives said his daughter wanted to play clarinet in school, even though the head of the music department recommended violin, Garcia replied, "I have kids—any time they express any interest in anything, I let them do whatever they want to do.") Briefly, the idea surfaced of distributing the records by way of ice cream trucks. "If somebody sent in a card and said, 'Here's $4, I want a new Dead album,' we'd send them a receipt, and they'd flag down a Good Humor truck and give them a coupon and get a record," explains Andy Leonard, the Barlow college friend and photographer (and new Weir acquaintance) who'd been hired at the label to help with distribution. "We'd pay the Good Humor trucks to carry twenty Dead albums a day. It wasn't crazy talk. It was a delivery issue." They never actually contacted Good Humor or any other such company, but according to Leonard the idea, which kicked around for a few weeks, wasn't dismissed as quickly as legend has it. Rakow went as far to fly to New Jersey to discuss it with John Scher, an East Coast promoter who was increasingly becoming part of the Dead's inner circle.

Once the First National Bank of Boston loan came through along with a cash infusion from Atlantic Records, which would handle the foreign distribution, Grateful Dead Records became a reality, and some of the first employees showed up for work in April 1973. (The deal wasn't announced in the music trades until late August.) Pigpen had died only the month before, and his passing, says Steve Brown, "cast a pall over the company—we started under a cloud."

The label was, naturally, unconventional; employees would recall going into meetings in Rakow's upstairs office at Fifth and Lincoln and finding a Hells Angel or two sitting in. At the outset many were in awe of Rakow's ability to set up the business. "In those days nobody lent money to rock bands," says Mike (nicknamed Josh) Belardo, the KMPX DJ who had interviewed the band at Hart's ranch in 1970 and later took a job at the label. Brown, one of Rakow's first hires, witnessed for himself the way in which Rakow's approach to business phone calls lit a fire under Garcia. "Rakow would have someone on the hook, doing the [aggressive] Bill Graham thing, and Jerry would be sitting back enjoying it," says Brown. "He loved this alter-ego bad-boy thing. Jerry couldn't bring himself to be that guy publicly or even privately, so watching someone else do it was fun for him."

If the Dead had seen themselves as paragons of a new, looser society in the previous decade, the launch of Grateful Dead Records (and its sister label, Round, devoted to side and solo projects) was proof that they were adapting to altered times. A few years later, in 1976, Tom Wolfe would dub the seventies the "Me Decade," and the Dead's new venture unintentionally tapped into the emerging solipsism of the decade—the sense that after the dreams of the sixties had died, it was time to hunker down instead of tearing down the walls. Rather than rely on anyone else to help them through the malaise, they would do it all themselves. Even the title of Grateful Dead Records' first release, *Wake of the Flood*, implied rebuilding after disaster. (According to a

Garcia interview in *Creem* magazine at the time, the working title was *We Are the Eyes of the World*.)

Wake of the Flood came three long years after the Dead's previous studio album, *American Beauty*, an eternity in that day and age. Recorded over the summer at the Record Plant in Sausalito and released in the fall, the album felt at times like a free-for-all: Weir's three-part "Weather Report Suite," a gorgeous composition blending an instrumental opener with alternately melancholic and rousing subsequent sections, was the most ambitious piece he'd ever attempted, and Keith Godchaux sang his first lead vocal on a Dead album ("Let Me Sing Your Blues Away"). The mood of the album was relaxed, not as airtight as that of *American Beauty* and *Workingman's Dead*; if the band felt restricted in any way while working for Warner Brothers, *Wake of the Flood* signaled the pressure was off. Some of the songs—especially "Eyes of the World," which swayed like a gentle island breeze, as well as parts of "Weather Report Suite"—felt ready to be opened up for jamming onstage. "Stella Blue," the lyrics of which Hunter had written at the Chelsea Hotel three years before, contemplated "broken dreams and vanished years," and Garcia set them to a languid melody that added an extra degree of ache to Hunter's words.

The album was too haphazard at times, especially in the sequencing: only the Dead would start such an important album in their career with a modest, slinky excursion like "Mississippi Halfstep Uptown Toodleloo," and placing the ballads "Stella Blue" and "Row Jimmy" next to each other almost canceled out the power of each. The album would have been better served had it started with "Eyes of the World" or "Here Comes Sunshine," a slow dazzle of a song with a chorus that sprouted open like flower petals.

As the initial release on an independent label run by people who'd never attempted such a thing, *Wake of the Flood* had its share of launch problems. Garcia told several different artists to devise cover art, then had Leonard deliver the bad news to the ones whose illustrations had been rejected. To acquire bags of virgin vinyl for pressings, Leonard had to risk life, limb, and potential jail time by driving a pickup truck into a particularly seedy part of Mexico. But the worst news was about to crash through their office doors. One day Leonard took a call from one distributor: the copies he'd received of *Wake of the Flood* sounded so bad, he said, that kids were bringing them back to the stores. Leonard thought it was a hustle—retailers wanting records sent to them for free—until he asked yet another grousing store owner to send him a copy of the supposedly flawed record. What arrived in the mail at the Dead office was a truly fake *Wake*: a cover that amounted to a mimeographed photo of the artwork and an LP with music that sounded as if it had been copied from a cassette, complete with hissing noises. They'd been bootlegged.

Theories about what happened ran amok in the office: Was it one of the major labels trying to make the Dead look bad? Or was it something slightly more sinister? One source says the label was told in advance by shadowy figures in Brooklyn that any release on Grateful Dead Records would be bootlegged and that they would have no choice but to go along with it—but, at least, it wasn't personal and the bootlegging would be limited. As if to prove the theory, the problem suddenly stopped and the fakes went away.

But in the ensuing chaos, which also included an unlikely-for-the-Dead visit from the FBI, the Dead lost a sizable chunk of money; they sold four hundred thousand copies of *Wake of the Flood* but could have sold even more without the bootlegs. "Here we are, a new fledgling company—we don't have the budget for someone to steal 25 percent of our income," says Belardo. "We almost didn't survive." Months later Leonard and McIntire, who were sharing a house in Bolinas, wound up with a box of *Wake of the Flood* fakes. They were so infuriated with the whole mess that they pulled out one of the ubiquitous guns that were part of the Dead world, set up the albums in a row outside, and blasted them to pieces. One of the shot-up *Wake of the Flood* bootlegs remained in Leonard's possession for decades to come.

* ◆ ■

The mere fact that they were playing an outdoor stadium like Mackay was one sign of the Dead's flourishing fan base. The record company was too young to be profitable, but the road was another, more financially rewarding story. Thanks to Cutler's relentless schedule and brutal bargaining, the band had begun raking in more cash each year on the road. Throughout 1969 they earned a few thousand dollars a gig. By 1971 the fees had edged up to between $10,000 and $15,000 a show, the latter at the Yale Bowl in New Haven, Connecticut. Some contracts called for three-hour performances; others, like the one at Yale, openly flaunted show times: "The Grateful Dead have the right to perform for any length of time that they feel is necessary," it stated bluntly. In 1972 they grossed $78,000 at Dillon Stadium in Hartford, Connecticut, which meant they took home about $25,000, a huge cash influx for the time. The following year they were handed a $25,000 guarantee (plus 60 percent of the gross, average for the time) in Tempe, Arizona, and $30,000 for Denver.

Their file cabinets began to bulge with statements like the one tucked away in early 1973. For four shows they would be paid, after expenses, $22,262.42. Their tour riders, including one for that year, specified requests for "sufficient light refreshments for fifteen (15) persons . . . Budweiser beer, coca cola, doctor pepper [*sic* lower case], and fresh fruit juice," along with "a grand or baby grand piano (preferably Steinway) tuned to A440 international pitch." As Sally Romano remembers, "What the Dead wanted, the Dead got. We had a huge advantage—we could dictate the terms of the contracts 80 or 90 percent of the time." Keith Godchaux might have been quiet and self-effacing, but he was also very particular about his pianos, as Cutler learned when he took Godchaux keyboard shopping in New York after the band hired him. "Keith wouldn't say boo to a goose, but once you got to know him, he wasn't so shy," says Cutler. "He had his feisty side. He played twelve different pianos and picked the one he liked."

By the time of the Reno show as well as subsequent gigs with the Wall of Sound, the coffers were still growing. In one month alone, March 1974, the Dead made a profit of $326,935, including $54,254 in gigs, $396,709 in royalties, and $17,379 in band earnings. Other barometers of the Dead's growing commerce sprouted up around them. Thanks to a well-placed note on the inside of the 1971 live album, *Grateful Dead*, asking Deadheads to write in, they now had forty thousand names and addresses of fans who would receive newsletters with band news. It was a logical step up from the few hundred names that Sue Swanson and Connie Bonner Mosley had collected for the band's first fan club mailing during the 710 Ashbury days. ("We thought, '150, wow!" says Bonner Mosley.) Grateful Dead Records employees like Brown began setting up booths at shows, giving away free posters and postcards and collecting more names and addresses. They would bypass the corporations and go directly to their fan base.

Because more product was needed to feed the record-company beast, the Dead started assembling at CBS Studios in San Francisco to make another album in early spring, 1974. (In the same *Creem* interview pegged to the release of *Wake of the Flood* from the year before, Garcia said the band already had two albums of material ready to go.) The loose-knit atmosphere of the Sausalito sessions for *Wake of the Flood* was out, replaced with a more professional undertaking that began with an in-house engineer, Roy Segal, who'd worked with fastidious record makers like Paul Simon and Art Garfunkel. Every day from 1 p.m. to 1 a.m. the Dead showed up for work and bore down, each session preceded by a full meal with wine, followed by cocaine later in the evening. "It felt more serious—it wasn't just hanging," says Brown. "They buckled down to get a hit album, hopefully." Between takes they'd hang upstairs at the offices of American Zoetrope, where they heard talk of a new movie that the company's owner, Francis Ford Coppola, was making about Vietnam, the film that would eventually become *Apocalypse Now*.

The signs that the Dead were serious about their business—or, at the very least, of knowing they had to sell records—were evident in the schedule: by April 30, just about a month after work had started, the album—*From the Mars Hotel*, in honor of a transient digs around the corner—was done. The album had the feel of a band that knew how vital it was to appeal to radio. Thanks no doubt to Segal, the tracks had the lightly buffed sheen of typical FM radio rock of the time. "U.S. Blues," a wry comment on the state of the nation during the Richard Nixon years, was an appropriately bouncy opener, ready to serve in arenas and stadiums. "Scarlet Begonias," Hunter's ode to his new love, Maureen, whom he'd met in England, had a Latin-on-acid groove, and Lesh's "Pride of Cucamonga" fit squarely into the truck-stop country-rock in vogue at the time. (Weir and Barlow's "Money Money" also had an FM-boogie feel, but its seemingly antifeminist lyrics were so reviled that it was quickly ejected from their stage repertoire.) The band also took advantage of the enhanced studio wares to stretch out. Hunter and Garcia's "China Doll," which could be interpreted as a conversation between God and someone who commits suicide by gunshot, had a chilling harpsichord arrangement, and Lesh's other contribution, the masterwork "Unbroken Chain," with lyrics by his old friend Bobby Peterson, was an intricate, tempo-shifting tour de force that blended in Tibetan bells, synthesizer, and one of Donna Godchaux's most sensuous harmonies.

As with any label, Grateful Dead Records hired people to talk up their records to disc jockeys and record stores, the industry networking that the band generally abhorred. Belardo was given the task of editing down "U.S. Blues" for the radio. Because he didn't know how to do that, he asked a CBS engineer, who put a razor blade to the song, nipping and tucking to make it a bit shorter. The fact that no one in the Dead raised any objections to editing their art was, for Belardo, a telling indication that the band was trying to play ball with the suits. "Previously nobody would have let anybody do anything like that to their music," says Belardo. "But then it was, 'Well, this is what you gotta do if we're gonna play in this league.' I don't think there was any excitement about it. It was, 'Okay, we gotta go to the dentist.'"

To promote the finished album, Brown conceived a clever idea—sending out promotional bars of soap tied in to the hotel theme of the title. But there would be a twist: the soap would be the gag kind that turned one's face black after a good scrub. When he heard the idea Garcia giggled; it appealed to his *Mad* magazine sensibility. Then they had second thoughts. It was all too easy to imagine an important radio executive using the soap and not being especially happy about it. In the end they dropped the idea; Garcia said he didn't want to feel guilty if the joke backfired. They could still be the freewheeling Grateful Dead, but now only up to a point.

As Peter Rowan saw for himself, there were less conventional ways to gauge the way the Dead had become an institution. In early June 1973 he and Garcia deplaned at Boston International Airport. Rowan, Garcia, and other members of Old and in the Way, Garcia's current Dead offshoot band, had just grabbed their luggage from the carousel and were on their way to find a taxi into town. Just then Garcia paused. "Wait a minute," he said, with a devilish grin. "I've gotta get Big Red."

A Massachusetts native who'd logged time as a member of Bill Monroe's Bluegrass Boys, Rowan had met Garcia by way of mandolinist

David Grisman. Grisman and Rowan had played together in a psyche-delic folk band, Earth Opera, and Rowan had subsequently joined the more rock-oriented Seatrain. After he left Seatrain, Rowan—who'd met Garcia earlier thanks to his brothers Chris and Lorin's group, the Rowan Brothers, whom Garcia had championed—moved to Stinson Beach, where he lived on the beach near his old friend Grisman. Having overdubbed mandolin on "Friend of the Devil" and "Ripple" on *American Beauty*, Grisman was peripherally connected to Garcia and the Dead world, so it wasn't surprising when one day he invited Rowan up to Garcia and Mountain Girl's hillside bungalow. "Jerry was standing in the garden in a T-shirt and jeans with a five-string banjo and a big grin on his face," Rowan recalls. "God, what a welcome." The jam sessions both outside and inside the house, accompanied by plenty of weed, eventually led to Garcia, Grisman, and Rowan forming a bluegrass band.

Garcia's new side project was an outgrowth of his new living ar-rangements, and both were early signs that Garcia was seeking his own space apart from the Dead. With a population that numbered only in the hundreds and a far-from-anywhere ambience that made it amena-ble to alternative lifestyles, Stinson Beach, tucked away on the curvy Highway 1, was the escape Garcia yearned for at the time. Eventually other members of the scene, including Rakow and Candelario, lived there, but for Garcia, Stinson Beach was a retreat. "It was hard to find safe places to live when you're a freak," says Mountain Girl. "And Jerry liked that drive to Stinson. He said it was the only time he had to him-self in his life. We needed a place where he could completely relax."

Also aboard the formative acoustic band was John Kahn, a tall, funny, and multitalented bass player who'd met Garcia at jam sessions at the Matrix club in San Francisco. Born in Memphis but adopted by Los Angeles–based parents—his new father was a talent scout—Kahn had grown up around show-biz royalty; according to Linda Kahn, later his wife, young John Kahn was once babysat by Marilyn Monroe.

Kahn, who developed a love of jazz in high school, was a very different bass player from Lesh, more rooted in blues and R&B, and he and Garcia clicked as friends, players, and movie fans. First with keyboardist Howard Wales, then with another keyboardist, Merl Saunders, they began a series of outside-Dead jam sessions at area clubs.

When Grisman and Rowan showed up, Kahn had no idea Garcia played banjo and was himself rusty on upright bass, but Kahn too was swept up in the casual energy of the new ensemble. Even though the musicians were all in their twenties, Garcia named it Old and in the Way, after a Grisman song. "We said, 'Of course, that's who we are!'" Rowan recalls. "That's the irony and joke of it. We were useless characters and the only way we could survive was to play music." First with Richard Greene and later Vassar Clements on fiddle, Old and in the Way went from a casual get-together to a performing and touring band, complete with Owsley tagging along to record shows. With Rowan handling lead vocals and frontman duties, Garcia was happy to play banjo and mostly sing harmonies on a repertoire that included Rowan's originals, traditional folk and bluegrass songs, and even a startlingly fresh cover of the Stones' "Wild Horses." During future Old and in the Way gigs Garcia would scowl when fans yelled out the names of Dead songs.

At their debut, at the Lion's Share club in San Anselmo in March 1973, Rowan received his initial taste of the cult of the Dead. After their first set the band walked back to the dressing room, still carrying their instruments; within the new band the rule was to keep playing and never put any of their instruments down. On the way backstage the musicians walked through a gauntlet of Deadheads—what Rowan recalls as "the most long-haired and bearded people you've ever seen in your life"—who were holding lit pipes and large joints. As Garcia passed them, they bowed in worship, and Garcia acknowledged them by stopping for a few quick hits of whatever was extended to him. "He seemed indomitable," says Rowan. "He had a constitution of iron."

Before a Dead show at RFK Stadium in Washington, DC, on June 10, Old and in the Way had flown into Boston for a set of their own at the Orpheum Theatre. When Garcia mentioned "Big Red," Rowan looked back at the luggage carousel—where, seemingly out of nowhere, a large red bag had materialized as if by magic. No one recognized it; it wasn't even tagged. "It had not been on the plane," Rowan recalls. "It was put directly on the carousel by somebody." Garcia grabbed it and, with the other band mates, made his way to their hotel, where other members of the Dead were waiting. Everyone gathered around the suitcase as it was cracked open, revealing a massive amount of quality pot. Along with the Dead, Old and in the Way grabbed plastic baggies and split up the booty. (The Dead weren't always so welcoming to Garcia's side players, as Rowan felt backstage at the RFK show: "It was kinda weird. It was like, 'You're not gonna take Jerry from us—he's *ours*.' They didn't say that, but that's the vibe I got.")

Rowan, who'd never heard the word "sensimilla" until that day, lit up a joint from the luggage stash. He'd smoked his share, but this joint was something else entirely: strong and mind-numbingly overpowering. "It was like, 'Oh, *this* is what the Grateful Dead smoke,'" he recalls. Where the luggage and its contents originated was never confirmed: rumors flew that a fan from either a local research lab (or even the government) sneaked it into the airport and onto that luggage carousel as a way to thank the Dead. That day Rowan learned another lesson about Garcia's world. "That's when I started to go, 'This Grateful Dead thing is really big,'" he says. "There was always stuff like that. They were living large."

■ ◆ ■

"Do I see a guy from La Honda out there?" Lesh called out to the thousands in Reno, seemingly recognizing a familiar face amid the throng in front of him.

Even if it were true—a pal from the Kesey or Acid Test days near the front rows—those days never seemed further away than they did now. The Wall of Sound and the swelling fan base were indications, but so was the repertoire. The bulk of the set, that night and during other performances during this period, was largely culled from the previous few, post-Altamont years. In Reno "Sugaree" was taken at a sultry, turtle-race pace; Garcia took a solo on "Tennessee Jed" that dug deeper and hit lower notes before he made his way back to his signature high, sweet pitch. (At New Jersey's Roosevelt Stadium in August an epic, nineteen-minute version of "Eyes of the World" showed how their collective musicianship could expand and swell like the roaring of the tides.) "China Cat Sunflower" and "The Other One" were played in Reno, but little else from the previous decade popped up. Now that Pigpen was buried, the band's early days, when he was such a prominent part of their shows, had left with him.

Whether it was the wind, the just-out-of-the-box sound system, or incoming burnout, the music also had more than its share of frayed edges. There was a raw, jumpy "Beat It on Down the Line" and a careening but inspired "Truckin'" in which Weir forgot some of the lyrics. Garcia accidentally switched up a few of the lyrics to "U.S. Blues." During "Greatest Story Ever Told," one of the songs from Weir's *Ace* album, Donna Godchaux's voice wandered out of sync and out of tune as she grappled with the dual-microphone setup and the Wall of Sound itself.

The arrival of a new, more industrialized Dead led to inevitable casualties. In early 1974 Cutler parted ways with the band after a tense meeting. Cutler (who by then had launched his own booking agency, Out of Town Tours, to handle the Dead, the New Riders of the Purple Sage, and other acts) claims the Dead wanted to avoid giving him a 10 percent cut by working with another party for half that rate. "That was just an excuse," he says. "I thought, 'I'm not gonna do it, simple.' I'd had enough. I was tired and I'd done my bit. I loved the band and the music, but I hated the politics—a bunch of hippies with nothing better to do than plot against one another rather than get on with the collective thing. There was more politics around the Dead than around the Stones." Given all the managerial types in their midst, which by now included McIntire, Rakow, and Garcia's then-solo manager, Richard Loren, the world inside the Dead was indeed beginning to grow tangled and territorial, and Cutler rubbed some the wrong way.

Owsley Stanley, too, was becoming increasingly out of place in the larger Dead operation. After the group bust in New Orleans in 1970 Owsley finally wound up in jail, and during that time he'd had only fitful interactions with the band. When he was locked up at Terminal Island, south of Los Angeles and near Long Beach, the Dead had rumbled in one day to play a concert in the prison's library. Band and crew found a seemingly clean and healthy Owsley, who introduced them to his fellow cons and helped them, as always, set up the PA. (To Parish's shock, no one at the prison searched the Dead's trucks and gear; the crew was just waved into the compound despite being, in his words, "psychedelized up.") As they were setting up, Owsley told Parish, "I've got to come back on the road with you," but he still had to serve additional time at Lompac, a low-security federal prison northwest of Los Angeles, where friends smuggled in tapestries, décor, and cassette copies of the *Europe '72* shows. Owsley was finally released from prison in 1972 after serving two years in federal jails, and before long he was indeed back in the Dead's employ.

While Owsley was in jail the band hadn't been able to gauge how he was holding up. At Terminal Island Weir was so busy preparing for the show that Bear's state of mind was hard to figure. "We got a little time with him, but I didn't get a great hit on what it was like to be in prison," he has said. "I was too busy getting the gig together." But once Owsley was a free man the impact of incarceration became more apparent. To Mountain Girl Owsley was "completely changed, and not in a good way. He was dark and dour. He'd lost most of his sense of humor. Prison was hard on him."

Back on the road with the Dead, Owsley was still Owsley. After checking into a hotel room, he'd unscrew every lightbulb, replace them with blue or red ones, and light candles. But adding to the difficulties was the role—or lack of a clearly defined one—Owsley had when he hooked back up with the Dead. To erect the Wall of Sound over the course of a tour more hired hands had been brought onboard, and they were rowdier and more boisterous than the band's original core crew, and each had a specific task. In the early days Owsley had a habit of tweaking the system—say, the EQ settings in the monitors—right before show time. The more tightly synchronized, professional Dead apparatus no longer knew how to handle such idiosyncrasies. "Bear would get these brilliant ideas, but the road was not necessarily the place to make that happen or test that out," says Candelario. "I learned so much from him, but we were more mechanized and more uniform when he came back out, and it was hard for him."

Owsley's quirks—enraging roadside chefs with his desire for super-raw meat, lathering himself up with creams in his hotel rooms—were intact. But, again, they were now seen less as quirks and more as distractions. "I'd be like, 'We're leaving for the airport, come on!'" recalls Parish, who always remained fond of Owsley. "He was at his own pace. There was Bear's world and then there was everybody else's." As Weir saw it, "We had a number of new faces on the crew, and Stanley was an acquired taste. A lot of new folks, especially the most country-bumpkin ones, could not relate to this guy. He traveled at a different altitude. There was a fair bit of constant tension there."

To writer David Gans, Owsley later complained there was "a lot of coke and a lot of beer and a lot of booze and a lot of roughness" in the 1974 Dead operation, adding, "I was very uncomfortable." And yet there wasn't much anyone could do to resolve the situation, since the Dead themselves were growing increasingly wary of laying down the law to their hired help. It was soon clear to everyone that Owsley's days with the band were numbered. Like Pigpen tangentially, he would be another casualty of the larger, more lumbering—and largely more institutionalized—machine the Dead had become. When the Reno show wrapped up an hour later with "Sugar Magnolia," that machine tore itself down and began the move to the next town and the next outdoor stadium.

Weir, Lesh, and Garcia (back to camera) working up
Blues for Allah *material at Weir's home studio, 1975.*
PHOTO: ROBBIE TAYLOR/THE BARNCARD COLLECTION

CHAPTER 8

MILL VALLEY, CALIFORNIA, FEBRUARY 19 TO MARCH 4, 1975

First came the jokes about what they would do if the cops showed up at their houses while something illicit was taking place. But on the night of February 19 they knew what they had to do: tap into their collective consciousness and create newfangled songs and soundscapes.

For a decade they'd tried making records in just about any way or place they could. And even with the occasional nitrous oxide tank at their disposal—even when they were fully prepared, as with *American Beauty*—the experiences rarely sat well with them. In the confines of an airtight studio, with a clock ticking, they tended to grow bored or distracted, and the absence of an audience left them feeling uncertain about what they'd come up with. They'd waste time or, as often happened with Weir, have trouble finishing songs in time to record them. But now they had Weir to thank for finally making them feel at home while cutting a record.

At the urging of Frankie, then still his girlfriend but not his wife, Weir had built a studio in his home in Mill Valley, which he'd purchased in 1972. Life at the Weir home was a scene of post-hippie domesticity, complete with a loving dog, Otis. He and Frankie had recruited Rondelle Cagwin, a kind-faced twenty-two-year-old friend of the band (she had met Garcia at one of his Keystone Berkeley solo shows) to cook, clean, and help run their house. To Cagwin, Frankie was "someone who embraced life with everything she had—she loved poker and one-liners, and Bobby gained a lot from her music-business sense." Weir struck Cagwin as shy and sweetly spacey, a "beautiful man inside and out," yet she also sensed how deeply he'd been affected by being adopted. She'd known others who'd been taken in by other families, and in Weir she felt some of the same guardedness. To Weir's specifications, Cagwin pressed the creases in his jeans.

Attached to the house, above a garage, the studio was equally idiosyncratic. Visitors had to navigate up a narrow, twisty road, then drive up a ramp that had room for only two cars. (To some in the Dead camp the incline felt very Evel Knievel, especially because he'd used a ramp for an unsuccessful jump over Snake River Canyon the year before.) Designed and constructed with the help of Stephen Barncard, the long-haired, bespectacled, and detail-oriented studio engineer who'd worked on *American Beauty*, the studio, called Ace's, had a skylight, a triangular-shaped control room not big enough for the whole band, and an open, if cramped, space for the musicians to play. Adding to the homey, tree-house feel of the place, the recording console, at Weir's request, was made of wood. Seeing the array of old-fashioned knobs used on the recording machines, Lesh, ever the science-fiction buff, exclaimed, "This looks like Buck Rogers!"

The neighbors weren't thrilled by the low-Richter-scale thumping that oozed out of Ace's, especially from Lesh's bass, and a few called the cops to complain. They were also less than pleased to look out their windows and see members of the Dead's crew parked at the bottom of the street—smoking weed and awaiting word on what gear the band might need to have hauled up to the studio. "If someone wanted us, they'd come down and yank our chain," recalls one crew member. "But we stayed out of trouble."

Inside Ace's, the windows blacked over and no hint of street noise to trouble them, the Dead were oblivious to all of it. That February night, once they'd gathered up their gear and settled into chairs, Garcia began wailing high notes on guitar, with Kreutzmann and then Lesh eventually joining in, making for a clattering power trio. Excitedly Garcia told them about listening to his new favorite album, the Beach Boys' *Smiley Smile*. Lesh soon pulled out an acoustic guitar and began strumming melodies that he openly admitted had been ripped off from old folk songs. Even the ever-particular Lesh had to agree the Dead were onto something new and that it couldn't have come at a more welcome time—the end of an exhausting and often frustrating few months that could have easily spelled the end of the band.

The largesse of the Dead operation had once seemed manageable, but no more. The previous summer at Roosevelt Stadium in Jersey City, New Jersey, Weir was being interviewed backstage by Gary Lambert, a young writer and Deadhead (and eventual Bill Graham employee), and the two gazed up at the Wall of Sound towering above them. "Did you think it would come to this?" Lambert asked. Weir looked skyward and said, flatly, "Yeah, there were times we had to cancel a show because we couldn't find an extension cord." (He was most likely referring to the free shows the band did in the panhandle in the sixties, which required their own electricity.) Inflated with carpenters, subcontractors, and other stage laborers, the crew was eating up almost as much money as the Wall of Sound itself. "We were playing hockey halls, and we'd have to go in a day early to set it up," Weir told *Rolling Stone* in 2011. "And we were down for a day while that was happening, so economically it wasn't a viable situation. We were selling out the hockey halls but barely breaking even. We had something like forty guys on the crew."

At a Marin County hotel in August, shortly after the Jersey show, a meeting of all Dead employees was called. Danny Rifkin—who'd quit as manager years before to travel but had returned to the fold to work with the crew—stood up and informed everyone that the band would be taking a break. He was so nervous that Swanson, who sat next to him, held his hand for comfort, just as she had with Jon McIntire the previous year when he had to make those dreaded calls about Pigpen. Following a few shows at Winterland in October the Dead would stop touring for a while. In a later newsletter to Deadheads, the band looked back at that moment and wrote that they'd gone "collectively insane . . . from pressures of traveling and devastating internal and external intrigue."

The topic wasn't openly discussed, but a topmost reason for shutting down the operation was to slim down a crew that had grown bigger and rowdier with the arrival of the Wall of Sound. "Everybody was too scared to fire anybody," says Grateful Dead Records employee Andy Leonard. "The guys from Pendleton had brought so many guys in, and I don't think there was anyone on the inside prepared to fire all his friends." Richard Loren, the former booking agent who'd been nicknamed "Zippy" for his East Coast energy, had been Garcia's personal manager since 1972, and in his temporary new role as the band's touring manager after Cutler's departure, Loren found himself bluntly telling Garcia that the Wall of Sound was going to break the band financially. "They had to stop," Loren says. "They had no choice." Garcia unhappily went along with the dismantling of the system. The promise of an autonomous era that began with Rakow's "So What" proposal was prematurely coming to an end. "We had turned into something we never were," says Swanson. "It was turning into this corporate structure."

Rock Scully sensed Garcia's disillusionment with the Dead machinery when he and Garcia were in the San Francisco airport and ran into, of all people, country-pop troubadour John Denver. To Garcia's amazement, Denver was carrying only a guitar case and a briefcase. "Where's your band?" Garcia asked. Denver replied that for this particular tour, he didn't have one; he was merely showing up in cities to play with symphonies, and he opened up his briefcase to show Garcia his sheet music. Afterward Garcia, marveling at Denver's relatively simple touring life, asked Scully, "Why aren't *we* doing that?"

A brief tour of Europe in September 1974 made it all too clear that a respite was desperately needed. If Europe in 1972 had been a working vacation, the trip two years later was simply work. They dealt with scurrilous promoters (one of whom had to be physically threatened before he paid them) and at least one canceled show, in Amsterdam. Meanwhile, the old standbys weren't working as well as they had. One promoter brought them low-grade coke, which made everyone snort more than usual to attain the same sensation.

As usual, they skirted authority as much as possible. Kilos of pot were stashed into the backs of speakers. A rental car containing a band member or two, a few crew employees, and some illicit goodies passed through the border from France into Switzerland, then stopped directly outside the checkpoint. Everyone went to the back of the vehicle, cracked open the trunk, pulled up the carpet, took out the stash, and had a good laugh. Still, employees like soundman Dan Healy and crew member Rex Jackson were increasingly disgusted with the amount of drugs everyone was consuming and tried to tamp it down. One day Jackson gathered together a bunch of cocaine in a garbage can and set it afire. ("But we still didn't run out of any—go figure," jokes Grateful Dead Records' Steve Brown.) Jackson threatened to leave, and Ram Rod talked him out of it. "The *clean* Grateful Dead," Garcia cracked to a friend after Jackson's coke blaze. The shows themselves were rarely inspired; one night Garcia shot Kreutzmann a "stink eye" for not being on the beat. By the end of the run they'd had enough of the whole operation.

Before they went their ways, permanently or not, they booked five farewell shows at Winterland in October 1974. Some things never changed: members of the Dead's extended family were tripping hard, and a Hells Angel asked for a special ramp up to the stage to accommodate his motorcycle. (Promoter Bill Graham had little choice but to agree.) All the while a multicamera film crew was documenting the event for a proposed concert movie. The movie would be a farewell to their past, perhaps in more ways than one. As Betty Cantor was listening to the tapes she'd recorded those nights, the oddest thing happened: she thought she could hear Pigpen in the mix, even though she knew he wasn't there. "I heard the organ, I heard the damn Leslie," she says. "It was in there and I said, 'Pigpen's playing!'" When she was reminded that he'd died the year before, she retorted, in her spunky way, "Well, I *know* that—but I heard him! I swear!" In some ways they could never escape their past.

■   ◆   ■

Later that night of February 19 more troubling news arrived. Rakow showed up to update them on their business. The Dead, he told them, had sold a total of 359,000 copies of various product the previous year. But they had to cut back whatever expenses they could.

The dream of the Dead's label was becoming a calamity faster than anyone thought. The bootlegging of *Wake of the Flood* had been a sizeable setback, but not a crushing one. In its first month out, *From the Mars Hotel* had sold a respectable 258,000 copies, but the single edit of "U.S. Blues" hadn't made converts of anyone in the pop world. A year earlier, in August 1974, Rakow had told the *Marin Independent Journal* that Grateful Dead Records was a "3 and a half to 4 million dollar company." But tonight the news was sobering: the Dead were hemorrhaging money. Among the band the must-own car became the BMW, several of which would wind up parked outside Weir's home studio. With their small size, reliable brakes, and overall stability when encountering hairpin turns, the cars were ideal for Marin County, but they also weren't cheap; a typical model cost $4,200, a considerable sum at the time. The band's requests for additional funding rarely let up. "They'd come back from the road and there would be a pile of money and somebody would say, 'I want an advance,'" says Leonard. "'Okay—for what?' 'Umm, I want to put a new board in my home studio.' 'Okay, here's $25,000.' Then everyone else says, 'I want an advance too!' There was a lot of that going on. Everybody had their own personal use for large chunks of money, whether to buy a house or use it recreationally."

By the second month of 1975 employees of either the band or the label had begun slipping out the back door, some never to return. On the heels of the *Wake of the Flood* bootlegging, the August 1974 meeting was the second red flag for promo man Belardo. "That gave me pause," he says. "The company was petering out. The dream was over." Belardo was also dismayed by the excesses: he once saw Garcia so incapacitated he couldn't function. To Leonard, the hiatus meant the company would have to rely on solo albums or side projects to move product, and everyone knew that none of those records—a projected Keith and Donna Godchaux album and Lesh's *Seastones*, his truly trippy electronic music collaboration with friend and keyboardist Ned Lagin—had the potential to sell as well as a full-on Dead album. "I said to Rakow, 'There is no Grateful Dead Records, because there's no Grateful Dead right now,'" says Leonard. "It was pretty clear after that meeting in August that this was not going to grow." Leonard was gone as well.

In what amounted to a humbling admission of defeat, the Dead had little choice but to hook up once more with a major label, this time

United Artists, to salvage Grateful Dead Records. "At the moment of financial crises we had no recourse but to turn our distribution over to the enterprise which could best serve our necessary market interests," the band announced to Deadheads in one of their newsletters. (They were even starting to *talk* like the companies they despised.) "United Artists seems as good as any and better in some technical respects relating to contractual obligations and distribution capability." It was hardly the most excited announcement, but at that point options were limited.

The UA contract did afford them a cash flow they might not have had on their own. Upon delivering their first album to the label, the Dead would receive $300,000 within ten days; each album to follow would earn them a $150,000 advance. The deal also came with restrictions. The first two Dead albums had to prominently feature Garcia (and, to a lesser extent, Weir), but no one else was specified. Garcia would receive a $125,000 advance for two solo albums, with Weir getting $85,000 for a record of his own. If the deal didn't recoup—if the label didn't earn its money back—Garcia would be required to make another solo album. Garcia was allowed to play on other musicians' records, but, as the contract read, "on the condition that Garcia's name is not featured more prominently than any other artist on such record." In a sign that UA was expecting radio-friendly material, the contract specified that albums couldn't be more than half instrumental. The paperwork also came with a subtle lifestyle warning: the Dead would be considered in default or suspended if their "voice and/or playing ability should become impaired" or if they became involved in any type of scandal involving "any act offensive to decency or morality."

The band laughed off the terminology ("it is with a sigh of relief we shake off our perpetual business hassles," they wrote in a newsletter), but attorney David Hellman, a tax and estate planning lawyer who'd starting helping out band attorney Hal Kant, understood the reason behind United Artists' last clause. "It was essentially a morals clause,"

Hellman says. "United Artists was a little nervous about the group and its reputation. They were new to this group."

More jarring were the departures of some of the band's inner circle. Cutler was just the beginning. Exhausted with the scene, Jon McIntire quit during the European tour. (Loren, who'd first met Garcia in 1970 in Stinson Beach, was now promoted to Dead manager.) The departure of Swanson, their beyond-loyal early fan who now tended to payroll and other office work, was a particularly devastating loss. While looking over the bills one day for purchases she realized someone in the organization (not a band member) was taking goods out of Club Front, a warehouse on Front Street in San Rafael, near the Dead's office, that had become their new rehearsal room. "It was the last straw for me," she says. Rather than tell anyone in the Dead or management because she didn't relish the role of being a rat, Swanson decided simply to quit and devote time to her two young children.

When Garcia heard she was leaving he stopped by Swanson's office to talk with her. But before she could say anything, a couple of strangers walked in and symbolically sat at Garcia's feet, distracting him. "All he would have had to do was say, 'Can you guys give us a minute?' and we could have shut the door and had a conversation," she says. "But it wasn't *my* place to do that, so we never really talked about it." She also left without talking to her old friend Weir. The scenario seemed like a depressingly fitting end.

■ ◆ ■

The Dead were on sabbatical, but most of its members weren't. The year before, Weir had approached his Atherton school buddy Matthew Kelly, who'd formed a band called Kingfish that leaned toward jammy country rock. Kelly was shocked when Weir said he wanted to sit in with them, and the band, with Weir in tow, recorded an album for United Artists that would be released in 1976. "It was fun for him because it was so different from the Dead," Kelly says. "In the Dead Jerry was more of the star. In Kingfish Weir was more or less the star of the band, and that was the first time he experienced something like that. He really enjoyed that role, but he handled it gracefully." Garcia, meanwhile, opened an office in Stinson Beach—right above Ed's Superette, a local grocery—with his new personal manager, Loren. His club-jamming with friends had evolved into a band, first called Legion of Mary and eventually simply the Jerry Garcia Band, and he and Loren began booking club and theater shows. The Garcia Band had less overhead, fewer crew members, and far less backstage and offstage drama than the Dead, all good reasons for Garcia to embrace the idea of the band in the early months of 1975.

Of all the band members Lesh may have been hit the hardest by the decision to stop touring after the Winterland shows. "I was never into taking a break," Lesh says. "But I knew why it happened. Jerry wanted to take a break. Jerry wanted to make the movie out of the Winterland shows. What are you going to do?" In his mind there was "no point" in voicing any disagreements. More and more Lesh began turning to drink, which, he says, was a direct result of the hiatus. "I didn't know whether it was ever going to start up again," he says. "I'll be honest with you—that drove me to drink. That fear. I didn't have a future. I didn't have any side bands. The Grateful Dead was my band. I helped create it."

In terms of home lives, Garcia's was particularly tangled. His second child with Mountain Girl, Theresa, or Trixie, had been born in the fall of 1974. (As with Annabelle, Garcia was on the road and unable to make it to the hospital for the delivery.) Yet to the dismay of many in the Dead scene, Garcia and Mountain Girl's relationship, so integral to the community, was melting down. Many knew Garcia slept with other women, especially on the road, but they hesitated to tell Mountain Girl for fear of hurting her. "It's very difficult when you're friends with two people and one is cheating and the other doesn't know," says Loren. "How most people dealt with it was by avoiding Mountain Girl. I hated that, because I liked her, but I didn't want to answer a question, 'Is Jerry with somebody else?' I could see that he was primed for something else." Mountain Girl was growing exasperated with Garcia, and she learned that when arguing with him, it was best to literally turn her back on him. "I really had no experience with expressing anger or really any strong emotions and found it safer to just not be all reactive," she says. "I was afraid to be angry. I didn't want to lose it. And he would turn on the charm, when needed, and I would be disarmed immediately."

Allan Arkush, the NYU film student who'd worked as a Fillmore East stagehand and had since relocated to California to start a film career, saw the growing tensions in the Garcia–Mountain Girl household during Christmas 1973. After an evening watching Howard Hawks's *Only Angels Have Wings*, Mountain Girl announced it was time for dessert and opened up the freezer, crammed with bags of pot. But one of their guests brought an unwanted gift—cocaine. Mountain Girl was suspicious of the drug, and Arkush saw her and Garcia have a tense exchange; Garcia made an excuse for using it and the conversation ended, at least for a short while.

Garcia was starting to see Deborah Koons, a Cincinnati-born filmmaker he'd met at a Dead show in 1973; she accompanied him to Europe on the Dead's fall 1974 tour. Compared to the out-front Mountain Girl, Koons was a more enigmatic presence, quiet and frequently dressed in black. The quasi-triangle blew up soon enough. At Weir's studio a few months later, in August 1975, Frankie Weir was in her kitchen with Cagwin. Both were accustomed to strange noises—usually musical ones—emanating from the studio, but this time came the sound of yelling and a door being thrown open.

Because it was Garcia's thirty-third birthday, Mountain Girl had dropped by with Annabelle in order to give him a present, only to find Koons there. Even though she and Garcia had been drifting apart for a while, with Garcia implying he felt constrained living in a two-bedroom home with three kids, Mountain Girl was infuriated; grabbing Koons, she dragged her out of the studio, pulling the door off its hinges in the process. After Garcia had spoken to them both to quiet them down, he wandered into the kitchen, sat down, and said to Frankie and Cagwin, "Women—I just don't understand 'em." The women exchanged knowing, he-has-a-lot-to-learn glances but didn't lecture Garcia.

By then a friend had arrived and wound up driving Garcia back home after the altercation. "I hate this shit," Garcia told him. "I can't tell you how much I hate it. I'm gonna get myself strung out to escape this shit." The friend couldn't tell whether he was joking or not, but Garcia was clearly out of sorts about the situation.

◆ ◆ ◆

Assembling on the night of March 5, they heard another bit of sobering news: Lenny had died about a month earlier. At first Garcia didn't know who they were talking about, but the response came soon enough: Mickey's long-departed father.

The story was true: just over five years after he blew out of Marin with so much of their money, Lenny Hart was truly dead to them in every sense. The Dead had hired private detectives to hunt Hart down, and they found him in San Diego as he was "baptizing Jesus freaks," in the words of *Rolling Stone* at the time. The Dead eventually sued Hart and were able to retrieve a portion of the stolen money; Hart was also convicted of embezzlement and spent half a year in jail. "When they sued him I was sitting outside the courtroom, and I said, 'How could you do that?'" recalls Joe Smith. "He said, 'The Lord has forgiven me—I hope the boys will.' I said, 'The Lord didn't lose seventy-five big ones.' He didn't know how to manage a band. Any story they wanted to hear, he would tell them." After his time in jail Hart was back in the area, although no one in the band was keeping track by that point.

Whether Lenny knew it or not during his last days on the planet, his son had worked his way back into his old band. Mickey Hart's four years in Dead Siberia had been difficult. One by one, most of those who'd crashed at this Novato ranch had moved on to other digs or left due to the increasingly tense, shadowy atmosphere. "I rarely went to Mickey's after 1970," says Vicki Jensen. "Things got dark there." Jerilyn Lee Brandelius, who'd met the band in 1968 and had subsequently worked for her uncle, an executive at Warner Brothers, was given the task of finding a ranch to hold a party for one of the label's acts. Flashing on Hart's home, she thought it ideal and called the house. An unnamed friend told her to come up from San Francisco but added she wasn't allowed to bring anyone with her. Making her way to Hart's front door, Brandelius was told he wasn't available. The same went for another visit. The third time Brandelius demanded to see Hart, who poked his head out from behind a door, a smirk on his face. They came to a financial agreement to hold the party there, but to guarantee Hart's isolation, Brandelius had to ensure no one would know or remember the exact address.

Not long after, Brandelius moved onto the ranch with her young daughter and, in doing so, saw how removed Hart was from the Dead scene. The band kept in touch with him. Hart was recording solo music there, including one album that was released (the all-star *Rolling Thunder*) and another that wasn't, but Hart still seemed in shell-shock. "He was a complete hermit, and he was very depressed and broken-hearted," says Brandelius. "I didn't meet his family for years. He cut himself off from everybody. He was so upset with everything that happened with his dad and the band. No one blamed Mickey ever, but *Mickey* blamed Mickey."

The week the Dead were playing their final shows at Winterland, in October 1974, the phone at Hart's ranch began ringing. Eventually Hart took the call and spoke with one of the Dead's crew. At first he hesitated, but on the last night Hart had a change of heart; throwing his drum kit in the back of a friend's car, he drove to Winterland in his Porsche and walked into the band's dressing room. To his and Brandelius's relief, everyone seemed happy to see Hart again, and someone asked whether he'd be up for sitting in during the second set.

Just then Kreutzmann walked in and was told Hart would be joining them for part of the show. "Oh, I don't know," he said, adding that the band was playing new songs Hart had never learned. Shrugging, Hart began walking out the door. "Bill was a bit on edge," Hart says. "He was probably surprised out of his fucking mind. He was holding onto something but never told me what it was." (The fact that Kreutzmann had been holding down the drum fort alone—and incredibly well— was probably a major factor.)

Fortunately, the suddenly tense backstage vibe didn't last much longer. Rex Jackson followed Hart and Kreutzmann out of the dressing room, and at the bottom of a backstage ramp he grabbed each by the backs of their necks and brought their heads so close their foreheads were touching. "You're playing together tonight—you got that?" Jackson barked. "You guys gotta get your shit together. Get . . . it . . . together." The matter settled—few wanted to pick a fight with the mammoth Jackson—Kreutzmann slung his arm around Hart, and the two walked out together during the second set. Taking it all in, Swanson said Hart resembled "a kid on Christmas morning—he was so happy to be back."

The pain and sense of betrayal Hart felt after his father bilked his own band never left him; decades later he would still sound grief-stricken. But after following his father's trial in the newspapers and hearing the news of his passing, Hart worked up the inner strength to visit the funeral home where Lenny's body lay. After asking members of his father's new family to leave the room for a bit, Hart pulled out a pair of his father's old drumsticks, played what he called "a drummer's farewell" on the casket, and put the sticks inside next to his father. But the son wasn't finished. Using a camera he'd brought along, he took a photo of Lenny. Later he printed it out, wrote "The Rat Is Dead" on it, and mailed it to a relative. "And then it was over," Mickey says. "That put the period on the sentence." Lenny's son would have the last word on a particularly traumatic period for himself and the Dead.

■　◆　◼

During his visit Rakow told them the album needed to be completed by the first week of May, which took them by surprise. In fact, the United Artists contract called for a delivery on July 10 for the first album of their new deal, followed by another to be handed in on October 31 and a third on January 31, 1976.

There was work to do, fast, but as was their want, they still took their time and worked at their idiosyncratic pace. Garcia would inevitably arrive first, as early as 7 a.m., and Cagwin would make a fresh pot of coffee for him and everyone else who showed up. As Cagwin recalls, "Bob's house provided a much more relaxed environment for those guys to work in." For dinner they'd order in steaks, send one of the Dead label employees on food runs, and smoke and snort whatever was around. Between takes they'd talk about their pets—the way Garcia's dog walked counterclockwise around his house—or the quality of Dead merchandise T-shirts. Lesh remarked that he was always inclined to give a ride to any hitchhiker who sported a Dead shirt.

Among those who stopped in were Hunter, Quicksilver Messenger Service's John Cipollina, and their old pal David Crosby, who lived in Mill Valley and had wrapped up a fraught Crosby, Stills, Nash & Young reunion tour months before. With Garcia avidly listening, Crosby expounded on his favorite type of pot and talked about the arrival of his upcoming baby. And at times they even found time to make music. One evening they spent hours working up a new Crosby song, "Homeward

Through the Haze," that Crosby had tried cutting unsuccessfully with CSNY, who were already falling apart again.

The sessions also revealed the Dead's personalities and how they'd changed—or, in some cases, not—over a decade. Lesh was the chattiest and most technical, calling out chord changes and chord names. Kreutzmann wisecracked the most, and Weir remained the most relentlessly earnest, talking in his slightly halting way about local loggers versus the Sierra Club or the *Wide World of Sports* TV show. When he was at the sessions, Hart kept a low profile and didn't talk much, reflecting the ways he was slowly working his way back into the fold. "I just hung out," Hart recalls. "I had a great feeling from everyone every day. You couldn't move in Bobby's tiny studio. It was really tight. But it felt the same. My relations with the guy was always the same. You didn't have to talk about these things." (People like Parish and Swanson felt that Hart seemed to be more tentative at this point, careful not to overassert himself as a way of mending fences and re-insinuating himself into the Dead.) A far more mysterious and fleeting presence was Keith Godchaux.

When Garcia spoke, everyone else would quiet down and listen. Even if he was just discussing a Don Reno and Chubby Weiss bluegrass show he'd attended, Garcia remained the unquestioned center of attention. He mentioned that the band had received an offer to play in the Middle East. Just a few weeks later, on March 25, Faisal would be assassinated, and the resulting album, *Blues for Allah*, would be named in his honor.

◆ ◆ ◆

They needed a rock 'n' roll tune, and late one evening Garcia volunteered, reminding everyone that "Loose Lucy," the slinky rocker off *From the Mars Hotel*, had taken him all of twenty minutes to write. But conventional rock 'n' roll, even in the Dead's loose definition of that phrase, wasn't what anyone had in mind as the days and weeks at Ace's gradually unfolded. Garcia wanted the band to sound fresh, to blow away all the musical and financial headaches of the last few years, and the solution was having *no* new material at all—to come up with it on the spot. A song might start with Lesh strumming chords on an acoustic guitar (or humming the melody to what would eventually transform into a song, "Equinox," that the band wouldn't attempt to record until their next album). It might launch with Lesh, Weir, and Garcia all playing simultaneously, sometimes for hours, trying to find the right new tone or direction.

Or, as it did on the night of February 26, it might start with Garcia playing a few, well-chosen guitar chords. When they found something, Hunter would show up and write lyrics along with the music, an atypical approach even for him. "It was comfortable being in Weir's house," says Candelario. "That was generally the mood in those days. They got along with each other. It was fun to hang out. Making records wasn't one of their professions, but that album was totally different." The less stressful atmosphere would be easily heard in the more relaxed, elastic song structures and rhythms in songs like "Help on the Way/Slipknot!" (which Lesh would later call "one of our finest exploratory vehicles"), the reggae sway of "Crazy Fingers," and the breezy "Franklin's Tower," partly inspired by the "doo-da-doo" chorus on Lou Reed's "Walk on the Wild Side."

As the weeks at Weir's studio continued, it became obvious that their enforced hiatus wasn't about taking a break from each other as much as it was from the overwhelming industry of the Dead. Even when the band was frittering away time, the experience at Weir's studio reinforced that music could still be their bond. Despite all the personal and business headaches swirling around the band, they could still come together in a small space, pick up their instruments, and continue the sonic journey they'd begun a decade before. In a heartbeat or something close to it, they could return to those days at Dana Morgan's music studio in Palo Alto, or the Acid Test nights, or the long days ensconced in professional studios creating *Aoxomoxoa* or *Anthem of the Sun*. And even better, they could still *enjoy* it.

Late the night of March 5, after almost a month of tossing around ideas and trying to invent a new sound, they began hitting on that mysterious, intangible new approach. Garcia suggested playing in unison, either a chord or just a note. The others guffawed or chuckled, as if in disbelief, but he continued: how about holding one note for two bars, then having two of the players shift to the third bar? The idea was to all play octaves simultaneously and musically hop around each other. It was an audacious thought, and they decided to go for it.

To demonstrate, Garcia played an F on his electric guitar; Weir and Lesh followed suit with the same chord, and finally Kreutzmann joined in. The result was a mammoth drone, a Wall of Sound in the studio, and everyone was palpably excited by it. They kept working on a piece—what would eventually come to be known as "Unusual Occurrences in the Desert"—and Garcia was thrilled, telling them he felt like he wanted to keep playing it forever. Even when the band would stop playing, Garcia rarely would; his guitar, that ambrosial sweet sound, would continue reverberating around the walls of the studio.

When would they complete the material, and when would they perform any of it live and work it up onstage? Those questions were still unanswered. As it was, they'd already committed to one show, a Bill Graham–organized benefit for SNACK (Students Need Athletics, Culture, and Kicks, a nonprofit founded by Graham) at Kezar Stadium. "Even though the band wasn't playing and everybody needed some breathing room, there was a large sense of family that never went away," says Debbie Gold, then working in the Garcia office with Loren. "They were around each other, and there were family events. It was a small community of people, but everybody needed some breathing room. Bill [Graham] willed that to happen. He said, 'I want the

Dead to play.' He was so passionate and determined and would not take no for an answer."

The Dead had agreed to participate, but not without chewing it over at Weir's studio. Weir wondered whether they would have time for a soundcheck before they went on, and Garcia assured him the pressure would be off given that the other scheduled acts included Bob Dylan, Santana, Neil Young, and Jefferson Starship. Plus, Garcia added, they'd only have to play an hour. The band cracked up. At last they could laugh about something, and more important, they could laugh about it together.

The new era, arising: The vast crowd and
empty boxcars at Englishtown.
PHOTO: HARRY HAMBURG/NY *DAILY NEWS*/GETTY IMAGES

CHAPTER 9

ENGLISHTOWN, NEW JERSEY, SEPTEMBER 3, 1977

As their helicopter whirly-birded toward the grounds, Garcia, wearing one of his customary black T-shirts, and Richard Loren, their manager of nearly three years, weren't sure what to expect. No one was. Along with John Scher, the gregarious, Jersey-based promoter who had started booking their east-of-the-Mississippi shows, both men knew that the corridor between Washington, DC, and Boston had been teeming with Deadheads. In 1970 alone the band played seemingly nonstop in the New York area and built up one of their most rabid followings.

But today's concert in Englishtown would nonetheless be a test and a gamble. The nearby raceway, its name immediately recognizable to anyone who'd grown up in Jersey and heard its ubiquitous "RR-RRaceway . . . *Park!*" radio ads, could hold up to ninety thousand people. Aside from their participation in festivals, the Dead rarely if ever played to that many paying customers, and no one was 100 percent sure whether that many *would* pay. The weather was another miserable factor: by the time all the members of the Dead began arriving in Englishtown the Jersey Shore's notoriously humid summer heat had blanketed Raceway Park.

The tickets had begun selling briskly, a positive sign for the Dead but bad news for local municipalities, who were horrified at the thought of tens of thousands of unruly rock fans descending upon their suburbs. Scher told authorities he'd be lucky to sell fifty thousand tickets, but that didn't mollify the politicians. "We were still in an era," he says, "where anything that smelled, hinted, or suggested Woodstock scared people." The towns sued to shut down the concert; when that failed, mysterious construction jobs on all the major roads leading to Englishtown suddenly materialized a day or two before the concert. Luckily for Scher, a judge ordered the towns to fill in the holes they'd already dug in the highways.

Not every Deadhead heard about the ruling, and starting the night before the show, many simply ditched their cars as close to Raceway Park as they could and began walking. To prevent gate-crashing, Scher devised a complicated but ingenious security plan—renting empty boxcars from local rail yards in Newark and connecting them in a large circle around the park. (The Dead's crew jokingly referred to the sight as the "Polish Railroad"—"it looked like a train, but didn't go anywhere," chuckles a friend who was there.) Fans couldn't squeeze in between the cars, nor could they climb up its slippery surfaces; if they did, they'd be greeted by security guards patrolling atop the boxcars. One fan managed to slip in, holding massive wire cutters, and was stunned to discover there was no fence to slice open even if he wanted to do it. Working to set up the stage throughout the day, Steve Parish and other members of the crew took in the spectacle. "From the side of the stage we watched the security guards repelling people all day long who were climbing up those things," Parish says. "It was just bursting at the seams."

But nothing—not highway snafus nor the oppressive summer weather that would normally drive East Coasters indoors—was keeping the cult away. As their helicopter made its way over Raceway Park, all Garcia and Loren saw was an enormous, swirling mass of bodies extending as far as they could see. "Oh, my God!" Loren said, turning to Garcia. "What a fan base we've got!"

At was his custom, Scher walked out onto the stage—with its massive Cyclops-with-a-skull backdrop—as the band was about to go on and introduced them, one by one. The Dead didn't ask him to do that, but Scher did it anyway, in part because he assumed most of the fans probably didn't know anyone's name other than Garcia's. Then he walked off, they started up "Promised Land," and the time came to see what would happen when the Dead tried to hold the attention of close to one hundred thousand people on the other side of the country from home.

■　◆　■

Given the burnout and stress that preceded their sabbatical from performing, the road back to the road had been measured. They'd only played a few times publicly in 1975—including the SNACK benefit at Kezar, previewing some of the more abstract new material they'd worked up—and released *Blues for Allah*, the album cut at Weir's studio, in September. Compared to *From the Mars Hotel*, *Blues for Allah* felt underproduced, almost drab at times. But starting with "Help on the Way/Slipknot!" the album had a cohesive, organic flow. With its cozy harmonies and languid chords, that song alone announced a more lissome version of the band, as did the instrumental second half, "Slipknot!," which incorporated jazz chording on guitars, bass, and electric piano. Written hurriedly by Weir and Barlow, "The Music Never Stopped" amounted to their first foray into rhythms that hinted at low-key disco, but the call-and-response vocals between Weir and Donna Godchaux never sounded more charged.

Blues for Allah presented the Dead at their most sociable, in "Franklin's Tower," and most eccentric, in "King Solomon's Marbles," a rubbery instrumental that gave Garcia and Keith Godchaux plenty of room to roam with their instruments. The latter felt less like a studio piece than an actual live performance, which was the key to *Blues for Allah*. For a band that notoriously had trouble translating its concert sound onto studio tape, the album felt especially alive. The experiment at Weir's studio, making something from virtually nothing, also resulted in the album-ending trilogy of "Blues for Allah," "Sand Castles and Glass Camels," and "Unusual Occurrences in the Desert," three pieces that collectively sounded like Marin County monks on an acid trip.

To launch the album, the Dead played a sparkling performance of *Blues for Allah* in its entirety at the Great American Music Hall in San Francisco. Because he'd used actual live crickets in "Sand Castles and Glass Camels," the ever-sonically adventurous Hart bought a box of crickets from a pet store in Novato and carted them to the theater. He wound up leaving them there, and a week later the owners angrily called the Dead office, complaining that the crickets had taken over, especially backstage; the Dead just shrugged and declined to help out.

The Great American Music Hall show (and a free show in Golden Gate Park that September with Santana and Jefferson Starship) became a warm-up for further reunions and reparations. The allure of playing together and earning a sizable living from it couldn't be denied, and they were reminded that time on the road could be preferable to time at home. Just a few months later, in early 1976, they'd congregated at Weir's house with Scher, who'd first worked with the band in 1972 at Roosevelt Stadium in New Jersey. The following year he began forming a tight connection with the band—Garcia in particular—when Garcia and Hunter were busted for pot (along with LSD and coke) in New Jersey while driving from Baltimore to Manhattan. "Go bail out Jerry Garcia? Come *on!*" was Scher's delighted reaction when the call arrived from management. In the middle of the night Scher drove over to his Capitol Theater in Passaic, opened the safe, and pulled out the few thousand dollars needed for bail; after Garcia and Hunter were freed they all drove back to Manhattan and stayed up talking until dawn.

At Weir's home the band talked about touring again, but under far more curtailed circumstances than in 1974. In a mailing to Deadheads that would announce the eventual release of *Blues for Allah*, they hinted at the stress of the road, announcing that they were considering "hit and run" shows "consisting of unannounced concerts . . . This will keep the size down and we will not feel obligated to play a place before announcing it if something else comes up." Those words were the germ of an idea that would be nailed down at Weir's home.

It was clear to Scher that the Dead still enjoyed playing together but that aspects of their touring business had to change. The Wall of Sound would have to go, along with some of the extra hired hands; rented gear and a small crew would now be the norm—to "make everything more compact," says Candelario, who survived that round of cuts. Over the course of hours of conversation Scher heard what the band wanted: multiple days at venues instead of arenas. "Bill Graham made the mistake [of thinking] they were a bunch of drugged-up hippies," says Scher. "But by the middle of the seventies, not suggesting they were straight arrow, they were sophisticated musicians and business people who agreed they wanted to participate in the business."

With that they began playing shows again in 1976, starting in Oregon in June. The performances sometimes felt tentative, as if they were still getting reacquainted. Hart had to learn material he hadn't played before, and he himself was easing his way back in personally. This time there would be no new album to promote other than *Steal Your Face*, a largely uninspired two-record live set culled from the Winterland shows in 1974 that helped fulfill the United Artists contract.

The Dead were working out their new life on the road, but the situation with their own company wasn't proving to be sustainable. In early 1976 the First National Bank of Boston wanted its debt repaid, and tension between Rakow and the band was mounting. Everyone other than Garcia was beginning to question the running of the business, and Hart had an outright confrontation with Rakow when Hart was recording *Diga*, the first album by his percussion ensemble Diga Rhythm Band, at Wally Heider's studio in San Francisco. Soon after, Rakow was fired. Hearing what had happened, Rakow, according to published reports, cashed a low-six-figure advance check from United Artists and paid off those owed for production of movie projects and other costs. He also kept some for himself that, he argued, would have been owed to him from an earlier contract with the band. As legitimate as it appeared, the news was still staggering to the Dead. As soon as he heard what Rakow had done, band lawyer Hal Kant called Hellman: "What the hell is going on here?" Everyone was as surprised as Kant.

Garcia, ever eager to avoid confrontation, didn't want to press the matter and draw attention to the band's financial chaos. (According to McNally's account, "They negotiated a settlement in which [Rakow] kept the money but retained no interest in the record company.") Within a few months Grateful Dead Records (and its sister label, Round) were history. Garcia's salary, which had been about $540 a week, according to Andy Leonard, was cut down to a little over $50 to penalize him and compensate for the depletion in funds. Garcia had been the one pushing for Rakow from the start and now had to pay the price for his decision. The fallout would have enormous implications for Garcia, his personal life, and the Dead.

◆ ◆ ◆

One day in late 1976 Keith Olsen, an LA-based record producer who'd overseen Fleetwood Mac's 1975 makeover *Fleetwood Mac*, found himself in the New York office of Arista Records head Clive Davis. Davis played Olsen a song by one of his acts, the Alan Parsons Project, then announced the real reason for the meeting: he'd signed the Dead and wanted Olsen to produce their first record for the label. "He said, 'I need an album that could be played on radio,'" says Olsen, who was admittedly ignorant of the band's music and immediately flashed on the one song he knew well, "Casey Jones." "I thought, it's the Grateful Dead—'high on cocaine'?'" Olsen recalls. "I didn't know their records. I was as far away from what they did as possible." After the meeting Olsen listened to a Dead album and focused on the sound of the dual drummers, which he thought was, in his words, "just slush—it wasn't a tight backbeat. It was just undefined. The guitar parts weren't together either, and I just thought, "How am I going to fix this?'"

Olsen wasn't alone in scratching his head over translating the Dead onto tape in a studio; even the band's management realized how difficult it was. "I don't think the Dead ever made albums that were anywhere near the excitement and what was going on in a gig," McIntire told writer David Hajdu. "Slightly off-key vocals are really going to stand out, whereas they don't when you're in the hall. And the lack of necessity of one note following another is lost when it's being recorded." Thanks to the largely freeform way in which it was made, *Blues for Allah* had been an artistic success, but the collapse of Grateful Dead Records had squandered that opportunity; the band now had to dig itself out of a considerable hole. They finally turned to Davis and Arista, the company he'd started after an acrimonious split with Columbia Records a few years before. At the time Arista was only three years old and best known for hits by Barry Manilow. But the label was also home to a small group of respected rockers and songwriters including Lou Reed, Patti Smith, and Loudon Wainwright III, making it a compatible potential home for the Dead. The band was also aware that Davis had been interested in signing them at least once before.

"We went and talked to Arista first," says Scher, who helped negotiate the deal. "They were the only people we negotiated with in any real way. Clive had signed the New Riders, and Jerry was very happy with the way that happened. So that was their first choice, and at the time Clive had an amazing staff. They felt if there was anybody they could work with in the industry, it would be Clive." With few alternatives, the Dead had almost no choice but to sign up.

Not wanting to alienate a powerful industry figure like Davis, Olsen agreed to give the Dead a fresh coat of sonic paint. "I had to do it," says Olsen. "It was an edict." With that command, he flew to the Bay Area and met with the Dead over dinner at his hotel. When he mentioned that Davis wanted a radio-friendly record, most of the band laughed, to Olsen's discomfort.

"No," he shot back, "the president of your record company really wants to have something in your album that's accessible to the marketplace and accessible on radio."

The band simply stared back quietly, except for Garcia, who said, "Hmmm—radio's good!" It was settled; Olsen would lead the charge.

By the fall of 1976 mainstream rock 'n' roll had never sounded glossier; tellingly, the biggest album of the year was Peter Frampton's *Frampton Comes Alive!*, a concert album by a journeyman British rocker who represented rock at its cuddliest and most family friendly. Punk was right around the corner; Smith had released her Arista debut the previous year, and the Ramones had launched in the spring with their own first missive, the low-selling but influential *Ramones*. But radio hadn't yet taken to punk rock—in some ways it wouldn't for decades—and only seemed amenable to records that had a studio-sheen glaze over them. In signing with Arista and then agreeing to work with Olsen, the Dead were conceding to the artistic and economic times around them. Weir, the band member most comfortable with mingling with record executives, had at least one meeting with Davis at the Beverly

Hills Hotel. "Bobby would do the networking for the band," says Janice Godshalk-Olsen, who was close to Weir during this period. "Clive was explaining that he wanted the band to go a little more Southern California—or, the word the band hates, 'commercial.' And he wanted them to work with his man Keith. Bobby was up for it more so than the rest of the guys."

Gathering in a circle soon after at Front Street, the band began playing as Olsen paced around, observing them at work. He couldn't tell whether they could hear each other, especially Kreutzmann and Hart, and he quickly realized their musicianship matched their personalities. "Mickey is pushing, pushing, pushing and on top of the beat," Olsen recalls, "and Billy was laid back; his backbeat was way behind." The way Lesh's bass jutted out to the forefront—rather than playing a reserved, supportive role in the way of most rock bass playing—was an indication of the leading role Lesh saw for himself in the Dead.

Olsen left the rehearsal depressed; he wondered how he was going to make a record with such ingredients, especially because the Dead didn't seem open to change. A subsequent visit to Front Street wasn't any better. The band played him "Estimated Prophet," a new Weir and Barlow song inspired by the sight of unhinged hangers-on at their shows; the narrator hears voices in his head and is awaiting his own personal apocalypse. The song would eventually settle into a groove that hinted at reggae, but at that early stage it still felt unformed. Olsen was praying Garcia had a few good songs to offer. Taking a seat, Garcia played snippets of different in-progress melodies—delightful pieces of music, but not finished works. After each one Garcia would pause and say, "Maybe I should finish one of these songs." At one point one of the crew leaned over to Olsen and joked, "You know those will *never* get done!" Olsen's heart sank until he suggested they fuse all of them into a suite. "Oh, like a symphonette?" Garcia said brightening. As Olsen recalls, "It was kind of brutal until I convinced them they needed more songs."

Whether they liked it or not, the band settled into preparing for the recording of their Arista debut. More so than probably any previous studio collaborator, Olsen put the band through its paces, making them rehearse and replay parts until they had them down as tightly as possible. Normally the Dead would have bristled, but not this time. "Keith was cracking the whip, but we liked it—it made us sharper," says Hart. "We became much more disciplined. We were trying to make a real record for Clive." Slowly the songs began taking shape: "Estimated Prophet," Donna Godchaux's ballad "Sunrise" (Garcia had strongly encouraged her to write a song for the album), and Lesh's "Passenger," the most rock-rooted song he'd ever written for the band. The pieces of music Garcia had previewed for Olsen had transformed into an epic Hunter-Garcia suite called "Terrapin Station Part 1," blending folk melodies, percussive interludes, and orchestration that, when finished, proved the Dead could pile on production without losing their essence. Once Olsen was confident the band had enough material for a record, the Dead moved into a motel in Van Nuys, close to Sound City, the mangy but first-rate studio where Olsen was working. And thus began the process of attempting to turn the Dead into a professional-sounding rock band, a chart competitor with the likes of Boston, ELO, and other lushly produced FM rock bands.

Not surprisingly given the match of producer and artist, the recording didn't start promisingly. Over the course of the first month the band insisted on playing simultaneously, but to Olsen, the result was a mess. Lesh's bass would often go out of tune. Keith Godchaux was mostly asleep on a couch in the studio; he'd wake up, play his part, and pass out again. Olsen felt the band had nothing usable after the first few weeks, and the band grew tired of hearing the producer's refrain—"not good enough."

Olsen, perplexed or frustrated himself, estimates that 25 percent of his time was devoted to rounding up the band: just when a few of them were ready to get to work, others would wander off. And even when he managed to gather them together, they didn't always stay in the same room for long. "Then it was, 'We've all gotta go to the bathroom' or this and that," says Olsen. "They would just *drift*. It was just taking forever." With the Dead's first round of 1977 concerts coming up fast, Parish and Ram Rod seized the moment and took control. One night in February the band bogged down in percussion overdubs. The roadies came up with a novel idea: nail the studio door shut. "We were under the gun, and it was taking *so* long for those overdubs," says Parish. "It was a joke, but it kept the guys in there, and they couldn't get out. It was a symbolic nailing that really worked." (Hart thinks they also hammered it closed because drummer and singer Buddy Miles, working in an adjacent studio, was stealing cymbals when the Dead weren't around.)

Gradually the project began to mesh. To Hart, Olsen was "too small to hit," so the drummer, among the most particular of the Dead in terms of sonic tweaking, let the producer have his way just enough. Olsen was impressed with Garcia's seemingly endless concepts for arrangements and guitar parts: "Jerry would have twenty ideas for everyone. He'd say, 'I got a bunch of ideas,' and we'd do them all." Godchaux's "Sunrise," a languorous ballad, required yet another musical pivot on the Dead's part; the soft-rock rhythm and feel of the song didn't come naturally to the band. Visiting Sound City one day, Allan Arkush—who recalls seeing a very young Annabelle running around and Garcia so wrapped up in album production that he didn't have time to play with her—heard "Terrapin Station Part 1" played back over the sound system and was impressed with how vast and far reaching it was.

In a strange way the finished album, *Terrapin Station*, was even odder than *Anthem of the Sun*: the sound of the Dead with some of its rough edges sanded down. They finally got around to cutting a studio version of "Dancin' in the Streets," the Martha and the Vandellas hit (usually called "Dancing in the Street") they'd been performing since the Pigpen days, but the song had been lent a disco beat fitting for the times. Within the band the reaction to the finished work was mixed. With tempered enthusiasm, Lesh later called the album "a fairly successful effort" that "varied wildly in terms of material." Hart lost it when Olsen overdubbed strings over one of his parts in "Terrapin Station Part 1" without telling him. "I wanted to strangle Keith," Hart says. "He took out all the timbales and put on those stupid strings. He thought the strings would supersede a beautiful unison part by me and Garcia. I couldn't believe it. After that we never really trusted Keith again. He tried to put a dress on the Dead, and it didn't fit."

At the Novato house of his Jefferson Starship friend David Freiberg, Garcia played a test pressing of the album for Betty Cantor. The two had a close, jocular rapport that allowed her to amiably bust Garcia's chops (she also regularly cut his hair during this time), and the production on "Terrapin Station Part 1," particularly the orchestration, gave her a perfect opportunity to rib her friend: "Oh, that's something Keith [Olsen] put on," Garcia said, less than excitedly. "I don't know."

Garcia began "making excuses," she recalls, and Cantor replied, "That ain't gonna fly with me, dear!" she said. To her, Garcia didn't seem all that happy with the finished album, but, she says, "He was trying to rationalize it somehow."

How the album would fare in the marketplace was another matter. When Olsen sent an early copy to Davis, the Arista boss labeled it, says Olsen, "a good compromise." (Davis, Olsen says, also instructed Olsen to make Weir's first Arista solo album, *Heaven Help the Fool*, more commercial than *Terrapin Station*, and starting with a Richard Avedon glam-boy cover photo, they did just that.) The Dead didn't have much time to sit and ponder what they'd just done. Once the album was in the can they would see how all the task-master studio work would pay off on the road, where the Dead always felt more at home and their songs always sprung to life.

■   ◆   ■

May 8, 1977, started as a warm spring afternoon but turned into a chilly night, and several inches of snow blanketed the campus of Cornell University in Ithaca, New York. The late-spring flurries didn't keep away five thousand Deadheads who crammed into Barton Hall, the school's field house. "All right now," a newly bearded Weir told them about halfway through the show. "We're gonna play everybody's favorite fun game—'Move Back.' Now, when I tell you to take a step back, everybody take one step back." Weir had to say it a few times, and bit by bit the fans shuffled toward the rear to alleviate the crush at the front of the stage. At least one other potentially hazardous crowd issue loomed. Arriving at the show from his Jersey office, Scher had to recruit security to make sure stoned Deadheads didn't accidentally plunge into one of several waterfall-like gorges that are part of the school's exquisite campus. "If you were too fucked up and walked off the edge of the gorge," recalls Scher, "you were dead." As a result of that last-minute chore, Scher missed the first twenty minutes of the show.

But once the playing began, little was amiss. All the hours the Dead had logged in the studio with a chart-minded producer had transformed the band into a monstrously strong unit. At Barton Hall "Morning Dew" was even more cathartic than before, "Deal" had an extra bit of strut in its step, and "New Minglewood Blues" growled. The relentless pace that Kreutzmann and Hart had been put through by Olsen resulted in tight, synchronized beats that gave the songs the firmest of backbones.

Later, beloved Dead archivist Dick Latvala would scribble excited notes on tape boxes of each show, especially Barton Hall. But that performance was just one of many highlights of an inordinately smooth-running group of shows. "That was just a magic year," says Parish. "All the gears meshed together for us at that time." Over the course of two tours, an Eastern-rooted swing in the spring and a Western and

Midwestern trek in the fall, the Dead played some of the sharpest, most consistently enjoyable shows of their career. Whether in college gyms, theaters, or arenas, they'd rarely sounded so well oiled, playing what Donna Godchaux called "regular shows like regular people did." At the on-campus coliseum at the University of Alabama they dug into a slow, mournful "High Time" and added dramatic flourishes to "Looks Like Rain." A beautifully burnished "Wharf Rat" in Hartford showed how they'd matured as a band without losing their loose and easy charm. During a particularly strong "Sugaree" in St. Paul, Garcia discharged a wild flurry of notes.

Fans also heard a new combination introduced onstage early in the year: "Scarlet Begonias" segueing into "Fire on the Mountain," written during a jam at Hart's studio as Hunter watched a blaze up in the hills that threatened to creep down. (The band cut a version of the song with Olsen for *Terrapin Station*, but no one was satisfied, so it was held for their next record.) They busted out a new cover, the festive New Orleans stomp "Iko Iko," which would become an almost permanent part of their repertoire. "We had all this new material that everyone was excited about playing," Donna Godchaux told *Rolling Stone*, "and everyone wanted to say, 'All right, this is the time to really make a statement and not just be a psychedelic weirdo hippie band.' And some of the other songs were more song oriented than jam oriented."

At New York's Palladium, a smaller venue that allowed them to work out some of the kinks in their set in the spring, "The Music Never Stopped" had especially crisper, more synchronized rhythms from Hart and Kreutzmann. Garcia sang the traditional ballad "Peggy-O" with heart-tugging sweetness and ripped off a solo in "Comes a Time" that burst with soulful, laser-beam intensity. The band embarked on "Terrapin Station Part 1," navigating its prog-like twists and turns with grace and nimbleness. Cantor, who sat by the side of the stage each night and recorded all the shows, heard a difference between 1977 and the previous year. "In 1976 it was seat of the pants," she says, "but in 1977, it got tight."

Moments of Dead craziness still abounded, of course. In Chicago Kreutzmann and Hart dressed up as doctors before they took the stage, with Donna Godchaux acting as a nurse, before the band played "Good Lovin'." ("I don't like this—what's going on?" Garcia said nervously before they started.) At the Palladium Hells Angels rode their hogs right into the band's dressing rooms, and one club member proudly brandished a knife and demanded they play "Truckin'." The bond between some of the Dead and the Angels remained amicable. Garcia was friendly with Sandy Alexander, who ran the club's New York City chapter, and their relationship nearly saved Garcia's life one night in the seventies. During a New York run an unhinged pimp sneaked into Garcia's hotel room and held a pistol on him; someone calling himself Garcia had been messing up some of the pimp's women. A rescue call went out to Alexander, who showed up with club members; before anyone could even remotely entertain the idea of calling the police, the Angels had located the imposter and brought him to the hotel, where he was dangled outside by his ankles. "I saw him once, when he was out the window," says one Dead employee. "They had to do what they had to do. Some things had to be dealt with."

Less burly guests also made it backstage at the Palladium. The Dead had befriended members of the *Saturday Night Live* cast, another group of nonconformist pop-culture rebels, and one night John Belushi appeared backstage, popping into Garcia's room to share some weed. Belushi also asked Cantor whether she wanted an impromptu tour of NBC right before she began taping the show. ("I said, 'I'm actually kind of busy right now, but thanks for the invite!'" she recalls.) *SNL* writers—and noted Deadheads—Al Franken and Tom Davis were also spotted wandering about; these would be far from their first or last Dead shows.

The Dead weren't quite mainstream, but something about them in 1977 felt almost acceptable to the nonconverts. When they arrived at the University of Alabama, marking their first-ever visit to a state not known for being friendly to long-hairs, the school's football team helped the Dead crew set up. "Female hospitality was wonderful," says Parish. "The girls on those tours in the South were incredible, man. Unbelievable. They were like sexual goddesses. They loved us, and we loved them." Most importantly Parish says of the band and crew, "We were still tight and had each other."

The Dead arrived at Raceway Park in a variety of physical and mental conditions, not all of them encouraging. Lesh was feeling better now that they'd returned to the road. "That fear had been assuaged," he says, but his life still felt out of sorts. He had started drinking more heavily and, tellingly, had married a woman he'd met in a bar. The post-hiatus Dead also rattled him in ways he couldn't ascertain. "When we came back after the break, it just was never the same, on some mysterious level," he says. "We hadn't evolved together. We'd evolved individually and separately. We had to get to know each other all over again, and, sadly, I don't think that ever really happened. We were all different people." Thanks to a daily breakfast consisting largely of beer, he'd put on an additional thirty pounds, and his vocal cords had strained, reducing his singing contributions to the band. "I lost my high notes, so I couldn't sing the high harmonies anymore," Lesh says. "Too much alcohol, advancing age. I don't know. Even after I quit they never came back."

For his part, Garcia rarely drank; one of the few times anyone saw him inebriated was on the Festival Express tour in 1970. But Garcia was increasingly besieged on numerous fronts, and his need to alleviate stress was growing. That year he endured a messy breakup with

Koons. (Inspired by Loren, Garcia had started carrying around a brief-case for his paperwork and, naturally, stash.) Garcia was also feeling guilty about the debacle of Grateful Dead Records and having not only brought Rakow into the fold but also stood up for him during the entire chaotic ride. It was as if he'd been entrusted to run the family but had let it run amuck.

To add to his workload, Garcia was also spending innumerable hours working on a movie built around footage shot at the semifarewell Winterland shows in 1974. Gary Gutierrez, a young animator who'd worked on public-television kids' shows like *Sesame Street* and *The Electric Company*, was hired and had begun working on the segments in the beginning of the movie. One idea, to feature Uncle Sam skeletons in time for the US Bicentennial in 1976, soon became outdated when the project stretched into the following year. The movie went way over budget, and Garcia, Loren, and promoter Scher came up with an idea to rent out movie theaters rather than work with an official distribu-tor and pay for expensive multiple prints. "We didn't have the money or inclination to do that," says Scher, "so we went to each of the big cities we knew were giant, found the best theaters, rented them out, and brought in a concert-level PA." When *The Grateful Dead Movie* made its long-overdue premiere at the Ziegfeld Theatre in Manhattan in June 1977, everyone dressed up: Donna Jean as Scarlett O'Hara, for instance. Deadheads who'd lined up around the block gave the band a standing ovation as they walked in and took their seats. At a hotel party after, Garcia played tic-tac-toe with Clive Davis, and a friend of the band watched as a female Deadhead barged in on Garcia and said, "Sign my arm!"

One of the few pieces of overt direction Garcia gave to Gutierrez was about the use of various bits of Dead imagery and iconography. "He said, 'We have a lot of artwork that expresses the idea of chance,'" Gutierrez says, "and he said he would like it to be about how, in life, things change directions this way or that way. He wanted to express the unpredictable randomness of life. I specifically remember him saying that." Even with a successful career as a rock star, Garcia's sense of fatalism had never deserted him.

The movie would be an invaluable document of the Dead onstage, but the workload, combined with everything he was juggling in his personal life, was proving to be too much for Garcia. Increasingly his affable, approachable image began working against him: anyone who needed a favor or a financial handout seemed to visit him backstage. "He had guys hounding him to do free shows," says Candelario. "They didn't come by to say, 'Hi, what's going on?' They came to tell him he needed to do a benefit concert or whatever. It was a hustle. He had all those kinds of things pounding on him. He wanted to be in that place where he could go in and turn the light off and just be quiet. Finally you can relax and take some time for yourself."

To reach that place, Garcia began turning to a strong Persian opiate that could be smoked rather than injected. Although some in the organization connected Garcia's alarming new habit to the fall of Grateful Dead Records, he had begun dabbling in heroin before that collapse. One Dead employee recalls seeing Garcia and one of the band's colleagues visit a brothel in 1974 so they could do heroin without any band interruptions; Parish first saw Garcia partake of the drug in the winter of 1975. "As far as I know, he started before the Rakow thing," says Lesh. "That was another reason I didn't think the band was going to start up again."

Sources differ as to who brought the drug into the Dead's camp: one recalls an outsider who would occasionally worked for their business. Garcia told Hart his connection was the son of an ambassador to a Middle Eastern country, who was using his diplomatic immunity to easily bring the drug into the states. For the time being, though, Garcia's habit wasn't debilitating, so it rarely set off alarm bells within the

Dead camp. Given the consistently brawny level of Garcia's playing and singing, especially in 1977, there was no reason for anyone to suspect anything was derailing. "In those days his music wasn't touched by any drugs in a negative way," says Parish. "He couldn't play or work enough in 1977. He was still functioning completely in those days." As Loren comments, "I'm just speculating, but I think it made him feel good, and when he felt good, he played well."

During a typical year band members would be home less than three months a year—a few days here and there before they were gone again on another leg of roadwork. By now Bill and Susila Kreutzmann's son, Justin, had grown accustomed to only seeing his father from time to time when he wasn't on the road. "He'd be home, and we'd have an attachment," says Justin, "and then he'd go away again, and that would be sad." Kreutzmann wanted his son to follow in his creative footsteps, to the point at which he bought Justin a Sonor drum kit for his bedroom. Justin wasn't all that interested—from an early age he was more intrigued with filmmaking than musicianship—and began noticing that, bit by bit, his drum kit would be missing a floor tom or cymbal. As it turned out, his father apparently needed them for his own drums, and Justin didn't seem to mind the missing pieces; the fact that his father had bought him a drum set to begin with was reaffirming enough of their bond.

Other members of the organization were dealing with loss in different ways. After more than five years Bob and Frankie's relationship was coming apart just as Garcia and Mountain Girl's had. Frankie was more than capable of standing up for herself, drinking and playing pool and poker along with any man on the scene. "I think she got bored," says Cagwin. "She called it the 'Marin Spin'—the same things that happen always keep happening." Frankie—and Weir as well—was turned off by the excessive drugging of some of the others in Kingfish. In the early months of 1976 Frankie moved out of her and Weir's Mill Valley home. "It wasn't a big dramatic scene," Kelly recalls. "It was all very calm, which was nice. I sensed they were both ready to go their own ways."

Sitting with her recording gear by the side of the stage each night, Cantor diligently recorded every gig on the 1977 tour. But she was also grieving over the loss of her husband. In September 1976 her partner, Rex Jackson, died after his car ran off the road near Mill Valley; he and Cantor had married in 1973 and had a son, Cole. (Donna Godchaux's "Sunrise" was partly inspired by Rex's memorial service.) The news was devastating to the community, and work became Cantor's outlet for coping with her grief. "I thought, 'I want to be here,'" she says of the road. "I was keeping busy. That's what saved my soul. Being creative kept me from getting depressed."

The band members in the worst physical shape, though, were Hart and Donna Godchaux. In an early morning in June Hart and his friend Rhonda Jensen, who'd come to live on his ranch with her sister Vicki at the end of the sixties, were returning from a concert to the nearby house of a friend in Half Moon Bay. Pulling up the dirt and gravel driveway, Hart punched the engine on his Porsche too hard, making the car swing out in the back. Because there was no guard rail, the car tumbled over the ravine next to the driveway, an incline so steep it was used for dumping trash. The car was caught in eucalyptus trees whose limbs looked like arms bent at the elbow, but the vehicle still slid down, and Hart was terribly bashed up. Climbing out of the wreck, Jensen told Hart not to move and ran to the house to tell everyone about the accident.

Firemen and police showed up soon, but some began debating how to rescue the car from its dangling tangle. "That's one of the Grateful Dead in there!" someone shouted in exasperation, snapping the emergency crew to attention. After the car was secured, Hart was pulled out and taken to a nearby hospital with a broken collarbone, smashed ribs, a broken arm, and other injuries; one of his ears was dangling by a piece of skin, causing a female friend visiting him to faint at the sight. The doctors didn't make any promises to visiting friends, but Brandelius told them proudly that her boyfriend was a "tough fucker." Making a rare trip to the hospital, Garcia looked at Hart and cracked, "You look like *shit!*" Hells Angels smuggled pot into Hart's room to ease the pain. Hart began a long, tedious physical rehab, which took six weeks and forced the cancellation of at least a few Dead shows just as *Terrapin Station* was about to be released in late July. The Dead's coffers still took a major hit.

Showing up at a band meeting at Fifth and Lincoln during this time, Donna Godchaux heard the band was planning to do a huge outdoor show in New Jersey. At first she balked for her own health-connected reasons. That summer she'd had an operation of her own and informed everyone it might be physically impossible for her to do the show: her stitches were still mending, and her doctor had warned her against even walking across the street. Garcia hung his head and said, "Well, I guess we just can't do it, because she sings on all the songs." With no arm twisting, Godchaux then changed her mind for the good of the band and began making arrangements to transport herself to Jersey by helicopter, limousine, and wheelchair; on site someone would have to physically carry her onto the stage and place her in a chair.

■ ◆ ▲

After opening sets by the New Riders of the Purple Sage and the Marshall Tucker Band, the Dead ambled onto the stage. They looked a bit older and chunkier than the last time fans had seen them; Kreutzmann now had wisps of gray sticking out of the side of his head. They also looked like they could have come from several different bands: Garcia's standard black T-shirt contrasted sharply with Weir's white slacks and aviator glasses. Half of the band looked as if they were conceding to the fashion trends of the seventies, and the other half seemed to be actively rebelling against them.

The show was adequate but not nearly as momentous as those that came right before and after that year. Self-conscious about his injury, Hart felt as if everyone in the crowd was watching him and his recovering shoulder. With the band's blessing, he played lighter than usual so he could cruise through the set. In his usual way he overdid it, and his shoulder began to ache. As often happened, Donna Godchaux couldn't hear very well and was further hampered by her own surgery, relegated to a chair near Lesh during most of the show. "It was like an out-patient clinic on stage," says Hart. "We weren't in the groove. We were stale. But we made it through. We did the best we could under the circumstances."

The circumstances around *Terrapin Station* were similarly wobbly. Despite its radio-friendly aura, the album wasn't proving to be the breakout hit everyone had hoped. Deadheads were deeply divided about the record, which only clawed its way to number twenty-eight on the *Billboard* album chart. Despite all the work put into it and its groundbreaking title suite, *Terrapin Station* became their lowest-charting album since 1970.

Yet the number of people who'd driven, walked, and shimmied their way between boxcars at Raceway Park told another story. When Scher double-checked the box office, he discovered they'd sold a staggering 102,000 tickets, more than double his estimate. The Dead had played before oceans of people before, at Woodstock and, in 1973, at Watkins Glen, the New York festival at which about 600,000 people showed up to hear them, the Allman Brothers Band, and the Band. Yet those were multi-act festivals, whereas Raceway Park was a Dead show (with two opening acts). The show was the most vivid demonstration yet that the Dead weren't just a large cult band but rather a phenomenon that couldn't be denied. "It said, 'We're a big band,'" Loren says. "It said, 'Yeah, the Allman Brothers, they're big, but they're not the Grateful Dead.' A lot of the industry stood up and said, '100,000 people at a Dead show—that's unbelievable!' And these weren't repeat [customers]—it was only for one show, not four. It wasn't the same people going over and over. And they didn't come to see Marshall Tucker." By then Deadheads were beginning to snap up tickets to multiple shows in the same cities, a development largely new to rock 'n' roll. Why would anyone want to see a band two nights in a row? It made little sense to those outside the community, but Deadheads knew how much the sets could change, even how the lengths of certain *songs* could vary show to show.

After the encore, an eleven-minute run-through of "Terrapin Station Part 1," they couldn't wait to return to their air-conditioned Manhattan hotel rooms. But everyone came away with one clear lesson: they could dismantle the band for a while. They could return, as they had the year before, without a new studio album to promote. They could make an album that would leave the fans ambivalent. They could force their fans to walk miles in the heat and then wait hours in the body-fluid-depleting sun to see them play. And when they did perform, as at Raceway Park, they could do it with two of their members physically incapacitated, hampering the music along the way.

Onstage and off, they could screw up as much as they wanted, yet none of it seemed to matter. The fans still adored them and would cut them enormous amounts of slack merely for the opportunity to see them play. The experience, the gathering, was as much the point as the performance. Just after Raceway Park Arista ran an ad in *Rolling Stone* with photos from the show and the copy, "A New Dead Era Is Upon Us." Even if they didn't realize it at the time, the era arrived with many new lessons.

*Unplugged at Radio City Music Hall in
New York, with Brent Mydland, far right.*
© BOB MINKIN

CHAPTER 10

NEW YORK CITY, OCTOBER 31, 1980

Even the union workers agreed: part of the wall had to go. After all, the Dead had a slew of shows about to begin, and their damn recording consoles had to be installed. If it meant a portion of a stairwell had to be removed—in a building that had just been given landmark status by the city of New York—so be it. On the occasion of the Dead's fifteenth anniversary, nothing and no one could stand in their way, not even Radio City Music Hall.

Just over a week before, the load-in had begun for the Dead's eight-night stand at the six-thousand-seat venue. On many levels the sight would have been unimaginable several years before. The venerable midtown building had opened its doors nearly fifty years before, in 1932, and by 1980 any tourist who came through the city seemed to be legally required to attend Radio City Music Hall's Christmas and Easter shows with the Rockettes or see one of the family-themed movies it hosted. But by the late seventies, with New York City in fiscal freefall, Radio City's future was suddenly shaky; movie attendance dropped, and plans to convert it into an office building or parking lot loomed.

Thankfully the interior of the building was granted landmark status in 1978, and its famed art-deco lobby and other interior design elements were refreshed for $5 million. During talks to save the building the idea of booking pop acts came up, and by the fall of 1980 Radio City Music Hall had presented one major pop star, Linda Ronstadt. Now it would host an entirely different kind of beast, the Grateful Dead, who were about to settle in for eight nights, October 22 to 31 (with the nights of October 24 and 28 off).

The band's clout became evident right away, when Deadheads converged upon Rockefeller Center, some camping out, and snapped up almost thirty-six thousand tickets priced between $12.50 and $15.00. In an ambitious move that recalled the special screenings of *The Grateful Dead Movie*, the last night, Halloween, would be broadcast live by a closed-circuit feed to fourteen movie theaters around the country; in addition, all the anniversary shows, both at Radio City and preceding ones at the Warfield in San Francisco, would be recorded for a live album or two. The entire undertaking felt like an event, especially when word trickled out that the band would be playing its first acoustic set in a decade, complete with their fairly new keyboard player.

To accommodate the recording the Dead needed two hefty Neve recording consoles, one rented and the other shipped out from their Front Street home base. Both had to be hauled up a flight of stairs to reach Plaza Sound, the studio that sat atop Radio City (and where punk bands like Blondie and the Ramones had recorded). The Dead's office had sent paperwork ahead of time to make sure the consoles would be able to make it into the building, but when the time came to install them, a problem arose: the consoles couldn't quite clear the stairwell. After some head-scratching, one of the union workers at the venue, with Hart's urging, said, "Oh, fuck it—we've gotta get this thing up here." With that they grabbed a sledgehammer and took down a few inches of the stairwell wall.

Promoter John Scher had no idea the "renovation" was happening until he heard from Betty Cantor, who would be recording the shows, and the thought of physical damage to the interior of a New York landmark rattled even Scher, who thought he'd seen it all with the Dead. "I remember Betty telling me after they'd already done it, after the fact," Scher says. "I was basically shitting in my pants until the shows were over." It wouldn't be the first time the Dead would encounter some pushback in their career, but this victory was significant. "I had no second thoughts about that," says Hart. "It was the thing to do. Nothing stops the Grateful Dead. Onward into the fog." They'd already made it to fifteen years despite adversity, busts, deaths, and fallow periods, and no one was about to let a bit of concrete stand in their way.

By then the bright memories of 1977 were starting to dim. Beginning the following year, the self-control and efficiency that had marked the previous year was beginning to slip out of the Dead's grasp, and the grind of touring was starting to wear them down. "When I first came along people were doing a little bit of everything," says Courtenay Pollock, the tie-dye artist now fully immersed in the Dead world on and off the road. "But with the demands of these tours, people started jacking themselves to keep up the pace."

Culturally the Dead were also now out of sorts. Thanks to the rise of punk rock and disco, the Dead, although only in their thirties, were now ensnared in what amounted to a sixties backlash; anything that even vaguely reeked of patchouli oil and weed was newly reviled or mocked. Even the country's hip, Dylan-quoting president, Jimmy Carter—who'd been elected in 1976, the same year the Dead returned to the road—was beginning to stumble. In the next election, a month after the Radio City Music Hall shows would wrap up, the country would embrace Ronald Reagan, a symbolic gesture of political and cultural change.

Eager to simplify themselves—and rejecting a return to the buffed sonics of *Terrapin Station*—the Dead hired Lowell George of Little Feat to produce their next album. The hookup sounded ideal: George had his feet planted firmly in American roots music, and the band could relate to him (and his funky, cutting-razor slide guitar) more than they could Keith Olsen. For extra comfort, the sessions wouldn't be held in Los Angeles but at Front Street, the Dead's warehouse in San Rafael. Although the band had been renting it for a few years, Garcia had used Front Street the previous year to record his Jerry Garcia Band (or JGB) album *Cats Under the Stars*. Maria Muldaur, the sexy-voiced former jug-band singer who'd had a hit with "Midnight at the Oasis" in 1974, sang on several tracks on the album, thanks to her relationship with John Kahn, Garcia's buddy and favorite non-Dead bass player. "Jerry and John were like spiritual brothers," says Muldaur. "It was musical, and it was something beyond that. Jerry respected John and the knowledge he had of other kinds of music. He liked his sensibility. They had this intuitive connection."

Kahn and Muldaur had been a couple since 1974, and now, years later, Muldaur was witnessing the craziness at Front Street for herself: recording sessions that started after midnight and were fueled by coke and wine. (Because she had a young daughter and woke up early each day, Muldaur took to carting along an espresso machine to help keep her awake late at night: "I called it Italian cocaine.") Yet Garcia's side band, which had started in 1975 during the Dead's hiatus and was now more or less known as the Jerry Garcia Band, was by now a legitimate and flourishing concern. With players that included Kahn, Elvis drummer Ron Tutt, and Keith and Donna Godchaux, with others to follow, the JGB allowed Garcia to revel in different rhythms and repertoire than the Dead. (*Don't Let Go*, a live album recorded in 1976 but released much later, was a prime example of the group's loose, funky Marin swing.) The sessions at Front Street for what would be Garcia's fourth studio solo album were especially productive. From Garcia's biting guitar on the pumped "Rhapsody in Red" to the enchanting story-song "Rubin and Cherise," about a love triangle set in New Orleans, the album featured some of Garcia's best outside-Dead work, and he would be justly proud of it for years after. Its lack of commercial success would also be devastating to him.

Months later at the same place, work on the Dead's new album, *Shakedown Street*, would prove far less satisfying. It was George's idea to tape the band at their rehearsal space, and with him they finally recorded "Good Lovin'," one of Pigpen's showcases, now with Weir singing lead. George did return the band to its dance-band roots with a modern twist; the title song leapt into a disco pool even more so than their cover of "Dancin' in the Streets" on *Terrapin Station*, and Weir and Barlow's "I Need a Miracle" roared in ways the Dead hadn't done in the studio before. With his white overalls, genial manner, and love of American music, George was seemingly a natural match for them. But the material was patchy, and the party atmosphere at Club Front wasn't helping; George was no stranger to cocaine, and he and some of the band members (and crew) indulged themselves regularly. "A lovely guy, but he was screaming on coke the whole time," says Hart. "He was killing himself. And, again, it was a desperation move. Nobody in their right mind would want to be the producer of the Grateful Dead. It's a death sentence. No one can handle that. They always crack up."

After school Justin Kreutzmann would show up to watch his dad work and, he says, "Everyone would still be up from the night before. Everyone was so unhealthy and the combination of Lowell and the Dead wasn't doing anyone any good." Weir invited his old friend and former Kingfish partner Matthew Kelly to play harmonica on "I Need a Miracle"; when Kelly showed up, George immediately lectured him. "Lowell came up to me and said, 'I don't allow any drugs at my recording sessions,'" says Kelly. "Which was ironic and somewhat hypocritical. Everyone was using them."

In the midst of that work one of their grandest adventures was taking shape. Thanks largely to their manager and booker, Richard Loren, they would be heading for Egypt for three nights of concerts in September 1978. The trip involved all manner of paperwork and diplomatic massaging, including trips by Loren, Lesh, and Alan Trist (now a longtime band employee) to Egypt and Washington, DC. Eventually they arranged it so the trip would be a fundraiser for two Egyptian charities (as opposed to a State Department–sanctioned trip that might raise eyebrows), and their dream of playing their most celestial music at the foot of the Pyramids became a reality.

In typically untidy Dead style they almost didn't make the trip. To raise additional funds (in part to help pay for all the friends and family who'd be joining them), they played a show at Giants Stadium in the New Jersey Meadowlands area outside of Manhattan. Because *Shakedown Street* wasn't completely finished (George had to leave the drawn-out sessions to return to his band and upcoming solo album), a few of them flew back to Front Street after the show for last-minute tweaks. Before anyone knew it, the whole band was back. "It was, 'Well, if *he's* coming back to fix this part, then *I'm* coming back too,'" says a Dead employee of the time. "They all snuck back." As a result, office worker Sue Stephens had to hustle and buy last-minute tickets from San Francisco to Egypt and make sure the band made it to the airport on time. By then a first plane, filled with Mountain Girl and various Merry Pranksters like Kesey and Ken Babbs, had already arrived.

Though it was bound to be an historic expedition, the Dead arrived in Egypt in various states of disrepair. Kreutzmann had broken his wrist beforehand. Garcia was suffering from withdrawal from heroin. Their regular piano tuner refused to join them after he felt one of the crew dissed him. "That put a kibosh on the show right there," says

Candelario. "The piano was out of tune. We had some other synthesizers and things, but not the nine-foot Yamaha Keith was used to, and he was bummed about it. That set the whole domino thing up." To kill all the mosquitoes and bugs in the air, trucks were spraying DDT all around their hotel, the Mena House in Cairo.

During the days leading up to their three shows at the Pyramids, everyone in the Dead caravan immersed themselves in the country and its culture: riding camels and horses, sampling the hashish openly sold on the streets, and visiting the King's Chamber high up in the Great Pyramid. (With its dusty, freewheeling ambience, the country was almost like an oversized version of Hart's Novato ranch during its heyday.) Healy and Owsley tried to create an echo chamber in the Pyramids. On the third night of performances, the Dead played during a full eclipse, with the moon and the nearby Sphinx scorching the sky. "That third night we brought the Egyptians down off the dunes in front of the stage," Hart says. "They parked camels and slowly started coming down." For most but not all of them the trip ended with a boat ride down the Nile, both to see the sights and to keep the band away from the Nubian porters who were trying to give them pure opiates.

Sadly the music was the least of it. Revealing their oncoming fatigue as well as their various ailments, the Dead played largely perfunctory sets. The shows were so unexceptional that Garcia would nix the release of a live album meant to pay off expenses. (It would eventually be released, but years after Garcia's death.) Egypt wouldn't be their first time messing up a high-profile event. They hadn't played all that well at the Monterey International Pop Festival in 1967; at Woodstock two years later, rain, technical delays, and hundreds of thousands of eyeballs watching them spooked them enough to result in a choppy performance. In the recording truck outside the Great Pyramid, which had been pulled in through the sand by truck, Betty Cantor was taping the shows as always, but, something felt off. "I thought, 'This seems typical,'" she says. "It was one of those things, one of those very big shows, like Woodstock, when they didn't play well. All the big ones, they would screw up. It would always baffle me." The erratic shows in Egypt, though, were indicative of something more ominous: the mighty Dead were once again starting to swerve a bit off course. In late 1979 the band pulled into New York's Madison Square Garden for three shows. On the first night a friend of the band laid out some positive-energy crystals onstage. At a previous show the crew had spoken to the friend about it, saying they appreciated the gesture but worried that the more light was added, the more darkness would be attracted. Sure enough, on the second night at the Garden a death threat was called in. The crew seemingly knew of what it spoke.

Tom Davis had an answer when someone at Radio City asked about the sketch with the LSD-dosed urine. "What are you guys afraid of, a little wee-wee?"

Before part of the wall in the Radio City stairwell came down, another issue had to be resolved about the live broadcast of the Halloween show: the matter of two forty-minute breaks. To fill up that time, and to the event producers (Loren and Scher) and director (Len Dell'Amico, who worked at Scher's Capitol Theater in Jersey), the answer was obvious: skits featuring Davis and his *Saturday Night Live* partner, Al Franken.

The bond between the Dead and *SNL* continued to be unbreakable. The Dead were frequent visitors to the Blues Bar, the scuzzy downtown hang-out run by Dan Aykroyd and John Belushi, and Belushi and Kreutzmann particularly hit it off. "It was a brotherhood of madmen," says Parish of the Dead and *SNL* bond. "We looked in each other's eyes, and we knew." During the *Terrapin Station* sessions Olsen watched as Belushi visited some later New York overdubbing sessions;

the comic performed a few cartwheels in the studio, hung out, then passed out. "He drank everything he could and took everything and then passed out in front of the console," Olsen says. "Everyone said, 'Don't bother him—let him be.'"

As writers and performers, the tall, gawky Davis and the short, frizzy-haired Franken couldn't have been more ideal for the assignment at Radio City. They shared a dark, cynical sense of humor with the Dead (among the rightly revered *SNL* skits they'd written were Aykroyd's Julia Child–bloodbath bit and Bill Murray's "Nick the Lounge Singer"), and both were Deadheads: Davis in particular had been to many shows starting in the early seventies. Thanks to him, the Dead had appeared twice on *SNL*, first in 1978 and then 1980. (According to Davis's memoir, producer Lorne Michaels was unsure about presenting the Dead the first time, and then-bandleader G. E. Smith told Davis the Dead were "not happening" at the time.) When Parish ejected Franken and Davis from one backstage area at a Dead gig, they turned the encounter and humiliation into an *SNL* skit, with Belushi playing "Parish." To kill time between sets, what better than skits along those lines? "If it hadn't been for Franken and Davis," says Rock Scully of the plans for Radio City, "I doubt the Dead would have done it."

The anniversary shows would officially kick off with a long run of gigs at the Warfield, and Franken and Davis flew in from New York to tape segments in advance, letting the Warfield stand in for Radio City. The duo's knowledge of the Dead and its music as well as the musicians' willingness to goof on themselves couldn't have made a better match. "Jerry's Kids" lampooned Jerry Lewis's muscular dystrophy telethons but with acid casualties; a pretend dressing-room visit by Franken and Davis allowed Weir to mock his fondness for his hair and blow dryers. Holding a microphone, Davis walked into the men's room at the Warfield to see whether people were "doing drugs," barged into a stall, and found one stoner, played by soundman Healy, who threw up (barley soup substituted for actual vomit). Other skits were rampant with drug and penis jokes, and Garcia mocked his own physical deformity by holding a box that contained his finger. "They made fun of themselves whenever that opportunity came up," says Dell'Amico of the process of sketch writing for the show. "They'd say, 'Go for that.'"

The skits pretaped at the Warfield were uniformly riotous, but someone at the Rockefeller Corporation, which owned Radio City Music Hall, wasn't so taken. Sue Stephens found herself frantically retyping scripts at the last minute with minor but telling changes. On the grand Radio City stage one day Dell'Amico and Franken were deep into rehearsal for a skit in which Franken, in thousands of dollars worth of makeup, would be impersonating former Secretary of State Henry Kissinger. With Kreutzmann joining in, Davis would "bust" the faux "Kissinger" for secretly taping the shows.

While they were practicing, "a phalanx of four men in black suits and carrying briefcases" watched by the side, according to Dell'Amico. The director was told to stop filming because the men—Radio City lawyers who supposedly represented the Rockefeller family—wanted to shut down the skit. As it turned out, Kissinger and Nelson Rockefeller were old friends. "I said, 'They can fuck off,'" Dell'Amico says. "And that was that. I think they looked at the paperwork and said, 'They're right, they're renting this room.' If you're working for the Dead, you've got muscle because of the money coming in the door." As Dell'Amico predicted, the skit aired in its entirety.

Early in the months of 1979, when the thought of playing Radio City was merely a pipedream, Kreutzmann and his son Justin, then nine, walked into the lobby of Club Front. Because the space had become a communal hangout, it wasn't unusual to bump into other band members there, and today it would be Keith Godchaux—bidding farewell.

"It's been nice playing with you," Godchaux said with a friendly, zero-hostility smile, and he and Kreutzmann shook hands. A few days later the Kreutzmanns returned to Club Front and, in nearly the same spot, met Godchaux's replacement, whose youth (he was twenty-six), shoulder-length hair, and beard made him look as much like a Deadhead as a fellow musician.

One night Godchaux asked a friend of the band to take him for a ride to a suspicious part of town. "Are you talking white or brown?" she asked him, meaning cocaine or heroin, and he was caught off guard: "Whoa, how did you know?" he replied. By the time of the Egypt escapade Godchaux's drug abuse and his and his wife's on-the-road difficulties were among the band's worst-kept secrets. Never the band's most thunderous player or most forceful personality in the band, Godchaux seemed to recede even further into the background as his addiction took over. (He would sometimes have a bottle of Pepto-Bismol on his piano to ease his nerves.) His zoned-out demeanor during the making of *Terrapin Station* barely changed as they recorded *Shakedown Street*; during the final stages of recording John Kahn wound up playing some of the keyboard parts himself.

Always more outspoken and opinionated than her generally subdued husband, Donna began confronting Keith about his hard-drug use; combined with the stress of trying to raise a young son, Zion, on the road, the couple was coming undone. Tales of their screaming matches backstage and a notorious car smashup outside Club Front were commonplace. During the Egypt trip Nicki Scully, Rock's wife, had to talk Donna down during a meltdown over one issue or another. During a Jerry Garcia Band tour in 1978 to promote *Cats Under the Stars*, Maria Muldaur would try to stand in between the couple onstage so Donna wouldn't be able to see when Keith would briefly stop playing and give his wife two middle fingers at once, which would often make Donna burst into tears. "Keith and I, we were wasted," Donna told *Rolling*

Stone in 2014. "We were exhausted. And the band was exhausted with us. Keith and I would be getting along, but then I'd be mad at him. All that kind of stuff in the mix. It was just a constant struggle because we needed to be a family and we were on the road all the time."

At a group meeting at the Godchaux's house in 1979 everyone came to a mutual decision: it was time for the couple to leave. "It was a relief, in a way," Donna said in 2014. "It was sad in another way. But it was what needed to happen. It was turning into being not profitable for anybody, and we needed to go, and they needed for us to go." According to a source in the Dead camp, the band had already begun auditioning replacements for Keith by then, but one in particular sprang to the head of the line. For his own Bob Weir Band, Weir had hired Brent Mydland, a young but experienced singer and keyboard player. Given the LA-pop feel of Weir's *Heaven Help the Fool*, Mydland was a natural for a band designed to promote the album. He'd already worked with two groups, Batdorf & Rodney and Silver, that were both far more soft-pop than the Dead would ever be.

In Mydland the Dead found themselves with another talented but hypersensitive keyboard player. Born in Munich on October 21, 1952, Mydland shared a military-family background with his first boss, Weir: his father, Didrick Mydland, hailed from Norway, moved to the States to attend Trinity Divinity School in Minneapolis, and later joined the army, where he served as a chaplain. Brent was born during one of Didrick's overseas duties. Once the family moved west when he was a baby, Brent was brought up in Concord, California; during one part-time job arranged by his father, he helped load bombs at a nearby military base.

In 1974 Mydland traveled down to Los Angeles to audition for a slot in the backup band for Batdorf & Rodney, the singer-songwriter duo best known for their cult FM hit "Home Again." According to John Batdorf, the twenty-three-year-old Mydland who showed up had a "monster singing voice," an affinity for jazz and blues, and one of the most intense stares Batdorf had ever seen. "Brent had those eyes," Batdorf says. "Some guys close their eyes when they sing, but his were open. He was a pretty scary-looking guy hitting all those high notes." Batdorf says the band would kid Mydland for that trait, but they soon learned they could take any ribbing only so far. During one sound check Batdorf sat down at Mydland's organ and began playing, and Mydland grew visibly upset. "We said, 'We're just having fun,'" Batdorf says. "We had to talk him down. You had to be careful what you said or he'd go into a shell. It was very odd. We had to walk on eggshells sometimes." When Batdorf & Rodney broke up, Mydland joined Batdorf's subsequent band, Silver, which cut an album for Arista that included a few of Mydland's songs.

During the Batdorf & Rodney era Mydland met Cherie Barsin, whose sister was married to Batdorf. In no time she and Mydland—then living in a van in Thousand Oaks complete with silverware, pots, and pans—coupled up. Silver's debut album was released on Arista in 1976—the same year the Dead signed with the label—but when it sold poorly, they were dropped, the band fell apart, and Mydland and Barsin moved north to a house in Concord owned by Mydland's father. Barsin recalls seeing Mydland butt heads with his dad and grow uncomfortable when he saw him drinking. At his own home Mydland preferred to write songs, listen to jazz and classical records, and play board games like Solitude and backgammon.

The call to join the Weir band came out of the blue, and Mydland quickly landed the job. At a party for Garcia's birthday in August 1978 Mydland and Barsin were invited along to meet the Dead at the house Garcia was now sharing with Rock and Nicki Scully, and Mydland and Barsin watched as everyone hung out and played guitars. Eventually Garcia emerged from his basement apartment and made Barsin feel immediately at ease by talking to her. A few months later the couple were invited to see the Dead's New Year's Eve show at Winterland, where they were told Keith Godchaux was going to leave the band. (Apparently the departure was already on the band's mind several months before the meeting with the Godchauxs.) Not long after, Mydland was invited to join the Dead.

In light of his musical preferences and background Mydland didn't seem the obvious choice. Batdorf found it interesting that Mydland, who valued rehearsal and precision, would join the far looser Dead, and Barsin has no memory of ever hearing Dead music played in their home prior to his being hired. (His preferences, she says, were "Chick Corea, Jeff Beck. Nothing with lyrics.") But the Dead needed a new keyboard player and a rebooted, post-Godchaux sound as soon as possible to continue touring, and Mydland needed a job. "His personality didn't fit in, but they all accepted him," says Janice Godchalk-Olsen. "The transition didn't seem to be much of a debate."

In April 1979, two months after the band meeting at the Godchaux's home, Mydland made his stage debut with the Dead at Spartan Stadium in San Jose. As soon as he joined, his predecessor came back to haunt him. "People would yell out 'Keith!' and that would piss him off," Barsin says. "He would say, 'Are they high, or am I just not that good?'" Yet Mydland's devotion to the job was instantly evident to those around him. "He put a lot of pressure on himself to be perfect," Barsin says. "There were jokes about it, like, 'How do you screw up with the Grateful Dead? Everybody's high and nobody's going to know.' But he was hard on himself. He didn't want to be a joke. If he could enhance what they did, that was important to him." Upon landing the job Mydland immediately went shopping for a fresh batch of hole-free T-shirts, and during one camping trip with friends Mydland, who'd grown up water skiing in the Delta area of Northern California, opted out; he didn't want to risk hurting his hands. The anxiety attacks he'd had as far back as the Batdorf & Rodney days—when Mydland would complain of chest pains or sometimes mysteriously disappear for days, what was known as "The Brent Special"—were at bay for now.

Coming after a period in which Keith Godchaux barely seemed to be playing onstage, Mydland injected the band with musical caffeine. His synthesizers and B-3 organ added upgraded textures to their sound, and his singing bolstered the harmonies, especially now that Garcia's and Lesh's voices were beginning to fray. When the time came for the Dead to make their first album with him, Mydland stepped up, writing two songs, "Easy to Love You" and "Far from Me," the former with lyrics by Barlow. "Easy to Love You" was such a straight-on love song that Arista's Clive Davis wasn't sure how it fit in on a Dead album (and rightly so), and as Barlow recalls, Davis asked them to revise a few lines to "make it sound more like the Grateful Dead." (Puzzled, Barlow tweaked a few words here and there to make what was once a straight-forward love song sound like what he calls "a bit more obscure.")

The jolt Mydland could bring to the band was heard when his organ revved up in the chorus on "Alabama Getaway," the Hunter-Garcia romp that became the first track on the new album, *Go to Heaven*. (Performing the song on *Saturday Night Live* after the album's release, the Dead came to life as rarely before on television, and Garcia spit out his Chuck Berry–derived solos with evident glee.) Thanks to producer Gary Lyons, who'd worked with the likes of Aerosmith and Foreigner prior to the Dead, the album was the most studio-tooled record the band would ever make. Not surprisingly, the Dead didn't adapt easily to that approach. Once, Lyons spliced a bunch of different Garcia guitar solos into one, thinking it would be a natural fit. When Garcia heard it, he demurred, "It's nice, but I wouldn't play it that way." Weir and Barlow's songs, "Lost Sailor" and "Saint of Circumstance," were moody companion pieces that blended soft rock and fusion as well as the Dead could, and the chugging remake of "Don't Ease Me In," from their early repertoire, had a jovial bounce. "Althea" made good use of the Dead's trademark shuffle. But the album's generic corporate-rock sound made the Dead, one of rock's most distinctive bands, sound strangely anonymous. Only when Garcia's voice and guitar slipped out into the forefront did the band sound like their old selves, and fans were put off by the cover photo of the band dressed in *Saturday Night Fever*–themed white suits. (The humor of the photo, or the fact that Garcia and Hart had gone together to see that movie, eluded them.) "As things got bigger and larger, the stakes went up," says Hart of this era, "and we stopped exploring so much."

According to Barsin, Mydland had long felt a sense of isolation: growing up in the Delta, he lived in a boathouse on the water while his parents and sisters resided in the main home. He once told Barsin he was haunted by a memory of not receiving an Easter basket as a child, even though his sisters had been given them. Now that he was in the Dead, though, he was no longer alone. Old friends who'd played with him in high school bands began reaching out to him, and a salesman at a local musical instrument store heard he was in the Dead and slashed the price, from $8,000 to $4,000, of a baby grand piano that Mydland was eying. Yet there were early signs that Mydland could be beset by it all. At a party at one Dead show Bill Graham had a Native American tent set up backstage. Everyone congregated inside it, and both Dead family members and outsiders approached the generally shy Mydland. "He seemed almost catatonic at times," Barsin says, "overwhelmed all of a sudden with the recognition." He would have to learn, sooner rather than later, how to handle it all.

◆ ◆ ◆

There would be more wee-wee to come. During the Radio City run, one of the Dead offspring was summoned into either a hotel room or backstage space. The almost-teenager thought something was wrong but was instead asked to urinate into some small plastic tips. From what the kid was told, the band had to take some type of drug test to satisfy the insurance requirements of the closed-circuit broadcast of the Halloween show. "God knows what they thought they were going to find, but someone thought it would be a good idea if I did the urine test," says the now-grownup. "I peed into the cups and thought, 'They're *never* going to believe this is us.'" (Director Dell'Amico, who doesn't recall the specifics of the story, says he can think of one instance in which a drug test might have been requested for those shows: "We could have realized we didn't have enough insurance or an insurer could have asked for it. That's how it could have happened.")

The story, or tall tale, was pretty amusing, but other, chillier winds were beginning to blow in the Dead's direction. At Radio City, members of the crew heard that a suspected dealer may have slipped backstage—through no one's precise fault—and reportedly pummeled him. The story was indicative of everyone's growing concern about Garcia's increasing fondness for what Loren calls "basically speedballing. You do cocaine and then you smoke that stuff, [called] rat. It's like a speedball." By 1980, as opposed to 1977, everyone knew Garcia was dabbling in the Persian opiate. It was not hard to notice: his hair was longer and stringier (and sometimes downright weirder, as when he wore it in pigtails during one of the shows in Egypt). More troubling was the impact of his addiction on the band's music. Garcia's voice was starting to sound strained, and during the *Go to Heaven* sessions he was spending more time than before in the studio bathroom. The usual reasons were trotted out: the pressures of celebrity, fallout from the Rakow debacle, his messy personal life. To others it may simply have been boredom. Driving home from a studio one evening with Vicki Jensen, Garcia gazed out the window and talked about how many of his good times were over. "He said, 'There's nothing fun to do anymore,'" she says. "All the things everyone was doing weren't happening anymore, like Playland [which closed in 1972] or free shows in the park. That stuck with me when he said that."

Even those who'd escaped the scene were still affected. After their departure from the Dead, Keith and Donna Godchaux moved back to

Alabama, where Donna had been born and raised, and they worked on cleaning themselves up after the previous eight years. They chilled by the Tennessee River, Keith began to relax, and the two formed the Heart of Gold Band, named after a line in "Scarlet Begonias." On a late July morning in 1980 Keith Godchaux and Pollock were driving back to Courtenay Pollock's house in San Geronimo, where the Godchauxs were staying while working on new music. To Pollock, Godchaux seemed at peace: "I've never been happy with my body," he told Pollock, "but right at this moment I'm the happiest I've ever felt in my life." Taking a longer route home so they could continue talking, their car came around a bend, and Pollock, who was driving, saw a rock truck in his lane and a propane tanker easing out of a driveway. On the other side of the road were kids playing ball. "There was nowhere to go, and I had a moment to make a decision," Pollock says. "There were trees on my right and all this blockage on the road."

Pollock heard Godchaux say, "Oh, Jesus," before the car slammed into the back of the rock truck. Pollock was seriously injured and on life support for several days but recovered; Godchaux never regained consciousness from his coma and was pronounced dead on July 23.

By the first night at Radio City, October 22, the nerves of the theater's owners were frayed. Deadheads had lined up around the block to buy tickets, preventing some Rockefeller Center employees from getting into the buildings. A minor stampede occurred when the ticket window opened. "The fans surrounded the place and took over," says Dell'Amico, who was observing from the sidelines. "They're doing drugs on the street. Management was freaking out."

The Rockefeller Corporation decided to retaliate. By way of Loren and Scher, they ordered the band to stop selling a commemorative poster for the event. The move took everyone aback: no one had thought the artwork would be a problem. Dennis Larkins, Bill Graham's stage designer and art director, had been assigned the task of illustrating a poster for the run of shows at the Warfield. He and Peter Barsotti, one of Graham's right-hand men, settled on featuring "Sam and Samantha," the iconic Dead male-and-female skeletons. The poster, which showed the skeletons leaning up against an illustration of the Warfield, was so well received that Larkins was told to design a similar one for the Radio City run. From "Sam" wearing an Uncle Sam top hat to the use of the skull-and-lightning "Steal Your Face" logo on the building, the poster was clever and witty, and the Dead signed off on it with no hesitation. "The figures weren't intended to be threatening, more like benevolent guardians," says Larkins. "They weren't intended to imply the death of *anything*. It was Dead iconography."

According to Rockefeller executives, though, no one cleared the illustration with them, and the corporation, possibly also irked by the Dead's wrangling over production costs, struck back. Interpreting the skeletons as a death wish for the hall and claiming the facade was a copyrighted logo, the corporation insisted the poster "suggests the Music Hall's impending death and is unpatriotic." The Dead, rarely accustomed to pushback at this point in their career, were stunned. "Here we are, saving Radio City Music Hall from its demise," says Loren, "and they're suing us for doing it." (Strangely, the slight damage inflicted on the interior stairwell wasn't brought up, probably since the Dead had warned the Hall owners about the specifications of the recording console.)

After initially demanding the entire run of shows be canceled outright, Radio City allowed the Dead to simply stop the sale of the posters at the venue and have the entire print run destroyed. The music, though, would proceed—but without yet another big-showcase glitch. Gathering onstage with their acoustic and percussive instruments for the final night at Radio City, with an audience at movie theaters from

Florida to Chicago watching them, they couldn't start: something was wrong with Lesh's bass. He would pluck, adjust, and start playing again, and still it didn't sound right. Finally Garcia said, "We're gonna start out with a little instrumental that doesn't involve Phil," and they launched into a vocal-less version of the title song of Weir's *Heaven Help the Fool* album. Lesh wouldn't fully join the rest until several songs into the set.

Backstage at the Warfield, before the first acoustic-set run-through at that venue, Dell'Amico witnessed band members wandering into Garcia's dressing room and expressing wariness about playing without electricity for the first time in so long. "It seemed like everybody was skeptical about the acoustic thing—they all thought it was crazy," says the director. "'Why are we doing this?' But it's something Jerry wanted to do, and he was laughing." (An Angel sitting somberly in the room also approached Garcia and passed along a greeting from Sandy Alexander.)

Judging from the technical snafu at Radio City, maybe they had a right to be worried, but in the end the acoustic segment, only eight songs long, was charming and lovely; the arrangements lent "It Must Have Been the Roses" (a bittersweet ballad that had first appeared on Garcia's 1976 solo album, *Reflections*, and had become a staple of the Dead's repertoire) and "Ripple" an autumnal feel not heard in previous performances of those songs. "Cassidy" recaptured the strumming gallop of the version on Weir's *Ace*. The plugged-in portion of the night started with "Jack Straw" and wound up with a mesmerizing electric version of "Uncle John's Band"; Mydland's vocal contributions, the way he returned the band to its three-male-voice harmonies of the *Workingman's Dead* era, were particularly evident on those two songs.

During the third set out came the concert segment that came to be called Drums. Percussion interludes had become a part of the concert ritual since 1968: sometimes during "Caution (Do Not Stop on Tracks)," during the start of "The Other One," or after "Truckin'." By the spring of 1978 Kreutzmann and Hart were given a percussion-bonanza segment all their own; by year's end it would often segue into Space. (The latter wouldn't have a name until *Dead Set*, the two-LP live album from the electric part of the Radio City and Warfield shows, was released in 1981; *Reckoning*, the unplugged companion album, came out first.) The back-and-forth interplay between Kreutzmann and Hart during Drums, which also included a battery of percussion instruments, could be captivating, and Space would present the Dead at its wildest, most free-form and spaciest, Garcia's guitar venturing into uncharted free-form territory in ways that recalled their early Acid Test shows. With those segments, Dead shows acquired even more breadth and adventurousness.

Another Kesey-like moment permeated the Halloween show at Radio City as well. In one live skit Davis pretended to drink the notorious acid-dosed urine backstage, and afterward he was seen wandering around onstage, even trying to climb the scaffolding, as Franken warned him, with an increasingly concerned tone, to be careful. Later Davis told Dell'Amico he actually *had* taken acid and was stumbling around onstage with good reason, but it's doubtful anyone informed Radio City executives of that either.

In fact, it's almost certain no one did. Once the shows were over the legal wrangling began. Radio City and the Dead haggled over who would pay the leftover production costs, which ultimately amounted to $146,000. Eventually Radio City filed a $1.2 million lawsuit against the Dead, largely on the grounds that its reputation had been damaged by Franken and Davis's sketches during the Halloween video broadcast. "Despite the Music Hall's strenuous and repeated objections, the band's representatives refused to remove small portions of the tape that were potentially damaging to the Music Hall's image and reputation and in violation of the standards mandated by the contract," read Radio City's filing. "Those objectionable portions either suggested that illicit drugs were being used in the Music Hall or were obscene, in bad taste or against good morals. For example, one segment, actually filmed in a San Francisco theater, reported to show men vomiting in a Music Hall restroom while another, also filmed in advance and without any reference to what was actually happening in the Music Hall, suggested that bad cocaine was being passed around the theater. . . . There is no doubt that the Music Hall was damaged by the simulcast." And yes, the skit in which "urine laced with LSD being consumed on stage" was also brought up. In its reply the Dead's legal team countered that "the Music Hall's lawsuit to enjoin use of the offensive videotaped segments and damaging poster were unnecessary because the dispute could have been resolved."

In the end the lawsuit was settled out of court, and everyone could claim one victory or another. Radio City Music Hall allowed the Dead to proceed with plans for a cable special of the show for Showtime, but thanks to the suit, the Dead wouldn't be allowed to use the now-outlawed poster or any Radio City logos on either *Reckoning* or *Dead Set*. For the Dead the shows would hardly be moneymakers. According to their own paperwork, they only earned $32,000 after spending $13,500 on road expenses, $3,134 on limos and cabs, and other bits and pieces. But much like the Wall of Sound, it proved the lengths to which the band was willing to go to push the technological envelope, often at their own expense.

One final disaster was averted Halloween night. In a truck outside Dell'Amico smelled a horrid, burning stench. He normally kept his cool under such circumstances, but on one of the previous nights at Radio City all the gear onstage had blown out the venue's huge brass electrical panel, never a good omen. Leaving the truck, Dell'Amico saw smoke on the street outside Radio City and briefly panicked.

Luckily, the source turned out to be a tire fire in New Jersey that was so pungent it wafted over into Manhattan. Although they came close on several levels, the Dead hadn't succeeded in destroying Radio City; if anything, they would make it acceptable for other major rock acts to play there over the next few decades. Once again, they laughed in the face of disaster and walked away untouched.

◆ ◆ ◆

Weir and Lesh at Fantasy Studios, Berkeley, February 1984.
© DAVID GANS

CHAPTER 11

BERKELEY, CALIFORNIA, LATE FEBRUARY TO EARLY MARCH, 1984

Hart was seated in a lotus position, preparing to stretch out his back, when a bottle of wine sailed past his head. He wasn't the intended target, but he was jolted nonetheless. It was that sort of day, that sort of week, that sort of *era*, in the ongoing saga of the Dead.

As work settings went, the band could have had it worse than Fantasy Studios in Berkeley. Home of the hits for everyone from Creedence Clearwater Revival to Journey, it was considered one of the Bay Area's most quality studios, worth the $150 an hour its owners charged. Studio D, where the Dead had set up, was outfitted with wood-paneled walls and parquet floors; the lounge where Hart was chilling had the requisite sofas and amenities. Their jumble of gear—Garcia's and Lesh's custom-made guitars and basses, Weir's graphite-neck guitar, Hart's and Kreutzmann's overwhelming collection of percussive instruments— were all in place. Outsiders and Dead haters—and by the middle of the eighties the culture had its share of the latter—may have seen them as anachronistic hippies, but the Dead were as ever up on technology and unafraid to use it. The array of instruments and effects loaded into Fantasy attested to that.

Starting on February 7 the Dead assembled to try something they hadn't done in four years: make a new record. It had been mutually decided they needed to leave their comfort zone—Front Street, their rehearsal space and ad hoc studio—for a less distracting, more focused environment. You never knew what you would find at Front Street. One day a member of the crew looked up, counted the studs in the wall, and said, "Yeah, right about *here*." He punched his hand through the sheet rock, reached inside, and pulled out a stash of crystal meth that, legend had it, Ken Kesey had dropped long ago and had fallen between the cracks.

Along with a new work space the Dead had a passel of new material to record. With its veiled reference to the notorious Chateau Marmont on Sunset Boulevard, where John Belushi fatally overdosed in 1982, Garcia and Hunter's "West L.A. Fadeaway" could have easily been about the band's longtime friend, even though Hunter's lyrics circled around the matter. (Not long before he died Belushi popped into a Dead show in Los Angeles, sweating and looking disheveled and drugged up; even the Dead were shocked.) Even the song's slow-rolling rhythm connoted sleaze. Weir and Barlow's "My Brother Esau" could have been interpreted as their take on the Cain and Abel saga, although a few months after these sessions Weir would tell the *New York Daily News* that it was "our most political song," calling it "an allegory about the treatment Vietnam veterans got when they returned home—though I'm sure it passes over a lot of people's heads." Another Weir-Barlow collaboration, an agitated rocker called "Throwing Stones," was among their most pointed and pessimistic songs: a depiction of a planet that looked beautiful from space but deep down was rotting away from lack of care, inept politicians, and pending darkness. Hunter and Garcia weren't writing together as much as they once had, but they did turn out another new song, "Keep Your Day Job," whose rollicking rhythm made it ideal for live shows. The fans weren't as taken with the words: almost as soon as the song was premiered onstage, in 1982, the fans interpreted Hunter's lyric as a call to *not* follow the band around on the road. (In fact, the song advocated supporting oneself while looking ahead to bigger, more fulfilling goals, but the title phrase tripped up the message.) In due time the outcry was so loud that the Dead dropped the song from their repertoire, but right now, at the beginning of the new album sessions, it was still on track to be included on the next record.

The Dead still equated working in a recording studio with something worse than a group root canal. "The recording process was very painful," says Hart. "The spirit didn't lie in the studio with no people. You're playing for the walls. It wasn't the Dead. There was a wild side of it that never came out in the studio." But given that they'd been performing a few of those songs for several years, the sessions should have been a creative cakewalk. And they could take their time; although Arista was anxious for new product, no one was pressuring the band at that point.

And yet, two weeks in, they were stuck for more reasons than anyone cared to ponder. The frustration was starting to affect everyone, including Weir. Typically the most agreeable and even tempered member of the band, Weir was happy to open up his home to others, happy to hobnob with record company executives. Walking into the studio lounge that day, Weir seemingly couldn't restrain his frustration. The problem wasn't the drummer; it had to do with the fact that, though the band was scheduled to work, the *only* person Weir saw there was Hart. As Hart watched in the lounge, Weir frowned and grabbed a bottle of wine. (With the Dead, quality food and drink were never far away, especially by the eighties; starting with their 1976 tour, manager Richard Loren made sure they always had quality catering backstage at shows.)

Hart was about ten feet away when suddenly Weir wailed the bottle like a baseball. Because some of the walls in the lounge were made of soft, porous materials, the bottle didn't shatter, but it slammed into the wall and remained there.

For nearly twenty years the Dead had lived by a credo: no one would lecture anyone about his or her lifestyle as long as it didn't affect the music. For what seemed like forever, that rule worked reasonably well; in spite of their excesses, records had been made and tours had been completed. At one time the hallucinogenic (or otherwise) enhancements had even helped in the process and enhanced their art. Besides, they'd lived with chaos for so long that it almost felt second nature. But now lifestyle choices, temptations, and recurring craziness were no longer cause for amusement; they were seriously beginning to affect the way they worked and functioned as a band. The dark was starting to over-take the light, and there would be no better reminder of that frustration than the wine bottle sticking out of the wall in the Fantasy lounge.

The fifteenth anniversary shows in 1980 should have augured a new era. Though few in the band or fan base were taken with *Go to Heaven*, "Alabama Getaway" had made a bit of noise on rock radio. The Dead pulled off a rare-for-them business coup: opening an office solely de-voted to mail-order ticket sales. Onstage Brent Mydland was becoming an electrifying force, pushing them in ways Keith Godchaux no longer had; a new generation of Deadheads were also pulled in by his songs, voice, and very physical performances. Other than Weir, Mydland was now the most animated player onstage.

Yet even by Dead standards, the years leading up to the wine-bottle moment had been difficult ones. Lesh's fears of the band never com-ing together again after the Winterland shows in 1974 had been allevi-ated once they returned to the road two years later. But of all the band members, Lesh was arguably also the least satisfied with the more radio-friendly music the band had started making with *Terrapin Station*. "Jerry and Hunter and Bobby and Barlow and I were still writing good stuff," he says, "but somehow it wasn't about the music anymore. That's the feeling I had. It was about the scene—being touring musicians, being rock stars. It just seemed less about the music and where we could take it." Regarding some of the studio albums that had started with *Terrapin Station*, he adds, "I wasn't deeply involved in those records. I felt like a sideman." As a result of his unhappiness, both with his band's music and his own life, Lesh began spiraling downward, medicating himself with drink. His marriage fell apart, and he wasn't having a particularly good time with a postmarriage girlfriend. Finally, in 1982 he met Jill Johnson, a local waitress, and was smitten. They would marry two years later. (As for Weir, the guitarist was never lacking in companionship, as Matthew Kelly witnessed during one backstage scene: "All the girls loved Bobby. When he would walk into a room full of attractive college girls, he would look around like a Roman emperor. It was hysterically amusing." Weir would happily confirm such stories in the 2014 documentary *The Other One*.)

In the few years leading up to the Fantasy sessions, Garcia and his issues had put the band through what seemed like a never-ending roller coaster ride. During a European tour of 1981 they'd written a letter to him accusing him of not being professional, but he'd ignored it. (Years later it was discovered crumpled up in an ashtray in his home.) Garcia was now living in that darkened basement apartment in Rock Scully's house in San Rafael, both men deeply ensnared in heroin use. The situation had grown so out of control that Scully's partner, Nicki, moved out in 1981. "I did everything in my power to keep Jerry in touch," Rock Scully says, "to the point where it drove my family out of my house because he wouldn't leave, and I'd have the band come into my living room and do the meetings there."

Dating back a decade, Allan Arkush had been accustomed to hanging out with Garcia, talking and watching movies (Garcia could recite all the dialogue from *Network*, for instance); in 1981 Garcia provided, via his guitar, the "voice" of a robot baby in Arkush's comedy *Heartbeeps*. By the early eighties, though, that interaction stopped. Rarely did Arkush pick up his phone anymore to hear Garcia's voice merrily say, "Hey, come over and watch movies." Instead, Arkush would call Garcia and hear his friend intone, "I gotta go meet Rock," implying drugs. "It was obvious what was happening," Arkush says. "Then he'd say, 'Call me' but never pick up the phone."

On New Year's Day 1982, at the Oakland Coliseum, Garcia and Mountain Girl, who'd reconnected as friends at the end of the previous decade, were belatedly married in a dressing room backstage; David Hellman, the lawyer who advised the Dead on tax matters, had suggested it for that very reason. Then living in Oregon, Mountain Girl only occasionally attended Dead shows with her children during this period. "I was out of the loop, deliberately," she says. "It was a dangerous place to be with kids at the time. So many creepy people around the band. I didn't want to be a part of that. It felt dreary to me. A lot of the life had gone out of it." Garcia's brother, Tiff, now a postal worker, stopped going backstage to visit his brother for the same reasons. A drug counselor who assessed Garcia's situation in 1983 decided he wouldn't be able to get fully clean in that atmosphere.

By 1983 Garcia was looking particularly sickly; on stage he was pasty skinned and ghostly pale, and at moments he barely seemed to move. (A Garcia Band tour that year was canceled for mysterious reasons.) Offstage he grew increasingly disconnected from his band mates, a combination of the drug use and a deepening resentment about the constraints on his time and the pressures of supporting the organization. When a friend asked why he didn't simply stop touring so much, he replied, "Gotta feed the bulldog."

To the increasing wariness of the other members of the Dead, Garcia was still spending time with Kahn and playing regularly with the Jerry Garcia Band. Garcia's close friendship with Kahn made many in the Dead less than friendly toward the bass player and the JGB, which the Dead saw as an unwelcome distraction. Kahn later admitted to writer Blair Jackson that drugs had crept into the JGB era of the late seventies, but added, "I really don't believe that drugs were as important a thing as it's probably perceived. Everything would have been the same. . . . Our relationship didn't have to do with that." Garcia clearly enjoyed playing and spending time with Kahn, and as Kahn's wife, Linda, says, "John and Jerry liked old movies and they loved to joke. We were an escape for Jerry." (Annabelle Garcia would concur, telling Jackson that the Kahns were "very sweet people" and provided her father with a "safe haven.")

A certain amount of unease also existed toward Bobby & the Midnites, the side project Weir had formed with the help of accomplished players like jazz drummer Billy Cobham and former Steppenwolf guitarist Bobby Cochran. The band had released its first of two albums in 1981, and Andy Leonard, the former Grateful Dead Records employee who was now managing the Midnites, would be lectured by Dead management about the importance of the "mothership." The sense of musical stagnation in the Dead, combined with Garcia's issues, was beginning to affect everyone.

The period was particularly difficult for Weir, who wasn't averse to a good time but also stuck to his exercise routines as much as possible. (When the band played a New York show Nicki Scully remembers seeing Weir leave their hotel for a run, and, she says, "all these girls were following him as he was jogging to Central Park.") Garcia's issues especially affected Weir, according to his friend Andy Leonard: "There was nothing he could do about it. Clenched-fist silence."

In 1982 the Garcia band and Weir's Bobby & the Midnites shared a bill at an outdoor festival. There, Leonard caught his first sign of

Garcia's transformation. "I had never seen a human being that color before in my life," he says. "He was the wrong color. I thought he was going to die onstage. It scared the crap out of me." As a result, Leonard suggested Garcia's set be cut short, and Garcia left the stage with no complaints. Afterward Weir broke down. Given the way Weir often kept his feelings to himself, it was a telling moment.

■   ◆   ■

"You're watching *this?*" Kreutzmann snapped, walking into the lounge at Fantasy and finding the band sprawled on couches and watching *The Rockford Files*, the TV detective show. "Come on—let's go play."

As always, the music should have saved them; it had before. In August 1982 they'd returned to a field in Veneta, Oregon, for a benefit for the then-struggling Springfield Creamery, an organic dairy company run by Chuck Kesey, Ken Kesey's brother, and his wife, Sue. They'd first played a benefit for the Creamery on a brutally hot day in 1972; the temperatures climbed to over 100 degrees, making their instruments lurch in and out of tune, and the facility almost ran out of water. In spite of the conditions, they'd rallied, playing a stunning set that included an epic "Dark Star" that would still make Ken Babbs, the Merry Prankster who served as master of ceremonies that day, swoon decades later. Staring at the thousands of stoned, naked fans in front of them, Lesh turned to the band and Babbs and cracked, "They'll be fucking on the ground in front of us."

The Dead who returned to raise additional funds for the Creamery in 1982 were not quite the same band anymore, but they could still catch fire: they could revel in "China Cat Sunflower," and Garcia's voice and guitar on "Tennessee Jed" retained the old spark. Peter Rowan, Garcia's friend from the Old and in the Way era, was booked to play on a side stage at the fair. He arrived with certain trepidations: he sensed lingering resentment within the Dead camp in light of the way Old and in the Way had taken Garcia away from the mothership almost a decade before. But at the fair Rowan felt comfortable—he had a blast hanging out with Weir—and eventually went in search of Garcia. Garcia's trailer, he learned, had been set up in the middle of the backstage area, in full sight of everyone. Getting in to see him was another matter, however. Rowan saw a Tibetan lama drop in, and then Rowan waited his turn. He waited outside for nearly two hours, and Garcia never emerged. Finally Rowan gave up and left.

Despite so much uncertainty enveloping them, the Dead still managed to play a number of exceptional shows during this period. (Dead historian and Garcia biographer Jackson maintains that the Dead's playing overall kept ramping up several notches during each year of the eighties, and they even slipped in "Help on the Way/Slipknot!" for the first time in many years.) Now came studio time. At Fantasy Phil Kaffel, an experienced recording engineer who'd befriended Hart during previous studio work, was hired to record the band. From previous encounters with them he knew the Dead could be fairly loose. They hadn't sent him tapes of the songs they might cut, and he hadn't had any swanky preproduction meetings or dinners with them the way Keith Olsen had before the making of *Terrapin Station*.

Kreutzmann's comment was apt: they *were* ready to play, at least some of them. Once the full band was set up in Studio D, Kaffel was impressed with their mountains of gear; it looked as if they were setting up to play a live show. With Garcia set up in his own booth, they'd started that day's session with "My Brother Esau," for which Weir offered up a fairly growled vocal. The take was fine, until Garcia hit a bad note toward the end. They took another crack at the song, and this time it sounded stronger, especially Mydland's organ and synthesizer parts.

Even so, the mood wasn't encouraging. "Well, it's not getting *worse*," Garcia muttered. The band took a five-minute break in the lounge before reconvening in the recording room, where they went at "My Brother Esau" one more time. It wasn't the easiest song to play: the rhythms had a tumbling, falling-down-the-stairs quality, and the song didn't have a genuine chorus to speak of. Yet bit by bit it seemed to be congealing. Lesh was bouncing on his toes, and Kreutzmann's rhythm was firm and steady. (Between takes Lesh complimented the drummer: "I've been trying to figure out how you swing for years, man.")

But again Garcia's musicianship was off, and "My Brother Esau" ground to a halt. During one of several subsequent takes Weir stood up, as if they were doing a show, and everyone had the feeling they were approaching a final, finished version of the song. "We're getting so close," Weir deigned to say, perhaps jinxing matters.

But it wasn't to be; the band took another break, and the lounge again beckoned.

■   ◆   ■

Other distractions were nipping at them as the Fantasy sessions were underway; by 1984, more members of their organization were falling away. Given Scully's role as a codependent in Garcia's life, the band was increasingly distrustful of the longtime former manager, who was now doing publicity for the band. Matters finally came to a head when Scully was called into a band meeting and accused of pilfering money during a New York trip with the Jerry Garcia Band. According to Scully, the hotel had mistakenly thought they'd overcharged the band, and Scully had walked out with roughly $2,600 in what he thought was honest cash. Few in the Dead office believed him, though, and office workers complained about unpaid hotel bills and other expenses. At the meeting Hunter spoke on Scully's behalf but to little avail; Scully was soon given what he called his "walking papers" and went into rehab himself.

Scully would be the latest stalwart of their organization to be gone by the summer of 1984. By then Mydland and Betty Cantor had been in a relationship for several years. With her encouragement and seasoned help, Mydland had started working on an album of his own songs, on which Garcia and John Kahn had guested. "He was trying to make a statement on his own, separate from the Dead and trying to prove himself," she says. "And it was really good work." But when the couple broke up, Cantor parted ways with the Dead camp soon after. "I had become an 'ex old lady,'" she says. "I thought, 'How could I be considered an ex-old lady? I've been working all through this.' They were afraid it would cause problems. They thought Brent would be uncomfortable. I thought, 'Okay, I'm going to get the hell out of Dodge.' I had to go on to a new life for a while." With that, another key member of their organization—in this case, on the technical and recording side—was no longer around.

In 1981 Richard Loren was beginning to feel fried after roughly a decade of managing Garcia and then the Dead. During a brief European tour that spring, when the band was playing Germany with the Who, Kreutzmann burst into his room and accused Loren of stealing money from the band and lying about it—and then fired him. (When Kreutzmann told Lesh what he'd done, Lesh, in his memoir, retorted that firing Loren was "a stupid move.") Later, back in California, Kreutzmann apologized and Loren kept his job, but the incident was a sign to Loren that managing the Dead in the new decade had become a tiresome, thankless job. Still, Loren had one more grand idea up his sleeve and decided to run it by the band. In what would amount to an Egypt-like experience but on American soil, he envisioned renting a riverboat and sailing down the Mississippi to New Orleans; the Dead would play and hold seminars, and well-heeled Deadheads would fork over hundreds of dollars for tickets. The whole endeavor would be filmed for a movie. It was, in Loren's words, "a no-brainer," and unlike Egypt, they would be paid upfront and have control over the event.

Attending a band meeting in May 1981, Loren made his case for the project, abetted by photos and cost estimates. He was under the impression Hart and Weir were willing to take part, but no sooner had he finished his presentation than Garcia intoned, "We don't want to do that." The gesture was striking: at board meetings Garcia rarely spoke first, preferring to let everyone else weigh in and then, peering over his glasses, weigh in yea or nay. Everyone would look to him for comment and gauge their moods by what he said.

Garcia's immediate dismissal of the idea stunned Loren; the concept was dead on arrival. Back home Loren tried to grapple with what had happened. Maybe, he thought, Garcia didn't like the idea of being holed up on a boat with Deadheads who would see his physical deterioration up close. Maybe Garcia was worried about how he would get drugs in such a setting. Whatever the reason, Loren came to a depressing realization. "The Jerry who rejected that presentation from me was a different man," he says. "It wasn't, 'Gee, that would be fun!'" With that, Loren parted ways with the Dead.

For all the psychodrama, the business of the Dead was increasingly robust, especially on the road. In 1983, thanks to Danny Rifkin, the Dead decided to take concert ticketing into their own hands because counterfeiting was becoming a major issue. The band opened their own ticket office to handle mail-order sales, and it worked: in 1983 they sold 24,500 tickets, and in 1984 the number spiked to 115,000. "We added $2 to each ticket as a service charge, and that's how we operated the ticket office," says Steve Marcus, who eventually ran it. "The ticket business never cost the Dead a penny, the only business of theirs that didn't." At first, employees worked out of an apartment in a building next to Front Street, where police would routinely arrive to deal with drugs, hookers, or domestic violence calls in other apartments. No one suspected that several hundred thousand dollars' worth of tickets and cash were in the small apartment downstairs. The first show sold through mail order was at the Warfield in March 1983, and it proved revealing of the fascinating, back-and-forth rapport between the Dead and Bill Graham, who continued to promote their West Coast shows. The Dead made sure their guests at that Warfield show had quality orchestra seats—and Graham's guests were relegated to further back in the balcony. The Graham people complained, deigning it unacceptable, but the Dead's people laughed it off. In the end, though, both camps respected each other, and the Dead's Graham-produced New Year's Eve shows, with Graham himself dressed as Father Time, were eagerly awaited annual events.

At a band meeting in 1984 sound man Dan Healy complained he was having trouble seeing the stage thanks to all the microphones being held aloft by audience tapers camped out in front of his board. Tapers had often been nuisances: in the old days Rex Jackson would walk out into the halls, see the microphone cables, and walk up and down the aisles, cutting the cables and stashing them in his bag. During the same period Sam Cutler made sure the contract riders for shows asserted that "employer will not permit recordings of the performance," although this dictum was largely aimed at unscrupulous promoters who wanted their own bootlegs.

The band had since become more lenient about fans recording the shows for themselves, but the increasing numbers of tapers was becoming an issue. Kidd Candelario, who'd been making quality tapes of shows for years, spoke up. He admitted to being irked by the tapers himself; at some shows friends who had guest tickets would approach him and complain that the tapers had taken over their seats. "The tapers were everywhere," Candelario says. "They were always picking on people who were there to see a show and have fun and scream and clap. And the tapers were like, 'You can't do that—no clapping, no whistling, no yelling.' They thought they had free rein to do anything they wanted."

At the meeting someone—no one remembers who—brought up stopping fans from bringing in recording gear altogether. But the band wanted the tradition to continue, so the idea of banning them was quickly shot down. Candelario and Steve Marcus of the ticket office suggested putting the gearheads in their own area, far from the sound-board, which evolved into talk of a regular, separate section for them. Perhaps that would be the best use for the 200 to 250 seats regularly not sold for each show because they were behind Healy and had obstructed views. Everyone, including the Dead, agreed it was the best solution—and also one that provided extra income no one had counted on. With the number of Dead employees continuing to swell, any additional dollars were welcome.

The tapers at the first show with an official section, at the Berkeley Community Theater, weren't particularly happy: at the last moment Healy moved the soundboard to beneath a balcony, where tapers didn't think the sound quality was as strong. But the night began the tradition of a small sea of what looked like miniature telephone poles sticking up at Dead shows. At least something in the Dead world was working.

By the early eighties little in pop music resembled a Dead concert. From the music to the audience, there was nothing punk, new wave, or disco about any of it, and the most diehard of fans, whether young or long term, were starting to follow the band around the country. Nothing like it had been seen in pop, even to an established veteran like, of all people, Joan Baez, the folk music institution with the vibrato-rich soprano.

By the time she shared a stage and studio with the Dead—and then entered into a relationship with Hart—Baez had her own scattered history with the band. During the Palo Alto days Garcia's first wife, Sara Ruppenthal, had met and befriended Baez, then a folk superstar, and Baez had asked Ruppenthal to join her on tour as an assistant. (She declined, opting to stay in the area with Garcia; today Baez has no memory of those encounters.) Almost twenty years later Hart and Baez met and became a couple, sharing, she says with a fond laugh, "different forms of insanity." The two would go motorcycle riding together, and one time she mounted one of his big Harleys by herself and took off up a hill. "I was a little iffy," she says of the ride. Her son Gabe became a Deadhead himself, traveling with fans around the country and bonding with Hart over drumming. It was, Baez says, "a family for Gabe," which she welcomed, given her own relentless touring schedule and time away from home.

While traveling with the Dead after she and Hart had hooked up, Baez took in her first show. Venturing out into the crowd, she accidentally stepped over a kid lying in the aisle, and what she calls her "Florence Nightingale side" jumped out. "I said, 'I'm going to save this guy,'" she recalls. Picking him up and setting him into a seat, she saw someone walking by with what looked like lemonade, grabbed it and offered it to the half-passed-out fan. "Is there anything in it?" he asked. When she said no, he was shocked: "Oh, shit!" (She didn't think he wanted to be *more* stoned.) The crowd, meanwhile, moved in what she calls "Ouija board dancing," calling it "a roomful of slow-motion robotic weirdness accompanied by the smell of heavy patchouli and drugs." It was, she says, a learning experience.

Baez was in the midst of her own self-proclaimed "period of confusion." For the first time in her career she didn't have a record deal—like many of her peers, she was now the victim of an industry that saw some sixties acts as dinosaurs, especially once MTV arrived in 1981. Since Hart had a studio, the couple decided to make an album using the Dead as her backup band. The idea didn't seem completely off the wall because both she and the Dead inherently loved folk music, and she had joined the Dead onstage for several disarmament benefits in 1981 along with their traditional New Year's Eve show. She and Weir dueted on "Me and Bobby McGee," which the Dead had been performing for some time, although Garcia walked offstage one night in the midst of one of her songs, which Baez didn't understand.

Working in Hart's Novato studio, Baez had her own dose of the world of the Dead. She heard rumors of a snake running around the place, and when she started nodding off after long hours trying to record songs, Hart would prod her: "Come on, Belle, you can sleep when you die!" Some of the band members played on the record, and they worked up some cover versions as well as a couple of Baez originals, "Marriott USA" and "Lady Di and I." "It was a strange combination," she admits, "but it kind of nudged me out of my comfort zone." The songs reflected the experience in more ways than one: written by Baez, "Lady Di and I" was an oblique commentary on her relationship with Hart. "It was about a 'hood guy on his motorcycle and the girl is saying, 'Hey, I'm the same age as Lady Di,' and comparing the two lives," Baez recalls.

Garcia mystified Baez, though. One time he was hours late and claimed he'd gotten lost in the fog on the way north. Baez had a feeling he wasn't comfortable in the situation but couldn't figure out why. Garcia didn't end up sticking around for long, and later work shifted to a different studio where Garcia would finally attempt to put down a guitar part for the song they were finishing. "He was *way* out there," Baez recalls. "He would noodle and get lost and start finding the part and go off into outer space, and it had nothing to do with that song." To her amazement, he found the right part in the end, but the process was one Baez was utterly unaccustomed to. "I was feeling quieter and duller and weirder by the minute," Baez says. Turning to Hart, she said, "What's going on?"

In a phrase she would long remember, he replied, "You're getting a contact *low.*"

The album was never completed nor released, although two of its songs would later wind up on a Baez retrospective, and Hart and Baez ended their relationship in 1982. For years, though, she would be struck by how the band stayed true to itself the entire time and after. "It's one of the few things that maintained a steadiness," she says. "Elvis Presley, the Beatles, the Rolling Stones, myself, Bob Dylan—we've all had these crashes, moments of 'What do I do now? How do I reinvent myself?' The Dead were probably invented in a special way, and they didn't really need to change much. I don't know any group that was so into its music."

■　◆　■

They thought they had a take. Or maybe they didn't. It was getting hard to tell. They gathered in the control room to hear a playback.

"Is this it?" Mydland asked to no one in particular.

"Not if Jerry wants a new 'Day Job,'" Lesh cracked. He then turned to Weir and said, "Promise me one more take." They all looked over at Garcia, who was still enclosed in his booth and noodling on his guitar. "Let him warm up," Lesh said. "Something might happen." The only problem was that Garcia had been warming up for a while already; at best it was wishful thinking.

The men straggled back into the recording room and took another stab at "Keep Your Day Job." Garcia's playing was flaccid, and when he was asked to take a crack at vocals, what emerged was a strangulated croak. During his interview with the *Daily News* Weir had almost predicted what was happening: "Since we haven't had phenomenal success that way, there's a certain amount of lethargy simply in going back to a studio. The question is whether the songs are strong enough to pull through studio torpor."

Observing the scene that day (and taking notes used here) was compact, wiry Dennis McNally, a self-proclaimed "army brat" now entrusted with writing the band's official biography. A graduate of St. Lawrence University who then received his doctorate in American history at the University of Massachusetts, McNally was fascinated with bohemian culture (his dissertation had been on Jack Kerouac, later the subject of McNally's first book, *Desolate Angel*, in 1979), and he attended his first Dead show in 1972. While working as a typist for court reporters after moving to the Bay Area, McNally had the idea of writing a book about the band and, in his words, "plotted to meet" the Dead by sending a copy of his Kerouac biography to Garcia. After writing a piece for the *San Francisco Chronicle* about the upcoming Warfield fifteenth-anniversary shows, McNally was tipped by Dead insiders to show up at the auditions for the "Jerry's Kids" skit for those shows, where he finally was able to meet Garcia. ("I said, 'What are you doing here—you're obviously too straight to be one of Jerry Kids," recalls Nicki Scully, who was helping to organize the auditions.) Garcia had not only read McNally's Kerouac book but also loved it; he later went along with the idea of McNally writing their official history.

In the early stages of researching his Dead book McNally was able to finagle his way into the session and witnessed up close the issues dogging them at the time. "When Jerry started playing, everyone stopped fiddling around," McNally says. "But the fact is, nobody was in charge. And certainly not Jerry, except on rare occasions."

Having worked with jazz musicians before, Kaffel realized that the Dead were more jazz than rock in the way they continually tweaked and rearranged their material. Watching the process was fascinating, especially compared to the way most rock bands would simply record the same takes of the same songs over and over. Kaffel knew it would be difficult to approximate the feeling of the Dead's live performances in a studio, yet he wasn't prepared for how largely unproductive the sessions were becoming. Managers and Arista types weren't calling in or stopping by to see how the work was going. Perhaps it was the setting: Fantasy, housed in the corporate headquarters of the Fantasy Records building, had a security guard in its lobby, the polar opposite of Front Street, where "security" amounted to the road crew camped out in the front office. The sessions didn't appear to have the slightest bit of urgency, and one of Kaffel's jobs—as it had been with Olsen seven years before—was to corral the band. "It was hard just to get them all in the room together at the same time," he recalls. "You'd get some of them, and then another one of the guys would be out of there."

Another factor, dating back years, was their last few experiences making records. They'd never been fans of recording; without an audience to play off and feed off, something felt wrong. Even working with like-minded Lowell George hadn't panned out as they'd hoped. "Those records are very painful for me," Hart says. "They were ill-advised. No one was happy being in the studio, and you can't play Dead music unless you're happy. We were in a rut in the early eighties. And I didn't do anything to stop it." At that point not even Hart's proactive attitude could help.

◆ ◆ ◆

By the time they began congregating at Fantasy Garcia was barely the Garcia they had known a decade before. He was now three hundred pounds with swollen ankles; his hair was increasingly white, long, and scraggly, and he seemed easily distracted. It wasn't unusual for him to arrive late and head for the bathroom, and he didn't seem to bathe with much frequency. One of his in-jokes around Front Street—"I stink, therefore I am"—was a particularly ghoulish slice of dark humor. Between takes at Fantasy Garcia would wander off again, and it was left to his devoted roadie, Steve Parish, to round him up and make sure Garcia was back at work.

That time had come once more, so they returned to the task at hand, and the troubles continued. Lesh's headphone cords became tangled up in his bass. Garcia tried singing a lead vocal on a song, but his voice was raspy and off key. Flipping through a bunch of Stax and Volt records in his booth, Garcia turned grumpy, snapping at the others, "None of you seem to remember it tonight."

"I'm searching for a part," Weir replied.

"Play a rhythm *fucking* part," Garcia snapped back.

The biting side of Garcia, especially during the music-making process, wasn't new to the Dead and their friends. As Sue Swanson recalls, "He could get pissy with the other band members during practice if someone was fucking up or not getting the notes or the timing right." As Swanson once witnessed firsthand, Garcia could also ramp up the anger if the time came. Back in Palo Alto in 1965, during one of the Warlocks' practice sessions in her parents' backyard, Garcia nearly came to blows with a friend who made some cracks about Swanson's family. "Cut it out!" Garcia snapped, almost punching the guy. To Swanson the incident showed Garcia's gallant side: "He really loved women. He was an old-style guy that way: 'Don't mess with women,' 'the weaker sex,' whatever you want to call it. With me it was 'Don't mess with someone's little sister.'" But it was also a sign of something he once said to her: "I could be the nicest guy on the block or the meanest guy on the block." She could tell from the tone in his voice that he meant it.

Equally telling were the conversations Garcia was now having about music. Few doubted he loved playing and singing his songs or other people's; it was the one place where everything felt right. Garcia was also known for his openness to music that didn't sound anything like the Dead's; he'd even tried to appreciate the rap albums his daughter Trixie played for him. But one day in 1984 he and Arkush sat around and listened to Prince's new single, "When Doves Cry." Uncharacteristically Garcia glowered: "There's no bass." He was right, but Arkush was struck by his response. "An earlier Jerry would have said, 'That's cool and interesting,'" he says. "This Jerry said, 'That's wrong.' The walls were going up."

Days and days into what were proving to be frustrating sessions, Garcia was spending so much time in the Fantasy bathroom that Hart suggested a microphone and recording wires be run right into the john so Garcia could record there. Hart later chuckled at the story, but Garcia, who didn't like to be confronted with issues about his personal life, gruffly dismissed the idea.

◼   ◆   ◼

It was time to stop, at least for the day. Nailing a finished version of "Keep Your Day Job" was still proving to be a Sisyphean task, and Garcia wasn't the only one irritated. During their next break Kreutzmann was clearly irked at something and, in the lounge, began swinging his arms in the air. Thankfully Kreutzmann told himself to calm down, and Garcia, always one to make sure the family held it together, jumped into the fray: he began chatting up Kreutzmann about different rhythm parts for the song and jazz drummers and rhythms, even thumping out a beat on a table to demonstrate how a boogie-woogie rhythm could be incorporated into the song. The tension defused, Kreutzmann gave Weir a friendly hug, and the two returned to the recording room. But Garcia was done for the day, and Parish took him home.

Throughout their time at Fantasy Kaffel tried to edit together different takes of songs for a complete, final version, or something close to it. It was a common enough way to make records, but even that approach wasn't yielding much. Kaffel thought a few of the songs were starting to come together, but the band never went back and finished them up. "With most bands you do a track and then do overdubs," he says. "With the Dead we never got to that point. You never got the feeling you were getting stuff done. Everything was always a bit up in the air. You didn't know if you had something or if you would come back to it. It's not like they were checking things off a list."

The next few weeks would play out along those lines. After a few more sessions, ending on March 10, hardly anything was accomplished. They'd spent almost five weeks in the studio, recording only half that time. (And even then sometimes the players would be only Kreutz-mann and Hart putting down drum tracks.) Kaffel would later have no memory of recording any vocals, although one track from that period, an early version of "West L.A. Fadeaway," would surface years later. For Lesh the sessions were particularly exasperating. "It didn't amount to anything at all," he says. "All these people were coming by, and they all brought their stashes. 'Break it out, break it out, break it out.' By the time we got through everybody's stash, we'd been there for eight hours and nothing had been done and everybody wanted to go home. That was a real joke." As one Dead office employee recalls, "It was called the Fantasy Record, because it was a fantasy."

Kaffel heard no out-front complaints: no one said he was unhappy, and no one expressed outright anger about what had or hadn't taken place. One by one the band members simply stopped showing up at the studio for work. It was if the wheels were coming off one spin at a time. The studio sat empty for a few additional days before the Dead's crew reappeared to box up all their gear and return it to Front Street. By the middle of March the only sign that the Dead had been there was Weir's bottle of wine, sticking out from the wall as a reminder of what could have been and what wasn't.

*A happy and recovered Garcia onstage during
the "Touch of Grey" video shoot.*
© JAY BLAKESBERG

CHAPTER 12

SALINAS, CALIFORNIA, MAY 9, 1987

They weren't entirely convinced they should be there. They'd endured grueling tours, Acid Tests, even moments behind bars, but few of those experiences compared to what was ahead of them. In a dressing room behind the Laguna Seca campgrounds, just east of Monterey, Lesh, Weir, and Hart gathered to discuss the unparalleled task ahead of them. Hart, always open to adventure and self-promotion, flashed a wily smile: "This is gonna be *it*," he enthused. Lesh's skepticism was apparent in his rigid body language and words. "Let's do one music video," he told them in a voice that made it clear the topic wasn't open for debate. "And be done with it."

As they were talking, golf carts had begun zipping around the campgrounds and national park in Salinas, accompanied by loud voices booming out of bullhorns: "We're going to shoot something, and everyone's welcome to watch!" The concert had ended about an hour before, and the echoes of the last song, "Iko Iko," had faded into the night. But a portion of the more than ten thousand Deadheads at the show began streaming back into the venue. There they saw cameras onstage, one in the audience, and a man in a baseball cap and black leather jacket—director Gary Gutierrez, who'd worked with the band on the animated portions of *The Grateful Dead Movie*. As hard as it was to believe, the Dead were indeed preparing for their first-ever video.

During the sessions for the album that came to be known as *In the Dark*, Garcia would pass the time watching hours of MTV at Front Street. One day a typical hair metal band of the era, complete with Spandex and puffed hair, blared on the set. Sitting nearby, Justin Kreutzmann, Bill's son, asked Garcia what he thought of it. "It's so . . . *mindless*," Garcia said, with genuine puzzlement. "They're not *playing* anything." Garcia spent hours watching junk-food television—he could stay up all night absorbing hours of Dr. Gene Scott, the white-haired, white-bearded quasi-hippie preacher—but music videos were far more inexplicable to him.

Up to that point the Dead hadn't bothered with them. When they rolled out their last studio album, *Go to Heaven*, MTV was still a year away from debuting. In the spring of 1987 that landscape had dramatically changed, and to the surprise of just about everyone, the Dead had agreed to make a visual counterpart to their new single. Part of it was economics—no video was a virtual guarantee your record could easily be ignored—and part of it was that rare commodity in the Dead world: positive vibrations. The previous twelve months, if not years, had been exceptionally rough; they'd almost lost their charismatic leader, along with a chunk of their income. In that regard the prospect of standing onstage for a few hours and lip-synching a song was the least they could do—even if, as Lesh indicated, they weren't planning on doing it very often.

Naturally it wouldn't be the world of the Dead without a degree— or two or three—of backstage drama. At a band meeting a few days before the taping employees began complaining about difficulties obtaining backstage passes for friends. No one questioned how hard the road crew toiled in preparing for each show—speakers, microphones, even precise rug placement had to be set up relatively quickly. Wives and girlfriends were allowed, but the crew were more than willing to bark at anyone they didn't know or, even if they knew them, felt they didn't belong. "We had eighty thousand tons of gear to get out onto the stage, and people would say, 'You're very uptight about stuff,'" says Candelario, who by then was in charge of Lesh's and Mydland's setups. "I would say, 'They didn't hire me to worry about guests. They hired me to do a *job.*' I didn't have time to worry about whether they were getting to see Phil or Jerry, and I'll admit it took me all day long to set that shit up and make sure it was all working and running. People said the crew had too much power, but the band would say no to us just like they did to everyone else."

Physically the crew weren't quite as wild-eyed and hairy as they'd been a decade or two before, but to some in the Dead organization they remained merciless when it came to anyone who wandered backstage without a pass. "We had to pick and choose a lot of times who we're going to have up there, who we were going to deal with," says Parish. "We don't *know* these people. If somebody was brought up and introduced properly and escorted around, that was one thing. But apparently all those people who worked for us, not in the band or crew, decided they had friends who belonged onstage." Parish maintains that Garcia had asked the crew to help with security as far back as a Winterland show in 1970, when he told them, "We're in front of the amps, and we'll take care of that—you guys take care of what's back there." Whether out of fear or a general laissez-faire attitude, the band rarely complained about the situation to the crew—but that hands-off stance changed with the meeting prior to the videotaping. The crew was told in no uncertain terms to oversee and protect the equipment and stop being stage guards. (In Lesh's memory, though, "We were trying to get them to *increase* security; we asked them to tighten it up.")

The crew listened, absorbed the comments and made a decision. "We said, 'Fine, we're not going to do [security],' and I called it off," Parish says. "It was a thankless job anyway. Let someone else do it." As the first set at Laguna Seca was about to begin, Dead employees and the Dead themselves noticed something odd: people they didn't recognize were wandering around onstage, sometimes within feet of the musicians. Bob Bralove, an affable keyboard player and synthesizer programmer who'd worked for years with Stevie Wonder, had been hired to sonically upgrade the band and had been invited to see the show at Laguna Seca. Watching by the side of the stage, Bralove saw "the stage fucking filled with people. The band would look around, and they couldn't find a familiar face or anybody they knew. It was hysterical."

Not everyone found the situation remotely amusing. Noticing a complete stranger standing beside him as he was playing, Lesh called Parish over to his side of the stage. "I was really pissed," Lesh says. "I said, 'What the *fuck* do you think you're doing?'" Lesh grabbed Parish by the bicep so hard that he left marks on his arm. The next day the bruise was still evident; when asked what had happened, Parish shrugged, "Bass player fingers." As Lesh recalls, "There we are: we're playing a show and there are all these hippies—not even hippies, *teenyboppers*—walking out onto the stage and staring while we're trying to work. It was outrageous."

After the show another meeting ensued—and tellingly, the band reneged on its earlier dictum. "We said, 'Hey, you said for us to just do our job without doing security,'" recalls Candelario. "They go, 'We got a lot of valuable shit up there. That's it—you guys are back on. Do your job and security.'" The matter was settled, and no one would again confront the men who toiled behind and around the band anymore. "It was all nonsense—no policy was made at all," Parish says. "It went away, and it shut everybody up. Nobody ever mentioned it again." With another dose of standard drama behind them, the Dead could get back to their new job at hand: convincing the world that they were no longer a dead issue, in any sense of the phrase.

■ ◆ ■

The rebirth had started the year before under the worst possible circumstances. On the morning of July 10, 1986, Garcia's housekeeper found him slumped over in the bathroom of the house on Hepburn Heights in San Rafael. Earlier that day he'd complained of being thirsty; now he was unconscious and was being rushed to the hospital. Someone in the Dead office called Kreutzmann, then living in San Anselmo, relatively close to Garcia's house. He and son Justin leapt in a cab and arrived at Marin General Hospital, tucked away on a tree-lined street in Greenbrae, near Mill Valley, just as the ambulance with Garcia was pulling up. Because no one else was around to check Garcia in, the elder Kreutzmann pretended to be his brother.

As the Kreutzmanns saw for themselves, Garcia was visibly discombobulated, arguing with the ambulance workers and unsure of where he was and what had happened; he would later claim not to remember anything between passing out in the bathroom and waking up in the hospital. The Kreutzmanns weren't allowed to see Garcia, who was wheeled in and vanished, so they waited in the emergency room. Bill called his third wife, Shelley, then visiting family across the country, to tell her the news. "Billy sounded pretty calm about it," she recalls. "He said, 'I want to tell you before you hear it on the radio.'"

To his son, though, Kreutzmann sounded far more disconsolate, telling him forlornly, "This is the end—it's over." After waiting to see Garcia and ultimately not being allowed into the emergency room, the two hitchhiked home because they couldn't find a cab. On their way out they saw the ambulance still parked outside, the emergency workers shaking their heads and saying, "Yeah, that was Jerry Garcia we just brought in."

The possibility of a Garcia collapse had been building for over two years, but few in the organization were in a position to challenge him, and Garcia himself either downplayed his addiction or fended off offers to help. "I was medicating myself so I didn't have to think about it," Lesh says. "I often think, 'If I'd tried to make a deal with him—I'll quit drinking if you stop.' And I was ready to do that at one point." According to Lesh, his attempt to talk to Garcia about the band's music during one of those confrontations was rejected by the intervention specialist, causing Lesh to walk out in disgust. "I was very frustrated," he says. "That was my last chance to have made that offer." Hart recalls confronting Garcia with some Hells Angels in tow, telling him to check into rehab right then or, as Hart recalls, "Angelo [one of the Angels] will take you right out." Garcia went along with the idea but checked himself out. "It was really hard," Hart says. "He would eat a hamburger and milkshake in front of you and laugh. We did about all we could possibly do. The heroin was stronger."

Finally, in 1984, over a dozen people—including the band, Mountain Girl, and Hunter—crashed Garcia's home for just such a discussion, and Garcia promised he'd go into treatment. To prove it, he and Lesh drove to a clinic in Oakland, where Garcia signed up and said he'd return later. But back home afterward he hardly seemed to take it seriously: he didn't say anything and acted as if their words of support had barely penetrated him.

The next day Garcia declared he was ready for change. On the way to a clinic he parked his BMW in Golden Gate Park. (According to a source, the car was only his in theory because it had been given to him by a fan and the paperwork hadn't been completed.) Noticing that the car's registration had expired the previous September, a cop approached Garcia, asking for identification; Garcia responded by "looking down at his hands in which he held a piece of tin foil paper that had a brown sticky-appearing substance on it," as the police report read. Clearly nervous and unsure what to do, Garcia tried hiding the foil on the right side of the driver's seat. When asked for his license and registration, he said he didn't have the former but did produce the latter. "I recognized his name, and he confirmed he was from the Grateful Dead band," the officer reported later. On the front passenger seat police found an open briefcase with more tin foil with brown residue, a glass cooker, seven cigarette lighters, eleven paper bindles with brown residue, and a plastic baggie with a yellow-legal-pad bindle with white powder (which, almost comically, was labeled "1/2 Gram"). Some speculated Garcia was simply in search of one last high before he committed himself to treatment; if so, it was ironic that a lapsed registration sticker undid his plans. (Decades later some would still wonder what became of that briefcase, which also contained music and lyrics of new songs.)

Garcia was arrested and booked, but afterward, back at home, he barely mentioned the incident and acted as if the bust wasn't cause for major concern. At his hearing a few Deadheads who appeared in court offered to spend time in jail on his behalf, but it wasn't necessary: Garcia, who didn't at the time think he had any sort of problem and rejected therapy, asserted he would seek treatment.

In spite of Garcia's health issues the Dead machine hardly slowed down. After a rehearsal at Front Street in December 1985, the band gathered in the front lobby to chill. Gradually talk turned to touring plans for the following summer—and how the Dead had no choice but to make the switch from amphitheaters and indoor arenas to vast outdoor stadiums. "Yeah, man, you're right," Garcia said with little enthusiasm, and everyone agreed, with varying degrees of reluctance. "The tone was resignation as much as anything," says McNally, who'd been hired as the band's publicist (Rock Scully's former job) in 1984 and attended the meeting. "Jerry did not want to play stadiums, but it was necessary. He said to me repeatedly, 'It cartoonizes the playing.'" (Fans sometimes agreed: as early as 1973 Deadheads wrote to the band arguing against playing stadiums like Kezar, saying they were too big and the sound systems were awful.) With that topic settled—the thought of bigger paychecks didn't hurt—conversation turned to the best possible coheadliner, Bob Dylan or Eric Clapton. Over the next decade the stadium decision would have enormous consequences, good and bad, but at the moment it was simply about making room for the unrelenting increase in fans. Even without a new album to promote, ticket sales rose each year.

Starting with first-rate shows the band performed in the summer of 1985, Garcia battled back, and by the time the Dead started a short tour with Dylan and Tom Petty and the Heartbreakers the follow-ing summer, Garcia seemed in better shape than he'd been in some time. He gradually kicked drugs, and his interest in art and sketches returned. But the shows with Dylan and Petty proved to be his un-doing. As straight as Garcia tried to stay, mysterious brown packets would still be handed to him in elevators, sometimes by strangers, and his mood grew less than pleasant. Taken to a dentist in one city for an infection, he was given codeine, which didn't help his drug jones, and he seemed to be urinating more than usual. During shows Weir would run around the stage like a bronco, partly as a way to compensate for Garcia's increasingly sedentary stage presence. At a hellishly hot July show at RFK Stadium in Washington, DC, Shelley Kreutzmann saw Garcia's condition for herself. "We were all in an elevator together, with a friend of mine who's a nurse," she recalls, "and she said, 'He doesn't look too good.'"

Back home on Hepburn Heights all Garcia seemed to want to do was drink beverages, preferably Orange Julius, and urinate, and soon enough, he'd collapsed. At Marin General the days and weeks that followed were unlike anything the Dead community had confronted before. "We watched all the tubes running in and out of his body," says his brother, Tiff, "and he was passing all this shit you don't want to know." Garcia's heart momentarily stopped after it was determined he was allergic to a type of valium, and his kidneys shut down for over a week. Dead employees were told his blood sugar level was off the charts and that Garcia was one of the sickest people they'd ever seen admitted to the hospital. He was in a coma—brought on by adult-onset diabetes, a new condition for him—for almost a week. (Scully says that right before Garcia's bust in 1985, he'd brought in a doctor who told him Garcia was on the verge of catastrophic diabetes, but the issue, perhaps due to disarray in the band's organization at that point, wasn't addressed.) In his hospital room with Tiff, Garcia watched the movie *Elephant Parts* at such a high volume that Tiff was worried they would irritate the other patients.

In scenes that recalled Vito Corleone's hospitalization in *The Godfather*, the Dead operation went into protective action. Told to report to the hospital and protect Garcia, the crew found Deadheads in the parking lot, some building makeshift altars in front of the emergency room, phoning the hospital relentlessly, and overwhelming the staff. Additional security, including some Hells Angels, was called in to stand guard at the hospital's front entrance to ensure Deadheads didn't enter the building. "They were crafty," says Candelario. "We'd find them in the stairwells. We weren't physical, but we had to say, 'This is not the time.'" Employees of the ticket office, including Steve Marcus, were stationed in the waiting room as extra backup and routinely went outside to ask fans to quiet down. When Marcus saw an unconscious Garcia himself one night, the sight was both disconcerting and encouraging: the tubes were there, but his complexion was healthy pink. "He was still in a coma," Marcus recalls, "but it was the healthiest he'd ever been."

People from Garcia's life, past and present, flashed before him: not just Mountain Girl, who flew down from Oregon, but also old Palo Alto friend Laird Grant and Garcia's first wife, Sara, and their daughter,

Heather. One early morning, around 3 a.m., Hunter showed up, telling Marcus, "I don't know why, but something told me I should be here." At that moment, Marcus recalls, a nurse emerged to tell them Garcia had just woken up and wanted to see a friendly face, and Hunter went in and spent time with Garcia. Still, Garcia could be an incorrigible patient: He would ask visiting friends and employees to bring him egg sandwiches or pork rinds from a nearby Chinese food store.

Popping into the hospital to visit his boss, Garcia's limo driver, Leon Day, looked down the hall and saw a slew of Angels. Day was shocked but not surprised by Garcia's health problems. A few months before, he'd gone to the house to pick up Garcia to drive him to a show, something Day had been doing since the early eighties. He knocked and knocked and rang the doorbell but received no response. Using his own set of keys, Day went inside and found Garcia lying in bed, looking comatose. "His mouth was wide open and he wasn't breathing," Day recalls. "The minute I got near him, he jerked himself out of it. He said, 'Glad you let yourself in.'"

The business of the Dead ground to a halt for the first time since the band had formed. Hart and Lesh called McNally into the conference room and laid him off. Fall concerts were canceled. Executives at Arista stayed away, hoping for upbeat reports from anyone in the Dead home office. Discharged in August 1986, Garcia returned to Hepburn Heights, now with his former family of Mountain Girl, Trixie, and Annabelle in tow. Trixie, a teenager very much a child of the eighties, down to dressing like Michael Jackson for a spell, had been in summer camp in Oregon when she'd been pulled aside by a counselor and told about her father. Until that point the Dead's massive popularity hadn't fully hit her. She'd regularly tease Garcia (whom she called "Jerry," not "Dad") about being a rock star who wore dirty T-shirts, and based on the band's name alone, most of her high school friends thought the Dead was a death-metal band to be avoided at all costs. ("Only the kids who'd grown up backstage could master the arena thing," she says. "I lost a couple of friends trying to bring them to Dead shows. So after a while I stopped trying.") At Trixie's summer camp in Oregon, though, Garcia's coma was major news. One day she found the entire camp, counselors and campers alike, standing together, holding hands, and saying a prayer for her father. "I thought, 'Wait, everybody cares? This is a big deal?'" she recalls.

Upon visiting the basement apartment in Hepburn Heights for the first time in her life Trixie saw what she calls "dirty little pieces of tin foil and straws" all around—good news of a sort because it meant her father wasn't shooting up. The refrigerator was filled with little but Tang, the fruit-flavored beverage powder, and the armrests in his favorite chair were covered with cigarette burns. Before Garcia returned, Mountain Girl and Grant went to work cleaning up the apartment. Grant hunted for leftover stash wherever he thought his friend may have hidden it. He found nothing inside album covers, but bits of heroin were taped to the bottoms of cereal boxes in the kitchen cabinets.

Garcia may have been back home, but rehabilitation was a dicier matter. With the help of Saunders, he slowly began playing the guitar again, but his progress was glacial. "Slowly he started to get his strength back," Merl Saunders told writer Blair Jackson, "but it sometimes took an hour or two for him to get even a simple chord down." One day Saunders brought by Bralove; the two keyboard players had collaborated before, and Bralove had worked on mixes for a new theme the Dead had cut for an updated version of *The Twilight Zone* series. Although hardly a newcomer to the pop world, Bralove was startled by what he saw—a bloated man smoking cigarettes nonstop and watching cartoons on a large-screen TV in a basement. "My reaction, was, '*This* is the guy?'" he recalls. "Jerry was vulnerable then. I couldn't quite understand it." Garcia seemed wary—he didn't seem to grasp whether

Bralove was a fan or a fellow musician—but he didn't turn grumpy and dismissive, which was a positive sign.

■ ◆ ■

Just after 7 p.m. that May night at Leguna Seca the fog rolled in, the temperatures began to fall, and the Dead returned to the stage to begin filming their first music video. The men who filed back onstage after playing a full show were middle-aged rock warriors, yet collectively they looked about as scrubbed, healthy, and camera-ready as imaginable. Garcia's hair wasn't as untamed as it had been during the worst days of his heroin addiction, and Mydland now sported a shag, replacing the shoulder-length mane from his earliest days in the band.

As the musicians took their places behind their instruments, Gutierrez noticed the first signs of the trauma the Dead had endured almost a year before: Garcia was wearing special padded sneakers for his swollen ankles, largely due to his diabetes. The director arranged a seat by the side of the stage so Garcia would be able to rest during breaks in the shooting.

The song that would be the basis for the video was "Touch of Grey." After hearing it and zeroing in on its "I will survive" refrain, Gutierrez had pitched the band on a clever idea for the video: depicting the Dead as rocking skeletons who'd morph into the actual musicians onstage. "It just seemed to fit with the song," Gutierrez says. "I don't know if the song is all about aging, but it's about the wisdom that comes with age." Garcia—who first asked the director to listen to the whole album they'd just finished and pick what he thought would be the single—instantly took to the idea, and the rest of the band went along with it. (If Garcia was happy, everyone else was too.) Plans were made to film it at one of the two shows at Laguna Seca, and Arista allotted a $150,000 budget to drag the Dead into the MTV age. Gutierrez's company bought anatomically correct skeletons from a medical supply company, asked the band members for their correct heights, and, with puppeteers Chris and Mark Walas (who'd done similar duties on the film *Gremlins*), got to work. The band was so game that Lesh donated one of his tie-dyed shirts for a puppet, Hart his Celtics jacket.

The months that had led up to this moment were agonizing for Garcia and everyone in the Dead camp. As soon as Garcia was able to play his instrument again, the Dead began rehearsing in October 1986 at Front Street, and the initial reports weren't encouraging. During visits to the nearby Dead office Hart and Lesh would shake their heads and mutter alarming comments like, "It's not there." Employees began to worry whether Garcia had suffered permanent damage and whether the Dead were effectively over. Finally, in late October, Hart returned to the office again and was smiling. "We just did a really good 'Dark Star,'" he told them, adding, "It's back." The Dead's ticket office booked comeback shows that same day, starting December 15 at the Oakland Coliseum. In early November publicist McNally visited Garcia's place on Hepburn Heights—Mountain Girl was cooking—and asked for his old job back, and Garcia just chuckled and rehired him. Flashing back to past employees, Garcia told McNally, "Usually when I get somebody a job there, they fuck up on me. But you didn't, so it'll be okay."

The newly buoyant mood continued at Thanksgiving. The days of congregating for a meal at 710 Ashbury were long gone, but a re-creation of a sort was arranged at the Log Cabin Dugout Bar in San Anselmo, part of an American Legion Hall built for Boy Scouts in the 1930s (and still decorated with flags and other patriotic Americana). Gathering at long tables, most of the band (save Mydland, who was absent), employees, and longtime friends like Sue Swanson shared food and laughs. Garcia arrived with a banjo, and eventually he and his longtime pals in acoustic music, David Nelson and Sandy Rothman, huddled together and played bluegrass for several hours. Lesh, sitting nearby with his wife, Jill, yelled out a request for "Wild Horses" from Garcia's Old and in the Way days. For once the air around the band wasn't tinged with tension and grousing; everyone's jobs were again secure, and the sight of Garcia with a banjo, which he hadn't played publicly in years, was another welcome sign.

The Dead played several well-received comeback shows the following month at the Oakland Coliseum, but the surest sign that Garcia and the band were fully in operational mode arrived January 6, 1987. Starting then and continuing through January 15, they recorded the basic tracks for a new album on the stage of the empty Marin Veterans Auditorium in San Rafael, in front of two thousand empty seats. Coming so soon after Garcia's collapse, the efficiency of the sessions was nothing less than miraculous. The reasons behind it were multiple. Except for "When Push Comes to Shove" and "Black Muddy River," they'd been playing most of the material for years and had settled into arrangements worked out on the road. Garcia's near-death experience had instilled a now-or-never urgency that had never permeated the Dead bubble before. Joining Garcia as coproducer was John Cutler, an astute, detail-minded recording engineer who'd worked with members of the Dead starting in the seventies. Cutler was comfortable with the Dead, compared with the name producers they'd worked with on their previous three studio albums, which made the recording even less stressful.

The songs were a relatively strapping lot. "Black Muddy River" had been written on Keith Godchaux's old piano at the Front Street studio. Garcia had begun playing in a gospel style and grabbed a stack of Hunter lyrics atop the keyboard; after leafing through them he had, in no time at all, written the song, which had the stately feel of a parlor ballad from the previous century. Thanks to changes in technology, they could record essentially live, playing together in a large room as if in concert. The borderline-toxic milieu from Fantasy Studios three years earlier were nowhere to be seen or heard. They even tackled—and nailed—versions of "West L.A. Fadeaway" and "Throwing Stones," both first attempted at the Fantasy sessions. The band had purchased an array of synthesizers and emulators and hired Bralove to help to operate them; the Dead were even ready to sound like a radio-friendly band.

In light of everything they'd been through—and the striking fact that they hadn't made a studio album in seven years—the energized brawniness of *In the Dark* was truly remarkable. (The album title derived from one Marin Vets session where the band played with the lights out.) Whether the lyrics were written by Hunter, Barlow, or Mydland, the songs were cantankerous, pessimistic, bleak, or a combination of all three. Teetering relationships, bondage-loving girlfriends, bikers, decaying planets, and sleaze ran through the songs. The eloquent finale, "Black Muddy River," felt like a weary farewell after a lifetime of travails.

Thankfully the music drove away the gloom and doom of many of the words. Bolstered by subsequent overdubs at Front Street, the Dead played with burly, confident energy; nothing about the tracks felt remotely defeated. The joyous swing in "Touch of Grey," with its soothing layer of Mydland organ, was just the start. With Mydland's barrelhouse piano pushing it along, "When Push Comes to Shove" had a similarly rollicking tone, and the band playfully snarled on "Hell in a Bucket" and "Throwing Stones." Despite everything it had been through, Garcia's voice held firm, and Weir let loose with a falsetto finale in "Hell in a Bucket." Rarely had the Dead been so primed to assert themselves on record, and rarely had they conveyed such pleasure at making music without an audience staring at them.

Keeping it as always all in the family, Justin Kreutzmann had been hired as an assistant and noticed some of the differences for himself. In the past at Front Street Garcia would disappear into one of the back rooms; no one was allowed in. Now he was once more accessible and engaged. During one session Bralove looked over and saw Garcia in a corner, snoring loudly. But this time, at least, they knew it was simply exhaustion.

$$\blacksquare \quad \blacklozenge \quad \blacksquare$$

The plan at Laguna Seca called for the Dead to lip-synch for several hours—monumentally torturous for a band who could barely keep it together for a photo shoot. (To ensure they wouldn't bolt those sessions, McNally would resort to reading gags from a joke book to keep them in a good mood and in one place.) "Everybody was all touchy about selling out," recalls Trixie Garcia, who, at twelve, was scampering around the set that day. "Jerry had his compass, and they would never dumb themselves down."

But as the band began to lip-synch, something wonderfully peculiar happened: most of them actually appeared to be enjoying the experience. Behind the drums, miming along with his part for "Touch of Grey," Bill Kreutzmann was actually caught smiling. (Before the shoot he'd even engaged in some animated quasi-standup for the crowd.) Lesh remained unconvinced about the job at hand. "I never understood why it was important to have some kind of visual analog to the song," he says. "And why people preferred to watch that than listen to the song. The visual is always going to dilute the impact of the song." Still, he and Weir joked with each other as they pretended to play their instruments.

The song they'd begun lip-synching had its own tangled, drawn-out history. Nearly seven years before, Hunter had written the lyrics to "Touch of Grey"—which could be interpreted as an ode to enduring day-to-day-struggles, although Dead historian McNally referred to it as "a superb rendering of the morning after a cocaine binge"—and with the help of Garcia and John Kahn, Hunter attempted a version of it for one of his own albums. But Garcia was intrigued: he asked whether he could rewrite the melody, and he could be heard wandering around the upstairs kitchen on Hepburn Heights happily playing the lick he'd devised for it. The Dead began performing the song onstage as early as 1982 in Maryland.

Hearing the band rehearse "Touch of Grey" one night at Marin Veterans, Justin Kreutzmann told Garcia he thought this song was the one—the hit that had always eluded them and that they'd deserved. "No one's going to like this song," Garcia scoffed, thinking the lyrics were too personal. "No one's going to get the significance of it." More troublesome, Garcia was also having trouble nailing the guitar solo, the result of lingering issues with his coma. "He just couldn't quite get it," Hart recalls. "He'd sit there and play it over and over. Endless takes. For some reason he had a hard time. He'd had to relearn his instrument and regain his confidence." Finally one night, as in the "Dark Star" moment, out it came, and they finally had the part and the song they needed.

Throughout this period Arista Records was removed from the process but patient. Although the label wasn't badgering the band for new product, they were still, in their way, keeping tabs on the band's progress. By chance an employee of the label's art department was a Deadhead who followed the band around on her summer vacations, and her cassettes, which she would pass along to Arista senior vice president Roy Lott, became the label's primary way of hearing the band's new material. When Lott received a tape from the band with the nearly finished "Touch of Grey," sent overnight to his home, he couldn't have been more pumped. Lott was immediately struck by how produced the song was. Starting with the switch from "I will survive" to "we will survive" in the end and the sense of uplift in the final verse, the Dead had somehow managed to concoct a follow-the-bouncing-melody song that could conceivably be played on Top Forty radio. (Some of that credit belongs to Bralove, who helped spruce up the sonics during overdubbing sessions at Front Street; he helped Hart overdub antique cymbals that sounded like bells.) Lott brought the tape to a Monday morning meeting and played it for the staff, and the reaction was uniformly positive; even those who didn't care for the Dead had to admit it was a hummable song.

Even before the "Touch of Grey" video was completed, the Arista wheels began turning in ways they never had before for the Dead. The label was stocked with executives who'd grown up with FM rock, were fond of the Dead, and related to the band more than to the label's MTV-geared pop. But *In the Dark* was the last release on the band's contract. Although Arista had come to be known as a pop label, thanks to its enormous successes with the likes of Whitney Houston and Barry Manilow, label head Clive Davis didn't want anyone to forget that Arista had fostered plenty of rock 'n' roll, dating back to Patti Smith, Graham Parker, and other acts of the seventies. Holding onto the industry-wary Dead became crucial for both the label's image and rock-press credibility. "We knew that if it didn't work, we would have lost the band, no question about it," says then Arista vice president Don Ienner, "and that gave us impetus."

In his job as aggressive head of radio promotion, Ienner began working "Touch of Grey" as soon as its video was underway. Convincing radio to play a song by a band that had never had a hit—and was the antithesis of pop in the eighties—would be tricky, but Ienner and his department were up for the challenge. To help his cause, Ienner wasn't above leveraging some of the label's biggest acts. "People were amazed that the Dead were still alive and [would say] 'Are you fucking serious? I haven't played a Dead song ever,'" Ienner recalls. "It was, 'If you want me to give you the next Whitney Houston single before I give it to the [radio programmer] across the street, you're gonna be dealing with this fucking Grateful Dead record.'"

But it was most telling that at that point in their career the Dead were willing to play ball with a business they'd normally viewed with antipathy or suspicion. But they now had wives, ex-wives, children, alimony, mortgages, and expensive cars. That turnaround became most apparent in the spring when, before a New York show, Garcia, Hart, and Weir had a brief meeting with Arista executives in a hotel conference room. At least for a moment the combative days of the past—the Dead versus the likes of Joe Smith—evaporated. Davis, Ienner, and Lott pledged commitment to the project; no one in the band objected. The one concern arose when Garcia turned to Lott after a discussion of obligations and said, "I don't have to do Dick Clark, do I?" They all laughed at the very thought of the Dead on Clark's Top Forty TV show, *American Bandstand*, but they also knew Garcia had his limits.

It wasn't only the musicians who had to adjust to the idea of a video. As the filming continued, McNally had the unpleasant job of wading into the audience and busting anyone with a flash on his or her camera. (At least the crew hadn't wrapped him in duct tape, part of his initiation hazing when he joined on as PR person.) One Deadhead thought McNally was hitting on his girlfriend and threatened to deck him; for the rest of the night McNally asked a security guard or two to follow him around.

Otherwise the filming was largely uneventful, one indication that the Dead were working hard to keep their past excesses at bay. Garcia's was the most dramatic rehabilitation, but he wasn't the only one who'd straightened his rudder. With his first baby on the way (Grahame, his first son, was born December 1986), Lesh had stopped using drugs and had seriously cut back on drinking. In terms of maintaining Garcia's recovery, Lesh and Weir laid down a law: no more cocaine on stage. ("That's possible," Lesh says of the story, "but I don't remember that.") Nitrous would still be allowed there, but it too was eventually banned during shows: "That *SSSHHHHHH* was coming through the microphones," says Bralove. "It wasn't doing anything for the music and it was destroying the sound."

In the way they were trying to straighten out the Dead were mirror-
ing the times as much as they always had. The all-for-one sixties were
gone, as were the solipsistic seventies that the Dead had reflected in the
formation of their own label. Now they were echoing the clean-and-
sober stance of many of their peers. Steve Winwood and Peter Gabriel
made themselves over as *GQ*-level cover models. David Crosby, their
old friend and partner in excess, had been busted for freebasing, had
served jail time, and was now living a healthier lifestyle. Former Eagle
Glenn Frey posed with his newly firm biceps in ads for a health-club
chain. The punk rock and new wave that had made the Dead and their
peers seem passé had outlived its welcome, and the sixties—even a
reunited Monkees—were resurrected. Unintentionally the Dead had
picked the ideal moment to connect with the masses.

The newfound and striking aura of professionalism around the Dead
extended to the conference room at their San Rafael headquarters. By
then the phrase "there is nothing like a Grateful Dead concert" was
part of fans' vocabulary, but there was little like a Dead board meeting as well. During band meetings in the seventies the floor would be
thrown open to anyone who wanted to express an idea or speak out.
"People would sit around smoking joints and saying, 'We should play
Cleveland after Chicago,'" recalls Sam Cutler of a typical early get-
together. "And someone would say, 'No, I like St. Louis, that's the best
place to play.' Amateur shit." Now that they were one of the highest-
earning corporations in California, their business gatherings took on
a more orderly air—as much as possible, anyway. They would begin
at least two weeks in advance, when office employee Sue Stephens, the
assistant to whomever was managing at the time and eventually also a
video producer, would begin calling the band members individually to
remind them of the upcoming gathering. After Garcia's coma, meetings
were restricted to band and crew, which didn't always mean they were
streamlined. Enthusiastic as always, Hart would throw out creative but
sometimes impractical ideas; Weir would have a suggestion that would

result in wisecracks from the other band members. Allan Arkush, who had by then known the Dead nearly twenty years and sat in on a few of these sessions, was struck by how unconventional they were despite the Dead's best efforts. "It was fascinating how there was absolutely no forward momentum in these meetings, no matter what the agenda," Arkush says, recalling one particular ideas meeting. "Mickey, Jerry, and Phil came in for a while. Bob came in for a few seconds and left. It was whoever was around. Whoever was there had a different idea. The roadies had ideas. You didn't know if you should pursue one person's idea or put them all together. It was hard to know how to deal with those situations."

One of the few who could grasp and work with the dynamic of the band was Jon McIntire, who had returned to the management fold after a ten-year absence. (In the interim he'd managed Weir separately, among other pursuits.) "In the Grateful Dead the term 'manager' doesn't mean what everyone outside thinks it means," McIntire told writer David Hajdu. "It's actually a lot more daunting than people would know, because of the lack of definition. Am I going to listen to the band? Yes. Is there a bottom line here? Yes, the bottom line is the band. But the band rarely would take a stand, first of all, that was unified, because they were just different individuals. But the individuals in the band would rarely have opinions so definite that they would preclude my making choices in what I was going to do. The one exception there would be Garcia, who occasionally would feel very strongly about something—like, 'hey, man, I'm not playing the *game*—stop that shit!' if I would be trying to make points that were a little bit too strongly in favor of business as usual out in the world, rather than creating our own game. Sometimes, I would go around to every individual in the band and take them aside, and I would explain what it was that I was trying to get them to see." With techniques like those, McIntire was able to get a few things accomplished and move the group's business forward.

Weeks after the "Touch of Grey" video had been filmed the meetings grew more focused and business-like. One concerned the marketing of long-form videos—*So Far*, a collection of performance clips and effects directed by Len Dell'Amico, and Justin Kreutzmann's documentary, *Dead Ringers*, about the making of the "Touch of Grey" video. Would the two products compete for fans' dollars? Bill Kreutzmann, who had been in charge of band finances very early in the Dead's life and still kept a watchful eye on the money (and the managers who oversaw it), could be laconic in meetings, but he also knew when to make sure his point was made. According to notes from the meeting, he "suggested working out the timing and price structuring to be able to market both items. The board agreed that they want to be able to market both, but wise strategy and communication are important."

Meanwhile Arista, sensing it might have an in-demand piece of music to market, began gearing up. The label prepared an initial shipment of 467,000 copies of *In the Dark* ("well beyond our most optimistic projections," wrote John Scher, still working closely with the band, to McIntire on July 9). Soon after came a memo from Arista marketing executive Sean Coakley to Scher recapping radio play for select songs on the album: "Week #3 on 'Touch of Grey' . . . can be described in no other terms than awesome. Album radio is dominated by DEAD air. If this were a hype it would be nauseating; since it's true it's enthralling." The label began planning a day-long celebration with MTV, to be called "Day of the Dead," to introduce the band to viewers who'd been born around the time *American Beauty* had been made.

The Dead finished their part of filming and lip-synching, a short break was taken, and at 11 p.m. the time came for the ghoulish marionettes. The attention to detail was impressive: each skeleton was the exact height as its corresponding band member. With the help of Parish,

Gutierrez secured one of Garcia's actual guitars, and together they figured out a way to protect the front of the instrument from being scratched by the skeleton hand. Gutierrez's company also suggested Weir and Lesh wear shorts "so that we can expose the skeleton's knobby knees!" read an internal memo.

Before the skeletons were wheeled out onstage, the musicians popped in backstage to inspect them and were suitably amused. They'd seen them in the early production stages, but now they faced their own macabre apparitions in their own clothes. Kreutzmann leaned into Garcia's skeleton and joked, "Keep on your diet and you'll be fine!" (For once they could laugh about Garcia's health scare.) Trixie Garcia recalls amusedly "the fake boobs on Jerry's skeleton to make him look beefy," and Garcia and Mountain Girl's daughter Annabelle helped assemble the skeletons by inserting wooden planks down the spine. On a large metal truss platform twenty feet above the stage, the puppeteers took their positions and began manipulating the skeletons, who were placed in the same spots as the band. To Gutierrez's surprise, the Dead stayed to watch the filming—not the entirety of the night but enough to prove they didn't have complete disdain toward the process. "The fog was coming in, and the lights were on the fog—it was just perfect," Hart recalls. "We couldn't have wanted a better setting. The skeletons were creative. The other videos were stupid, but that one was fun." When the marionettes started, the crowd roared as if they were watching the actual band. "They had all the same enthusiasm," Gutierrez marvels. "We had the real Grateful Dead reaction to the marionettes."

In the early hours of the morning the filming began to wrap up. Gutierrez and his crew would be there until just before dawn, although the Dead themselves were able to leave earlier—and, to some of them, not soon enough. Vans carried everyone back to their hotel, with some residual grumbling about all the hours they'd spent in the cold, lip-synching their song. "It was a long night, and it went on and on, and it was, 'We're dying here!'" recalls Mountain Girl, who was out in the crowd with Annabelle for most of the shoot. "Everybody was completely burnt out. It was a long drive down there, and then we do all this crazy shit. Everyone was beside themselves." She noticed that Garcia seemed to be "very pissy" at that point, although she couldn't always tell whether it was about their relationship or the work.

Gutierrez and his company would have just over a month to turn the video in to Arista—the deadline was June 8—so editing began almost immediately. When a rough cut was finished the director took the clip to Front Street, where by now the band was rehearsing for an upcoming tour with Bob Dylan. Gutierrez and his crew brought along a tape deck and monitor and set it up in the front office space, and the musicians took a break from rehearsing and gathered around to watch themselves in a music video. Culminating in the charming moment when the skeletons transformed into the live Dead, the resulting clip was clever and self-aware, and it captured the Dead's sense of humor. The macabre aspect of it—the sight of a Garcia skeleton in an imitation of his clothes, just about a year after he almost died—wasn't lost on anyone. When it came to his documentary, Justin Kreutzmann thought all the outsiders who wandered onstage actually enhanced his project: "With all those people up there," he says, "it made for an interesting shot."

When the "Touch of Grey" screening was done, applause and approving comments followed; as was often the case, Garcia loving it was good enough for everyone. In the back Dylan said nothing, but he nodded and smiled at Gutierrez, in what seemed to be tacit approval.

■　◆　■

The video would be merely the first of a new list of industry chores on the horizon. The band had to put finishing touches on *In the Dark* and rehearse for the tour with Dylan. *Forbes*, the business magazine that normally couldn't have cared less about anything Dead, was requesting an interview for a lengthy story about the industry of the Dead in 1987: the ticket office and sales, the six thousand calls a day received by the hotline. Despite a few grumbles now and again, the Dead went along with it all. They *had* survived, and what better time to remind everyone that they had and then sell a few records in the process? As buzz for "Touch of Grey" and the Dylan tour began building, a palpable tingle enveloped the Dead office: they'd been hearing for twenty years that they could be a huge band, but that level of success suddenly felt within reach. Talking with *Rolling Stone* at the time, Hunter, giving a rare interview, wondered aloud whether the incoming tidal wave would be good for them all. "By all indications, we're going to get the record-company backing all the things that are necessary to have a hit, and it's a little frightening. Are we going to be eaten now? . . . I'm excited by it, and I have misgivings. I would like the world to know about the Grateful Dead; it's a phenomenal band. But I don't think the Grateful Dead is going to be as free a thing as it was."

Only time would tell, but for the moment a few positive omens were in the air. During the "Touch of Grey" shoot they'd had the idea of filming a dog running off with the leg of the Hart marionette. One of the producers waded into the crowd, found a group of dog candidates, and set up an audition area for the owners to show off their pets' tricks. One canine stood out and was hired. As it turned out, his name, recalling another heyday of the band, was Tennessee Jed.

Onstage in Pittsburgh, far from the turmoil outside.
© ROBBI COHN

CHAPTER 13

PITTSBURGH,
APRIL 3, 1989

They'd trundled into the place six times before, dating back to 1973. And starting with its silver dome—which could pass for a spaceship that had crashed and half-sunk into the ground—the Pittsburgh Civic Arena had looked about the same. Tonight would seem to be no different—with one minor but telling change. As soon as he stuck his head out the backstage door, Dennis McNally, now in his fifth year as the band's publicist, immediately had a feeling something was off. He was accustomed to seeing Deadheads milling about before shows, waiting to get in or eager to score tickets, but tonight, so *many* of them seemed to be out there.

As the Dead began wrapping up their third decade as a road machine, their operation was as clockwork and regimented as that of any major corporation. At each venue the crew would generally arrive first, before lunch, to begin the arduous task of preparing the Dead's flotilla of gear, ensuring everything was in the same spot every night. The onstage Persian rug had to be rolled out and set in its precise location or else someone in the band might notice and take offense that it was a few inches off. Eventually the band would arrive by van or limo and be driven into the generic cement catacombs of whatever arena or stadium they'd be playing. The crew, which included Ram Rod, Parish, Candelario, and Robbie Taylor, a longstanding, loyal employee since the seventies, would begin the process of screening anyone who wanted to get backstage, not always a pretty sight. (As Parish had predicted, there was no fallout from the incident at Laguna Seca two years before.) Allan Arkush was always able to pass muster and make it backstage to Garcia's area, where he witnessed another part of the ritual: unfamiliar faces streaming in with homegrown pot. "They'd hand him some in a box and say stuff like, 'I crossed it with this type you really dug,'" Arkush says. "It was like a *High Times* centerfold." After the roadies tested it first, Garcia generally accepted the gift with a smile. Because the dressing rooms rarely had adequate ventilation, Arkush would sometimes tumble out higher than when he'd walked in.

About a half-hour before show time management would pop in to the Dead dressing rooms to give each man the thirty-minute warning. Tonight the person handling that chore would be Cameron Sears. In 1987 Jon McIntire had again left the Dead, replaced by Sears, his right-hand man. A bearded former river raft operator, Sears had entered the Dead world in standard head-scratching manner: after he had taken some of the Dead office staff on several river expeditions, McIntire had called Sears with a job offer—despite Sears's lack of experience working in the music business.

No matter the city or venue, other aspects of the Dead road experience always remained in place. There was the matter of figuring out something approaching a set list, or at least an opening song. With that began another part of the ceremony: the ribbing of Weir. As Arkush watched one night, Weir might suggest a song to start the second set, only to be greeted with mocking retorts. Someone else might then yell out the name of an incredibly obscure track from their back catalog, at which everyone would agree—before circling their way back to Weir's original choice. Even though Mydland was younger, Weir remained the little brother who needed to be given a hard time. The crew would relentlessly tease him for the way he'd show up early for soundchecks and spend an inordinately long amount of time working on achieving the correct tone for his guitar. "It could be brutal," says one. "It seemed like he would play the same note forever just to get the tone right." (Luckily, the results generally paid off: the guitars *would* sound good.) The increasing brevity of Weir's onstage shorts also egged them on. Weir took the mocking in stride, rarely if ever losing his cool. Like friends who'd met in high school and were frozen in time, they clung to their own interpersonal rituals.

During Drums everyone but the percussionists would retreat to his own space, and during Space anything offstage would be possible. (During one New York–area show Hart left his percussion area, walked over to guest Al Franken, seated by the side of the stage, and offered him a drink—all in the middle of the show.) The rituals would continue outside, where campers and vendors set up in the psychedelically festooned area that came to be known as "Shakedown Street." Inside, tapers would gather in their now-established area and begin installing their recording gear. The security and safety guidelines were so ingrained that Ken Viola, promoter John Scher's head of security, wrote up a pamphlet distributed to local promoters about how to deal with the crowds in and around the venues.

Following each show, once the Dead had left in their limos or vans, the promoters and band reps would gather for the inevitable backstage settlements, factoring in overtime costs, catering bills, and whatever other expenses were incurred. Alex Cooley, who promoted a number of Dead shows in Atlanta, recalls that the band would always walk out with 70 percent of the gate, anywhere between $250,000 and $700,000 per show, depending on the year. (The Omni had 17,000 seats but only sold 14,000 because the sound system took up the rest of the space.) After the show, assuming they had to move onto another town right away, the crew would begin the task of tearing everything down and loading it back into the trucks.

When McNally opened the stage door in Pittsburgh he was tending to one of his own regular jobs: escorting in local TV crews or photographers who wanted to shoot footage of the show. Although he noticed the gathering mob, he didn't have time to ponder what was taking place. Like everyone else in the organization, he had an assigned task that had to be taken care of. Even if something went wrong, everyone involved assumed that, as always, the Dead would find a way to resolve it and carry on. That too had been de rigueur for decades.

Nearly two years earlier, in September 1987, McNally had been confronted with a wholly different and far more onerous task. To celebrate the success of *In the Dark*, executives from Arista, along with Scher, had gathered backstage at New York's Madison Square Garden to have their photos taken with the Dead. Here was a standard industry ritual of its own: pose with the suits, hold up your gold records, smile, and watch as the photo of the victory lap was reprinted in the music trade magazines. But as McNally was learning, sometimes in the most excruciating way there was only one hitch: the band couldn't be remotely bothered with those sorts of customs.

As many on the Arista business side had anticipated, *In the Dark* had become that rarity, a million-selling Grateful Dead album. The label's promotional muscle—and the urge to ensure the record's commercial success so that the Dead wouldn't flee for another company—had worked in ways it never had before. It was almost impossible to turn on MTV and not see the "Touch of Grey" video, and the single climbed to number nine. *In the Dark* itself sneaked into the Top Ten, smirking alongside albums by Whitney Houston, Def Leppard, U2, and Mötley Crüe. Even when the album began slipping down the charts after peaking at number six, an issue of the Deadhead fan newsletter *Terrapin Flyer*, distributed free at shows, urged Deadheads to "call MTV to tell them how much you love the video" in order to "give the Dead's new album a needed sales push because it has slipped slightly on the charts." The fans could be as organized as the office itself.

A few months before, McNally had entered a backstage room where the Dead had all gathered shortly before going on stage—Garcia in his trademark black T-shirt and, as always, practicing scales—and broke the news that "Touch of Grey" was now a Top Ten hit. Glancing up from his guitar, Garcia cracked, "I am appalled" and went back to playing. The rest of the band exchanged quizzical looks, a collective *hmmmm*—the sound of men deciding how to respond to news about entering foreign territory. Not the worst feeling in the world, and yet so alien they couldn't quite grasp it.

In 1986 the Dead was in need of a new business manager because their finances, especially after Garcia's coma and their canceled shows, were in shambles; they were also behind on their tax returns. The band approached Nancy Mallonee, a CPA with experience in the music business. During her job interview at a band meeting Garcia chuckled and said to her, "I don't know why anybody would want to do this job, but if you want it, it's yours." Mallonee saw for herself the way their finances turned around the following year. "Things changed dramatically after *In the Dark* was released," says Mallonee. "The business took off after that. It was surprising how much things changed from 1986 to 1987. Huge. They made a lot of money off *In the Dark*."

Record sales were merely one indication that the Dead's business was erupting around them in the wake of "Touch of Grey." By now touring income amounted to 80 to 90 percent of the Dead's gross income; the Dead grossed $26.8 million in 1987 alone. In 1987 mail-order ticket sales hit 450,000, more than ten times from a few years before. Enough requests had come in for their 1987 New Year's Eve show at Oakland Coliseum to fill that venue six times over. Some promoters didn't even bother advertising for shows; because the fans knew ahead of time, it was just wasted money.

Sensing they had the upper negotiating hand for the first time in their careers, the Dead barreled into the renewal of their contract with Arista with a rare sense of boldness and self-assurance. With their savvy, poker-champ lawyer Hal Kant leading the way, they demanded and received a higher royalty rate, about $3.50 per CD. They floated the idea of releasing a series of live albums from their vault on their own label, to be curated by in-house archivist Dick Latvala. Arista wasn't initially taken with the idea—they feared it would compete with live albums the label was planning to release—but the company agreed, as long as the band limited the pressings. "I said, 'You can't sell more than twenty-five thousand units,'" Arista vice president and general manager Lott recalls. "'If you have live recordings and want to sell twenty-five thousand to the hardcore, go ahead.'" (That series became *One from the Vault*, launched in 1991 after soundman Dan Healy convinced the band to dig into the archives and release the famed Great American Music Hall gig in 1975. That release was followed in 1993 by the launch of the two-track recording series *Dick's Picks*, helmed by Latvala, Candelario, and John Cutler.) Busting Arista's chops a bit more, Kant insisted the contract be as boiled down as possible and limited to only five pages at most, about ten times shorter than the usual music business paperwork. To squeeze in all the details and numbers, Arista lawyers had to extend the page margins and make the point size as small as they could and still have it be readable. But for the Dead post–"Touch of Grey," it would be done.

Playing by the industry's rules had never been the band's forte, as was immediately evident during their five-night run at the Garden starting September 15, 1987. To the puzzlement of Clive Davis and his troops, they only played "Touch of Grey" two of those five evenings. One top executive was also baffled when Garcia would start a solo but stay put where he was rather than walk to the front and engage in some watch-me-play showboating—standard rock procedure for nearly every other arena band in the world. Garcia would have none of it.

McNally received a lesson in industry politics himself when Garcia, Weir, Mydland, and Scher dropped by New York's iconic rock station, WNEW-FM, to hang out and chat with Scott Muni, the gravel-voiced DJ legend. As Scher watched, surprised but helpless to stop them, the band and Muni began playing cards on the air. "I was jumping out of my skin," Scher recalls. "Every time Scott took a break, which was not very often, a lot of advertisers got screwed. I remember saying, 'Hey guys, we're on the radio—it's not television! Nobody can see what you're doing!'" Unfortunately no one in the Dead organization told anyone at the label that the Dead were dropping by the station for some lackadaisical promotion, and back at his hotel room McNally received a furious call from an Arista executive who hadn't been informed of the Dead's plans until he'd turned on his radio. McNally had to apologize for the oversight. "It wasn't intentional," he says. "It just didn't occur to me to coordinate with the record company. I hadn't even *talked* to the company until those meetings in the spring of 1987."

Backstage at the Garden the time had come to honor the Dead's promise to pose for photos with the higher-ups at Arista while holding sales awards for *In the Dark*. McNally began hitting one dressing room after another. But schmoozing with record industry people— those who Garcia would regularly refer to in a David Letterman–esque way as "weasels"—still wasn't especially appealing. When McNally began making the rounds, the responses were, to say the least, mixed. Weir, agreeable as ever and also the most cognizant of the value of face time with label folks, emerged readily. But with the rest McNally found himself begging and cajoling the Dead, sometimes on his knees, to leave their rooms and shake a few hands: "We promised!" McNally implored. Finally Garcia begrudgingly agreed, and he, Hart, and Weir trudged into the Arista-filled room, where they gathered with Davis and his troops, smiled, stood still for a few photos, and then almost immediately left. McNally would later describe the experience as "brutal," leaving him frazzled and exhausted after what he called one of his worst days on the job.

■　◆　■

The first night at the Pittsburgh Civic Arena, Sunday, April 2, had gone reasonably well. The set included a slew of the band's usual grab-bag of covers, from blues ("Little Red Rooster") and New Orleans romps ("Iko Iko") to covers of what were now being called classic-rock songs (Dylan's "Queen Jane Approximately," Traffic's "Dear Mr. Fantasy"). There were few surprises, which sometimes rankled Garcia. "There's a certain amount of laziness," Garcia would tell *Rolling Stone* later that year about the band's repertoire during this time. But the ebullience that infused the 1987 and 1988 shows largely continued into the new year, and in Pittsburgh the crowd did hear a few new songs that had yet to appear on an album: Mydland and Barlow's "We Can Run" and a relatively new Hunter-Garcia song, "Foolish Heart."

By now a new generation of devoted Deadheads had begun following them gig to gig, town to town, and Dan Ross, who had a ticket for both Pittsburgh shows, embodied that new breed. Born the year the Skull and Roses (*Grateful Dead*) album was released, Ross was raised in the Detroit suburbs. In the early eighties a friend had given him an unwanted copy of *Dead Set*, and even though Ross was more inclined toward punk bands like the Dead Kennedys and the Misfits, he was captivated by the Dead; because his father had served in Vietnam, both the culture and counterculture of the sixties resonated with the eighteen-year-old. And because the Dead were far from in vogue when he first discovered them, his classmates shunned Ross in some quarters, but his fascination with the band didn't dim.

In April 1988 Ross finally made it to his first Dead show, at the Joe Louis Arena in St. Louis. He'd been to other concerts before, including one by Kiss, but his St. Louis experience was like none other. The crowd of strangers was uncommonly welcoming—to the point of dosing him—and he noticed how the crowd would erupt at even the tiniest of Garcia's gestures. The interaction between band and fans was like nothing he'd seen. Arriving home, he was so stoked that he woke up his parents at two in the morning to tell them about it; they seemed happy, if sleepy.

Like many before—and many to come—Ross was immediately hooked on the band's music, culture, and mythos. Deciding he had to attend every Dead show on their summer and fall tour that year, Ross, who was still in high school, made an unusual deal with his parents: if he maintained an honor-roll average for the remainder of the academic year, his mother would give the school her approval for him to miss certain days in the spring. His parents would also put aside $60 a week, which he'd receive if he maintained that average. (He eventually used that money to support himself as he followed the Dead around for every tour from then on.) Ross graduated on time but couldn't attend the ceremony; the Dead were playing that night in Foxboro, Massachusetts. When he stopped by his school later on to pick up his diploma, a teacher asked where he'd been. "Dead show," he said. "Yeah," the teacher shrugged, knowingly.

Ross wasn't a "Touchhead"—a derogatory term old-timers used for those fans who'd never heard of the Dead until their radio-welcomed hit—nor was he a grizzled veteran. To demonstrate he wasn't a newbie, he quickly adapted to the unwritten rules of how to behave at Dead shows: no gate crashing, no scalping, no dosing without the consent of the person about to get dosed, and no sneaking ahead in line for shows at the same venue the following nights. "It was basically the same behavior you would expect or condone in any other community," he recalls. "Be a good neighbor."

Those rules were still in effect and honored, but a new, less informed swarm was beginning to descend upon Dead shows. MTV initiated the rush with its "Day of the Dead" broadcast in the summer of 1987 as part of the promotional push for *In the Dark*. With its footage of partying, tie-dyed fans in parking lots (and the implied message of vast quantities of drugs in the vicinity), the show sent out an intractable message: *Come here and party, even if you don't know much about this band or its history*. As Steve Marcus of the Dead's ticket office says, "It was the beginning of the end."

Initially the influx of new followers didn't faze the band, who rarely if ever ventured out into the crowd once they were ensconced in the belly of the arena beast. "We became immensely popular, and from what I could see, our popularity jumped by 20 percent," Weir has said. "We were already taking venue security into account before *In the Dark*. People were crashing fences and stuff. People were getting hurt. We had to be very careful the way we plotted our moves to avoid trouble. And when we had a hit record suddenly with *In the Dark* it had the potential to take us into a fairly troublesome space. But we were already so well versed at handling crowd situations that it wasn't much of a blow."

During this initial wave of mainstream popularity comical sights abounded: the lawyer in the three-piece suit who zipped into the parking lot at RFK stadium in his BMW, all the while screaming at his female companion about the judge who'd kept him in court too long and made him late for the show. Jumping out of the car, he yanked off his vest and jacket, revealing a tie-dyed T-shirt underneath; popping open his trunk, he pulled out shorts and flip-flops. Instantly he became a Deadhead, making Don Henley's lyric from several years earlier—"I saw a Deadhead sticker on a Cadillac"—come to life. Meanwhile Candelario would hear from Deadheads who'd begun monitoring his every move on stage as he and the crew set up, which he found odd and unnerving.

As amusing as such moments were to those who worked with the Dead, they also portended an invasion for which no one was fully prepared. In 1988 the Dead played three shows in Hartford, but the people who camped out at Bushnell Park left it a paper-clogged mess. Although plastic bags had been distributed to help clean up the trash, few were used. The next day Jim Koplik, the local promoter, received a call from the Hartford city council, which banned the Dead from the city. (Memories of a 1975 riot at a Dead show there, where five thousand fans tried to barrel into a show that wasn't even sold out, were still dogging them.) The city publicly ordered the Dead to pay for cleanup. The Dead refused, but privately the band forked over $2,500 in the form of a donation to Bushnell Park, thereby putting a good face on an ugly situation. The Dead would eventually play Hartford again, but not until several years of income had been lost at one of their most profitable venues.

By the time the Dead were preparing to go onstage the first night in Pittsburgh, Deadheads had already been camping out near the Civic Arena. Police reporters at the *Pittsburgh Post-Gazette* began hearing about cops growing increasingly anxious and infuriated by fans who'd begun setting up tents in vacant lots in the adjacent Hill District, a poor and drug-addled area to begin with. Tensions were gradually escalating, and the traffic cops patrolling the Deadheads were a special, aggressive breed at the time, down to their black leather jackets and boots—"fucking storm troopers, and they dressed like them," recalls one *Post-Gazette* reporter. The situation hardly seemed rosy, but then the Civic Arena had hosted hundreds of rock shows before this, including the Dead's, with few incidents.

■ ◆ ■

The guest lists at Dead shows reflected their newfound roles as mainstream outlaws. Walter Cronkite, Speaker of the House Tip O'Neill, various members of the *Saturday Night Live* cast—the range of guests revealed their growing range of followers. After John Kennedy Jr. worked as a ranch-hand at Barlow's Bar Cross ranch in Wyoming, he and his sister, Caroline, attended at least one Dead show (the Capitol Theater in Passaic, New Jersey, in 1978), and John took a seat next to Weir at one band after-show dinner. Jill Larson, one of the stars of the soap opera *All My Children*, was invited to sit onstage after one of the Dead and his wife took a tour of the set of the show. (Before she had a chance to compliment Garcia on Cherry Garcia, the Ben & Jerry's ice cream flavor, one of the crew warned Larson not to mention it—something about it was still a sore point.) At a later '90s show, Bralove looked over and saw, next to him, Tipper Gore (then wife of Vice President Al) and a retinue of Secret Service agents; Al himself was on the other side of the stage. The Dead's long, strange trip was only becoming stranger.

At a show at the Forum in Los Angeles early in 1989 a familiar face, partly covered by a hoodie, was wandering in the back of the hall—Bob Dylan. When Dylan had toured with the band about two years earlier the results had a certain oil-and-water quality (although the Dead's own sets were largely stellar), and the live album that came from it, *Dylan and the Dead*, was so anticlimactic (especially compared to the looser rehearsal tapes of the Dead and Dylan at Front Street) that Arista didn't fight when Dylan's label, Columbia, wanted it. "Columbia insisted that the album be on Columbia, and I remember not being disappointed," says Lott. "We could have gotten into it—'You can't have the Dead'—but I didn't think much of the album, and we were coming off a high with 'Touch of Grey.'" In the crowd at the Forum Dylan spotted Debbie Gold, the friend of the Dead who'd also worked for him and was wading through the crowd. "Take me to Jerry!" he said. As she led him up to the stage, Dylan enthused, "I get to play 'Dire Wolf!'" He wound up sitting in with them for more than one song, playing guitar alongside them but never singing. Even knowing

Dylan, the Dead were baffled; during the intermission one of them wondered what the hell was happening. According to Dead legend, Dylan called the Fifth and Lincoln office the Monday after the show and asked whether he could join the band, but at least one member of the Dead nixed the idea—assuming it was even a serious one to begin with on Dylan's part.

By now the backstage area was also filled with a few new family members. In his limo one day in the middle of 1987 Garcia broke some news to driver Leon Day. "He said, 'I guess I'm fathering a child,'" Day recalls. "I said, 'You *guess* you are? You don't know? What are you doing about it?' He said, 'Well, it would be nice to know the kid's okay.'"

That night Day met the mother, Manasha Matheson, a Deadhead who, by coincidence, had grown up in Englishtown, New Jersey, the site of the Dead's mammoth 1977 show. As a child Matheson had played in the same field where the show was held and even attended the concert herself as a teenager. (Even before the Raceway Park show her first Dead experience was at the 1973 Watkins Glen extravaganza, where she says she was struck by the "sound and clarity" of Garcia's guitar.) Matheson had met Garcia in a roundabout way. While she was studying abroad at Oxford, by way of her own Chicago school, Shimer College, a friend attended a Dead show in Illinois in 1977 and brought Garcia a pumpkin with a playful note inside that read, "Manasha says hi."

The following year Matheson was back in the States at Shimer and preparing to see the Dead at the Uptown Theatre in Chicago. Before the show she'd been listening to *Terrapin Station* while working on figure-drawing sketches when a friend visited, holding a topographic map of Illinois. "I noticed an area called Terrapin Ridge," she says. "As serendipity would have it, Jerry's voice came through the stereo speaker at that moment singing, 'The compass always points to Terrapin.'" Matheson tucked the map and some red roses into a carved-out pumpkin she'd bought from a farmer, took it to the Uptown, and, walking up to the stage just as the show was beginning, presented it to Garcia. "It made him smile," she says. "He thanked me and gently put the pumpkin on his amp." By way of a pal of Hart's, she and a friend met Garcia the next day at his hotel. After talking about Catholicism, among other topics, Matheson said to him, "I think you are a saint." Garcia chuckled and replied, "How are you defining 'saint'?" Despite their nearly twenty-year age differences, the two had certain things in common: Matheson's father was a clarinetist, like Garcia's dad, and thanks to her parents, Matheson was interested in visual arts in much the way Garcia was.

By the mid-eighties Matheson was living in California and working at a health food store in Fairfax in Marin County. When she heard about Garcia's coma, she hitchhiked to the hospital; there she met Hunter, who, she says, told her Garcia was "drifting in and out" and that she shouldn't see him in that condition. When Garcia woke up from his coma she heard he'd evoked her name. During his recovery Garcia called her at her parents' house in New Jersey and asked her to come back to California, sending her a plane ticket so she could visit him in Los Angeles (where he was working on the *So Far* long-form video). Although he and Mountain Girl were living together at his apartment on Hepburn Heights in San Rafael, Matheson and Garcia went to the Dead's Easter weekend shows in Irvine before returning to Marin. By the Dead's summer tour the two were a couple.

Garcia insisted to Matheson that his relationship with Mountain Girl was platonic, but when Manasha became pregnant Sue Swanson saw the hurt look on Mountain Girl's face. (To writer Robert Greenfield, Mountain Girl would add, of the baby, "He really enjoyed that little girl. . . . For him, the magic was in this relationship with that little girl, and there was nothing I could do about those things so I just let go. That was extremely hard to do but it did get done.") Friends had nothing but praise for the way Mountain Girl had helped Garcia through his recovery after his coma. "MG kept people away from him," says Linda Kahn.

"She was able to protect him. I'm not sure how much he appreciated that after a while, but for the time, he did." But as Parish would later note, Garcia had a habit of ending one relationship by diving into another; unpleasant confrontations were to be avoided as much as possible.

Other additions backstage were more musically oriented. After Bruce Springsteen temporarily dissolved the E Street Band, Clarence Clemons relocated to the Bay Area in search of new opportunities. Given how much he loved music, sitting in with bands, dropping into clubs, and partying, it was inevitable that he and some of the Dead would intersect, and they did, running into each other at clubs like Sweetwater in Mill Valley. It wasn't long before Clemons was backstage at Dead shows. At the Oakland Coliseum a bag of mushrooms was passed around backstage. Seeing the container on a table, Clemons exclaimed, "I wanna get high with the Grateful Dead!" Handing him the bowl, Garcia cracked, "Well, here you go!" Big and gregarious, Clemons dropped to his knees between Weir and Garcia, reached into the batch of mushrooms with his large hands, grabbed a handful, and tossed them down. Clemons seemed fine—until he sat in with the band and, halfway into the set a large, confused smile overtook his face.

Clemons responded both to the band's musicianship and especially their blues and R&B covers, and according to Weir, the saxman would have loved to have joined the Dead full time. Weir and Garcia were actually amenable to the idea, but not everyone else in the Dead was. "A couple of our guys hate the saxophone," Weir has said. "So not everyone else would have gone for it. In the Dead back then anyone in the band had the power of veto." Sensing the objections, Weir didn't push too hard for Clemons to join. Still, Clemons sat in with the Dead and the Jerry Garcia Band a handful of times in 1989, and even stranger, he floated an unusual idea to Weir and Garcia. Clemons suggested the three of them move in together for what Weir says would have been "a bachelor pad." As odd as the idea sounded, Weir has said he and Garcia gave it serious consideration, at least for a while; after all, all three loved a good party. "It would've been a lot of fun," Weir has said. "But I don't think anyone would have survived. That would've been a toxic environment." In the end, they passed on the idea—yet another example of the surprises that could await them backstage.

■ ◆ ■

Shortly before they hit the road again they needed to record new material for their all-important—at least to Arista—follow-up to *In the Dark*.

"Can we do it a few more times?" Weir asked about a new song, "Shit Happens."

It had been another long night at Club Front, and as Justin Kreutzmann watched, one of the Dead cast a withering glance at his band mate. "I will play that song twice," he said, "and if I play it a third time, it will curdle my blood."

The growing, sometimes unruly crowds at their shows were one thing, but even in the studio the Dead universe seemed to be off its axis compared to the preceding two years. The first hurdle was obvious: they hadn't road-tested the fresh songs as much as they had the material on *In the Dark*—a lovely Hunter-Garcia song, "Standing on the Moon," had made its stage debut only in February. But they had to maintain the momentum of a hit album, and Arista convinced the band and management that an October 1989 release date would be ideal, if only in terms of marketing. (Halloween! Dead!)

At Club Front and George Lucas's nearby Skywalker Studios they again tried to play the songs live as a band. But something wasn't clicking, and they opted to painstakingly overdub each of their parts onto basic rhythm tracks. Anyone stopping by Club Front would have encountered the unusual sight of Garcia, headphones clamped down onto his silvery mane, sitting by himself and adding leads, or Weir doing the same, with no one else around. John Cutler was back, assisted this time by Bob Bralove, who'd graduated from helping them with electronics on stage (he was practically an unofficial seventh member of the band) to taking an associate producer role on the album. Onstage Bralove continued to stand near the drummers and help with MIDI and other sonic enhancements to make the Dead sound more high-tech than they had before.

Bralove had grown accustomed to the Dead's unpredictability and sonic adventurousness. On his first tour with the band, during their summer 1987 shows with Dylan, Bralove watched, stunned, as Hart began smashing pedals with a metal pipe during one Drums segment. "I thought, 'Oh, my God!'" he recalls. "Everything was in the red and distorted. I went, 'Oh, there's a different reality in performance for these guys.' I was trying to figure out what the hell was going on. This was education by fire."

In theory the new recording plan could have worked. Dating back to *Anthem of the Sun*, the Dead had used the studio as a large instrument, and technology had vastly improved since 1968; with Bralove's help, they could use digital recording, MIDI, drum loops, and other effects far more effortlessly. "It was, 'Maybe we should try this—who knows? We've never done it that way!'" Bralove recalls. "That was all part of it. I saw it as a desire to experiment. For a band that comes off as so casual about so much, the desire to improve sound quality and production techniques was huge."

For their part the Dead were trying their best to stay on a relatively even keel and be good boys. Yet tempers, frustrations, and old habits intruded as the band attempted the arduous task of piecing together an album practically note by note. Garcia was looking haggard again, and that newly darkened mood cast a pall over the sessions. "The camaraderie was still there," recalls Shelley Kreutzmann, "but it was all contingent on how well Jerry was doing and if he was chasing the dragon. The healthier he was, the better everyone got along." Worn down after repeatedly playing to a click track that would keep him on the beat,

Bill Kreutzmann snapped, "I'm done playing this—I'm going home." (And, according to his son Justin, he did.)

For his central contribution, Weir brought with him "Victim or the Crime," lyrics courtesy of Gerrit Graham, an actor who had come into the Dead world by way of a mutual friend, Andy Leonard. The song was melodically complex to start with; for all the teasing he endured, Weir was now the one pushing the band into the most unexplored song-structure territory. But according to Graham, at least half the band were unhappy with the use of the word "junkie" in the song; Graham assumed it had to do with band members afraid of using it in Garcia's presence. "We were all supposed to understand automatically what the problem was and why Jerry must be protected from this unthinkable offense," Graham later wrote. "Words like 'inappropriate' and 'unsuitable' were getting heavy workouts."

The ensuing storm made Weir want to stick with the song even more, which only made the sessions tenser. "They wanted to use the studio as an instrument, but it wasn't as much fun," recalls Justin Kreutzmann, again hired as an assistant. "It was very un-Dead-like, and people lost patience. I remember days and days of 'Victim or the Crime'—days and days of that chord progression. You start to shake after a while." Hart was spending enormous amounts of time at his home studio piecing together percussion parts. Lesh would later dub the making of what came to be called *Built to Last* "a nightmarish briar patch of egotistical contention." That was especially the case with "Shit Happens," a mediocre Weir-Hunter collaboration; the band took two stabs at cutting it and then canned it altogether. It was never completed nor included on any Dead album.

It fell to Mydland—and his recurring lyricist partner, John Perry Barlow—to write the bulk of the new material, especially with a deadline looming closer than the band was accustomed to. "Nobody was writing songs," Barlow says, "and we had a commitment." An instinctively creative musician, Mydland could pump out a melody in as little as a half-hour, and before long he and Barlow had finished a handful of songs. How his songs fit in with the Dead would be open to debate: comparisons to pop-soul singers like Michael McDonald were apt. Yet Mydland's creativity on keyboards clearly enhanced their music; during the sessions for the new album his parts on "Picasso Moon" and "Foolish Heart" made the songs three-dimensional.

At the same time, Mydland was also showing signs of distress. Just before the album was mastered he turned up at the studio in no shape to work but desperate to remix "I Will Take You Home," the touching ballad he'd written for his daughters. (By now Mydland and girlfriend Lisa had wed.) Even though Bralove had to leave for Los Angeles with the master tapes the next morning, somehow they got it done despite Mydland's condition. His troubles were hardly a secret to the Dead, but few knew how bad they would get in the months to come.

Assuming their positions on stage at the Civic Arena on the second night, April 3, the Dead were a study in subtle contrasts, grown men who revealed the different ways they were handling middle age. Wearing a sweater, Lesh looked like a nicely coiffed college professor. Weir was in stylish gray slacks, his long hair pulled back in a ponytail. As always, Garcia was sporting a black T-shirt, of which he had a closet full, and his white hair was swept up over his forehead and cascaded down to his shoulders. Even though he was parked in front of his synthesizer and B3 organ, Mydland remained the most animated member of the band. At times he seemed to be heaving himself onto the keyboard with a desperate, almost manic energy, as if an electric-shock switch had been inserted under his piano bench.

The Dead rarely if ever rehearsed before packing their suitcases for the road, and some of the early shows on this spring 1989 tour reflected that; the band sounded tentative or just average. Yet at some point along the way the beast awakened and began to roar, and Pittsburgh was one of those moments. Garcia was now standing next to Mydland (he and Lesh had switched places onstage), and the two alternated expressive solos on "Blow Away," one of the new Barlow-Mydland collaborations. Mydland sparkled on a keyboard solo on "Greatest Story Ever Told," the galloping Weir-Hunter song from *Ace*, and his harmonies continued to boost warhorses like "Uncle John's Band," which ended with a dramatic, chord-crashing crescendo before leading into the Drums and Space segments. "We were real tight," Weir opined to *Rolling Stone* in 2013. "We could hear and feel each other thinking, and we could intuit each other's moves readily. And at the same time, our vocal blend was at its peak. Jerry and Brent and I, we all individually reached new plateaus as singers. And when we were all singing together it was pretty strong. We packed a punch. For me that was our best era, the late eighties. There was a lot of electricity going on onstage besides the stuff that was plugged in."

Garcia's voice continued to show the strains of his debilitating lifestyle of the previous decade; on "Crazy Fingers," he sounded creaky. Flashes of his old strength came and went, and his guitar solos retained the quality of stones skipping over the water. The previous fall the Dead had broken out a new song, a loping Hunter-Garcia collaboration called "Built to Last" about healing, hope, and reconciliation that brought out the best in the band's casually bubbly Kreutzmann and Hart rhythms and Garcia's still-sweet delivery, and the song became a high point of the second night at the Civic Arena. Inside the arena Deadheads reveled in it all, roaring when Garcia stepped to the mic for "Bertha," his first solo vocal of the night, or when the spotlight hit Lesh for one of his rare turns as lead singer, this time on a cover of Dylan's "Just Like Tom Thumb's Blues."

Yet outside the arena was another, far less blissful story. By the time the Dead kicked into their first song of the night, another part of the touring routine was in effect: the hundreds upon hundreds, sometimes thousands, of fans who'd come without tickets and opted to hang out and party in the parking lot. Depending who was asked, the number without tickets for the second night in Pittsburgh swelled to anywhere between three and ten thousand, all circling an arena that held sixteen thousand. Hearing the music emanating from inside, those who already had tickets began swarming in to the few glass doors that were open (or were cracked open by fans inside, which happened sometimes).

The police on duty panicked because there weren't enough of them to adequately corral the fans. With memories of the tragedy at the Who's 1979 concert at Cincinnati's Riverfront Stadium in mind—eleven fans died of asphyxiation when the crowd rushed in—the cops called for backup, and in roared the traffic police on their motorcycles. The result was a perfect horrible storm. A small number of people, stoned or drunk and unfamiliar with the unwritten rules of a Dead show, began throwing bottles, and a handful of police decided enough was enough. One cop, later claiming a fan grabbed his arm too tightly and refused to let go, punched that fan in the face as he was being led to a police van, all of it captured on video by a local TV news crew. Other cops on duty kicked a fan in the head (allegedly for having pissed on a police motorcycle); another fan had his head slammed against a van. In the end twenty-two others were arrested on charges of drinking and drugging, and even a local TV reporter was briefly detained.

The immediate aftermath of the chaos ranged from ridiculous to infuriating. Sophie Masloff, Pittsburgh's seventy-one-year-old mayor, was well known (and sometimes beloved) for her malapropisms; Bruce Springsteen was, in her words, "Bruce Bedsprings." When she weighed in on the Civic Arena mess she referred to the band as the "Dreadful Dead" and added, of their loyal fans, "I don't want those Deadenders ever back again." According to local reporters, Pittsburgh bike cops at the time had a history of aggressive behavior, but they accused the city of not preparing enough for the fans. Deadheads insisted fans hadn't attacked police, whereas others pointed to newbies who shouldn't have acted out or been there in the first place.

On the basis of videotape of one cop slugging that one fan as well as other clips of the chaos of that night, three officers were brought up on disciplinary action. The judging panel consisted of fellow officers, as per procedure, and their defense lawyer argued that the issue was "whether the force used was necessary under the circumstances. That tape was not, in and of itself, enough to show that." Under the circumstances it was hardly a shock when the charges were dismissed. Mayor Masloff said she disagreed with the verdict—but added that she wouldn't pursue another hearing because "another trial board would have had the same results."

■ ◆ ▲

In terms of the Dead's relationship with Pittsburgh, the repercussions of the fuzzy events of that night would be relatively minor. The Dead would continue to play there, albeit at Three Rivers Stadium, which held many more people. (Even though they tried to avoid uncontrollable outdoor stadium shows, they always wound up being pulled back into them.) The incident itself was seen within the organization as a fluke based on unfortunate planning. The show was the Dead's only date in the Northeast until the summer, and given the enormous number of Deadheads who still lived in the New York–Washington corridor, it was inevitable that many would converge on Pittsburgh to catch the band's only local performance of the season. With a guileless smile Weir told MTV, "If it gets really bad, then we'll go to Europe or Asia or something and play over there, wait for things to cool down."

But they couldn't talk away the growing perception that Dead shows were a problem, even when they weren't. Managers of the Riverfront Coliseum in Cincinnati, where the Dead were scheduled to play five nights after Pittsburgh, immediately beefed up security. During a later

Philadelphia Spectrum show Scher spied cops with billy clubs; when he ran up to them and started screaming for them to put them away, he was picked up and heaved out the back door. A little over three weeks after Pittsburgh ninety-one people were arrested at the Irvine Meadows Amphitheater, charged with drugs, "alleged assaults," and other instances. (Deadheads countered by saying that drunken yuppies were to blame.) By comparison, earlier incidents—like the Houston teenager busted for LSD at a show in 1984 whose probation mandated that he couldn't attend any Dead concerts for five years—seemed frivolous.

At a June 1988 band meeting in San Rafael the Dead grappled with the influx of new fans—and what they were leaving in their own wakes. The goal was to craft a carefully worded statement warning ticket holders to tidy up and not flaunt anything even vaguely illegal in the vicinity of the show. But the band had to be careful: How to get the message across without patronizing their fan base? Now the time had come to get serious. Before the Dead's shows at Giants Stadium in July 1989, management at the venue informed the band they couldn't accommodate overnight parking (a euphemism for "camping out in the lot," as most Deadheads knew). That practice meant the venue would have to provide local city services—medical tents, portable toilets, medical supplies—for a miniature city of the ten thousand that everyone predicted would take over the lot.

Faced with the potential of losing out on yet another profitable venue, the band decided they had to tamp down on camping and reluctantly agreed to break the news themselves to the fans. When the Dead office sent out tickets for a later show, they attached a letter, written by McNally and signed by the band: "We're going ahead with camping and vending this summer full of doubts as to whether we can continue them," it began, adding, "we're running out of places to play. . . . Camping and vending have turned it into a largely social scene that is potentially a real and ominous threat to the future live performance of the music itself." The letter then announced "a limited amount of on-site camping available at each gig." Vending booths would be limited to an area the size of a blanket.

The letter made the rounds and made a degree of impact. "They were coming without a ticket," says Hart. "There would be more people outside than inside. And we said, 'You're going to kill the thing you love the most—you're going to put us out of business. We can't go out there and fight cops and gate-crashers.' So we made a real appeal to them, and they responded. They actually calmed down." But not all of them knew there was a problem. At Alpine Valley in Wisconsin, one of the Dead's cherished regular venues, over 40,000 fans showed up nightly for their July 17–19, 1989, residency. Afterward the Dead were banned for the foreseeable future.

Scher says he didn't freak out when he heard about the venues that no longer wanted them: "There were always other places to play," he says. Still, the message had to be stronger. When the next batch of mail-order tickets went out, for fall shows in New Jersey, Miami, Charlotte, and Philadelphia, a sterner letter was stuffed inside those envelopes: "We've all seen how the camping and vending have attracted people there for a party, not for the music—if the outside scene interferes with the music inside, it's gotta go." Then in capital letters no one could miss on the page, the anvil came down: "AND IT'S GONE; THERE WILL BE NO VENDING AND NO CAMPING ON THE TOUR." The letter (written, again, by McNally but credited to the band) ended with: "If you're a Dead Head and believe in us and this scene, you will understand what the priorities are. Thanks for understanding." Kidd Candelario was now charged with enforcing rules against bootleg merchandise outside the venues, and he would get injunctions to go after anyone doing so. "A lot of people were doing simple stuff from show to show, and that was okay," he says, "but there were Jamaican gangs and fucking criminals who were bootlegging." Ironically, with the help of the law, Candelario would have the illicit, unauthorized goods impounded.

In general, though, the band was befuddled and unsure what to do, and overcrowding became more of a discussion at their board meetings. "We're getting that same rap from nearly everywhere now," Garcia told *Relix*'s Steve Peters that fall. "There's very few places that welcome the way the shows, the way the audience and so forth, has defined itself previously." Eliminating the problem without offending Deadheads was becoming trickier than anyone thought. During a radio interview to talk about the edict, McNally, in his role as band spokesman, received a taste of what the band was facing in laying down any sort of law. On the air he made the band's case: Deadheads weren't living in a bubble, there were consequences for their actions, and the "Shakedown Street" area was subject to the law of the land just as much as anyplace else in the country. As fond as he was of Deadheads, McNally was still stunned that they could walk around outside the venues yelling "Doses! Doses!" and not expect any repercussions. During the interview McNally finally blurted out he thought the fans were "just plain dumb" (or words to that effect) to ignore that reality.

When the interview ended, McNally didn't think much more about it. After being in the job five years and having attended Dead shows even before he worked for the band, he thought he could gauge the temperature of the crowd. But this time he was wrong. In the growing world of online chat rooms, McNally was excoriated by Deadheads, who compared him to a spokesman for a malevolent cigarette company. McNally was completely taken aback by their vitriol; like the crowds at the shows, it was another new aspect to the scene that few had witnessed before. (In fairness, the rules were new to fans, too.)

By year's end other problems would plague them. In October the body of nineteen-year-old Adam Katz was found near an overpass outside the Brendan Byrne Arena in New Jersey after a Dead show. During an investigation it was determined that Katz was killed by a "blunt instrument," but little else was clear: two medical examiners' reports had conflicting information about the drugs in his system (one said he had them, another didn't), and allegations that overzealous security had played a role in the death were never proven despite a statement by a sixteen-year-old who said one of the guards told him security had smashed Katz's head against a van and "just dropped him off someplace." At the Inglewood Forum in California in December Patrick Shanahan, a nineteen-year-old business major at the University of California, Santa Barbara, walked outside to go to a medical tent; he'd taken some LSD and wasn't feeling well. Police said Shanahan was being difficult—"yelling and rolling around," in their words—and had to be restrained by eight cops, but in the van on the way to the police station Shanahan stopped breathing. Later it was determined he'd died of "compression of the neck during restraint," strongly implying homicide. No criminal charges were brought against the police, but the Inglewood City council settled a lawsuit by Shanahan's family and paid them $750,000. Although the city denied any wrongdoing, some saw the money as an admission of guilt.

In the aftermath of those horrific events as well as the Pittsburgh situation, the Dead were eventually banned from Maryland's Meriwether Post Pavilion and UC Berkeley. Their annual shows at Stanford were canceled; the school cited camping, drug arrests, and "general unruliness" as reasons why. During shows in Foxboro, Massachusetts, the National Guard, with the approval of the Pentagon, conducted drug raids; several dozen Guard troops, wearing night-vision goggles, spread out around the parking lot and stadium, and forty people were arrested.

Even as their performances sharpened and stayed on track, the Dead were attracting their two least favorite forces—police and ill-equipped newcomers—and were caught in their crossfire. Such was the result, at least for the Dead, of having a taste of popular success. "In the end it backfired," says Scher. "Once 'Touch of Grey' hit some people were there because they had a hit single and everyone says they're cool. The amphitheaters couldn't take that pressure of thousands and thousands of people without tickets outside. The security line is a fence, and there's no fence in the world that's gonna keep a couple of thousand kids from bringing it down." Employees of the Warfield in San Francisco would grow so tired of the inundation of Deadheads during a run of solo Garcia shows that they hung a Garcia doll from the rafters in the kitchen and beat it with sticks to vent their frustration.

After the second and last night in Pittsburgh the Dead returned to their hotels, largely unaware what had happened at the venue. They had to keep moving, as always, but no one could deny that the mania that had started nearly two years before, with MTV's "Day of the Dead" broadcast, was affecting them in ways no one had predicted or wanted; the only question was whether it was permanent. "From then on it was just a matter of holding on for dear life and appreciating any show in which only ten or twenty people got arrested," says McNally. "The fact that it was going to be a constant recurring pattern—I don't believe we were aware of it at that time."

Garcia and Bruce Hornsby onstage, May 1991.
© ROBBI COHN

CHAPTER 14

BOSTON, SEPTEMBER 20, 1991

Any other night Bruce Hornsby would have been more than content to spend time chilling out in Garcia's backstage space. Since joining up with the Dead about a year before as an official unofficial member, the earnest, ever-eager pianist and singer had wiled away many an hour in Garcia's room. The two men couldn't have looked more different: Hornsby clean cut and chisel faced, favoring crisp, white shirts onstage, and Garcia chunky and graying, sporting one of his ubiquitous black T-shirts. But then Garcia would crank one of his Jerky Boys or Henny Youngman cassettes, and the two men, separated by thirteen years, would yuck it up together over the Boys' prank phone calls or Young-man's Borscht Belt one-liners.

On this first of six nights at the Boston Garden, as in other arenas or stadiums that hosted them, each member of the Dead has his own separate room behind the stage thanks to the "pipe and drape" setup common for convention trade shows. No matter the venue, the arrange-ment was always the same, with Lesh's room on the left, Hart's on the right, and everyone else's in between. "Everything was set up the exact same way," recalls a family member who frequented backstage. "Everyone had their exact room, and the same pattern of how they did things. Each room was the same size, set up the same way, with the same stuff in it. Nothing changed. Here on one hand was a band based on freeform music, with nothing planned, and yet every other single aspect of what they did was completely choreographed." (Adds Hornsby, "It's almost like they had this detailed schematic to recreate it—it was so meticulous.") Thanks to the setup the musicians didn't have to wander far during set breaks or the inevitable Drums and Space segments; Garcia in particular was still grappling with swollen feet and ankles. "There were times," says promoter Jim Koplik, "when it was easier for Jerry [to visit his tent] than to take a walk all the way to his dressing room and back."

The precision of their backstage design, complete with surf-and-turf dinners, Asian cuisine, or whatever the Dead might want to eat that night, was merely one of Hornsby's many eye-opening moments now that he was performing regularly with the band. Five years after scoring his first hit with "The Way It Is," recorded with his band the Range, Hornsby was no stranger to fame and its perks, and his mark was still being felt on the charts and the radio, thanks to his piano playing on Bonnie Raitt's "I Can't Make You Love Me" and his 1989 collaboration with Don Henley, "The End of the Innocence." Hornsby had already sat in many a limo and stayed at many swanky hotels; on tour a separate truck carted around his Baldwin grand piano. But for him little compared with the Dead experience, starting the first night he officially played with them in 1990: after finishing a show with the Range in Connecticut, he was immediately picked up by a limo and driven all the way into Manhattan, where he checked into the Dead's residence, the Ritz-Carlton.

Before they took the stage the band's chef would ask each musician what he wanted to eat afterward, and no matter what city or what time of night, the order was always filled: Hornsby knew that as soon as he walked offstage after the last note a paper bag with sushi or his favorite Ben & Jerry's ice cream flavor would be handed to him. (He always wondered what was in some of those *other* bags, food or otherwise, but he didn't ask.) If Hornsby wasn't available due to his own touring schedule, he was no longer surprised when the Dead approached the promoter of his show and, at a significant six-figure cost equivalent to a cancellation fee, would buy him out so Hornsby could join the Dead that night.

Hornsby also knew this Boston Garden run should have been celebratory. The Dead hadn't played there since 1982, but the city and its local businesses were now happy to see them back, especially because Boston's unemployment rate had swung up to its highest level in decades, with over twenty-five thousand out of work. To the locals, injecting cash into the local economy by way of hotels filled with Deadheads had never sounded more appealing. (The Dead themselves had grossed $22 million on the road for the first half of 1991.) The Dead were still finding their sea legs with two new keyboardists now in the band—Hornsby and Vince Welnick, who had signed up during the same time as Hornsby—but the highs, like a storming set in Greensboro in March, made up for the bumpier nights.

As Hornsby also knew, the previous year had been one of the band's most trying. No one talked about it in any specifics, and certainly no one talked about what had happened with Mydland. At Garcia's request Mydland's B3 organ wasn't even on stage at that point. In contrast, the lackluster sales of *Built to Last*, the album they'd released in the fall of 1989 after the platinum-level *In the Dark*, were a trivial matter. They'd all been given yet another reminder of how demanding and intense the Dead world could be. Not to mention mercurial: Hornsby truly felt something fresh and invigorating had been happening onstage between him and the Dead, but he also sensed something was beginning to fray around the edges, and the time had come to speak up. Walking past

Steve Parish, Garcia's ever-loyal and vigilant tech and right-hand man, Hornsby stepped into Garcia's curtained tent to confront the elephant in the Dead's room.

■ ◆ ■

It hadn't been remotely easy, but the Dead had managed to complete their next album, *Built to Last*, in time for the planned Halloween 1989 release Arista had strongly advocated for. For all the struggles that had gone into its creation, the album revealed another way in which the Dead mirrored their world, this time musically. By the dawn of the nineties, pop albums had never sounded busier and more produced, slathered with synthesizers and drum machines, and such was also the case with *Built to Last*. The precision-tooled album wasn't simply the sound of the modern Dead but also the sound of pop music.

And based on the album, the person yanking the Dead into the future was Mydland, whose keyboards and synthesizers were far more prominent than on *In the Dark*, and he also contributed the most songs—four. Mydland's electronic-pop touches worked well with his songs, especially "We Can Run," which blended a soaring chorus with a pro-environment lyric by Barlow. But the same approach somewhat gummed up some of the other songs, especially Garcia and Hunter's three contributions. "Foolish Heart" merged a bubbly melody with a lyric that warned against impending heartbreak; the elegant "Built to Last" felt like an oblique comment on the band and its ever-complex personal dynamics; and "Standing on the Moon," of which Hunter was especially proud, injected a rare bit of political commentary into the Dead's repertoire. But the production on all three songs was too busy for the songs' own good. The band had managed to make a record out of "Victim or the Crime," complete with Gerrit Graham's use of "junkie," but the track was still unwieldy. (Like so many other Dead songs, it managed to work itself out on stage.) Despite the quality of some of the songs—even the hooky charms of "Picasso Moon," a collaboration between Weir, Barlow, and Bralove—the album felt weighed down, as if a heavy backpack had been slung onto it.

The band put a good face on the record, talking up the diffuse recording process in interviews. But away from the media they were less than happy with the results. Listening to it at Arista's headquarters in New York, executives realized soon enough that another *In the Dark* was unlikely. "It wasn't as good an album," says Roy Lott, then the label's executive vice president. "You didn't have to be a genius to know it wasn't as strong. It was, 'This is their next album—let's do our best by it, let's go to work.' It sold what it should sell. It didn't have a 'Touch of Grey.'" The label didn't have the opportunity to reject the album since the band's contract enabled them to submit and release a record without any revisions from the label.

In another sign of the way they were willing to work with the business if need be, they willingly went along with the filming of a video for the first single, "Foolish Heart." Once again Gutierrez was recruited to direct, and he and Garcia met at the director's studio to talk about it (and were promptly locked into the office when a latch broke). On the soundstage the Dead changed into costumes, including Victorian clothes; Garcia grabbed a black jacket to augment his usual dark T-shirt. Lesh made it clear in his body language that the last place he wanted to be was in a studio miming and lip-synching for a music video, never his favorite pastime, but Gutierrez caught a moment when Lesh began laughing from what Gutierrez calls "the corniness of him wearing those clothes."

During the shoot Gutierrez saw how much Garcia had aged in the two years since "Touch of Grey": his hair was now completely white—striking for someone only in his late forties—and he was still wearing specially prepared shoes to help his swollen limbs. The director wanted to do a close-up of Garcia's hand playing the guitar solo, a challenge in itself. "He was struggling to remember what he had done in that solo so it could match up in the close-up," Gutierrez says. "He was struggling, but he was laughing too." As it always had, the chance of redemption still hung in the air.

●   ◆   ▲

On a late July morning in 1990 Hornsby was in Seattle, preparing for a radio interview to promote his latest album, when his production manager, who knew the Dead, broke the news: Brent Mydland had died. After the interview Hornsby was walking down the street when someone approached him and said, "Hey, Bruce, are you gonna join the boys?" Hornsby was taken aback: Was the rumor mill already spinning, just a few hours after the news?

In the decade leading up to that day Mydland had not only grown into his role as a member of the Dead; to the new generation of Deadheads who'd discovered them in the eighties, before or after "Touch of Grey," Mydland had also become a centerpiece of the band. He was closer in age to those fans than the other members were, and his voice was stronger and more commercial sounding than Garcia's or Weir's (a vital consideration for music fans who'd grown up hearing more polished rock and pop). To newcomers Mydland's songs, especially those that dwelled on romantic turmoil, were the most relatable. Mydland was the voice and face of the new Dead, and his onstage animation and energy made him a beloved figure. Within the Dead community he especially endeared himself to Justin Kreutzmann, then a teenager dealing with family issues. "My dad and I would have father-son dramas," says Justin, "and Brent came to me and said, 'Your dad loves you.' Brent was the craziest guy I've ever met in my life, but he was sweet and loving."

Yet to the consternation of those in the Dead world, little of that love and recognition seemed to sooth Mydland's increasingly troubled soul. By 1990 he'd been on a slow-motion downward slide for several years. During his time with Cantor she would notice how he was riddled with self-doubt, afraid that Deadheads were relentlessly comparing him to his predecessor. "Brent always felt like, 'The fans hate me—they want Keith,'" she recalls. "I would say, 'Bullshit—these guys are *loving* you.' But Brent had a big fear about being the replacement guy. I kept trying to reassure him: 'Your playing is marvelous—you rock the organ!' Jerry would say, 'Oh, we finally have a singer in the band!' But Brent was very insecure." Barlow felt the songs he wrote with Mydland weren't well recorded—perhaps, in Barlow's mind, because other members were threatened by Mydland's output. "They weren't great songs necessarily," Barlow says, "and they didn't get done in a way that made them as good as they were. There was a certain reluctance to let Brent step forward."

Unfortunately Mydland's shaky self-esteem led him to into increasingly difficult behavior backstage. In 1986, at the Berkeley Community Theatre, boards were set up backstage for fans to leave handwritten comments for each band member. Mydland's comments totaled almost two hundred, of which only two were negative. ("Who asked you to sing?" read one.) Glancing over the list of comments, Lesh asked Steve Marcus of the Dead's ticket office to transcribe them all and give a copy to Mydland so he could see how popular he was with the fans. When Mydland saw the comments, he ignored all of the encouraging ones and zeroed in on the two negative remarks and began screaming and ripping up the board. For a number of years crew member Kidd Candelario attended to both Mydland and Lesh onstage, but the job was growing even more demanding now that Mydland's demons were flailing away. When Mydland would demand a drink onstage, Candelario knew after a while to fill it mostly with orange juice and a shot on top; Candelario thought Mydland would take a few sips of the watered-down drink and resume playing. But Mydland instantly knew what he was drinking and would hurl the cup back at Candelario. More than once Mydland would take his pricey synthesizer programming books and throw them into the audience.

Mydland's wavering sense of self-worth wasn't helped by reviews of *Built to Last*, like the *Washington Post* write-up that claimed "his efforts range from barely tolerable to downright intolerable" and said his songs had "a rinky-dink blandness." That review also called "I Will Take You Home," Mydland's ballad to his daughters, "the most embarrassing thing ever to appear on a Grateful Dead album." And yet soon after the album's release one of his contributions, "Just a Little Light," was chosen as a single—a milestone for Mydland—and in late 1989 the band assembled at a Marin soundstage to make a video for it. As they had with "Touch of Grey," the Dead again endured hours—five, in this case—of lip-synching. Mydland seemed happy and comfortable as the star of the video, and Gutierrez interpreted the single and video as the band's way of affirming his vital role in the band. "Doing that song was the band's way of telling Brent he was an important member of the band," says Gutierrez. "It was a way of bringing him in." (To others in the organization it was simply the most radio-friendly song on the album.)

The song itself, its lyrics cowritten by Mydland and Barlow, addressed dreams fulfilled and unfulfilled, the downside of fame, and trampled-underfoot love; the chorus had a heavy-hearted hook. The director interpreted the song as a depiction of the battle between light and dark in Mydland's own soul. "He told his story in that song," Gutierrez says. "It was about what was going on with him." To match the lyric Mydland was surrounded by hundreds of candles. At the end of the video, for dramatic effect, the candles were blown out.

In December 1989, around the same time as the "Just a Little Light" video was shot, Hornsby returned to his home in Virginia to find a message from Garcia on his answering machine: "Hey, man, it's Garcia—give me a call. I want to talk to you about something." Hornsby phoned back, but no one answered at Garcia's home. Months later Garcia flew down to Los Angeles to film a video for a song on Hornsby's album *A Night on the Town*, on which Garcia had guested. During a break Hornsby had the chance to ask Parish about the mysterious call and heard the explanation: Mydland hadn't been doing well, and the band had wanted to hire Hornsby to replace him. Hornsby was stunned, but he was also told the storm had passed, at least for now. "The desire to replace Brent obviously didn't continue," Hornsby says. "Parish said something like, 'Yeah it's okay—Brent's doing better.' I didn't pursue it at all." Hornsby never brought up the conversation to Garcia, who didn't mention it during the video shoot.

The call to Hornsby hadn't come completely out of the blue. That same month manager Cameron Sears received the news he'd been dreading: Mydland was in jail, having overdosed at home. Hurriedly Sears managed to pull together enough cash for bail and rushed to the jail in San Rafael, where he and publicist McNally found Mydland milling about in the lobby, angry that he'd been arrested. (The paramedic, realizing Mydland had drugs in his system, had alerted the police.) Sears and McNally drove Mydland back home, where they refrained from scolding the keyboardist for his habits; in the Dead world no one told anyone else not to indulge. But they at least wanted him to admit he had a problem, which Mydland resisted. Because he and his wife, Lisa, had separated and she had left their home with their children, Mydland would be alone for the rest of the night; fearing he could ingest more of whatever he'd already taken, Sears and McNally stayed with Mydland until he fell asleep and crashed at the house themselves.

The time had come for a long-overdue band meeting to confront Mydland's downward spiral. Band and management gathered around a nineteen-foot-long solid-oak table—complete with wood-carved chairs, one for each band member, skulls carved into the end of each arm—and read him the Dead's version of the riot act. Mydland wasn't fired or threatened with such action, but he was firmly told he had to get himself under control. Contrite and embarrassed, Mydland said he'd rein in his excesses and pull his life together, but no one was fully convinced. The crew began monitoring backstage visitors, especially anyone who even remotely resembled a dealer.

At one of the Dead's first shows after Mydland's overdose and arrest, at the Oakland Coliseum, Kreutzmann's limo pulled up right behind Mydland's. (At this point Mydland had had so many DWIs that he could no longer drive.) The drummer jumped out, grabbed Mydland around the neck, and said, "If you die, I'm gonna kill you!" The two men had bonded many times before on the road, partaking in antics and practical jokes. But this moment felt different. Because neither the Dead nor the generally private Kreutzmann were known for touchy-feely exhibitions, the drummer's comment to Mydland, as gruff as it was, felt like an expression of genuine concern.

When the Dead inevitably resumed their road work just before the official start of spring in 1990, Mydland's wrist-slapping appeared to have paid off: his keyboard work—fanciful piano on "High Time," B3 organ fills on "Estimated Prophet" and "Cold Rain and Snow"—and singing remained robust, even if the huskiness in his voice now had a ravaged edge. (In that regard he really did seem like a true member of the Dead now, no longer the long-haired newbie who'd joined up eleven years before.) In what many would agree was the band's last first-rate tour, the Dead sounded revitalized, ready to shake off the crowd-control and business hassles that had built up around them over the previous few years. Even Garcia's voice, heard in renditions of "High Time" and "Crazy Fingers" at various stops on the tour, rediscovered its sweet spot. At a March 1990 show at Nassau Coliseum on Long Island, jazz saxophonist Branford Marsalis sat in with the band—at Lesh's invitation—and pushed the band to new improvisational highs, as he also would during later sit-in jams with them.

Still, Mydland looked as if he were barely holding himself together during most of his time onstage. To Deadhead Dan Ross, who attended every one of those shows and felt a particular kinship with Mydland, the concerts were unsettling. "Brent looked horrible," he says. "You knew about his separation. You're looking at this person who was falling apart." By their last show, in Tinley Park, Illinois, on July 23, Mydland appeared puffy, his trademark stare even more startling than usual. During an encore they played a relatively recent addition to their repertoire, the Band's "The Weight." Garcia, Lesh, Weir, and Mydland each sang a verse, and Mydland's included the line, "I gotta go, but my friends can stick around." The show was ten years to the day after Keith Godchaux's death.

On the plane ride home the next day Bralove, sitting next to Mydland, had to stomach Mydland's alcohol odor for several hours. Bralove was fond of Mydland but was saddened by the state he was in, and like everyone in the organization, he didn't quite know how to help. "He was in rough shape," Bralove recalls. "He had his demons, and they didn't rage all the time, but they were raging during that tour." Bralove had noticed that during that summer run Mydland had been getting heavily into video games, and that worried him too. "It was isolating him more," he says. "It felt bad to see him playing a little golf game or whatever he was playing."

On the morning of July 26 an ambulance was already at the house in Lafayette, a suburb just west of Berkeley, when two police officers responded to a report of a possible fatality. Walking into the bedroom, they found a man dressed in slacks, wearing a long-sleeve blue shirt and sneakers with white shocks. He was lying on the floor in between the TV and the bedroom; the TV was still on and set to a Nintendo game. The controller for the game was lying nearby. Friends at the house admitted to police that Mydland had a heroin habit and had overdosed before and that they hadn't heard from him since he'd arrived back home from the tour on July 24. Police also spoke to a couple who lived in the house but hadn't been there in a few days.

One of Mydland's friends called the Dead's office to relay the grim news. Nancy Mallonee, now the organization's chief financial officer, had the unfortunate job of calling some of the musicians. The Dead operation was stunned and saddened—if not completely surprised—by the news. Garcia was at his home in San Anselmo when the call arrived, and he was, in Manasha Matheson's words, "visibly shaken." Weir was angry, Lesh saddened, and some office employees cried. That same day John Cutler, Justin Kreutzmann, and engineer Jeffrey Norman were working on the band's forthcoming live album, *Without a Net*. They'd just isolated Mydland's piano track on a terrific, rousing version of "Cassidy" in order to give it a better listen when the news of his passing arrived. With the band's consent, an immediate decision was made to include a Mydland-sung song on the album, and the Dead signed off on a version of "Dear Mr. Fantasy" that included the keyboardist's lead vocal.

Starting with the Associated Press, the media reported that Mydland, who was thirty-seven, had died of "undetermined" causes, since nothing was confirmed and the autopsy report had yet to be completed. When the toxicology report came out a few weeks later his passing was attributed to "acute cocaine and narcotic intoxication"; due to "a recent needle puncture mark" and the presence of a mix of cocaine, morphine, and codeine in his blood, it was clear Mydland had injected himself with a speedball. Compared to the initial news, though, the final results didn't get as much play in the media, and McNally sensed how relieved the band was not to have to talk about a drug overdose in the band. In the Dead organization Mydland's lack of intellectual curiosity was often cited as a root cause of his ability to find satisfaction beyond fame. As Garcia told *Rolling Stone* a year later, "He didn't have much supporting him in terms of an intellectual life. . . . Brent was from the East Bay, which is one of those places that is like *non*culture." But it was also clear that Mydland was still desperately eager to be accepted as more than the "new guy" and that keeping up with the band's lifestyle may have been his way of earning their respect. And like Godchaux before him, he paid the price for not being as road-hardened as those around him.

As word continued to spread, few were shocked. "We saw it coming," Hart, his voice a mixture of anger and resignation, told Gutierrez when the director stopped by Hart's house a few days after Mydland's death. (Garcia said something similar in his *Rolling Stone* interview a year after Mydland's death.) Hart told Gutierrez the band had tried interventions and even made threats about his livelihood, yet there seemed little they could do.

Once again, as they had for Pigpen in 1973, the Dead congregated at a chapel for a funeral service for one of their own—yet another easily rattled keyboard player who couldn't control his excesses. The Dead squeezed in together in a front row, across from Mydland's mourning family, as a tape of "I Will Take You Home," which now felt heartbreaking, played on a small sound system. "They were all quiet," recalls Mydland's former girlfriend, Cherie Barsin, who attended. Unable to fully address his death, the Dead joked around with the casket in a back room, almost dropping it. At the cemetery in Lafayette a member of Mydland's family pointed to his house and told Trixie Garcia that Mydland would sit on his porch with binoculars and zoom in on burials. ("He loved his family, his music and his friends," read Mydland's own tombstone.)

Trixie, still a teenager, also grappled with Mydland's death; she'd come to think of him as her "little buddy." But a far more sobering thought crossed her mind the day of his funeral. "That was when I realized Jerry was probably going to die early," she says. "I had to think that Jerry lost hope or was unhappy."

From the moment he heard the news Garcia clearly took Mydland's death particularly hard. Onstage the two men had an intriguing dynamic—Mydland's vigor and musicianship would frequently bolster Garcia's own, especially coming after Keith Godchaux's increasingly lethargic concert presence, and he forever seemed to be looking at Garcia to receive a quick nod indicating Garcia was happy with something he'd just played. A few days after Mydland's death the Dead's ticket office held its annual barbeque on Garcia's birthday. Normally Garcia would've been on the road, but in view of the tragedy, the Dead had canceled shows, and Garcia was back home. The ticket office's Steve Marcus invited Garcia, who, to everyone's surprise, showed up and spent two hours at the party.

Before Garcia arrived, Marcus warned his coworkers not to mention Mydland; no one wanted to accidentally depress Garcia. But once he showed up and took a seat at a picnic table, Garcia brought up the topic before anyone else could. "What should we do?" he asked the employees. He told them he dreaded the idea of going onstage and not having Mydland there, but the Dead had shows lined up at the Shoreline Amphitheatre in Mountain View. Perhaps boldly, Marcus suggested that the band should take a six-month break and examine its scene, which would involve shutting down the ticket operation. Garcia took it in but didn't decide one way or another.

A little over a week after Mydland's death Hornsby and the Range were playing the Concord Pavilion—by eerie coincidence the same town where Mydland and Keith Godchaux had both grown up. Before the show Hornsby had received a call from Lesh that he and Garcia were going to drive down to see the show and talk with him. Along with Sears, they all huddled in Hornsby's dressing room and offered Hornsby a job with the Dead.

Almost immediately Hornsby had mixed feelings. A part of him relished the thought: as a young music head, he'd been a fan of jazz and Leon Russell and had seen his first Dead show in 1973. But it wasn't until the following year, when he saw them at the William and Mary Hall at the University of Richmond, that he became truly entranced. Between the Wall of Sound and the band's music, Hornsby was swept up in the Dead. "What really got me on board," he says, "is that at the end of the night, Bob walks up—I've never seen this before or since—and says, 'Hey, we had such a good time playing tonight, we're gonna come back tomorrow and take out the seats and party.'" Hornsby was one of many who returned the next day and heard the band play a completely different multihour set. With that, he says, "I was totally on board. I wasn't a Deadhead, because I was immersed in other music too, but I loved it."

Thirteen years later Hornsby found himself playing an opening set at a Dead show—the same Laguna Seca performances where the "Touch of Grey" video was filmed. (Because he left after his set, Hornsby didn't witness any of the backstage tumult involving the Dead's crew.) The Dead's East Coast promoter, John Scher, a fan of Hornsby's music, had sent a copy of his debut album to the Dead, who signed off on the idea of Hornsby and his band as an opening act; it might have helped that Hornsby was covering "I Know You Rider" in his set. Over the next few years the bond between the group and Hornsby gradually strengthened. Having played in a Dead cover band in Virginia, Hornsby was fairly well versed on the band's repertoire, so it felt natural when he was asked to sit in on piano or accordion. "They said, 'Come on and play!'" Hornsby recalls. "And suddenly I'm standing next to these guys. Garcia said, 'We don't let just *anyone* play accordion with us.' They were a bunch of smiley faces. It was surreal." Early on, Hornsby also learned how demanding the band's fan base could be: at the Laguna Seca shows he played the identical songs both nights, and Deadheads responded by yelling out, "Same set!"

For all his interest in hooking up with the Dead, Hornsby's own career was thriving. The previous year "The End of the Innocence" had hit the Top Ten, and his schedule was starting to fill up; he'd already been in the studio with Dylan and Crosby, Stills & Nash, and Raitt was next. As flattered as Hornsby was about Garcia and Lesh's offer at the Concord Pavilion, the timing wasn't right. "If they had gotten to me four or five years before, I would've said yes," he says. "And I would've been their keyboard player for good, and it would've been great. But I had my own thing going pretty well." A few days later Hornsby called back to say he wouldn't be able to become a full-time member but offered to help with their transition to another keyboardist; he would be, in Garcia's term, a "floating member."

Now the band had to scramble; a fall tour was set to start in early September. The last thing anyone in the Dead wanted to do was break in a new member, but they dutifully called in a range of keyboard players, including T. Lavitz of the Dixie Dregs and former Jefferson Starship member Pete Sears, and jammed with them, all in a single grueling day. When word leaked that the band was auditioning players, Weir, through a mutual friend, was approached by Vince Welnick, a thirty-eight-year-old Arizona-born journeyman player and singer.

On paper Welnick wasn't the odds-on favorite. He'd grown up immersed in the same genres the Dead loved—jazz, boogie-woogie— but was best known as a member of the Tubes, the campy-decadent seventies San Francisco prog-punkers who were the polar opposite of the Dead. But unlike some of his competition for Mydland's seat, Welnick could sing the high notes. (As Welnick later told *Relix* publisher Toni Brown, "[Bob] said, 'Bruce Hornsby is in the band now, and we want a synth player who can sing high harmony.'") "I remember the band sitting around going, 'Wow, he could play the hard parts,'" recalls Bralove, who attended the rehearsals. "He had all of Brent's high harmonies, which made it possible for them to keep doing what they were doing vocally. The idea of rearranging the vocals to accommodate a new voice would have been very challenging." Welnick could also hold his own instrumentally: when the band jammed with Welnick on

"Estimated Prophet" Kreutzmann was impressed that Welnick didn't "give up the seven"—referring to the song's 7/4 time signature. After anxiously waiting a week to hear whether he was in, Welnick got the offer, and he became the Dead's new keyboard player. As Welnick would later recall in several interviews, the band flashed its dark humor by asking him, "Is your insurance paid up?"

The decision was relatively quick; the Dead, in typical style, decided to keep working rather than confront its internal issues. As always, it was best to move on without dwelling much, if at all, on what had just occurred. "Band morale was so low," recalls Justin Kreutzmann. "It was, 'Oh, God, we gotta do this again?' I remember Jerry saying, 'I'm never going to teach all these songs again—this is it. We're not going to start up all over again with someone new.' It really sucked to be the new guy after Brent." When McNally asked the band about releasing a statement on Welnick's hiring, they decided against it; as Garcia told McNally, "Enough already." The thought of talking up a new member —and talking about the one who'd just passed away—was beyond dismaying. By way of the *San Francisco Chronicle*, which had covered the Dead for many years, the news eventually broke. But no official press release about Welnick would ever make it out of the Fifth and Lincoln office, right up to his debut with the band in Ohio in September.

A few weeks later Hornsby made his official debut as part-time member—and discovered soon enough that the Dead machine, although efficient and militaristically organized, was also eccentric. That first night Hornsby didn't rehearse and had to wing it. He only knew how to play about thirty Dead songs, which left another hundred-plus that could pop up in the repertoire. (Adhering to a bit of rock concert protocol, they did compile set lists the first few months for Hornsby and Welnick; Welnick especially was far less up to speed on Dead songs than Hornsby was, so the band sent him their back catalog and even a CD player.) When the time came to walk onstage Hornsby would be pumped, but he was surprised by how casual the rest of the band could be. "Eight o'clock would come and go, and they wouldn't give a shit," Hornsby says. "At 8:15, I'd say, 'Hey, you guys wanna go out there?' They didn't want to be pushed." Soundchecks were also rare, and at times he found himself standing onstage with the Dead as everyone adjusted their levels and prepared for the show as a stadium or arena full of fans watched. "Other bands would be freaking," he says. "That never happened, which was really nice, really refreshing. No pressure."

Once the music began, Hornsby at times grappled with the band's overwhelming sound, now augmented by not one but two keyboard players. It was, he says, "so friggin' loud," especially Lesh's bass, that Hornsby felt the music ripping through his torso. As a result, he would sometimes play the wrong changes and, after the show, be told what chord he should have been playing. Hornsby even stood out physically: recalling one show in the summer of 1991, Hornsby jokes, "I look like a choir boy out there, or like I'd just come from playing with Tony Orlando." And although Hornsby didn't mind the smell of pot wafting around him during concerts, he gave the band and crew a strict warning: if he were dosed, he would leave. "I didn't want to deal with that," he says. "But they were good with it."

Yet Hornsby was a natural fit for the band's music. His playing was luminous and animated, and his sparkling acoustic piano runs recalled not just Godchaux's finest work with the Dead but also Chuck Leavell's vibrant playing with the Allmans in the seventies. With Hornsby on piano and sometimes accordion (and Welnick on synthesizer alongside him, augmented by Bralove's sonic embellishments), the band felt as reborn as it could after enduring yet another internal tragedy. "Suddenly there was Hornsby, who from a talent point of view was Garcia's equal," says Scher, "and Jerry recognized that immediately." Hornsby's crystalline piano revitalized everything from "Franklin's Tower" to "Let It Grow."

Unlike Mydland—or Godchaux or Pigpen, for that matter—Hornsby was extremely self-assured and could give as much as he could take. He quickly keyed into the crew's snarky, sarcastic tendencies. Whenever Hornsby's regular-folks friends from Virginia attended a show, the crew would invariably refer to them as "Bruce's geeks." That crack amused Hornsby, but he was less than tickled when a crew member barked "Get the fuck out of here!" when one of Hornsby's friends was standing in the wrong spot. Hornsby admonished the employee and received an apology.

Beyond the music—including many songs he'd never played before—Hornsby also had to adjust to the fact that by 1991 there seemed to be two Jerry Garcias in the house. Garcia's drug use and health issues had continued, on and off, since 1989. At one of the ticket office's Christmas parties he'd walked in and began scoping around the office, clearly searching for something. "Are you looking for nitrous?" an office employee asked him. "Yeah," Garcia replied. For his part Hornsby had few dealings with addicts, but during some of the band's shows the summer of 1991 he noticed certain signs: Garcia immobile onstage, hunched over his guitar and staring at the floor, barely playing. When he switched to accordion, Hornsby was able to walk over to Garcia and yell, "Sounds great!" to boost his energy or pump him up.

What Hornsby didn't know at the time was that at the end of their summer 1991 tour the band had conducted yet another intervention with Garcia, resulting in a stint at a methadone clinic. (The confrontation, held at Front Street, had finally allowed Lesh to air his grievances toward Garcia, even if his longtime friend and band mate clearly didn't want to hear them.) One day that fall, over drinks in a bar after a gig, Weir sat down with Hornsby and Welnick and gave them the news: Garcia was using again. To Hornsby, Weir seemed more resigned than angry. "He just told us, 'This is what's happening, Jerry's having a problem again,' and I went, 'Okay,'" Hornsby says. "He was matter of fact. He was very even toned." (Bralove noticed changes too: one time, as the band was preparing for a show, Garcia walked onstage and began intently talking to Bralove, and as Bralove says, "He seemed very lit.") Although Hornsby also sensed Garcia was doing drugs again, he felt, as a "good friend but a new friend," that it wasn't his place to take him to task for it. At another band meeting Garcia retaliated, saying it was no longer fun to play with them and that they'd been "running on inertia," as he later told *Rolling Stone*.

For all those warning signs and offstage debates, Hornsby still admired Garcia's musicality, and onstage Hornsby and Garcia would exchange runs and, frequently, smiles. Hornsby remained drawn to Garcia's personal warmth, which he saw firsthand when, during a later stint with the band, he brought along his baby boys, Keith and Russell. Backstage the infants were greeted with an array of musicians who would make most classic-rock fans drool: the Dead, Hornsby's friend Don Henley, and Sting, who was opening the show. Each time the babies broke out into anguished screams—until they encountered Garcia. For once, the kids quieted down. "He was the only one who they let hold them," Hornsby says. "Those little babies just had a vibe."

One of Hornsby's most cherished memories would be the time he flew into Marin for a Dead rehearsal and stayed at Garcia's house. Giving Hornsby a tour of the digs, Garcia brought him into a room with the least likely of sights: a treadmill. "Let me show you how to use it, man," Garcia said. In his black sweat pants, black sneakers, and black T-shirt, Garcia was dressed for a workout, even if he didn't look especially healthy. Climbing onto the machine, he "walked" a few casual minutes and then stopped: "There you have it—that's how to do it," he shrugged to Hornsby. It was, Hornsby would later recall, "a vision you never thought you'd see." Yet the bigger question—whether the healthy or the unhealthy Garcia would win out—remained unanswered.

■ ◆ ■

As McNally saw, Garcia could still revel in the music, even if they weren't the ones playing it. On a flight with the band a few months before the Boston Garden run, McNally walked over to Garcia's seat with a Walkman; he'd just listened to something completely out there that Garcia had to hear. Putting on headphones, Garcia listened, and soon a big grin overtook his face. "That's a trip!" he said. And it was: a cover of "Ripple" by, of all bands, Jane's Addiction, the kings of sleazy Los Angeles punk-metal. Nor was it a standard cover: lead singer Perry Farrell sang Hunter's words while beneath and around him the band played a whirlwind version of "The Other One." Farrell himself had chosen "Ripple." "The melody of that song makes you feel better, and the lyrics are beautiful," Farrell says. "It was a song I zoned in on."

Next to Garcia on the plane was Manasha Matheson Garcia. In the summer of 1990 Garcia had nervously asked her, "Honey, would you come with me for a drive?" As she recalls, "At sunset we drove west toward the ocean over Mount Tamalpais. When we reached the Pacific he took my hand and proposed to me." Garcia suggested Easter 1991 as a wedding date, but Matheson preferred, she says, "to marry free of legal convention. I was a hippie." Garcia went along with the idea, and on August 17, 1990, the two were wed in what Matheson called "a private spiritual ceremony" at their home in San Anselmo, with Garcia in a black T-shirt.

On tour with Manasha, Garcia seemed to revel in family life: visiting the Art Institute of Chicago with her, taking a boat ride on Lake Geneva, Wisconsin, and going on carriage rides in New York. With their daughter, Keelin, born in December 1987, the family saw the Radio City Rockettes show one Christmas. When the Dead toured Europe in 1990 Matheson referred to it as their "little honeymoon," and she says she and Garcia discussed opening a "bookstore-theater coffee shop" in San Anselmo. People in the Dead world would often scratch their heads over the relationship, but Garcia seemed, at least for now, happy.

In April 1991 the Jane's Addiction version of "Ripple" was unveiled as part of the first-ever Dead tribute album. Overseen by producer Ralph Sall, *Deadicated* featured covers by an impossibly eclectic lineup, ranging from the expected (Los Lobos, Dwight Yoakam) to the left field (Jane's Addiction, Elvis Costello). The Dead had little to do with the album but were tickled by it: when Hunter heard Jane's re-invention of "Ripple," his jaw dropped and his mind was blown, and it became one of his favorite covers of a Dead song.

Deadicated wasn't simply a lark that allowed closet Deadheads like Costello to finally revel in their fandom. (Despite his punky early days, Costello had been a fan as far back as 1972, when he sat in the mud at the Bickershaw Festival show on the 1972 European tour, and he, Garcia, and Weir had shared a stage or two in the previous decade.) The album also had a specific nonmusical purpose: a way to counter the bad press the band had been receiving. "The success had caused everyone to focus on the parking lots and the death at Giants Stadium and all this negativity," says Arista's Roy Lott, who approved *Deadicated* once Sall had pitched the idea. "And I wanted people to remember that it all started with great songwriting and artistry." As an added public relations bonus, the royalties would be sent to the Rainforest Action Network. (In 1988 the Dead had given a press conference about the foundation at the United Nations, another sign of how legit they'd become in the aftermath of *In the Dark*.) The album received kind reviews, and for once, the press talked up the band's music rather than horrid incidents taking place near their shows.

The album also served to inject some Dead-related product into the market. By the time *Deadicated* had arrived it had been almost two years since *Built to Last* had been released, and there were few signs that an all-new Dead album was on the way. An executive at Arista floated the idea of the band playing an acoustic set for MTV's then in-vogue *Unplugged* series. But the project, a missed opportunity if there ever was one, never got off the ground.

■ ◆ ■

The first set in Boston hadn't gone well—and, to Hornsby's mind, neither had most of the previous nights at New York's Madison Square Garden. To him the Dead, especially Garcia, seemed lackluster; the sparkle and interaction evident in his earlier sets with them had dimmed considerably. With a year under his belt, Hornsby had learned it was often best to lay back and wait for space to open up before he played, a particularly crucial point because the band now had two keyboard players for the first time in two decades. But in Boston he was forced to change tactics; to him the band felt so lackadaisical that he pounded forcefully, as many notes as possible, to jack up the faltering energy.

Stepping offstage, Hornsby was steamed, and the time to vent had come. He knew Garcia could have an occasional off night, like every other musician, but this was one time too many. "I thought, 'Okay, well, *fuck* it—I need to do something here, for my own sanity,'" Hornsby recalls. By the time he stepped into Garcia's backstage tent he had worked himself up into righteous anger. "Hornsby's a perfectionist," says Scher. "He wanted to be great every time he was out there. And you can't do that by yourself."

Many times Hornsby had witnessed a version of Garcia in his tent, including the time Owsley Stanley—who remained in touch with some of them, especially Lesh—had stopped by. For reasons Hornsby didn't understand, Garcia snapped at their old friend. Tonight, though, Garcia was good-natured and effusive, telling Hornsby how much he loved the more forceful, aggressive style the keyboardist had adopted in the first set. "Man, I love the way you're playing tonight," he told Hornsby. "It's the best."

Rather than softening Hornsby up, though, the remarks set him off. Hornsby retorted in a way he'd never done before to Garcia, and others rarely did. "Motherfucker, I *hate* the way I'm playing," Hornsby snapped. "I'm playing too much."

Garcia seemed puzzled: "What do you mean?"

Hornsby didn't let up, telling Garcia he was only playing that way—"triple forte at all times"—to inject some life into the set. "You're just phoning it in," he said to Garcia. "You're not there. You're not really delivering."

With that Garcia's friendly façade faded, and he muttered the phrase that would haunt Hornsby for decades afterward: "You don't understand twenty-five years of burnout, man."

Even so, Hornsby didn't let up. He told Garcia how busy he was, with only six days off that year, and that he was "fried half the time" from shuttling between studios and road work. Despite that pace, Hornsby said he still tried to play at a high level, and Garcia didn't seem like he was even trying—and that Garcia was letting the fans down. Steve Parish, who popped in and out of the tent during the exchange and caught moments of it, was a bit surprised someone would challenge Garcia like that. Everyone knew Garcia struggled at times, but, Parish says, "It's something that was never said but was under the surface." The conversation settled down, and the topic didn't come up again, at least not with Hornsby.

Outside the dressing room Manasha Garcia was prepping a soothing honey-ginger drink for her partner. After Hornsby left, Garcia told her about the conversation. According to her, Garcia had a flu-related respiratory issue that night. "He wasn't feeling well at all," she says. "He was also a bit exhausted from playing the nine-night run of concerts at [Madison Square] Garden." Yet, she says, "I can understand how Bruce may have missed that Jerry was not feeling well that evening. Jerry rarely complained publicly about his health and always preferred to continue on with the show."

Hornsby knew Garcia didn't like to be confronted about his lifestyle and its impact on his playing. In the short term, at least, the exchange may have helped. During the second set at the Boston Garden "Fire on the Mountain" in particular felt spunkier, and on subsequent nights at the venue the Dead and Hornsby played ferocious versions of "Hell in a Bucket" and "New Minglewood Blues." Later some Deadheads would refer to the six nights in Boston (which alone grossed just over $2 million) as the band's last first-rate string of shows anywhere. A day that had promised so little wound up delivering more than intended.

Yet the night would signify the beginning of the end for a potentially promising new era for the Dead. "Jerry didn't think, 'This is gonna change my life that Bruce Hornsby is giving me this lecture,'" says Parish. "But Jerry felt bad about it, and he knew Bruce felt that way. After a year of playing with them, Bruce realized there were some days when people were having problems. After that time he tried to distance himself from the Dead." Within a few months Hornsby would no longer have the same role in the band.

■ ◆ ■

The gathering darkness: Fans overtaking the
fence at the last show at Deer Creek.
© JEREMY HOGAN

CHAPTER 15

NOBLESVILLE, INDIANA, JULY 2, 1995

Three songs into the show, the house lights still on, the time had come for "Dire Wolf," but with a perverse twist no one had anticipated. Twenty-five years had passed since the Dead had recorded that song at Pacific High studio. They'd played it innumerable times since, occasionally slowing it down a half step. But tonight, in the middle of Indiana, they again injected it with the crisp, merry gait of the recorded version, and even the song's refrain harked back to its original impending-death inspiration. "Please, don't murder me," Garcia sang again, now in a voice weathered by age and abuse, as cops pivoted their heads, hoping to catch sight of the man who'd vowed to kill Garcia before the night was over.

Along with the likes of Alpine Valley Music Theatre in Wisconsin, the Deer Creek Music Center had become a destination spot, a revered haven, for the Dead and their fans alike. Springing up amid cornfields and cow pastures a half-hour north of Indianapolis, the amphitheater was, like the band, an enclave unto itself. Out there the straight world never felt so distant. Although the Dead had played Deer Creek six times before without major incident, tonight began on a sour note. On their way from their hotel (north of Indianapolis) to the venue word filtered down to band and its management: a death threat had been called into Deer Creek's box office. Similar calls and warnings had arrived before, but this one felt creepier. An anonymous person had called local police claiming to have overheard the distraught father of a young female Deadhead. The information was unclear, but the implication was that the girl couldn't be found and had run off on the road with them, and that the father was planning to attend the show and shoot Garcia.

Huddling backstage with Ken Viola, Scher's head of security, the band grappled with what to do. Verifying the threat was difficult, but Lesh, the most immediately concerned because his family was there, made the case for canceling the show and heading out. "I was not going to stand up there and be a target," he recalls. But Garcia brushed it off, saying he'd dealt with crazies before and wouldn't let this one stop him. "Would you sacrifice yourself for the music?" Hart recalls of that night. "All those things run around in your brain. But I remember joking, 'Jerry, could you move over six inches onstage? At least *I'll* make it!' We were screaming laughing. The decision was made and everyone came around. We were worried, of course, but we didn't want some lunatic to shut us down." Indiana state police made their way into the crowd and the stage pit; there they were joined by other Dead employees, including publicist Dennis McNally and Steve Marcus of Grateful Dead Ticket Sales, all nervously glancing around for . . . *something*. No one knew what the supposed shooter looked or dressed like, and no one even knew for sure whether the threat was real. But they weren't about to take any chances.

Ironically, the show opened with "Here Comes Sunshine," the twinkling kaleidoscope of a song that was dropped from the repertoire after 1974 but had returned starting in 1992. With Welnick playing synthesizer, the song was rearranged, sounding tighter and firmer but still evanescent. After Robert Johnson's "Walkin' Blues," Garcia swung into the honky-tonk intro notes of "Dire Wolf." At one point in the show a piece of electronics gear began misbehaving, and Bob Bralove, who usually stood behind the keyboards or drum riser, was forced to walk to the front of the stage to fix it. He'd performed the task dozens if not hundreds of times before, but never before had he felt as if a bull's eye was plastered on his chest. "You could *feel* it," he says. "This was normally the place that was always safe and you felt the love from the audience. But all of a sudden I'm realizing I'm standing next to the guy they said they wanted to kill. It was very, very intense." After tending to the repair Bralove quickly retreated back to the darkened part of the stage.

For years they'd defied the odds; so many times they'd been written off creatively, physically, or economically, only to return, sometimes as vital as before. But the last few months had made even those closest and most loyal to the Dead wonder whether they, Garcia especially, would be able to pull back from the darkness. During a set break Garcia called his loyal driver, Leon Day. "I had a threat on my life," he told him. Day joked back: "I got your back—you got mine?"

Still, Garcia sounded unnerved. "He'd gotten threats before," Day says, "but for some reason this one seemed to hit home." The driver made plans to pick up Garcia at the airport when the tour finished in a few more days. Then, as Garcia was beginning to tell members of his inner circle, he would finally consider rest, recuperation, maybe even a serious stint in rehab. Thirty years after the Warlocks had played Magoo's pizza parlor, they all needed to reassess what everything had come to.

■　◆　■

Just over two years before, the past had circled back to Garcia in a far more intoxicating way. The day before New Year's Eve 1993 he'd jumped on a plane to Hawaii, where he'd been scuba diving and escaping the Dead world regularly since 1988. Joining him were two companions from the comparatively carefree early days in the Peninsula, two reminders of the time before relentless touring, deaths in the Dead family, and other complications and tragedies.

First was Barbara Meier, Garcia's long-ago girlfriend from the Chateau era three decades before. Then living in Colorado, where she was painting, writing, and working with the Naropa Institute, the Buddhist-inspired college in Colorado, Meier had built a completely new and separate life since she and Garcia had broken up. (She loved *American Beauty* but hadn't kept up with most of the band's other music.) When she published a collection of poetry Hunter came across a copy in a bookstore and passed it along to Garcia, who sent a letter to her, by way of her publisher, that read in part, "I've always loved you and still do." The two connected backstage at the Shoreline Amphitheater in May 1991. The last time Meier had seen her old boyfriend he'd had black hair and a black goatee and was trim; now the man facing her reminded her of Santa Claus. He told her he felt they'd lived parallel lives and that she was always part of his "psychic future." In what seemed like a heartbeat, they'd reconnected; Garcia went onstage to do the second set, and Meier sat weeping in her seat, overcome by the reunion and its possibilities.

Although she was in the midst of working toward a graduate degree, Meier took the Garcia plunge again. As an excuse to see him again, she interviewed him for *Tricycle: The Buddhist Review* magazine and began visiting Marin. Driving with director Len Dell'Amico in his BMW one day, Garcia unexpectedly announced he was in love with, he said, "Barbara, this girl I knew a long time ago. She's like the sun." Hearing comments like those, the Dead community geared up to re-insert Meier into Garcia's life.

When Meier arrived at Hunter's house on December 30, 1992, according to Lesh's account, she found not only Garcia and Robert and his wife, Maureen, but also Phil and Jill Lesh. Garcia had left home that morning without telling Manasha anything about his plans to leave her for Meier, but he had to say *something* about what he'd done, so his friends helped him write a note, then had it hand-delivered to Manasha by Garcia's assistant, Vince Di Biase. "I immediately sensed it was not written in Jerry's voice," Manasha says, but there was little she could do. The next day Dead crew members whisked Garcia and Meier to a Holiday Inn near the airport to spend the night before being flown to Hawaii. "They had all the logistics lined up like a military operation," Meier says. On the flight out the couple chuckled when the pilot walked back to first class and told Garcia, "Usually, I'm at *your* gig on New Year's Eve."

Along with the Hunters and the Leshes, Garcia and Meier settled into a condo complex in Maui, and the heady, creative rush of almost thirty years earlier appeared to breeze back in. Garcia and Meier took strolls on the beach and went scuba diving together. After a mini-studio was set up in his room, with recording gear and a keyboard, Garcia and Hunter sat down to pen new material. The two had written together only sporadically since the early eighties, but the stress-free atmosphere, removed from Marin and the Dead community, seemed to inspire them. Soon enough they'd finished "Lazy River Road," a lively stroll inspired by Garcia and Meier's reunion. "The more beautiful world tapped us on the shoulder again, so we thought we'd have a second chance," Meier says. "And we all felt it. It felt like, 'This is right.'"

The sense of renewal couldn't have arrived at a better time for Garcia and the Dead. In the months after confronting Garcia backstage in Boston, Bruce Hornsby had continued playing with the band, but his enthusiasm seemed to wane with each show. "Let's be honest here," he says. "Jerry was in and out of his problems. There were times when he was all there, but other times he wasn't. Jerry was my main reason for doing it." As the *New York Times* noted of a 1991 show, the two-keyboard setup could result in overbaked arrangements: "The band is clearly still trying to figure out what to do" with Hornsby and Welnick onstage together, wrote critic Peter Watrous, adding, "With four chordal instruments onstage, the sound at times became clotted and busy."

Feeling Welnick could handle the parts by himself and wanting to spend more time with his twin sons, born January 30, 1992, Hornsby found a nonconfrontational way to quit his part-time job with the Dead. By way of management Garcia found out before Hornsby had a chance to tell him, but Hornsby was still able to have an amicable conversation about it with Garcia. "I said, 'I think Vince has it—you don't need me anymore,'" Hornsby recalls. "I felt my role was to be the transitional figure between Brent's death and the time Vince got comfortable. But I also felt there were too many nights it didn't have that spark. I didn't tell that to Jerry, but it was definitely a reason for me."

Garcia took the news well, but Scher, still the band's principal promoter and a trusted adviser, was taken aback. He knew Hornsby had little tolerance for sloppiness or lack of rehearsal and would practice piano several hours every day. Hornsby had been complaining to Scher for some time, but Scher never expected the keyboardist to pull the trigger and leave. "It was a big disappointment to me and a great lost opportunity," Scher says. "They were a better band with Hornsby in it. Bruce loved Jerry, and he liked most of the guys in the band. But at that stage in their career, when they were being sloppy and weren't playing well often enough, he got disillusioned."

Lesh would later write that the band's less-than-polished approach to playing Hornsby's own songs was an issue, and Hornsby generally agrees. "They wanted to play some of my songs, so I arranged them for the Dead shuffle style," he says. But unless the songs were rigorously rehearsed and played repeatedly, Hornsby realized the band would often forget the arrangements. "By the seventh time playing

'The Valley Road,' it was really rough," he says, "and I went to them and said, 'Hey, come on, guys—unless we rehearse it, let's not do it anymore. It's nice that you want to play my songs, but I've got this other forum, so it's okay.' And they said, 'Oh, no, we'll rehearse.' But we never really did." After his last official shows with the band, at the Palace in Auburn Hills, Michigan, in late March 1992 Hornsby was gone as a full-time member, although he would join them for select performances in the future, easily gliding back into his role.

With the Dead back to a single-keyboard lineup, Welnick did a capable job playing and adding harmonies. (He even led the band on arguably its least likely cover ever, the Who's "Baba O'Riley," starting the summer of 1992.) But because the Dead world would never be entirely settled, other troubles sprang up soon enough. Still in a relationship with Manasha as of the middle of 1992, Garcia had moved with her and their daughter, Keelin, into a luxurious ten-acre home in Nicasio. (In a sign of how economically far the Dead had come, this was the same town where the ragged, woodsy Rukka Rukka Ranch had once been home to Weir, crew members, and anyone else who needed someplace to crash.) At that house in August Garcia crumbled from exhaustion soon after returning home from a Garcia Band tour, which had followed a short run of Dead performances. "It was too much for him," says Manasha. "He had a hard time saying no and just went along with the program until he collapsed." At Garcia's request, Manasha called the Dead office and told them he wanted to cancel the band's planned fall tour.

As it had six years before, after Garcia's diabetic coma, the brakes were suddenly slammed on the Dead organization. This time no one in their office was laid off, but concerns mounted as never before. According to Nancy Mallonee, staffers were worried either about Garcia dying or the band giving up touring or winding down altogether: "People would ask, 'How long do you think it's going to be?'"

With a small crew of healers—two holistic physicians, an acupuncturist, a dietician, and an alternative-medicine homeopath—the hospital-wary Garcia began to physically improve at home. He drank fresh organic juices prepared daily by Manasha, avoided fats in his diet, became a vegan, and lost about sixty pounds. In an even more hopeful sign, he announced he wanted to give up smoking, his longtime passion, and was soon down to only a few cigarettes a day, according to Manasha. He granted Manasha durable power of attorney for his heath decisions and, to keep himself busy during recovery, invited Bralove to their house to help him score black-and-white films and print out his computer artwork. Garcia's dark sense of humor remained untouched: watching *Nosferatu* and *The Cabinet of Dr. Caligari*, still-creepy 1920s horror films about the undead, he looked at Bralove and said, "This is too close!"

But Garcia's most restorative retreat from his workaday world was Hawaii, where he'd been introduced to diving by Vicki Jensen; the former Dead family member (and Hart ranch worker and resident) was now living on the Big Island, where she'd become a dive master. On his first dive Garcia had to take it slow; Jensen noticed his legs were nearly purple from lack of circulation, and he primarily stayed in one spot in the water and did 360 turns. He was so overweight that, on that and later dives, he had to be weighed down with thirty-two pounds (more than usual) to make sure he stayed below the surface. (In diving, weight makes people more buoyant.)

But in stark contrast to his increasingly sloth-like stage presence, both with the Dead and the Garcia Band, Garcia seemed to come alive in the water. "It was so wonderful to see him dive and see that sparkle again," says Jensen. "It was, 'Oh my God, he's back.' He was roly-poly, but his face glowed. The grapevine was saying the diving's going to kill him. But I thought, 'No, he might be around *longer.*'"

Garcia immersed himself in diving with the same intensity as when he was learning banjo or guitar decades before; in effect, it became

his new addiction. He took dive classes, bought a diving suit, and had prescription lenses put into his mask in order to clearly see underwater. Within time he lost enough weight to need only an additional eighteen pounds attached to his gear, and over the years he went on over five hundred dives. "He could be the Jerry he used to be," says Candelario, who accompanied Garcia on numerous trips to Hawaii. "To see Jerry in Kona was a totally different guy. He was happy and not on drugs and not having people hit on him. On that dive boat nobody bothered him." When Manasha and Keelin joined him, he'd bring them seashells and return from dive trips with stories of seeing sea turtles and whales. Even then Garcia remained a risk taker. During one night-time dive Jensen saw him trying to befriend an eel, even though she'd warned him to be careful around them and not stick out his fingers. "I thought, 'God, I don't want to be responsible for him losing *another* finger!'" Jensen says. "But the thing accepted him."

By the early nineties the members of the Dead weren't seeing much of each other off the road; they were business partners but rarely socialized. "When they got home they shut each other out a little bit after so many years of working together," says Trixie Garcia, who stayed in the Bay Area and went to community college after Garcia and Mountain Girl split up again post-Manasha (Mountain Girl returned to Oregon). "Typically Jerry would be pretty exhausted for a week after a tour. Almost catatonic. He wanted a simple existence. He didn't want to go anywhere or have visitors. Very shuttered." Hawaii helped to change that dynamic for the better; on various trips Garcia invited along Weir, Hunter, Hart, Kreutzmann, and crew members like Candelario and Parish. (Noticeably absent from pre-1990 trips was Mydland; no one ever recalls seeing him scuba dive with the band.)

After he'd left Manasha, an old romance renewed and new songs being crafted with his longtime friend and creative cohort, Garcia struck Meier as relatively happy, and his devotion to his new hobby was more than evident. Settling into the water as if it were his second home, he showed her how to slow down her breathing and not waste oxygen in the tank. Underwater, away from the pressures of the Dead, the two held hands and watched giant sea turtles swim by, and he told her not to be scared when sharks passed them. "Jerry was very Buddha-like in that underwater world," she says. "He was buoyant, free of his body. It was as if he belonged there."

■　◆　▲

The tickets for Deer Creek announced a 7 p.m. start time, but as always, the devoted—and those who simply wanted to have a good time—began arriving early for parties outside the venue. Those who'd been to Deer Creek before and didn't have tickets knew that one of the best spots to hear the band was at the bottom of a hill outside the venue, and several thousand people and their cars began congregating there.

From his car Chris Clair, wearing a tie-dye shirt and sporting a curly Afro, could see the prohibitive wooden-slat fence that separated them from the Dead and the inside of the Deer Creek Music Center. He could see the security guards driving around in golf carts keeping an eye on anyone who might want to run up the incline and into the venue. He could smell the pot in the air and hear Dead tapes blasting from sound systems in the thousands of cars parked in a semicircle around him.

Having gone to his first Dead show in 1989 when he was nineteen, Clair, then attending college at Indiana State, was part of the post-"Touch of Grey" wave of Deadheads. He loved Hunter's lyrics, the sound of Garcia's guitar, the sight and sound of two drummers, and, especially, Mydland's voice and energy; he actually preferred Mydland's singing to that of Garcia and Weir. Yet he was starting to feel that Dead concerts hadn't been the same since Mydland's death. At twenty-six, a veteran of roughly fifty shows, Clair now felt like a grizzled veteran compared to the nitrous-inhaling teenagers around him. "I was looking at the young kids and feeling they were ruining the party," he says. "They were coming for the drugs and didn't know much about the music. They were raining on the parade." The music was straining his loyalty as well: the sound of Garcia's weakened voice made him sad, as did the sight of Garcia not remembering lyrics. To Clair, Welnick was no Mydland. Clair began growing nostalgic for an earlier era: "I used to talk about the eighties," he says, "the way other people talked about the sixties."

Clair wasn't the only one to notice that a younger, rowdier, or more inclined-to-excess crowd was starting to take over Dead shows as the nineties dragged on. In 1992 Steve Marcus started joining the band on the road; counterfeiting had become such a problem that Marcus set up "Ticket Verification" tables to differentiate the genuine stubs from the ones supposedly forged by the mob in New Jersey. At Rich Stadium in the Buffalo suburbs that June he was confronted with an equally worrisome problem. As he examined tickets outside the venue Marcus saw a large group heading in his direction "like a pack of wild animals," he says. After running around the parking lot, they made straight for one of the entry gates, smashing it open. Grabbing his walkie-talkie, Marcus reported to security inside and heard the chilling response: "Get your table and get the hell inside."

Moments like that were still largely the exception: more common was the amusing sight at a show in Maine, where a state trooper holding a police manual was hurriedly flipping through it to learn whether or not he should arrest a fan for having nitrous. But the aggressive tactics of 1989 made a comeback at the start of the Dead's summer 1995 tour at the Franklin Valley Field in Highgate, Vermont. A show at the same venue the previous year had gone off without problems, but tonight promoter Jim Koplik heard kids were trying to pull down the chain-link fence around the venue. Grabbing a few security guards, Koplik raced to the scene and saw tens of thousands of kids on the other side of the metal links, pushing to get in. "It shocked us," he says. "It was definitely not Deadheads." He'd thought he and his crew could hold on to the fence and keep it in place, but realizing they were overwhelmed, Koplik ran in the other direction. To avoid the riot and spare the fences, organizers had no choice but to open the gates and allow thirty thousand crashers—about twice the number who could fit into a typical indoor arena—in for free. As they rushed in, Gary Lambert, then working for the Dead's merchandising office, saw portable toilets knocked over with people still inside.

For now, at Deek Creek in Indiana, the calm held. When "Dire Wolf" finished, the Dead dove into a cover of Bobby Womack's "It's All Over Now," followed by Robbie Robertson's exquisite "Broken Arrow," sung by Lesh. Then, as Clair and his friends at his car watched, a handful of people in the parking area suddenly ran up the steep hill. Two of them stopped, cupped their hands together, and hoisted the other three up over the fence. "Wow, they got over the fence," Clair heard one of his friends say. Another group followed, hoisting the remaining two who'd been left behind. And then another group of ten, and another group of twenty after that. Five or six waves of fans jumped over, all without damaging the fence. Security guards began shouting, "Get off the hill!" But for now there wasn't much more they could do.

■ ◆ ▮

Inevitably Garcia had to leave Hawaii and return to the mainland, and the Dead road machine cranked up again. The band's schedule was set in particularly hardened concrete: tours each spring, summer, and fall, with spring shows in the Carolinas and up through New York; summer stadium shows, then the multiple fall runs at arenas in Philadelphia, New York, and Boston. Specific dates, even venues, were reserved as much as a year in advance. The labor paid off: in 1993, according to the concert-industry outlet *Pollstar*, the band was the top-earning touring act, pulling in over $45 million, and the following year the number jumped to $52 million. Tickets were almost always sold out in advance, thanks to a mailing list that had started in the early seventies with 26,000 names and now including more than 200,000. After Garcia's collapse in 1992 additional shows had to be added the following year to compensate for the loss in revenue. The band had had to deal with another crippling blow in October 1991, when Bill Graham died in a helicopter crash. "That was a big deal," says Trixie Garcia. "He was a mentor, friend, and uncle figure."

As the band well knew, their success came with a Faustian bargain. Grateful Dead Productions now employed thirty people (including the band), some who'd worked for the Dead for decades. Another fifteen worked at Grateful Dead Merchandising, and GDTS (Grateful Dead Ticket Sales) was home to another few dozen. In 1973 total monthly salaries for the band were $60,769. By 1995 the band's monthly overhead, including salaries, rent, and insurance, could top $750,000 when the Dead toured stadiums (less when they were doing indoor shed or arena tours). "We were no longer just a band," Hart says. "We had a payroll and families. We weren't getting that much money; we were spreading it around. We couldn't stop. We were a snake eating its tail. There was no way for us to take a rest. We were locked into tour, tour, tour. I'm sure I wanted to take a break, but there were no options." Garcia had a high overhead himself, which included monthly $20,833 payments to Mountain Girl from their divorce. The couple had amicably met behind closed doors at the office of lawyer David Hellman in 1993. When Hellman questioned the number Mountain Girl proposed, Garcia said he was fine with it.

A degree of midlife stability had settled over the band. By now Lesh and his wife, Jill, had two sons, Brian and Grahame. In 1989 Hart had struck up a relationship with Caryl Ohrbach, a San Francisco public defender who'd previously been an environmental lawyer, and the two married soon after. Weir was in a relationship with Natascha Muenter, whom he'd met at a Dead show years before but didn't hook up with until later. As they settled into their late forties and midfifties, some health issues dogged them. Realizing it was time to leave Front Street in favor of more professional digs, the Dead decided to buy a former Coca-Cola building on Bel Marin Keys Boulevard in Novato. At over thirty thousand square feet, the space was huge and could accommodate a recording studio more advanced than the one at Front Street. According to McNally, the band members were required to take physicals for insurance on the property, and what came back were diagnoses of high cholesterol, hepatitis, and other ailments. Polygram, which owned part of Scher's Metropolitan company, took out a death-and-disability policy on the Dead. The paperwork didn't stem from overt concerns about the Dead's well-being; corporate policy dictated that key executives as well as recording artists who had influence over the business had to be insured. In this case only Garcia and Weir were included because someone assumed that the primary lead singers were the key to the Dead's success.

Far more troubling was the moment during one of Garcia's Hawaii trips when Vicki Jensen found Garcia talking about hard drugs again. "He said something like, 'There were some really *good* things about it,'" she recalls. "And I thought, 'Don't delude yourself, man.'" But he had, and Manasha soon learned that Garcia had fallen back into old habits. She never saw him use heroin or other opiates, and he was never "visibly addled," she says. But in 1992, she says, Garcia's doctor, Randy Baker, informed her that Garcia was "inhaling small quantities of opiates" and that he was a "maintenance user," a term she'd never heard before. Garcia's drug use and how it would affect Keelin, then five years old, became Manasha's foremost worry. "It was my concern that Jerry was getting into a pattern that would not end well," she says, and for a few days she considered leaving him. "Honey, if you go, I'll find you and bring you back!" she says he told her, which made her decide to stay. "We talked about the situation, his health, and the future," she says. "We shared a very intimate loving evening together." Then a few nights later came Garcia's hand-delivered note.

Garcia and Manasha Matheson Garcia had at least one more conversation. Right before Easter 1993, she says, Garcia called her from the road, saying, "I miss you" and asking whether they could reunite for the holiday. "Although I loved him deeply, I still had unresolved feelings about seeing him right away, given the circumstances of our separation," she says. "I said, 'I'd like to wait' and explained I'd made Easter weekend plans already with a friend who was visiting from the East Coast." Garcia replied, "I'm going to keep trying." It would be her last conversation with him. A week later Manasha called him back, and according to her, a woman answered the phone, said "very impolite words" to her, and hung up on her.

Garcia's reunion with Meier proved short lived. She noticed how snappish he could be and, after speaking with his doctor, realized he was an addict. "I remember thinking about it and naïvely saying to myself, 'Well, we'll take care of that! That won't get in the way!'" she recalls. "Words like 'the golden era' were being thrown around. Now, do you say no to that?" When she talked about it with Garcia, Meier learned he wasn't particularly open to such discussions, and their relationship ended almost immediately after. ("He would say, 'I'm fine—I'm *fine*,'" recalls photographer Herb Greene, who brought up the topic with Garcia during this period. "He didn't like people talking to him about that stuff.") In another jarring twist in years filled with them, Garcia also told Meier he'd run into another ex-flame, Deborah Koons, and couldn't stop thinking about her.

During a band rehearsal at Front Street in December 1993 Garcia pulled McNally aside and said he needed some help. As everyone soon discovered, he and Koons had not only reunited but were going to marry. The news came as a surprise to nearly everyone, especially members of Garcia's own family. "We were all excited," says Trixie about her father's reunion with Meier. "'He's going to marry his high school sweetheart! How sweet is that?' And all of a sudden he's with Deborah Koons. And we were like, 'Who's *that*?'" A good chunk of the Dead community dutifully attended the couple's wedding in Sausalito on Valentine's Day, 1994. (Garcia didn't make it to his bachelor party and therefore missed strippers and nitrous tanks.) When a bearded, long-haired guy in a car with a Dead sticker drove by the church during rehearsals, McNally ran out and begged him not to tell anyone, and the man apparently complied; the wedding wasn't besieged with Deadheads.

Even newly remarried, Garcia remained everyone's concern, especially when his stage performances during 1994 shows grew increasingly erratic and slothful. "The nineties was my least favorite period, because of Jerry's declining health," says Hart. "He was missing so many damn notes." Hart says he soon learned one of the reasons why Garcia was making those mistakes. Garcia told him that due to clogged arteries, he could no longer feel his guitar pick, which was starting to freak him out. Garcia was also grappling with carpal tunnel syndrome and diabetes. At a show at Giants Stadium, most likely in 1994, Bralove watched as the band started "Crazy Fingers" and Garcia began playing the opening riff again and again, as if in an addled loop. "Jerry couldn't get out of the beginning triplets," he says. "He got stuck in this groove. I remember thinking, 'Did he have a stroke?' I thought, 'Oh, it could happen this way, where he just keels over in front of forty thousand people.' There were other times when he was taking solos when I thought, 'What's going on? What's he doing?' Maybe it was one fret off, so he was a half-step off the whole solo. He was going through some routine—the physiology of it—but not actually listening." Bralove would look over and see pained expressions on band members' faces, especially Lesh. Fans began writing into the Dead office com-plaining that Garcia was forgetting lyrics. Ever willing to invest in new technology, the Dead began using in-ear monitors that allowed them to press a foot switch and speak to one another without the audience overhearing. Garcia's impatience now had a vocal outlet: "The chord is *A minor*," he was once heard saying in the middle of a song.

Around the country promoters heard the ominous rumors and speculation about Garcia's health. Shows would often be preceded by a series of unsettling phone calls. "I'd ask, 'How's Jerry doing?'" re-calls Atlanta promoter Alex Cooley. "They'd say, 'It's gonna go—he's going to play. Just do it.' There was no show without Jerry, so we relied on people's words. We were dealing with millions of dollars, and peo-ple were giving me verbal okays over the phone. It was scary." Koplik would tell his team, "Don't worry about it—it's going to happen or not happen. You don't have control over it." It was about all anyone in his position could say. In one of Garcia's guitar cases his old friend Laird Grant left a poignant note: "Hey Jerry, please take care of yourself out there. Your friend, Laird."

■　◆　■

The new contract they'd signed with Arista in 1989 demanded an even-tual album, and by late 1994 the time had finally come to assemble one. For any other band the scenario would have been promising. They chose the Site, a studio tucked away in the postcard-ready hills of Marin County, and arrived with nine new songs, each road tested. "Lazy River Road," the Hunter and Garcia song inspired by Garcia's fleeting reunion with Meier, was one of them, but their two other contribu-tions were even deeper and more soulful. Worked out in the pool house of Hunter's home, "Days Between" felt utterly innovative for them: a slow, meditative crawl of a song, comprised of four verses of four-teen lines each, its lyrics autumnal and reflective. The same late-in-life ambience ran through "So Many Roads," which continued the majestic feel of "Black Muddy River" but with a new coat of world weariness.

As with *Built to Last*, the other songs were a grab bag of approaches and sensibilities. "Way to Go Home," a collaboration between Welnick, Hunter, and Bralove, locked into and sounded most like the Dead when Garcia's guitar burst out into a solo. (The same went for Welnick's other song, "Samba in the Rain," which attempted to weld the rhythms in its title to the Dead's trademark groove.) The blues—thicker, growlier, and more dramatic—also inhabited Weir's "Eternity," cowritten with Rob Wasserman and blues legend Willie Dixon. The song was more musically grounded than Weir's other contribution, "Easy Answers," which continued the tangled, tempo-shifting feel of "Victim or the Crime" and other consciously adventurous later-period Weir songs. For the first time since "Box of Rain" Hunter and Lesh were about to commit one of their collaborations to record; atypically pop and breezy, especially for Lesh, "Wave to the Wind" struck fans as either a lovely diversion or one of the corniest songs the Dead had ever written. Lesh also brought along his more complex, solo-written "Childhood's End," its title but not subject borrowed from Arthur C. Clarke's sci-fi novel.

First in November 1994 and again three months later the band settled into the Site to transform the motley collection of songs into a record. But in an unfortunate reminder of the Fantasy sessions of a decade before, little usable work emerged from it. The Site's isolated setting was amenable to recording, and Welnick's acoustic piano never sounded better. But Garcia would often show up late, carting along egg creams and egg salad sandwiches with extra mayonnaise, despite his health issues. "Jerry was pretty fucking smooth," says Bralove. "He would come in, apologize, have an excuse. He was a charmer. But he was in rough shape." When the work began, whether due to drug use, his diabetes, or other ailments associated with his smoking, Garcia wasn't always up to the task. The band would run through the songs, but according to Lesh, Garcia played only a total of "a few minutes" during the entire run at the studio. Eventually the band decided to record tracks without him and overdub his guitar parts later, yet even that plan was never realized.

Garcia had appeared tired and increasingly disoriented during shows in 1994, but as the band entered its thirtieth year in 1995, his descent became more obvious. Visiting her father at his home in Tiburon during the early months of the year (he and Deborah Koons maintained separate residences), Trixie let herself in and found Garcia lying face down on the bed. When she playfully tickled his feet to wake him up, he leapt up, startled. "He was passed out in the middle of the day on his bed, and he was probably high," she says, "but I didn't put it together." Around the same time, Garcia agreed to be interviewed for a history project, *Silicon Valley: 100 Year Renaissance*, produced and directed by John McLaughlin, the Palo Alto native who'd taken drum lessons from Kreutzmann long before. Garcia was friendly and chatty, but with his creased, sagging face, he looked at least twenty years older than he was, and every fifteen to twenty minutes he'd ask for a break to go into the pantry to, as he put it, look for his car keys. Given the rumors around Garcia and his past issues, it was easy enough for the film crew to assume he was taking one substance or another during those breaks. Lesh grew deeply concerned when, right before the summer 1995 tour, Koons fired Garcia's assistants, Vince and Gloria Di Biase, who saw to his day-to-day needs; the last thing anyone in the Dead world wanted was Garcia left to his own devices.

Meanwhile band and family grappled with what was ailing Garcia. He clearly wasn't healthy and was coping with lung and heart issues. Was he happy? Was his live-for-the-moment fatalism coming into play? What could anyone do about it? Kreutzmann would later admit that Garcia had been worn down by the Dead's predictable touring regimen. "Jerry had gotten kind of bored with the Grateful Dead, and it was sort of like a marriage that had maybe gone on too long," Kreutzmann told *Rolling Stone* in 2012. "I think a lot of it, I hate to say, was really a financial obligation. He needed to earn the money for some things." To Allan Arkush, Garcia referred to touring as "homework, a chore—it was like doing a term paper every night." (Speaking of his 1992 setback, Manasha says, "I personally think what was being demanded from Jerry in terms of working, touring, et cetera, contributed to his need to self-medicate.")

The perks of the job continued unabated: large homes, BMWs, home studios. On tour the Dead sometimes flew in a private Gulfstream III plane complete with a bar and made-to-order food. But to some friends or intimates Garcia would make his wishes known. Before his breakup with Meier he told her about a $125,000 payment he'd received from Ben & Jerry's for use of the Cherry Garcia name. (Garcia hadn't objected to the usage at first, done without his permission, but attorney Hal Kant convinced him to ask for a percentage of the sales.) Garcia mentioned how he'd love to quit the Dead and live off the ice-cream money; when she asked him why he didn't pursue that option, he mentioned all his employees. (When she wondered why he didn't simply get rid of the deadwood, he didn't respond.) Garcia told Candelario he wanted to move to Italy, sign up for art classes, and only play with the Dead on weekends. "We were so excited," says Candelario. "That was his dream. He wanted to put the Dead on sabbatical. There was plenty of money to be able to do that."

The time had come to address not just the machinery of it all, but everything that had built up over the last three decades: the sometimes-overwhelming intensity (and devotion) of their fan base, the live-and-let-live philosophy within the band, and, equally important, the way it was affecting the music. At band meetings the thought of shuttering the unwieldy Dead operation and allowing Garcia to regain his health would be brought up. (Garcia canceled the second half of a Garcia Band show in Phoenix in the spring of 1994 after he felt sick backstage.) According to Lesh, a three-point plan was laid out after Garcia's breakdown in 1992. If the Dead played only Bay Area shows for the rest of that year, they would cut back on salaries and equipment and "hopefully go back to full salaries in January," according to an internal report. If the concerts didn't resume at all until December, salaries would be cut in half in November, rather than by one-third (as in the first plan), before eventually returning to normal pay levels. In the third proposal, which assumed the band wouldn't play at all for the rest of the year, salaries would still be cut, but expenses would be reined in by "laying off everyone except for those necessary to maintain office and operations until we regroup in 1993."

That outline was the closest the Dead came to mapping out a specific plan of action. Otherwise, band and management would meet in the Dead's conference room and grapple with if, when, and how to leave the road, at least temporarily. Garcia's inconsistency onstage—weak performances followed almost immediately by strong ones—also confused matters. (At a show in Albany, New York, shortly before Deer Creek, his guitar had moments of ageless beauty even if Garcia himself—looking drawn and frail, his long white hair drooping forlornly to his shoulders—seemed prematurely aged.) "They talked about it, but they never made a decision to do it and figure out exactly how to do it," says Mallonee. "Jerry felt he was on some kind of assembly line and needed more time at home, and the band knew it was hard on him. But they were stuck in this pattern. They'd laid people off in the seventies, but [the machine] wasn't nearly as big then." Recalling similar discussions, Scher says, "There were a couple of times—and, believe me, they were not serious confrontations—if the band said, 'We're not going out until you get yourself together,' he just would have gone out with the Garcia Band. He said, 'John, I play guitar every single day. I might as well get paid for it.'" Indeed, the JGB, still anchored by Garcia and Kahn but also by now featuring keyboardist Melvin Seals, was still a going concern up through the early months of 1995.

Ironically, one of the non-Garcia-related problems the band was increasingly facing—outsiders who crashed the shows and made the road less enticing—could have been their salvation. According to Weir in *Rolling Stone* in 2013, "The last year or two, we were actually faced with more than just the possibility that we'd have to knock off for a while and let things cool down. There was a lot of trouble we had to deal with, the crowd-control problems." Far more so than the crowds in Pittsburgh and at other troubled cities in 1989, this new breed of concertgoer seemed less interested in the music and more attuned to the party—and more eager than ever to crash that party without paying. But again, canceling entire tours would, in their minds, be more difficult than coping with bad shows. Garcia would wonder aloud whether some of their employees, given how long they'd worked for the band without any other experience, would even be able to find work anywhere else.

Swanson saw the hugeness of the operation when she returned to their fold in the late eighties to work in the merchandise office. She'd never seen so many limos before, and the Dead office in San Rafael was now packed with employees. Swanson also noticed the band's mixed feelings toward their success. "They could have called it at any time, but none of them did," she says. "They could say it was all about the machine, and all of that was true. But fame is a sort of seductress, and they were seduced—staying in really nice places in New York City and taking limos back and forth. It was hard to walk away from that, and they treated everybody well. Once you do that, you can't go back."

In the meantime road work beckoned, as it always did. When driver Leon Day picked up Garcia for a soundcheck at the Silver Stadium in Vegas in May of 1995, he had to throw pebbles at his boss's window to get his attention. Finally Garcia came down, looking bedraggled and tired. "Oh, come on, you'll outlive us all," Day joked. Garcia replied, "I won't see the end of the year."

■ ◆ ■

The next group who clambered over the fence at Deer Creek didn't simply want in; they wanted destruction. Instead of jumping over and heading toward the music, they settled atop the fence and began shaking the wood slats back and forth. As Clair and a friend watched in astonishment, the barricade began breaking down, splinters of wood flying through the air. "They were like monkeys, hollering," Clair says. "You could hear people inside the stadium yelling, 'Get off the fence!' But the majority of the people outside were cheering them on, like, 'Go, go!'" Although Clair heard security radioing for backup, it seemed shockingly clear that no one had a plan if the fence was attacked.

Suddenly but inevitably, a huge chunk of the barrier crashed down completely, and with it, the people in the parking lot transformed into a stampede, running up the hill and into the venue. Clair had no interest in jumping a fence, but now that all gate-crashing hell had broken loose, what was the harm in following everyone else in and catching the show? "I'm not proud of it," he says. "I thought, 'These kids who just came for the drugs and the scene got into *my* show in *my* hometown. That's not fair. I should be in there too.'" Clair and his girlfriend looked at each other, didn't say a word, and made a run for it.

Sergeant Scott Kirby of the Noblesville police department was among the first to arrive at Deer Creek. On the police radio he'd heard a few dozen cops at the venue desperately calling in for help: from what he could gather, they'd never seen any part of the fence dismantled before, and police were now outnumbered. When Kirby drove into the venue on a side road he saw the situation for himself and was stunned. He'd worked security at previous Dead shows and knew the community welcomed Deadheads, if only for the extra revenue they pumped into the economy. But tonight thousands of people were walking on the road, barely moving out of the way of his squad car. "It was like running a gauntlet," he says. "They were everywhere. I had never seen that many people there before." Kirby managed to reach a command post on one side of the venue, but even there rocks and bottles began bouncing off the police cars.

Kirby realized two different groups—the Deadheads who rarely caused problems and what he calls "the party group" looking for trouble—were vying for control, and the latter were winning. Every so often someone would burst out of the crowd and taunt the cops; when police advanced, the kid would run back into the crowd to cheers. Realizing they were hugely outnumbered—fifty to thousands—the police made a decision: they wouldn't fight the mob. "It was, 'We've lost the venue and we're not going to get it back,'" Kirby says. "We needed to take another tack." Hearing the Dead, Kirby and the other police hoped they'd stop playing, giving the people less impetus to cross the road that separated the crowd from the cops. But the band thought otherwise and continued; Lesh later said the band thought the rioting would only worsen if the music ended.

Clair had almost reached the top of the hill when the tear gas canisters and pepper spray hit him. By then other police had arrived and begun following the mob up the embankment from the parking area. Clair had been running alongside his girlfriend, but now he grabbed her, did an about-face, and began scurrying back down, holding his breath the whole time. With the air thick with tear gas, he felt as if he were driving with a fogged-up windshield. Back down at the bottom the smoke wasn't as thick, and Clair and his girlfriend could see people screaming, vomiting, and holding twisted ankles all around the hill. To Clair it felt like a war zone.

■ ◆ ■

The band had just started into Bob Dylan's "Desolation Row" when a very different wall of sound hit them. Because the crowd was still lit up by the lights, due to the death threat, the Dead could see what was happening in the distance, and the sight of thousands of fans smashing through a fence and rushing in their direction astonished even the most hardened road warriors among them. "I looked up, and they were *pouring* over the fence," says Bralove. "Bodies were flying. And you realized that all precautions were gone. All this stuff based on trust between the band and the audience had this energy of paranoia at that moment. Now it's like, 'These are the people who could be bringing the guns.' It was very freaky." Lesh had a look of disgust, Weir of shock, and the song momentarily stopped. The band said nothing to the crowd and eventually resumed playing, a noticeable snarl heard in Weir's delivery.

The Dead soldiered on, took a typical break between sets, and finished the show. Sears, walking in the crowd, was hit with bottles; with his walkie-talkie, he was mistaken for a cop. When the show was over the band's exodus quickly began: women and children were sent out first through the crowd in vans—which struck one member of the organization as a strange type of decoy—while band members and crew clambered aboard a bus that took them out the back of the venue. Gazing out the windows, those inside could see fans lighting fires and banging on the bus, and the more zoned-out wandered in front of the moving bus like zombies. "People were so fucked up they were almost daring the bus to run them over," says McNally. "It was eerie." Adding to the weirdness, the driver opted for a side road to get to the freeway, and the bus ran into a ditch. After the crew were unable to pull it out, a tow truck eventually yanked the bus out of the hole, and the Dead finally were on their way back to their hotel.

Back at his car in the lot, Clair took a swig of vodka to clear his throat—it was the only liquid in sight—as angry fans around him, those who hadn't jumped the fence, berated him: "You shouldn't have done that—the show is over!" and "Thanks for ruining the party, asshole!" The crowd dispersed, and Clair made it back to the apartment he was sharing with roommates. The smell of the tear gas, or whatever it had been, lingered in his throat and eyes. When he told his Dead-hating roommates what had happened, they simply laughed, and Clair had trouble sleeping that night.

A second show at Deer Creek had been scheduled for the following night, but local police told Dead management that if problems arose again, officers would only be on duty to direct traffic, not defend the venue. Because no one wanted a repeat performance of the riot, the show was canceled, and everyone in the Dead camp was told to assemble in their hotel lobby at 1 p.m. to leave early for the next show in Missouri. In his job as spokesman, McNally drafted an open letter to fans from the band about what had happened and the consequences of gate-crashing. Titled "This Darkness Got to Give" and signed by each band member, the letter was more emphatic and angrier in tone than the messages they had sent to fans after the troubles of 1989. "At Deer Creek, we watched many of you cheer on and help a thousand fools kick down the fence and break into the show," it read near the start. "We can't play music and watch plywood flying around endangering people. . . . Don't you get it? . . . A few thousand so-called Dead Heads ignore those simple rules and screw it up for you, us and everybody. We've never before had to cancel a show because of you. Think about it." The letter went on to warn against vending and against coming to shows unless people had tickets: "This is real. This is first a music concert, not a free-for-all party. . . . Many of the people without tickets have no responsibility or obligation to our scene. They don't give a shit. They act like idiots. They think it's just a party to get as trashed as possible at." It warned that allowing "bottle-throwing gate crashers" would only "end the touring life of the Grateful Dead. . . . A few more scenes like Sunday night, and we'll quite simply be unable to play. The spirit of the Grateful Dead is at stake, and we'll do what we have to do to protect it."

Arriving at Deer Creek the next day fans saw the letter posted at the entrance. That same morning Kirby spotted a group of Deadheads at a local grocery store, stocking up on food for the show. When he told them it was off, they initially refused to believe him, then gathered around a car radio to hear the news for themselves. Some looked dejected; others began crying. Kirby didn't quite understand it, but he'd never seen anything quite like it before and realized how vital to their lives those tours were.

Four shows remained—two at Riverport Stadium in Maryland Heights, Missouri, and two at Soldier Field in Chicago—and the Dead managed to slog through them. But catastrophes of varying scales dogged them. Before Deer Creek, lighting had struck three Deadheads in a parking lot at the show at Washington, DC. After Deer Creek 108 fans at a campground miles away from St. Louis were hurt when a porch they'd crowded onto collapsed. (One other died of an overdose in the same campground.) By the time the band reached Chicago for the last two shows, July 8 and 9, eleven TV crews had arrived to chronicle any further calamities, and John Scher flew in from New Jersey after hearing the Deer Creek news. Even though Garcia would sometimes flinch when Scher tried to talk with him about his smoking, Garcia admitted he knew his health was teetering and told Scher he was going to Hawaii after the tour to relax and recuperate. Compared to past conversations, Scher was pleasantly surprised and hopeful, even if the scene around the Dead still appeared shaky. "Things were pretty fractured at that point," says Scher. "Everyone was a bit on edge and tired of what was going on, at, and for Jerry. It had all gotten out of hand."

The final night in Chicago, July 9, didn't feel right from the opening notes—and not only because, thirty years before, a Ouija board in the band's rented house in Los Angeles had announced that day as some kind of finale. Starting with "Touch of Grey," Garcia's voice wavered in and out of key, and the harmonies were shaky. When Garcia peeled off a solo the tone was spry and fluid. Roaring out the "we will get by" refrain at the end of the song, the crowd seemed eager to voice its own positive outlook toward him and the Dead. The rest of the show was typically spotty, but at moments—especially on a version of "Lazy River Road"—Garcia's voice settled into its deeper, lower register as if he were sinking into a comfortable old sofa. The slower, more elegiac songs were clearly speaking more to Garcia, made jarringly clear to Steve Marcus when he and some coworkers watched closely as their boss sang "So Many Roads," with its desolate Hunter lyrics about easing one's soul. "We were looking at each other like, 'What's going on with Jerry?'" Marcus says. "He was putting more into that song than we'd seen him do for years."

Standing at the soundboard, Caryl Hart looked up at a screen broadcasting a close-up of Garcia's drawn face and was saddened. Dan Ross, the Michigan Deadhead who'd attended 423 Dead concerts since 1988, did something he'd never done at any of the shows he'd seen: finding the experience of watching his beloved band in such a weakened state, he headed for the parking lot before it was over. "When I left," he says, "I was thinking, 'It's time.'"

As the band ended the show and prepared for an encore, word filtered out through crew walkie-talkies of a double encore: "Black Muddy River" and then, at Lesh's suggestion for a more upbeat ending to the show and tour, "Box of Rain." For three decades the band had put itself through a seemingly nonstop cycle of ups and downs: rejuvenation followed by collapse or near-collapse, followed by another renewal. The pattern was as much a part of their story as their music, and it was only natural to assume that the pattern would continue, that Garcia would again rise up.

On the flight back to San Francisco Hart sat next to Garcia and watched as his band mate of twenty-eight years nodded off, falling into a deep sleep, accompanied as always by his thunderous snore. (That peculiarity could be useful: when he fell asleep in hotel rooms on the road it was a way for the organization to tell he wasn't dead.) At one point in the flight Hart looked over and saw Garcia's heart literally beating through his T-shirt. "I went, 'Wow, have I ever seen that before?'" Hart says. "His brave heart was beating on, but that baby was really tired." After such a difficult run of shows, everyone needed a rest, but no one more than Garcia.

The Dead reunited backstage (with Warren Haynes, second from right) at the Gramercy Theatre, New York, 2009.
PHOTO: BENJAMIN LOWY/GETTY IMAGES REPORTAGE

NEW YORK CITY, MARCH 30, 2009

On an inordinately chilly dawn-of-spring night they were back to doing what they'd perfected night after night, year after year, for over three decades. This time they were backstage at a midsized theater in midtown Manhattan. Bent over a coffee table, Lesh, now a lean sixty-nine-year-old, was jotting down a list of songs they'd be attempting that night. The first issue literally on the table was the length of the set; in a very un-Dead-like scenario, they'd only have an hour to play.

"We'll start out and see where it goes," Lesh said. "If we have to cut, we cut."

"Are we gonna be pitch-forked off the stage if we play too long?" Kreutzmann asked.

No one answered, but Hart, looking at the list, interjected, "This is do-able." Weir remained quiet, soaking it in.

The accommodations at the Gramercy Theatre weren't as lush as the Dead had long been accustomed to. They were gathering in a blandly decorated room stocked with a refrigerator, a couch, and a fruit-and-cheese display. Gone, for nearly fifteen years at that point, was the larger-than-life, reluctant frontman whose presence still lingered over everything they'd done and would ever do.

In about a month the group, now simply calling itself the Dead, would start its first tour together in five years. They'd been through much in their lives, good and bad, and the accumulated lifestyle mileage and rock 'n' roll wear and tear was evident on men now in their sixties; skin cancer scars and hearing aids were in evidence. Kreutzmann's hair, white as a new snowfall, was partly hidden by a backward baseball cap; Weir's chin of whiskers was also graying. Other than guitarist Warren Haynes—a recurring member of Lesh's solo band who'd have the unenviable task of filling in for Garcia on the tour, vocally and instrumentally—Weir was still the youngest at sixty-one. Despite the weather outside, he still wore his trademark sandals and short pants.

To help promote the upcoming tour they'd agreed to a promotional stunt: playing three one-set shows at three different venues in one night, with free tickets given away to fans on the Internet. The day had begun with Weir, Lesh, and Haynes appearing on the morning talk show *The View* (cohost Whoopi Goldberg was a longtime Dead fan), for which a line of Deadheads stretched down the street at the show's Upper West Side studio. "It's hard to get used to it without Jerry," said Don Moore, who scored tickets to all three gigs, "but I know the music must go on." Hours later the three men started the evening at an acoustic trio show at the five-hundred-seat, churchlike Angel Orensanz Center on the Lower East Side, playing "Cumberland Blues," "Casey Jones," "Dire Wolf," and "Ripple." On a version of "Bird Song" that extended to almost a half-hour, the three men were caught in a loop-like trance that threatened to derail at any moment but never did.

Now they had arrived at the second venue, the larger Gramercy Theatre, and had to figure out the set list. "Well, so far so good," said Weir earlier in the evening, settling into a couch as he and Lesh awaited the arrival of Hart and Kreutzmann. "We actually established a dynamic for the acoustic portion. That's another whole palette. It was fun. And we can go there now, and that's huge. You know, we haven't done it for thirty-five years or something like that."

"We did it at Radio City," says Lesh, referring to the long-ago 1980 show.

"Right, we did it at Radio City," Weir repeats, nodding. "The approach we're taking now is much different, and it's much easier to *hear*. And as Phil pointed out, we've also learned to listen to each other. So this time around it's really very different."

Moments later Kreutzmann and Hart walked in, and hugs and warm greetings were exchanged. "How was *The View?*" asked Kreutzmann, who sheepishly admitted he'd been napping after a long flight from his home in Hawaii when the show was aired.

"It was good," said Lesh, adding, with a frown, "[Bill] O'Reilly was there, though."

"Yeah, it was kind of *interesting* that he was on the show!" Kreutzmann cracked. "My joke to myself was, I wonder how the green room was."

"He was civil," Lesh said. "So were we."

"Phil put on Keith Olbermann and cranked it," Weir joined in, and Kreutzmann laughed.

"Well, Ann Coulter is a Deadhead," added Lesh's wife and manager, Jill, standing nearby.

"Yeah," Weir said. "She came to one of my shows. A year or so ago. A Ratdog show."

The road to this moment had been a tough one for each of them—fourteen often difficult years of shock, depression, health issues, business disputes, and reunions. Five months before, they'd reconvened for a benefit, and it had gone well enough that they were now about to take to the road together again. Old issues remained, yet they were doing their best to make nice publicly. "I've got a great-sounding drum set up there," Kreutzmann enthused, kicking back in a chair. Lesh indicated he was thinking of going onstage early to tune up even though Deadheads were already streaming into the venue.

"Well, there are a few people out there who'd love to see you!" cracked Kreutzmann, who still flashed signs of his untamed, looseygoosey energy.

"Oh, it's okay," Lesh added. "I don't mind."

First, the newly reformed Dead would need to get through twentytwo concerts, starting with winnowing down their first set of tonight to sixty minutes. In words that summed up what lay ahead for them, Hart said, with a manic gleam in his eye, "It's all going to change pretty radically. Stay tuned."

■ ◆ ■

On that grim day years before—August 9, 1995—everyone who heard the news thought it was just another rumor. At his home in New Jersey longtime Dead promoter and confidant John Scher was awoken by a reporter calling for a comment on Garcia's death. Scher barked that he didn't know what he was talking about—Garcia was in Hawaii, just as he'd told many in the Dead organization after the last show in Chicago the previous month. But the reporter was certain, and Scher called Cameron Sears in the Bay Area, who was equally taken aback. Garcia's former assistant Vince Di Biase phoned publicist McNally, who in turn called the county coroner's office. The rumor was true: at fifty-three, Garcia had been found dead in a rehab facility not far from his home.

When the Dead returned from Chicago after the "Tour from Hell" in the summer of 1995 a scheduled fall series of shows was still on the agenda, although they could have been canceled at any minute. Management hoped the same crowd-control issues wouldn't continue at places like the Boston Garden or Madison Square Garden, indoor venues in cities that didn't attract the same hangers-on outside. Before that run of shows took place, though, Garcia had decided the time had come to clean himself up. Koons has said that she became aware of Garcia's addiction early in 1995 and that the two agreed he should go into treatment when the summer tour was over. With the help of Koons and his personal manager Steve Parish, Garcia checked into the Betty Ford Clinic outside Los Angeles; as he told his driver, Leon Day, "They tell me Betty Ford's good for me." Garcia indicated to Parish he was ready for a change and that he was weary of both his addiction and hiding it from Koons.

Shortly before Garcia left for the clinic Bruce Hornsby had called to check in on him. They'd kept in touch even after Hornsby's departure from the band in early 1992, and despite his earlier concerns, Hornsby had sat in with the Dead at several shows afterward. "He said, 'I'm gonna do this and this is what needs to happen and I'll be okay and I'll be there for a month or five weeks,'" Hornsby recalls. "He sounded fine."

Two weeks later Hornsby called back, and to his surprise Garcia himself answered the phone. "Yeah, I left," he told Hornsby. "I got all I needed in two weeks." (The plan called for a monthlong stay.) Around this time Garcia ran into Peter Rowan, his former Old and in the Way bandmate, at a record store in Mill Valley; Garcia struck Rowan as upbeat and almost ebullient. But Garcia had slipped back into heroin use and decided to check into Serenity Knolls, a five-year-old rehab facility in Marin County, not far from his home.

Garcia kept his plans fairly private. (When he stopped by the home of close friends John and Linda Kahn before entering Serenity Knolls, he left them with the impression he was going to leave much from his past behind, including, presumably, the Dead.) Just before Garcia arrived at Serenity Knolls, Sears spotted him in his BMW driving out of a local Wendy's; Garcia smiled and waved at Sears and his wife, Cassidy Law. (Fast-food wrappers were later found in his car.) When Garcia's daughter Trixie heard where her father was, she called the facility but says she wasn't allowed to speak with him.

After admitting himself, Garcia called driver Leon Day to wish him a happy wedding anniversary and asked whether he wanted to go with him to Hawaii when he got out. That night Koons visited him, and the two reportedly had dinner at an Italian restaurant in Mill Valley before Koons drove him back to Serenity Knolls. At just after 4:30 the next morning a nurse making the rounds checked in on Garcia's room; earlier he'd been snoring, but now he was silent. When he was found not to be breathing, a paramedic was called, but it was too late.

According to rumor, word first slipped out when an ambulance driver called his wife and asked her to guess who he'd just picked up there, and the spouse supposedly called a local DJ. Whatever way it leaked, everyone soon heard. Lesh was driving his son Grahame to camp when he received the call; Weir was at a hotel in New Hampshire, where his side band Ratdog would be playing at the Casino Ballroom in Hampton Beach, and his longtime friend and bandmate Matthew Kelly saw Weir react emotionally. CNN crews showed up, and Deadheads held a candlelight vigil all the way down the road to the beach from the club.

Back in San Rafael, Hart, Lesh, and Welnick gathered at the Dead office at Fifth and Lincoln, the site of so many rollicking times but now a somber place. TV crews were beginning to appear outside, as were Deadheads. The band members seemed shell-shocked. "It was like they had been whacked by a two-by-four," says McNally, who was also in the house. "They were just looking at each other and wondering what the future was." For once there would be no mocking comments about death and caskets. When none of the band offered to go outside to make a statement, McNally did it by himself. The musicians and Koons were driven to a mortuary to view Garcia's body.

For those who worked with Garcia, regret and second-guessing seeped out. "From my perspective the aura around Jerry was such that clearly we needed to stop touring a couple of times and say to Jerry, 'We're not going to tour until you go to rehab or a doctor and get yourself straight,'" says promoter Scher. "But nobody, me included, had the balls to really confront Jerry." No easy answers existed, and the days and weeks after his death were sometimes fraught. Organized by Koons and held at a church in Belvedere two days after Garcia's death—the place was called, coincidentally, St. Stephen's—Garcia's funeral was attended by many of Garcia's partners, closest friends, and colleagues, from his fellow Dead players to Hunter, Barlow, Hornsby, Ken Kesey, and even Dylan, who flew up from Los Angeles. Outside—or simply not invited—was another cast of players, including Mountain Girl and Rock Scully. John Kahn managed to sneak in and stand in the back with his wife, Linda. Hunter recited a moving poem. Walking by the open casket to pay their final respects, some stopped to talk to Garcia, others to kiss him on the forehead. Dressed in a flannel shirt, Dylan stood for a few moments and appeared to be talking to Garcia. (As one musician walked out he was overheard saying, "That guy in there, he's the only one who knows what it's like to be me.") When Hornsby and Weir walked up, Weir took a look at Garcia and, recalls Hornsby, said, "Nobody home."

When the autopsy results were released soon after, Garcia's death was ruled a heart attack. That he'd used heroin a few days before was less a factor than the two of three largely blocked arteries to his heart. (Two had 85 percent blockage; the third was 30 percent.) As Weir later said, "Jerry had it in mind to clean up. Christ, he died in a rehab place. Right after his first major health issue [in 1986], for a couple of years he was in great shape, and then he slowly slipped back into the dope. But he missed [his good health] and wanted that back and that's what he was going for when he checked out. His body couldn't handle it. He was being kind of aggressive about cleaning up and his body just couldn't handle it." The fact that Garcia checked himself into a nonmedical facility also indicated that he may not have fully grasped the overall state of his health; the facility was so remote that it would have taken an ambulance a good chunk of time to reach him and rush him to a hospital.

The outpouring for Garcia—TV news broadcasts, tabloid coverage, a public memorial in Golden Gate Park just three days after the private service—was overwhelming and fitting for his iconic stature. Online bulletin boards were overwhelmed with messages of grief from Deadheads: "I just woke up . . . I wish I hadn't," "I don't know what to do with myself," "I can't survive . . . I'm devastated." The WELL (the Whole Earth 'Lectronic Link), which hosted online forums for Deadheads back to the mid-eighties, was so deluged it had to shut down for a while.

Reflecting an often messy and chaotic personal and business life, the landscape after Garcia's death was contentious and litigious. His estate, run by Koons, was hit by millions of dollars of claims from his ex-employees and partners. Although a judge ruled that Carolyn Adams (Mountain Girl) was still entitled to the financial agreement she'd reached with Garcia a few years before, Koons appealed, leading to a televised lawsuit. (In the end Adams agreed to a settlement.) A few weeks after their father's passing, Trixie and Annabelle Garcia went to visit Koons and asked whether they could grab a few of their father's belongings. Koons agreed, and Trixie left with a pair of sweatpants with an "NYPD" logo, a jacket, a traveling bag, and a manicure box. In April 1996, about nine months after Garcia's death, his ashes were dispersed—some in India, some in the waters outside San Francisco. For the surviving members of the Dead the difficult part would be next: what to do with themselves, their future, and their body of work without the man around whom it was all centered.

■　◆　▲

"One of the things we discovered is that the last time we took a swing at this, I think we overstocked the pot," Weir said backstage at the Gramercy Theatre. "The band we put together this time around is smaller and way more agile. This is a shakedown cruise here. There's less traffic on stage than we had last time around. It's different."

"It's pretty calm right now," Lesh added. "But we always have the same expectations, which is magic. When we walk out onstage, anything can happen."

"And we *invite* it to," Weir emphasized. When asked about the last time they had come together, five years before, Weir didn't know quite what to say: "I don't *remember* that tour," he finally shrugged.

In the months after Garcia's death various tour ideas were floated, from having Carlos Santana or Los Lobos' David Hidalgo fill in for Garcia or propping up Garcia's guitar onstage, lit by a spotlight, while the rest of the Dead would play. In the end all were rejected. Finally, in December, four months after Garcia's death, the surviving members met again, this time in the same conference room where Garcia used to peer over his glasses at certain ideas. Kreutzmann, by then living in Hawaii, called in to say he was finished with touring; Lesh seconded that emotion. The name "Grateful Dead" would be formally retired, and each man would go his separate way.

During that same meeting the band's business manager, Tim Jorstad, brought up the business of the Dead. "They were kind of tired of being together," Jorstad says. "But I was looking at them and saying, 'You have a company here, with merchandise and a record company—that's a real, live business that will carry on whether you guys release new music or not.' They were fine with letting the business go along." In a sense they had no choice. As soon as Garcia had died, the band's merchandise office was flooded with requests for T-shirts and other memorabilia, so much so that a bank of new computers had to be purchased the following day to keep pace with the orders. (For

Sue Swanson, who had returned to the Dead fold to help with computers, the additional work was a mixed blessing: "It was so busy that I couldn't drown in what was going on. I could only grieve in bits and pieces.") With no concerts on the horizon, the merchandise wing, once considered the stepchild of the operation, suddenly became the company's main revenue stream. Still, the income wasn't enough to support the dozens who worked for the Dead, and a round of layoffs and salary reductions swept through their office. Over fifteen people in Grateful Dead Productions, about a third of the staff, were out, including members of the road crew and Bob Bralove; others were put on retainers.

Starting the following year, 1996, the surviving members began what would become a ritualistic dance of re-forming for a tour, trying to reconnect with an audience and each other, and attempting to rekindle the magic without the man around whom it had been built. First came the Furthur Festival, which featured Weir's Ratdog—a side band and result of his collaborations with bassist Rob Wasserman that had, ironically, started its first full tour right before Garcia's death— and Hart's band Mystery Box. (It was also the name of a fine, rhythm-nation solo album, with lyrics by Hunter and guest appearances by Weir and Hornsby, released in 1996.) According to Hornsby, who was invited to participate, Garcia's death didn't come up much backstage. "It wasn't talked about much," he says. "It was plow ahead, full steam ahead, and let's make the best of this situation." Both that tour and one the following summer had their moments, but ticket sales were shaky, and Lesh's absence—he was still in retirement mode—made the shows feel less than celebratory.

The dance continued in 1998, when another permutation, cleverly dubbed the Other Ones, toured, this time with Lesh but not Kreutzmann, who decided to stay home in Hawaii. Invited back into the fold, Hornsby, who had remained on good terms with all the Dead, felt an immediate change with Lesh back in the picture. "The Dead never wanted to rehearse," Hornsby says. "Maybe a few days at Front Street in late summer. But for all practical purposes, we never rehearsed. With Phil back on the scene, we rehearsed a *lot* for the Other Ones tour. Phil was more determined on a rehearsal level to make it right. He was willing to put in the time. He was asserting himself more."

In December 1998 Lesh, who was living with Hepatitis C, had liver transplant surgery that took him out of commission for several months. In 2000 Weir, Hart, and Kreutzmann partook in another Furthur Festival, and by then Lesh had returned to performing, but this time with his own outfit. First launched in 1999, Phil Lesh & Friends presented an ever-evolving lineup—with notable players like Haynes, Phish's Trey Anastasio, drummer John Molo, guitarists Derek Trucks and Jimmy Herring, keyboardist Rob Barraco, and many others—offering up faithful, well-played, extended-jam versions of the Dead repertoire. In that regard Lesh became the keeper of the flame, as Herring learned when he was invited to rehearse with and then join Lesh's band in 2000. "Phil thought of it like a flock of birds or a school of fish—he'd use those analogies," Herring says. "In Phil's world a solo was a group conversation, not a single person going off and doing their thing while the others played a backing track behind him. Sometimes you might be in front and sometimes in the back or middle or side. He never wanted you to find yourself in your own space, and that was hard. Most of us come from a place where you play the song and back up the vocals." Herring soon realized the fans wanted that too: on this first tour with the band that spring, the audience would largely stay in their seats and not head out for a beer. Not surprisingly, Lesh & Friends became the shows that attracted increasing numbers of Deadheads, and in 2002 the group recorded a credible studio album, *There and Back Again*. The ascendance of Lesh and Friends, compared to Ratdog, initially confused some promoters: Why were so many people buying tickets to their shows? The business types didn't realize—but the fans did—that Lesh's bass was as integral to the Dead's legend as Garcia's voice. Even after all those decades Lesh's jumpy rumble remained distinctive and embodied the sound of the band as much as any other player in the group.

With Ratdog, especially in its first half-dozen years, Weir took the opposite approach: internalizing his grief, he threw himself into touring and decided not to turn Ratdog into what amounted to a Dead tribute band. A few Weir-penned Dead songs would enter the set—"Victim or the Crime," "Throwing Stones"—but he rarely played his best-known Dead songs, instead relying on covers of blues, R&B, and Dylan songs. To those who worked with him, that decision was baffling. "There was this void, and we had a choice of which way to react," says Kelly, who played with Ratdog for a period after Garcia's death. "Everybody felt, 'Well, we'll never take the place of the Dead, but let's do something to fill that void.' Bobby took a strong stand on not doing any Dead songs. People in the audience were devastated. The audience needed so badly to be healed, and they were looking to us—you could see it in their faces. It broke my heart. It was almost unbearable. The rest of the guys were pleading, 'Bobby, you *have* to do this for no other reason—they're *dying* out there.' He wouldn't go there." (In 1998, Weir told *Rolling Stone*, "I carry his [Garcia's] memory with me.") Early on, Ratdog didn't even have a lead guitarist, another way of avoiding Dead comparisons.

In 2001 Weir and Lesh played together at Sweetwater in Mill Valley under a fake name, playing rarities like the *Workingman's Dead* outtake "Mason's Children." "It was awesome to look onstage and be standing there with Bobby and Phil but not having it called the Dead or the Other Ones," says Herring, who joined them that night. "It made it less pressure. No one had any expectations other than friends playing together, and it was fun." In 2001 Ratdog coheadlined a few shows with Lesh & Friends, and the following year Lesh joined up with the Other Ones for a tour that featured some of his players.

In 2003 and 2004 the four surviving members united once again for two summer tours but now billed as the Dead. During the 2003 tour, in a quaint sign that some things hadn't especially changed with the fans, Tampa, Florida, police seized a small quantity of chocolate lollipops that were blended with mushrooms. Musically the tours had plenty of high points, but the four founding members were still trying to adjust to life without Garcia and determine who would lead the charge. Garcia had been their bond, and without him they weren't simply missing the musical center of the band; they were sometimes lacking the principal connection they had with each other. By the time the tour wrapped up in May 2004 at one of the Dead's longtime favorite venues, the Shoreline Amphitheatre in Mountain View, California, the Dead had grossed $17.9 million, but were weary of each other. But as Hart would later recall to *Rolling Stone*, "We had to let this thing rest. These things take a lot of time, the ability to see beyond the struggle of being the Grateful Dead and who we are. This isn't an easy thing. This is really hard."

∎ ◆ ∎

"Everybody *remembers* things really well," says Lesh as he and his wife, Jill, were driven to the next venue, the six-hundred-seat Gramercy Theatre in midtown. "It's in our bones now."

As they always would, reparations between the musicians after the 2004 tour eventually arrived, with one more bump along the road. Around 2005 Grateful Dead Productions began entertaining a new round of offers to manage its recordings, merchandise, licensing of likenesses, and any other physical and digital assets (excluding its publishing, which remained with their longtime company, Ice Nine). Several big-name rock managers expressed interest, but in 2006 an agreement was struck with Rhino Entertainment, with the Dead retaining creative control over any decisions. In a move that was very Dead, Rhino executive Mark Pinkus had to pass a test first during a meeting at a hotel in Marin County: To make sure he knew their material well and was the right man for the job, the band asked him to sing the tricky "Victim or the Crime" from *Built to Last*. Luckily Pinkus, a genial and Dead-loving guy, knew the song.

Starting in the mid-nineties Deadheads had been uploading fan-taped Dead show tapes to the Live Music Archive, the concert tape section of Archive.org, a San Francisco–based website. But with a new business arrangement in the works, the question became: How to adhere to the group's free-trade legacy while ensuring its financial future? (A similar issue came up about five years before, when Lesh disagreed with the other band members about giving over their assets—their recorded legacy—to a new venture-capital company, but the dot-com collapse put an end to those plans.) In 2005 the band ordered Archive.org to pull the band's soundboard recordings, although audience-made tapes would remain available for streaming and downloading.

The scenario was tricky for all involved. As one source in the Dead world says, "The Dead were caught in a difficult place. The market ethic of the band was always to give performances away. It worked as long as there were infinite shows. When Jerry died, all that music became their financial future. So now it was, 'Maybe we *can't* give this away.' It was a very complicated position." Unexpectedly, Lesh issued a statement that read, in part, "I was not part of this decision-making process and was not notified that the shows were to be pulled. I do feel that the music is the Grateful Dead's legacy and I hope that one way or another all of it is available for those who want it." Deadheads signed an online petition, after which the Dead allowed audience tapes to be available for download, while the band's own soundboard tapes would only be streamed. The confusion of the moment embodied the difficult ways in which everyone was adjusting to life after Garcia.

The reparations eventually arrived. With the Rhino arrangement in place—and someone else taking charge of their business, which always seemed to get between them—tensions within the band began to ease. Lesh and Weir ran into each other in Mill Valley, and before long the two men, along with Hart, played a benefit for Barack Obama at the Warfield early in 2008. Lesh's son Brian had been an Obama volunteer worker, and when the group was invited to headline an Obama benefit in the fall, all four musicians tabled their differences and agreed to come together again. "It was, 'This is a man who we think is worthy,'" said Hart to *Rolling Stone* at the time. "The idea is to put the consciousness in their heads." Haynes, who had played with Lesh & Friends and the Allman Brothers Band as well as on one of the Dead's reunion tours (and his own band, Gov't Mule), was called in, as was keyboardist Jeff Chimenti, a versatile, jazz-influenced Northern California–born keyboardist who'd joined up with Ratdog in 1997 and played on the Dead's subsequent reunion tours.

Held at Penn State's Bryce Jordan Center in October 2008, the concert—the first public performance by all four members in four years—found them playing everything from "Dark Star" and "St. Stephen" to "Touch of Grey," and afterward Lesh was heard raving about Weir's singing, an early sign of détente. The drummers again clicked: "Mickey and I are getting along better now," Kreutzmann told *Rolling Stone* after. "The egos are out of the way." Immediately and perhaps inevitably, talk of a reunion tour was ignited, and Live Nation, the touring-business behemoth, came aboard to organize and promote it.

The sextet reconvened in Mill Valley and rehearsed for two weeks, and the full-on tour began in April. At the start, interband relations were steady; no one wanted to taint the legacy of the Dead, and everything from the standards to more obscure and trickier pieces like "King Solomon's Marbles" from *Blues for Allah* were worked up. Haynes and Chimenti were unobtrusive and agreeable, each bringing a new instrumental palette to the band: Hayes was more blues rooted than Garcia and had a throatier, hoarser, more aggressive style of singing and playing, while Chimenti's piano could sparkle in ways that recalled the work of all the Dead's previous keyboardists.

* ◆ ▲

In New York that night in March they were doing their best to carry on the traditions of the band, and so were the fans, who snapped up the free tickets to all three shows. At the Gramercy Theater they played an abbreviated career-spanning set that included "Playing in the Band," "Franklin's Tower," and "Viola Lee Blues." A roar went up when Lesh sang a verse from "Franklin's Tower," recalling the "Let Phil Sing!" signs of Dead shows past. The musicians then jumped into a van and headed uptown to the Roseland Ballroom, the largest of the venues, with three thousand ticket holders. "It's like a show split up by cab rides," cracked Weir.

"People are listening to each other more, as opposed to taking the other person for granted," Hart said at Roseland. "Sometimes you don't tell people you love 'em after a show or say, 'That was good!' We used to get off stage and that was it. But now we're interacting on a personal level very well and that can only bode well for the music. We try not to be confrontational. We try to work it out in the music."

Staring at the set list backstage, though, Hart was initially skeptical of what he saw. "Yeah, that will never happen," he said, shaking his head. "We could probably play 'Dark Star' for an hour. This is nuts. I think Phil did it. Phil probably just had a cup of coffee—that's what that's about. Phil's dreaming if he thinks we can play that set."

Weir wandered in. "Bob, look at that!" Hart said, showing the sheet of paper to Weir. "We'll never get to all that," Hart said. "If *half* of it gets played, we'll be lucky."

In the wake of Garcia's death each of the four men had grappled with the aftermath in varying ways. Kreutzmann stayed largely in Hawaii, away from the music business. "I was lost in every direction," he told *Rolling Stone* in 2012. "I didn't know what to do." Keyboardist Vince

Welnick seemed the most devastated after Garcia died. Initially he'd joined Ratdog but came across as troubled and depressed during a tour with them. On the road, band members had talks with him to "try to bring him out of his funk," says Kelly. "He was constantly talking about suicide on the tour. We were worried about him." Before one show they found Welnick unconscious on a tour bus, an empty bottle of Valium nearby. Welnick left the tour soon after. In 2006, feeling excluded from the Dead's post-Garcia lineups and unhappy with his career, he slit his throat at his Marin home. The curse of the Dead keyboardists didn't really exist—Hornsby and Constanten were still alive—but here was a particularly grisly reminder of it.

Dating back to the band's earliest days, Weir had always kept the most in shape. He'd had lower back problems starting in the seventies, which had led him into running and eventually to try weights, yoga, and bike riding. He now had a regimen—a half-hour of wind sprints on an elliptical trainer, followed by weights—but was also suffering from shoulder pain from throwing around a football all his life and took painkillers "for a number of years," he has said. A few months after the 2009 Dead tour he told *Rolling Stone* he was using what he called "an industrial-strength vibrating massager" to work on his shoulder and loosen it up. ("You would not want to use this thing in bed, though," he cracked.)

Weir, who had grown a bushy white beard, still had that twinkle in his eye and remained the courtliest of the four. (Few if any rock stars give their cell phone numbers and e-mail addresses to reporters, as Weir often did.) For the ever-pensive Weir, Garcia's presence always hung in the air. "He shaped the music," he told *Rolling Stone* in 2013. "His hand is still there. I can hear him out of the corner of my ear. I can hear his harmonic development. I can hear what he registers he's going for. It never went away. It just became a little more ethereal. I don't mean to wax hippie metaphysical, but that's how it is for me. It always has been."

■ ◆ ■

At Roseland that March 2009 the Dead finally were able to play a fairly long set. The younger fans who pushed up against the stage barricades had hair longer than the original members of the band. Haynes and Weir sang the songs Garcia once had, and some of the old trademarks remained, like Weir forgetting a few of the lyrics. (He knew right away and pounded himself on the head as soon as he did, to the loving cheers of the fans who tolerated it.) They jammed on "St. Stephen" and threw themselves into an "Eyes of the World" that was brightened, as always, by Chimenti's glistening piano.

The Dead tour would begin the following month and last about four weeks. When it was over, so were the Dead, at least for a few more years. Given their history, clashing personalities, and the directions their post-Garcia music had taken them, it was probably inevitable that a reunion wouldn't last long. (A completed tour documentary was also shelved.) In a surprise move, Lesh and Weir, who had had their share of ups and downs, decided to carry on together. In the summer 2009 they recruited John Kadlecik and, at Weir's suggestion, called their new band Furthur. Kadlecik, a guitarist and singer who'd grown up in the Midwest, had been in one early Dead tribute band ("China Cat Sunflower" was the first Garcia-Hunter song he'd learned to play) and, starting in 1997, had fronted Dark Star Orchestra, the country's leading Dead tribute band. He'd first seen the Dead live in 1989 and had caught his share of shows after. With his gentle demeanor, long, dark hair, and, especially, the way his guitar style recalled Garcia's, Kadlecik helped Furthur recreate the sound of the Dead more than any previous post-Garcia combination. "Yeah, it's a little spooky in some ways because he's internalized the essence of Jerry's approach," Lesh told *Rolling Stone* in 2010. "Not so much the notes, although he's really good at pulling *that* out. Also, his voice can be very similar to Jerry's. Every so often he'll sing something in a certain way and it's just like déjà vu. I love that. It's been a *long* 15 years."

For the next four years Furthur became a juggernaut, touring regularly and playing songs from the Dead canon and even entire album sides. Dark Star Orchestra continued without Kadlecik, still brilliantly recreating specific Dead shows, but Furthur became, in their way, the leading Dead homage—and, in doing so, unintentionally rode a business wave in rock 'n' roll. More and more, classic rock bands—Journey, Foreigner, Styx—were touring without their key front men but with younger vocal ringers. Yet when Furthur was on—at intimate shows at Sweetwater in Mill Valley in early 2013 or a headlining triumph at Madison Square Garden in late 2011, to a sold-out crowd that spanned generations and stayed on its feet the entire time—it transcended nostalgia and brought the old songs back to life. By the time Furthur had run its course in 2014, the four surviving members had returned to their separate corners. Hart, who had two Grammys under his belt (for his *Planet Drum* and *Global Drum Project* albums), had his own pop-worldbeat band, the Mickey Hart band, and was working on projects that included turning light waves into sound. Still based in Hawaii, Kreutzmann applied his drum skills to a series of jam bands starting in the early 2000s, including 7 Walkers (fronted by New Orleans–based singer-guitarist Papa Mali) and, in 2014, Billy and the Kids. In 2011 Weir opened the Tamalpais Research Institute (TRI), a recording and broadcast facility based in San Rafael; he would also return to Ratdog, with whom he'd cut the sturdy 2001 album *Evening Moods*. Lesh had his own venue, Terrapin Crossroads, in San Rafael, an intimate venue inspired by Levon Helm's Midnight Ramble barn shows in Woodstock.

What remained, more than anything, was the Dead's broad legacy. For a bunch of outcasts and outliers who'd come together from widely varying economic and musical backgrounds, playing music that rubbed against conventions (and the industry) from the start, the Dead had left a startlingly huge footprint on the culture. The world of improvisational jam bands had become a genre unto itself, complete with annual festivals and extended improvising that used the Dead as its blueprint. One could easily trace a line from the Acid Tests to the flourishing electronic dance music world that had become mainstream by the second decade of the new century. As with the Tests, electronic dance music (EDM) events were less about the performers (DJs, in this case) and more about communal (and actual) ecstasy. Both focused on waves of sound and delirium. Their impact could be even more day-to-day. In Japan during a later tour with Ratdog, Weir was confronted with the band's reach when he visited an ancient temple. "We stopped into this little Japanese restaurant that had been in the family for hundreds of years," Weir told *Rolling Stone* in 2013, "and the head chef was a huge fan. He recognized me right away, and he was acutely knowledgeable of many aspects of our lives. He served us a lot of sake."

For a band that never quite knew how to deal with the business until later in their career, the Dead's influence on the music industry was also profound. With the virtual collapse of the old-school music business in the new century, bands like Radiohead and Nine Inch Nails began releasing new work on their own labels, much like the Dead had thirty years before (but with not as much success). The Dead had a connection to the formation of social networking: first with its direct band-to-fan communications in the seventies and then by way of the online Deadhead forum in the WELL (cofounded by Stewart Brand). Thanks to devoted Dead archivist David Lemieux, the music kept coming in the form of elaborate boxed sets of particular tours and the *Dave's Picks* series of vintage concerts that picked up where the late Dick Latvala's *Dick's Picks* series had left off. There were now Grateful Dead conferences, snowboards, and video games. The industry of the Dead, considered in such peril after Garcia's death, carried on—but, luckily, so did the band's music, preserved better than ever for future generations to dissect and analyze. As for future reunions, Weir wouldn't rule anything out. As he told *Rolling Stone*, "Unfinished business, and there always will be with us, until enough of us are gone that it's off the table. But until then, it's always going to be on the table. The Dead is going to do what the Dead is going to do, and that's always there."

The Roseland set of the evening finally ended, and the four surviving members, along with Chimenti and Haynes, gathered in a backstage area to finally rest after a relentless day. "Interesting band," Hart said with a smile. "It's like a box of chocolates—you never know what you're going to get." Behind him, the musicians shared a collective end-of-the-night joint. Garcia was gone, but some of the rituals—along with the songs, the melodies, and the flashes of group harmony—remained. The vans soon arrived to transport them to one more hotel room and return them, once more, to the twisty road that had changed music and their lives.

BIDDING YOU GOODNIGHT (OTHERWISE KNOWN AS ACKNOWLEDGMENTS)

As mentioned at the start of this book, attempting to shed new light on a subject as deep, expansive, and multitentacled as the Grateful Dead can be challenging, to say the least. Start with the reams of information already devoted to the band, much of it scrupulously researched. Add in conflicting memories of Dead family and friends who are still around— what one former Dead employee called the "fog of war" when offering up his own, different version of one particular event—and the result is rock 'n' roll Roshoman unlike any I've ever encountered. The best one can do is talk to as many people as possible, acquire as much documentation as exists, and attempt to untangle history as best as one can.

Thankfully I had expert guidance from the start. As soon as I reached out to him for advice, David Lemieux, the band's knowledgeable, devoted, and vigilant archivist, was supportive of my idea of writing a book on the Dead. David was considerate enough to put out the word to the camps of the surviving Dead members, and in time we heard they were all fine with me embarking on such a project. They also agreed to my stipulation that I would have control over the finished manuscript. I want to thank Phil Lesh, Bob Weir, Mickey Hart, and Bill Kreutzmann and their peeps for allowing yet another journalist to tackle this saga and, in doing so, for affording me access to friends, family, and archives, all with no strings attached. The many roads they all traveled together were both smooth and bumpy, and I especially want to thank Phil and Mickey for not flinching when I asked about both the highs and lows of the remarkable Dead saga. I would say I'm grateful, but that would be too easy.

Unless specifically cited in the text, quotes in this book are from interviews I conducted in person, by phone, and by e-mail between 2011 and 2014. The majority were specifically for this project, although in some cases, particularly Bob Weir, the comments are from Dead pieces I wrote for *Rolling Stone* between 2008 and 2013.

After the band, my next major tip of the hat extends to the family members, former employees, and longtime Dead associates who graciously allowed me into their world and tolerated my ongoing series of nitpicky questions over the years it took to research this book. In alphabetical order, my eternal gratitude to Carolyn Adams (Mountain Girl), John Perry Barlow, Bob Bralove, Jerilyn Lee Brandelius, Matt Busch, Rondelle Cagwin, Kidd Candelario (extra thanks for the driving tour of Dead sites), Betty Cantor-Jackson, Tom Constanten, Sam Cutler, Manasha Matheson Garcia, Tiff Garcia, Trixie Garcia, Laird Grant, Caryl Hart, Bruce Hornsby, Vicki Jensen, Justin Kreutzmann, Shelley Kreutzmann, Jill Lesh, Richard Loren, Steve Marcus, Bob Matthews, Rosie McGee, Brigid Meier, Connie Bonner Mosley, Steve Parish, John Scher, Nicki Scully, Rock Scully (who, sadly, passed away as this book neared completion), Cameron Sears, Sue Stephens, and Sue Swanson.

For their time, insights, memories, and laughs, many thanks to Alex Allan, Allan Arkush, Joan Baez, Ken Babbs, Cherie Barsin, Mike Belardo, Stewart Brand, Steve Brown, Buddy Cage, Jack Cassady, Chris Clair, Kip Cohen, Alex Cooley, Stan Cornyn, Paul Curcio, Jim Cushing, Leon Day, Len Dell'Amico, Don Douglas, Vance Frost, Janice Godshalk-Olsen, Herb Greene, Gary Gutierrez, David Hellman,

Jimmy Herring, Don Ienner, Tim Jorstad, Phil Kaffel, Linda Kahn, Denise Kaufman, Jorma Kaukonen, Matthew Kelly, assistant Noblesville police chief Scott Kirby, Jim Koplik, Dennis Larkins, Jill Larson, Andy Leonard, Ed Levin, Roy Lott, Carol McKernan, John McLaughlin, Nancy Mallonee, Maria Muldaur, Keith Olsen, Tom Paddock, Mark Pinkus, Courtenay Pollock, Sally Mann Romano, Peter Rowan, Phill Sawyer, Tim Scully, Joe Smith, Starfinder Stanley, Michael Stepanian, Alan Trist, Norm van Maastricht, Michael Wanger, Jann S. Wenner, and Baron Wolman. Several sources spoke only on condition of anonymity, and I thank them for their assistance as well.

The very thought of producing a book that could complement the work of the iconic Dead scholars—Dennis McNally, Blair Jackson, David Gans, and Steve Silberman in particular—was incredibly daunting. Their books and articles, listed in the Select Bibliography that follows, are essential reading for anyone in search of the building blocks of this long and always strange trip. In particular, Dennis's epic, extraordinarily detailed *A Long Strange Trip* and Blair's soulful and insightful *Garcia: An American Life* are essential, prodigiously researched volumes with a wealth of information, from the early Palo Alto–Menlo Park years of Garcia, Hunter, and their friends up through the big-business Dead of the nineties. To my everlasting gratitude, each of these four men were supportive, welcoming, and encouraging during the course of my own research, and I can't thank them enough for their time, ruminations, and suggestions. (Dennis graciously made available his notes from the 1984 recording session in Chapter 12.) Thanks so much, guys, and keep on truckin', if I can say that without making each of you wince.

Extra special thanks to Debbie Gold, who went far beyond the call of duty by pointing me in many right directions (and ensuring I didn't wander in the wrong directions either). Her guidance, contacts, and constant support were priceless.

My friend and colleague David Hajdu kindly allowed me to dig into the transcripts for his 2005 *Rolling Stone* story on the origins of the Dead, and words can't express what a treasure trove those pages were. In addition to the journalists named above, a big shout-out to other longtime Dead scribes whose brains I picked over the course of this book, especially David Fricke, Robert Greenfield, Jesse Jarnow, Gary Lambert, Michael Lydon, and Peter Richardson. Corry Arnold helped me nail down certain specific dates, and his wonderfully obsessive journey to ascertain places and dates can be found on his blog, http://lostlivedead.blogspot.com. Much respect to Dan Ross, Denny Horn, Mike Schein, John Zolidis, and the many other Deadheads I met and spoke to on this journey.

The Dead universe is lucky to be blessed with archivists who are not only fans but also consummate professionals. David Lemieux fielded more research and chronology questions than any sane Dead sonic archivist should have to handle, and each time he did it with professionalism and patience. At the Special Collections department at the University of California at Santa Cruz, home to the Dead's archives, Nicholas Meriwether was every writer's dream. From start to frenzied end of this book, Nicholas waded through files, folders, and papers in search of historical documents that helped support or enhance existing information. The Dead—not to mention Deadheads and the many future Dead chroniclers, scholars, and academics to come—are fortunate to have both of these hard-working men in their corner.

J. C. Flyer endured years of nudging calls and e-mails, always promising he would deliver—and he did, and I thank him for staying the course. For putting me in touch with the appropriate parties, thank you, Marc Allan and Kevin Monty Red Light; Howard Cohen; Rose Solomon; Jason Elzy at Rhino; Josh Sapan; Mike Courtney; Peter Kliegman; Ambrosia Healy; Cash Edwards; Jim Flammia; Bob Merlis; Anthony D'Amato at Shore Fire; Harriet Rose; Ethel Berdah of

City Winery; Diane Richard at the Pittsburgh Bureau of Police; Mark Spector; Brehanna Sawyer; Bob Kaus; Thom Duffy; Tina Williams at the Noblesville, Indiana, Police Department; Laura Cordes; Laura B. Cohen; Rachel Sachs; Aaron Schlechter; Mark Pucci; David Prentice; Jeffrey Wood at Fantasy; Dan Goodrich; and Mike Fuoco and Lexi Belculfine of the *Pittsburgh Post-Gazette*.

Thanks to Deborah Dragon for her fantastic photo research, and an extra shout-out to Sacha Lecca for pitching in with his picture skills too. Corinne Cummings and her fact-checking acumen ensured I wouldn't embarrass myself too badly, and Dan Hyman dug into old newspaper microfilm with a vigor I couldn't help but admire.

Huge five-star thanks to the Wenner Media crew for their encouragement and the occasional work breaks that allowed me to finish this book, and I mean you, Will Dana, Nathan Brackett, Jason Fine, Sean Woods, Christian Hoard, Caryn Ganz, and Simon Vozick-Levinson. Elsewhere at *Rolling Stone* and *Men's Journal* Andy Greene, Brian Hiatt, Alison Weinflash, Cady Drell, David Fear, Patrick Doyle, Nick Murray, Mark Healy, Rob Fischer, Ryan Kogh, Tyghe Trimble, and Marielle Anas were never less than supportive too.

For their contacts, feedback, and brain-picking, thanks to Dan Ouellette, Peter Guralnick, Sheila Weller, Eric Alterman, Ed Bakos, John Chuldenko, and Steve Knopper.

My ever-supportive (and far cooler than me) agent, Erin Hosier of Dunow, Carlson & Lerner, smartly pressed me to do this book when I first mentioned the idea, and my editor, Ben Schafer at Da Capo, may be one of the few in book publishing who can boast of seeing the Dead at Alpine Valley—the first of many reasons he was, as always, the man for the job. (His own deep knowledge of the Dead was a great reason too.) Thanks to Josephine Mariea for the edit, and to my friend Kathy Heintzelman, who gave the manuscript a thorough red-pencil read in a relatively short time. My wife, Maggie, had to endure endless hours of the Dead SiriusXM channel—highly recommended for those who may not have plugged into it—and learned to love it along the way. She remains an inspiration. Our daughter, Maeve, doesn't know much about the Dead yet, but she's intrigued by the dancing bears and skeletons—a good start for any potential future Deadhead.

SELECT BIBLIOGRAPHY

Back issues of the following publications were consulted: *BAM*, *The Golden Road*, *Marin Independent Journal*, *Pacific Sun*, *Palo Alto Daily News*, *Palo Alto Times*, *Palo Alto Weekly*, *Peninsula Times Tribune*, *People*, *Rolling Stone*, the *Los Angeles Times*, the *New York Times*, *San Francisco Chronicle*, *San Francisco Examiner*, *San Jose Mercury News*, and the *Washington Post*. In particular, Blair Jackson's and David Gans's work at *BAM*, Joel Selvin's and Ralph J. Gleason's at the *Chronicle*, and Paul Liberatore's at the *Marin Independent Journal* were invaluable.

A huge nod to the Grateful Dead Archive and associated collections and research material, Special Collections and Archives, University Library, University of California at Santa Cruz. Special thanks to Nicholas Meriwether. Thanks to Dennis McNally for permission to reference his taped interviews with Frankie Weir and Jon McIntire.

Portions of Chapters 10 and 17 appeared, in different form, in *Rolling Stone*.

Among the many websites I clicked on and continually pored over were the Dead's own, Dead.net, along with Corry Arnold's aforementioned Lost Live Dead and its sibling site, http://hooterollin.blogspot.com; Jerry Garcia's Middle Finger (http://jgmf.blogspot.com); Dead Essays (http://deadessays.blogspot.com); and the Modern Deadhead (http://moderndeadhead.blogspot.com). Blair Jackson's late, lamented, but still invaluable Blair's Golden Road blog never fails to enlighten. The JFK Library site, JFKlibrary.org, was a treasure trove of Cuban Missile Crisis documentation.

As any Dead scholar will tell you, the number of books, articles, and blogs devoted to the band could practically fill a library. It's nearly impossible to cite every book and newspaper or magazine piece about the band, but below is a sampling of ones that were especially useful for this book.

ARTICLES
Brown, Toni. "An Interview with Vince Welnick." *Relix*, June 1991.

Browne, David. "Rolling with the Dead." *Rolling Stone*, March 31, 2009.

———. "Still Truckin'." *Rolling Stone*, November 13, 2008.

———. "The Dead Recall the Colorful Life of LSD Pioneer Owsley Stanley." *Rolling Stone*, March 30, 2011.

———. "The Dead's Greatest Year." *Rolling Stone*, June 26, 2013.

———. "Donna Godchaux's Long, Strange Trip." *Rolling Stone*, March 4, 2014.

"California: End of the Dance." *Time*, August 18, 1967.

DeCurtis, Anthony. "The Music Never Stops: The *Rolling Stone* Interview with Jerry Garcia." *Rolling Stone*, September 2, 1993.

Eisen, Benjy. "Grateful Dead Drummer: Jerry Garcia 'Wasn't Really Happy Playing' at Band's End." *Rolling Stone*, January 17, 2012.

Emerson, Paul. "Medics Add Folk Singing to Menu." *Palo Alto Times*, January 22, 1963.

"Fan of Rock Concert Killed by the Police, Coroner Rules." *New York Times*, December 30, 1989.

Foege, Alec. "Funeral for a Friend." *Rolling Stone*, September 21, 1995.

Fong-Torres, Benjamin. "15 Years Dead." *Rolling Stone*, August 7, 1980.

Fricke, David. "The Dead's Working Man." *Rolling Stone*, April 21, 2014.

Gans, David, and Blair Jackson. "Talking with Garcia." *Record*, June 1982.

Gilmore, Mikal. "The New Dawn of the Grateful Dead." *Rolling Stone*, June 16, 1987.

Goodman, Fred. "Jerry Garcia: The *Rolling Stone* Interview." *Rolling Stone*, November 30, 1989.

Graham, Gerrit. "The Crime and Its Victims." *Annotated Grateful Dead Lyrics* (2004).

"Grateful Dead Ungrateful; Sued." *Rolling Stone*, July 26, 1969.

Greenfield, Robert. "Owsley Stanley: The King of LSD." *Rolling Stone*, July 12, 2007.

Gupte, Pranay. "Panel Suggests 'Rescue' Plans for Radio City." *New York Times*, January 9, 1978.

Henke, James. "Alive & Well: The *Rolling Stone* Interview with Jerry Garcia." *Rolling Stone*, October 31, 1991.

Himes, Geoffrey. "Grateful Dead, Alive as Ever." *Washington Post*, November 1, 1989.

Hinckley, David. "This One Is for Deadheads." *New York Daily News*, October 16, 1984.

Hopkins, Jerry. "The Grateful Dead Hit Europe." *Rolling Stone*, June 22, 1972.

Isikoff, Michael. "Interest in Dead Was Not Musical." *Washington Post*, August 14, 1990.

Jackson, Harry. "On Tour with the Dead." *Zygote*, July 22, 1970.

James, George. "Possible Drug Link to Rock Fan's Death Cited by Prosecutor." *New York Times*, November 18, 1989.

Lydon, Michael. "The Dead Zone." *Rolling Stone*, August 23, 1969.

"New Orleans Cops and the Dead Bust." *Rolling Stone*, March 7, 1970.

Ong, Mark Stuart, and John Walker. "The Roy Kepler Story." *Kepler's Review*, December 1991.

Pareles, Jon. "The Dead's Gamble: Free Music for Sale." *New York Times*, December 3, 2005.

Pavlis, Timothy. "Tangent Turns to Ethnicism." *Stanford Daily*, January 23, 1963.

Perry, Charles. "A New Life for the Dead." *Rolling Stone*, November 22, 1973.

————. "The Deadhead Phenomenon." *Rolling Stone*, Winter 1980.

Peters, Steve. "Built to Last: A Conversation with Jerry Garcia." *Relix*, December 1989.

"Pop Records: Moguls, Money & Monsters." *Time*, February 12, 1973.

Shepard, Richard F. "Radio City Music Hall Returns." *New York Times*, June 1, 1979.

Sidon, Rob. "Bob Weir, Gratefully." *Common Ground*, November 2014.

"St. Michael's Alley Has Matured, But Stays True to Its Bohemian Spirit." *Palo Alto Times Tribune*, November 24, 1991.

Watrous, Peter. "The Grateful Dead's Continuing Metamorphosis." *New York Times*, September 12, 1991.

Weitzman, Steve. "A Chat with Jerry Garcia." *Rolling Stone*, April 1, 1976.

Young, Charles M. "The Awakening of the Dead." *Rolling Stone*, June 16, 1977.

BOOKS

Allen, Scott W. *Aces Back to Back*. Outskirts, 2014.

Brandelius, Jerilyn Lee. *Grateful Dead Family Album*. Warner, 1990.

Brightman, Carol. *Sweet Chaos: The Grateful Dead's American Adventure*. Simon & Schuster, 1998.

Brown, Toni, with Lee Abraham and Ed Munson, eds. *Relix: The Book—The Grateful Dead Experience*. Backbeat, 2009.

Conners, Peter. *Growing Up Dead*. Da Capo, 2009.

Cutler, Sam. *You Can't Always Get What You Want*. ECW Press, 2010.

Davis, Tom. *39 Years of Short-Term Memory Loss*. Grove, 2010.

Dodd, David, annotations by. *The Complete Annotated Grateful Dead Lyrics*. Free Press, 2005.

Dodd, David G., and Diana Spaulding, eds. *The Grateful Dead Reader.* Oxford, 2000.

Editors of *Rolling Stone. Garcia.* Little, Brown, 1995.

Gans, David, and Peter Simon. *Playing in the Band: An Oral and Visual Portrait of the Grateful Dead.* St. Martin's, 1985.

Gans, David. *Conversations with the Dead: The Grateful Dead Interview Book.* Da Capo, 1999.

Garcia, Jerry, Jann S. Wenner, Charles Reich. *Garcia: A Signpost to New Space.* Da Capo reprint, 2003.

Graham, Bill, and Robert Greenfield. *Bill Graham Presents: My Life Inside Rock and Out.* Doubleday, 1992.

Greenfield, Robert. *Dark Star: An Oral Biography of Jerry Garcia.* William Morrow, 1996.

Harrison, Hank. *The Dead Book.* Links, 1973.

Hunter, Robert. *A Box of Rain.* Penguin, 1993.

Jackson, Blair. *Grateful Dead Gear: The Band's Instruments, Sound Systems, and Recording Sessions, From 1965 to 1995.* Backbeat, 2006.

———. *Grateful Dead: The Music Never Stopped.* Putnam, 1983.

———. *Goin' Down The Road: A Grateful Dead Traveling Companion.* Three Rivers, 1992.

———. *Garcia: An American Life.* Viking, 1999.

Lesh, Phil. *Searching for the Sound: My Life with the Grateful Dead.* Little, Brown, 2005.

Loren, Richard, with Stephen Abney. *High Notes: A Rock Memoir.* East Pond, 2014.

Lydon, Michael. *Rock Folk: Portraits from the Rock 'n' Roll Pantheon.* Citadel reprint, 1990.

McGee, Rosie. *Dancing with the Dead: A Photographic Memoir.* Tioli Press & Bytes, 2013.

McNally, Dennis. *A Long Strange Trip: The Inside History of the Grateful Dead.* Broadway, 2002.

Parish, Steve, with Joe Layton. *Home Before Daylight: My Life on the Road with the Grateful Dead.* St. Martin's, 2003.

Scott, David Meerman, and Brian Halligan. *Marketing Lessons from the Grateful Dead.* John Wiley & Sons, 2010.

Scully, Rock, with David Dalton. *Living with the Dead: Twenty Years on the Bus with Garcia and the Grateful Dead.* Little, Brown, 1995.

Shenk, David, and Steve Silberman. *Skeleton Key: A Dictionary for Deadheads.* Doubleday, 1994.

Stanley, Rhoney Gissen, with Tom Davis. *Owsley and Me: My LSD Family.* Monkfish, 2013.

Trager, Oliver. *The American Book of the Dead.* Touchstone, 1997.

Various. *Grateful Dead: The Illustrated Trip.* DK Publishing, 2003.

Wolfe, Tom. *The Electric Kool-Aid Acid Test.* Farrar, Straus and Giroux, 1968.

INDEX